SQL Server® 2008 Administration
Instant Reference

Michael Lee

Mike Mansfield

WILEY

Wiley Publishing, Inc.

Acquisitions Editor: Agatha Kim
Development Editor: Candace English
Production Editor: Rachel McConlogue
Copy Editor: Judy Flynn
Editorial Manager: Pete Gaughan
Production Manager: Tim Tate
Vice President and Executive Group Publisher: Richard Swadley
Vice President and Publisher: Neil Edde
Book Designer: Maureen Forys
Compositors: Maureen Forys and Craig Woods, Happenstance Type-O-Rama
Proofreader: Publication Services, Inc.
Indexer: Nancy Guenther
Project Coordinator, Cover: Lynsey Stanford
Cover Designer: Ryan Sneed
Cover Image: iStockPhoto

Library of Congress Cataloging-in-Publication Data

Lee, Michael, 1966-
  SQL server 2008 administration instant reference / Michael Lee. -- 1st ed.
    p. cm.
  Summary: "Perfect companion to any SQL Server 2008 book, providing fast, accurate answers on the
spot for millions of IT professionals System and database administrators, IT consultants, and database
application developers often need quick answers and practical solutions for SQL Server issues. This
convenient guide offers you quick referencing for the product and database topics you need most. If
you're an IT administrator looking for the essentials in the day-to-day tasks of administering SQL
Server 2008, you'll appreciate this book's design for providing quick and easy look up of solutions
and tables, lists, and step-by-step instructions for answers on the spot. SQL Server 2008 Instant
Administration Reference is a guide that you want to keep within reach. SQL Server is Microsoft's
bestselling database manager; the 2008 version offers enhanced security and high availability,
encouraging users to upgrade Features thumb tabs, secondary and tertiary tables of contents, and
special heading treatments to provide quick and easy lookup, as well as quick-reference tables and lists
to provide answers on the spot Covers installing, configuring, managing, and maintaining SQL Server;
optimizing server performance; and troubleshooting SQL Server 2008 Administration Instant Reference
answers the questions you encounter most often in your daily work"—Provided by publisher.
  ISBN 978-0-470-49660-2
  1. SQL server. 2. Database management. 3. Relational databases. I. Title.
  QA76.9.D3L4275 2009
  005.75'85--dc22
                                    2009024947

Dear Reader,

Thank you for choosing *SQL Server 2008 Administration Instant Reference*. This book is part of a family of premium-quality Sybex books, all of which are written by outstanding authors who combine practical experience with a gift for teaching.

Sybex was founded in 1976. More than 30 years later, we're still committed to producing consistently exceptional books. With each of our titles, we're working hard to set a new standard for the industry. From the paper we print on, to the authors we work with, our goal is to bring you the best books available.

I hope you see all that reflected in these pages. I'd be very interested to hear your comments and get your feedback on how we're doing. Feel free to let me know what you think about this or any other Sybex book by sending me an email at nedde@wiley.com. If you think you've found a technical error in this book, please visit http://sybex.custhelp.com. Customer feedback is critical to our efforts at Sybex.

Best regards,

Neil Edde
Vice President and Publisher
Sybex, an Imprint of Wiley

To the children of Bikers Against Child Abuse (BACA).
You are the real heroes.
—Michael

To my father, Bill Mansfield, who joined the angels this year.
I am thankful that he always kept my good data,
and never seemed to recall the bad.
—Mike

Acknowledgments

Every time I finish a project like this, I am always humbled by all of the effort that it takes the team to put something like this together. It may be my name on the cover, but my effort is only a portion of the work that went into this book. The entire team at Sybex is amazing. Agatha Kim kept everything on track and gave me encouragement throughout the process. Candace English is a phenomenal editor who was able to repair my problems without removing my personality from the work. To all the rest at Sybex, including Rachel McConlogue, and to Judy Flynn, I am truly grateful. A special thanks to Neil Edde, who has been willing to give me these opportunities over the last 11 years.

Also, thanks to Mike Mansfield, who did a fantastic job as a tech reviewer for this work. He was also willing to write a few chapters when the schedule got tight. I appreciate his help. To Jon Hansen, Bob Taylor, and Tim Davis, my mentors and friends who have helped me along life's road, I am thankful. Finally, to my family, who always support me: my wife, Raelynn and son Myles. Thanks for the love and laughter that you bring to my life.

Finally, on a very personal note, I want to mention that a portion of the royalties from this book are being donated to the Nevada Chapter of Bikers Against Child Abuse (BACA). Thanks to Sybex for helping this to happen and to BACA for the fine work that they do. It is my honor to call you my brothers and sisters. You can get more information about this organization at www.bacausa.com.

—Michael Lee

This is my first book with Sybex. I have always had a passion for database work, and Sybex helped me take that and turn it into something that can be shared. The entire team made the experience extraordinary. Even when difficulties arose, Agatha Kim and Candace English kept helping me through them. I am not exaggerating when I say without them, I could never have been successful in this project.

I particularly wish to thank Michael Lee, who I have had the pleasure of knowing for most of my years as a trainer. Michael and his lovely family are exceptionally giving and caring folks; I feel truly blessed to know them. I also especially thank my family: brothers, sisters, uncles, and aunts whose support I have always deeply appreciated. My wife Cindy must also be acknowledged for her patience and love that keeps me going.

—Mike Mansfield

About the Authors

MICHAEL LEE (MCT, MCPD, MCITP, SCJP) has spent the last 15 years in technology training and consulting. Most of his career has been spent working with companies and helping them ease the transition to new technologies and practices. With a degree in Business Finance from the University of Utah, Michael discovered early that he enjoyed the IT aspects of business and built a career bringing together businesses and IT professionals, helping them understand each other and improve communication.

His beginnings in IT were a bit dubious, having worked as an intern with IBM in 1988 on the FAA modernization project (AAS), which has been dubbed one of the greatest project failures in IT history. He learned a great deal from that experience; since then, his focus has been bringing together business and technology interests. As a former Microsoft Regional Director, he was heavily involved in the rollout of Visual Studio 6.0 in 1997 and made a career out of melding business and technology into a unified strategic front.

Currently, Michael is employed with the Clark County Court System in Las Vegas, Nevada, where he still gets his hands dirty in all kinds of technology, applying his passion to the public sector. When he is not coding, writing, or spending time with family, you can usually find him on his Harley, looking for that next great American Road.

MIKE MANSFIELD is a Senior Technical Trainer for Signal Learning in Indianapolis, Indiana, and holds many 2008 product certifications. Mike began teaching at Missouri State University in 2003. Prior to 2003, he worked in production environments and as a consultant for nearly two decades. In 2007, he went to Signal Learning to design a program for retraining workers who had lost their job and the initial training of recent high school graduates. These programs focus on enabling people to achieve a certified Web developer or certified SharePoint administrator status, and at this point enjoy an 83% success rate.

Mike has authored or designed many courses and special training, including a Kimball-based data warehouse architecture class for many high-level data personnel in the state of Indiana. He has trained data staff at the Assembly of God world headquarters, delivered courses on clustering to Navitair.com and Target stores world headquarters in Minneapolis, as well as many others. Mike currently resides in Carmel, Indiana, where he enjoys spending time with his beautiful wife Cindy and his interesting cat named Earl.

Contents

Introduction

This book has been a little bit different than others that I have worked on. Instead of long discussions of architectures and deep illustrations of technical concepts, this book is designed primarily to "prime the pump." The goal is not necessarily to provide every possible detail about every subject. The book that you hold in your hand is obviously much smaller than that. Our objective is to give you what you need to get going as quickly as possible so that you can start moving forward and not get caught up by the little things.

You will notice that the book is organized specifically to help you find information quickly. It is organized into parts that categorize topics into major groups. Then each chapter deals with a specific subject. In the beginning of each chapter, we tell you exactly what we will cover and where you will find it in the pages. We hope that this organization will assist you in finding the information that you need to solve immediate problems or begin a process as painlessly as possible.

Our goal from the beginning was to create a book that would be part of your everyday tool belt, something that you can pick up whenever you need a quick reference or a reminder. If the pages become worn and the cover torn, we have met our objective. Good luck in your SQL Server projects. We're right there with you.

Who Should Read This Book

Our target audience is the database professional with some SQL Server experience that is doing one of the following:

- Trying to ramp up skills on SQL Server 2008
- Transitioning from another RDBMS to SQL Server

If you have read through the Microsoft marketing materials on SQL Server 2008 and would like to see what is behind the hype, then this book is for you.

This book is primarily targeted to the database administrator. While there are some development topics addressed, they are brief and only deep enough to provide context for the administrator. If you are a database administrator looking for a quick reference guide to common tasks, then this book is a very good match for you.

Finally, if you are very experienced with other database products and want to simply get up and running with SQL Server as quickly as you can, we hope that this book will help. We have tried to remove all of the fluff and give you what you need to get the job done.

How to Contact the Author

I welcome feedback from you about this book or about books you'd like to see from me in the future. You can reach me by writing to feedback@leeteched.com.

Sybex strives to keep you supplied with the latest tools and information you need for your work. Please check the website at www.sybex.com, where we'll post additional content and updates that supplement this book should the need arise.

PART I

SQL Server Basics

IN THIS PART ▶

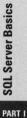

1

Installing SQL Server 2008

**IN THIS CHAPTER, YOU WILL LEARN TO DO
THE FOLLOWING:**

E ach new version of Microsoft SQL Server brings new tools and features that make the daily lives of the database administrator (DBA) simpler and more efficient. Past advances in the SQL Server feature list include elements that have become part of the core toolkit, such as the SQL Agent service and the full-text indexing tools. When it comes to including new features, SQL Server 2008 is no exception. You will find many new features in this tool. Some, such as the Transact SQL (TSQL) MERGE functionality and policy-based administration, are sure to take their rightful place beside these other tools as the new standard of SQL Server functionality.

Being a competent DBA on any product, SQL Server included, requires you to have a firm grasp on the tools, features, and architectures of the system. You would never think about starting a long journey without a road map as your guide, so also you should review the "terrain" of the SQL Server enterprise world before you begin to plan your system architectures. This book will hopefully become that road map as you work your way to a successful SQL Server 2008 implementation.

Every journey starts with a first step. In this chapter, we will address the first step, installing SQL Server 2008. To begin, we will introduce you to the role of SQL Server 2008 in the enterprise architecture and compare the various editions available for licensing. This will set the foundation upon which we will draw to discuss the specific tasks and issues relating to SQL Server installation.

Prepare for Installation

Before we dive into the installation, a little background is important. Some of the decisions you will make at installation, such as how many servers to install, where to install them, which editions to use, and so forth, will depend entirely on how you intend to use SQL Server within your organization. In the following sections, we will lay the groundwork for installation, covering such topics as understanding SQL Server's place in the enterprise, choosing the appropriate edition for your needs, determining licensing requirements, and reviewing the requirements for the actual installation.

SQL Server in the Enterprise

Prior releases of SQL Server were a bit hard to defend as truly enterprise systems. The significant architectural transformations that Microsoft implemented in the transition from SQL Server 6.5 to SQL Server 7.0 laid the basis for the enterprise system that we have today. While releases like SQL Server 2000 were essentially transition builds, SQL Server 2005 finally approached what many would begin to label as a true enterprise system. There are many features that the seasoned DBA would identify as requirements for an enterprise database platform, including these:

Interoperability   In many cases, SQL Server data must be available to applications outside of your Microsoft Windows infrastructure. With the strong presence of mainframe systems, Unix and Linux environments, Java platforms, and so on, data interoperability requirements may be extensive.

Performance   Performance often means different things to different people. To the end users, it is typically about how fast they can get their data. For an administrator, the primary concern is maximizing overall throughput. These are often conflicting goals, and the database system must be able to balance them

Security   The integrity of your data is only as good as your ability to secure it, but security these days goes beyond the typical authentication/authorization issues of the past. We must also be able to manage things like encryption processes and backup security and at the same time be proactive to prevent the security exposures of tomorrow.

High availability   What good is having the data if it is not available to the people who need it when they need it? A good enterprise framework must ensure that we have adequate redundancy and the means to minimize downtime. Every second that the data system is not available can mean lost revenue—and in some cases, legal repercussions.

Automation   The more complex and larger a system becomes, the more important it is to be able to automate routine tasks and proactive maintenance to ensure that data availability and integrity is maintained. Otherwise, the typical DBA will be completely overwhelmed with day-to-day maintenance.

Centralized reporting   Storing data isn't of much use if you can't get it when you need it in the formats that you need. A number of reporting environments are available. Whichever one you use, it is essential that the reporting tier be efficient, be flexible, and have the lowest possible footprint in terms of resource consumption.

This is definitely a short list. You could certainly add more to this list with a little thought; however, the important lesson here is that there is much more to an enterprise database platform that just handling basic Data Manipulation Language (DML) statements. Yes, it must do that, but it must do so much more as well. So let's take a closer look at what SQL Server 2008 really offers to the enterprise.

NOTE   The term *enterprise* can be a little vague and often means different things to different administrators, depending on their implementation environment. In our examples, we will assume that *enterprise* refers to any large distributed database solution. Usually there will be multiple client applications driven from the same database structure. Also, most enterprise systems will generally distribute logic throughout the tiers, adding a presentation tier and business logic tier to the application. The database is therefore just one component in a much larger architecture and must work in concert with these other components to provide a stable and efficient environment for the end user.

SQL Server 2008 Enterprise Features

This is could be a very extensive list, and again, depending on your definition of *enterprise*, some features may be more or less important to you than to another DBA. However, some of the most prominent enterprise features are listed here:

Policy-based management   Policies make it easier to enforce best practices and standards. You can have policies such as naming conventions, configuration standards, and coding standards. You can enforce these centrally for the entire organization. Not only does this simplify enforcement of standards, but it also allows central modification of policies as needed.

SQL Server Integration Services (SSIS)   SQL Server Integration Services (SSIS) provides exchange/transform/load (ETL) functionality for SQL Server 2008. SQL 2005 took a significant step forward from Data Transformation Services (DTS) when it was released, providing not only more intuitive designers, but also a native .NET execution environment. SQL Server 2008 continues that process with significant pipeline scalability improvements as well as the ability to provide persistent lookups, which is a significant data warehousing enhancement.

SQL Server Reporting Services (SSRS)   Although not a new feature, this is, in our opinion, one of the most important enterprise features that SQL Server provides. The tight integration with SQL Server and the exposure of the reporting engine through a standard web services interface make Reporting Services one of the most compelling reporting solutions available for SQL Server 2008. Enterprise features such as web report distribution, subscriptions, and infinite click-through make this one feature you should definitely evaluate for inclusion in your enterprise data architecture.

SQL Server Service Broker   The new buzzword in enterprise architecture is SOA, which stands for Service Oriented Architecture. Creating software as a set of independent and reusable services can reduce the number of "one-off" software components that add to the maintenance costs of software. The SQL Server Service Broker is a component that facilitates the integration of data-based software services through a message delivery paradigm. This tool can reduce the complexity of distributed data services by tying them all together through a common message-based programming model. This tool made its first appearance in SQL Server 2005 and has acquired a loyal following since that time.

Full-Text Search services   Full-text indexing and special query syntax let you effectively search large text blocks for patterns, word forms, proximities, and other elements. SQL Server 2008 provides some compelling enhancements to the full-text set of services. They include features such as improved full-text index management, customization tools, and performance enhancements. If you haven't at least played with Full-Text Search, you owe it to yourself to spend a few minutes learning what it has to offer.

Business intelligence   Business intelligence (BI) content is critical to the success of SQL Server 2008. The BI agenda for SQL Server 2008 was very aggressive. One of the reasons that the schedule slipped for SQL Server 2008 was that the BI features needed a bit more polishing.

The cornerstone of this version's BI functionality is SQL Server Analysis Services. Supporting data warehousing through multidimensional data models (data cubes), Analysis Services provides mechanisms for analyzing and mining the large data volumes that most organizations have collected over the years. It is also highly integrated with other services, relying on SSIS for warehouse loading and SSRS for reporting on multidimensional data, including ad hoc reporting through Report Builder.

SQL Server in the Microsoft Enterprise

Data is the foundation of most enterprise applications. Whether the application is a data management system or an administrative/productivity utility, there is generally a need for data somewhere in the architecture. Microsoft has leveraged SQL Server significantly to play that role in its enterprise framework. To say that Microsoft's enterprise strategy relies on SQL Server would be an understatement. To a large extent, SQL Server represents the data foundation of Microsoft's entire strategy. For this reason, the following Microsoft tools and utilities depend directly on SQL Server data services:

- Team Foundation Server
- Systems Management Server/System Center Configuration Manager
- Office SharePoint Server
- Office Project Server
- Operations Manager Server
- BizTalk Server
- ADO.NET

TIP   Pay close attention to SQL Server capacity and licensing options as you plan your enterprise strategy. Many administrators consider the data needs of their applications as they plan their data infrastructure but fail to include the data services required for supporting systems such as Team Foundation Server or Microsoft Operations Manager as they lay out their plans and requirements. Remember that SQL Server is pervasive in the Microsoft enterprise. Look under every stone to see if there is another SQL Server requirement lying there hidden before you finalize your data plans. It is easy to have SQL Server implementations run away with all of your resources if you do not plan for them effectively.

The important lesson here is that we need to be careful to expand our definition of what we mean by "data services." While the tendency is to think of data services as those database systems that support our client applications, the reality is much different. Data is everywhere, and in the Microsoft enterprise world, SQL Server is typically the repository for that data. This affects the following aspects of your job as a DBA:

- Capacity planning
- License management
- Network management
- Security
- Performance tuning
- Disaster recovery

SQL Server Editions

The first step in enterprise planning is knowing what your options are. From the SQL Server perspective, that means familiarizing yourself with the various editions of SQL Server, including their features, benefits, and limitations. In the ideal world, you may have unlimited resources. It would be nice to be able to buy large-capacity servers and enterprise licenses for every machine, but in the real world, this is rarely an option. Maximizing your resources requires you to understand what each edition of SQL Server offers and matching those features with the specific requirements for each application. Although this sounds simple, performing this task at the lowest possible cost while allowing for expected growth and increase in capacity and balancing the needs to the users and other systems can be a difficult process.

SQL Server 2008 Editions

The list of SQL Server 2008 editions is very similar to that of SQL Server 2005. While there have been some changes in the features and limitations of each edition, the basic logic behind SQL Server 2005 licensing continues on in SQL Server 2008. Table 1.1 provides a list of SQL Server 2008 editions and their standard capacities.

Table 1.1: SQL Server Editions

Edition	Number of CPUs	Memory	Database Size
Enterprise	OS maximum	OS maximum	Unlimited
Standard	4	OS maximum	Unlimited

Table 1.1: SQL Server Editions *(continued)*

Edition	Number of CPUs	Memory	Database Size
Workgroup	2	4GB	Unlimited
Web	4	OS maximum	Unlimited
Developer	OS maximum	OS maximum	Unlimited
Express	1	1GB	4GB
Compact	OS maximum	OS maximum	4GB

Microsoft has targeted each edition to a specific computing scenario. The intention is to provide support for the basic services that fall under a scenario without paying for services and components that you will never use. As a result, choosing the best edition is more than just matching up the CPU and memory requirements of the application with an edition. You must also understand the feature list for each edition and determine which features are critical to your application or if the computing scenario is acceptable.

NOTE   We have included only the most prominent features in this discussion, so for a complete listing of features for each edition, please consult SQL Server Books Online. This documentation is part of the SQL Server installation if you wish to copy it locally, or you can get the most up-to-date documentation online. At this writing, the URL for the U.S. English version is http://msdn.microsoft.com/en-us/library/ms130214.aspx. However since this may change, the most reliable way to locate the Books Online is to navigate to http://msdn.microsoft.com, click the Library tab on the top of the page, and then navigate to MSDN Library\Servers and Enterprise Development\SQL Server\SQL Server 2008 in the tree view on the left of the Library page.

The following list provides details of each edition.

Enterprise Edition   SQL Server 2008 Enterprise Edition is designed for those applications that need the highest level of resource management and scalability. With no hard limit on either CPU or memory, you can throw whatever the OS allows at your application. The Enterprise Edition also provides a number of additional tools related to business intelligence, redundancy, and scalability not found in other editions. Some of the more prominent features are listed in Table 1.2.

Table 1.2: Enterprise Edition Features

Feature	Description
Table partitioning	Organize a table into multiple partitions broken across physical resources.
Data compression	Consume less physical space on disk by compressing SQL Server–managed data structures.
Backup compression	Conserve disk space by compressing backup data.
Resource Governor	Balance system resource consumption to prevent resource starvation.
Database snapshots	Read data that is locked by a transaction from a snapshot instead of the live data page, preventing inconsistent reads.
Online indexing	Manage indexes, including clustered indexes, without having to take the database offline.
Online restore	Restore database backups without having to take the database offline.
Hot add memory and CPU	Add resources without taking the server offline.
Transparent database encryption	Transparently encrypt and decrypt data as it is written to and read from the database.
Business Intelligence	A wide array of BI features are exclusive to the Enterprise Edition (see Books Online for details).
Failover clustering	Supported with nodes limited only by OS maximum.

Standard Edition   The SQL Server 2008 Standard Edition is adequate for most applications that do not require the highly specialized tools offered by Enterprise. Although the Standard Edition is equivalent to Enterprise in terms of data processing, it lacks some of the administrative and business intelligence features that set the Enterprise Edition apart. There are also many features supported in the Standard Edition and higher that are not present in other editions:

- Analysis Services and the Business Intelligence Development Studio

- Failover clustering with two nodes

- Most SQL Server Integration Services (SSIS) support

- Replication publisher support

- Dynamic Address Windowing Extensions (AWE) memory configuration

Workgroup Edition   This edition supports small workgroup database scenarios. Since it is limited to two CPUs and 4GB of memory, it lacks the scalability of the Standard Edition. However, applications with light database needs and smaller transactional requirements may be perfectly suited for this edition. Since this edition also supports acting as a replication subscriber, it is well suited as the replication target for remote sites that do not have to act as a replication publisher.

Web Edition   This is a specialized edition of SQL Server that is licensed only for web workloads on Internet-facing applications. This edition is light on the extra features and tools but packs a punch for delivering scalable data services at a reasonable cost.

WARNING   Pay attention to the licensing requirements of the Web Edition if you make this choice. You are allowed to use this edition only in web application hosting scenarios, and most traditional non-web-based client server application implementation would be a violation of the license agreement. If you are doing web hosting, however, this can be a good choice because it provides the best feature set for web applications at the most reasonable cost structure

---

Developer Edition   This specialized edition of SQL Server is functionally equivalent to the Enterprise Edition, but it is only licensed for development and testing. It is not connection or resource throttled in any way, providing you with the perfect tool for true enterprise testing without having to pay for an enterprise license. It is, however, against license terms to use this edition for production services, no matter how small. The license terms are per developer, allowing a licensed developer to install this edition on as many systems as necessary for their development and testing needs. It is also possible to upgrade a Developer Edition installation to an Enterprise Edition without a complete reinstallation. Upgrades to Standard Edition are not supported.

Express Edition   The Express Edition is one of the two free editions of SQL Server. Intended primarily for educational use and independent software vendor redistribution, this edition is extremely limited in terms of features and capacity. There are three versions of this edition:

- SQL Server 2008 Express

  - Contains only the core data services

  - Targeted for small deployments and redistribution

- SQL Server 2008 Express with Tools

  - Includes the services of SQL Server 2008 Express

  - Also includes a basic version of the SQL Server Management Studio interface

- SQL Server 2008 Express with Advanced Services

  - Includes the data services and tools

  - Support for full-text indexing

  - Support for basic Reporting Services

Compact Edition   While primarily intended for mobile devices, this edition also works very well for supporting embedded database solutions. It supports only a subset of the features of the other editions, but its small footprint and easy distribution make it a perfect choice for solutions where there is a zero maintenance requirement for a standalone system

---

NOTE   SQL Server Data Services (SSDS), in beta as of this writing, is Microsoft's cloud-based data solution. This is a hosted data service, using standards-based interfaces such as SOAP, supporting a service-based implementation of SQL Server. This approach to data services offloads the need for a customer to supply its own hardware and host its own solution. The data store and maintenance is outsourced, and clients interact with the data source using cloud-based (Internet) interfaces. This is an exciting new phase of the SQL Server product life cycle with far-reaching ramifications for true distributed computing.

Operating System Support

SQL Server 2008 supports a variety of operating systems. Different features are available depending on your operating system choice. The biggest choice that you will have to make is whether to go with a 32-bit or 64-bit platform. This is more than a simple operating system choice. It can have extreme ramifications on enterprise scalability, particularly relating to memory utilization. Not all editions of SQL Server support all of the same operating systems as well, so it is important to match up your choices to make sure that you get all the benefits that you are hoping (and paying) for.

To get the full benefit of a 64-bit operating system, you should use an appropriate 64-bit version of SQL Server. When you run a 32-bit version of SQL Server on a 64-bit platform, it executes in a mode called Windows on Windows (WOW64). WOW64 is a subset of the 64-bit OS architecture that creates a 32-bit Windows environment on the 64-bit platform, thus enabling 32-bit applications to execute. The core of this subsystem is a kernel translator that transforms calls between 64 and 32 bit. These calls include all memory addressing and processor interaction. This approach is most often used for legacy support and does not fully leverage the capabilities of 64-bit Windows.

Table 1.3 provides an overview of SQL Server 2008 operating system support. This not a complete list but rather indicates the most common operating system choices in each category. Please consult SQL Server Books Online if you have concerns about a specific OS/SQL edition pairing that is not in the table.

Table 1.3: SQL Server 2008 Operating System support

SQL Server Edition	Processor Type	Operating System Options
Enterprise IA64	Itanium	Windows Server 2008 64-bit Itanium Windows Server 2003 64-bit Itanium Data Center Windows 2003 64-bit Itanium Enterprise
Enterprise X64	AMD Operton AMD Athlon 64 Intel Xeon and Pentium IV with EM64T support	Windows Server 2003 SP2 64-bit x64 Standard Windows Server 2003 SP2 64-bit x64 Data Center Windows Server 2003 SP2 64-bit x64 Enterprise Windows Server 2008 64-bit x64 Standard Windows Server 2008 64-bit x64 Data Center

Table 1.3: SQL Server 2008 operating system support *(continued)*

SQL Server Edition	Processor Type	Operating System Options
Standard X64 Web X64	AMD Operton AMD Athlon 64 Intel Xeon and Pentium IV with EM64T support	Windows XP Professional x64 Windows Server 2003 SP2 64-bit x64 Standard Windows Server 2003 SP2 64-bit x64 Data Center Windows Server 2003 SP2 64-bit x64 Enterprise Windows Vista Ultimate x64 Windows Vista Enterprise x64 Windows Vista Business x64 Windows Server 2008 x64 Web Windows Server 2008 x64 Standard
Workgroup X64 Express X64	AMD Operton AMD Athlon 64 Intel Xeon and Pentium IV with EM64T support	All X64 Standard Options plus: Windows Vista Home Premium x64 Windows Vista Home Basic x64
Enterprise 32-bit	Pentium III compatible or faster	Windows Server 2003 SP2 Standard Windows Server 2003 SP2 Enterprise Windows Server 2003 SP2 Data Center Windows Server 2003 Small Business Server SP2 Standard Windows Server 2003 Small Business Server SP2 Premium Windows Server 2003 SP2 64-bit x64 Standard Windows Server 2003 SP2 64-bit x64 Data Center Windows Server 2003 SP2 64-bit x64 Enterprise Windows Server 2008 Web Windows Server 2008 Data Center Windows Server 2008 Enterprise Windows Server 2008 x64 Standard Windows Server 2008 x64 Data Center Windows Server 2008 x64 Enterprise
Standard 32-bit Web 32-bit	Pentium III compatible or faster	All Enterprise 32-bit options plus: Windows XP Professional SP2 Windows XP SP2 Tablet Windows XP x64 Professional Windows XP SP2 Media Center 2002 Windows XP SP2 Media Center 2004 Windows XP Media Center 2005 Windows Vista Ultimate Windows Vista Enterprise Windows Vista Business Windows Server 2008 Web

Table 1.3: SQL Server 2008 operating system support *(continued)*

SQL Server Edition	Processor Type	Operating System Options
Workgroup 32-bit Express 32-bit	Pentium III compatible or faster	All Standard options plus: Windows Vista Home Premium Windows Vista Home Basic

NOTE   Developer Editions are functionally equivalent to the Enterprise Edition but with different licensing restrictions. Therefore, you can select from the same operating system list for a Developer Edition as for an Enterprise Edition but also allows for XP and Vista installations.

SQL Server 2008 Licensing

Microsoft provides for three different licensing schemes for SQL Server 2008. The costs for these licensing options will depend on your selected edition plus any specific arrangements that your organization may have with Microsoft, such as a volume license agreement or special pricing for government or education licensing. Table 1.4 provides an overview of the licensing options along with recommendations as to which option to select based on your intended use. For specific license questions and pricing, contact your Microsoft reseller.

Table 1.4: SQL Server Licensing Options

Licensing Option	Description	Best Suited For
Per Processor	Each available processor must be licensed. If a processor in a server is configured to be inaccessible to SQL Server, it does not have to be licensed. Licensing is done per socket, not per core/logical CPU	High client-to-server ratios and Internet-accessible applications
Server plus Device CAL	Requires a license for each server, plus a CAL for each device accessing SQL Server within your organization.	Shared devices such as shared workstations or kiosks

Table 1.4: SQL Server Licensing Options *(continued)*

Licensing Option	Description	Best Suited For
Server plus User CAL	Requires a license for each server, plus a CAL for each user accessing SQL Server within your organization.	Limited number of users needing access to the server, especially if they connect with multiple devices

Installation Requirements

Before installing SQL Server, you must consider all of the prerequisite requirements. Not only are there specific hardware requirements, there are also software, security, and other prerequisites. It is important to make sure you have anticipated and planned for these requirements before you perform an installation.

Hardware Requirements

In addition to the processor requirements provided in Table 1.3, there are hardware requirements. Each SQL Server installation requires a computer with the following devices:

- A CD or DVD drive if you are installing from disk media. Not necessary if you are performing a network installation.
- A VGA or better display with a minimum resolution of 1024 × 768.
- A mouse or other pointing device.

Additionally, there are memory and hard disk requirements that are specific to the edition of SQL Server you are installing. Table 1.5 provides a list of memory requirements by edition, and Table 1.6 provides a list of hard disk requirement by feature.

Table 1.5: Memory Requirements

SQL Server Edition	Min / Recommended / Max Memory
Enterprise IA64	512MB / 2GB / OS max
Enterprise X64	512MB / 2GB / OS max

Table 1.5: Memory requirements *(continued)*

SQL Server Edition	Min / Recommended / Max Memory
Standard X64	512MB / 2GB / OS max
Workgroup X64	512MB / 2GB / 4GB
Express X64	512MB / 1GB / 1GB
Web X64	512MB / 2GB / OS max
Enterprise 32-bit	512MB / 2GB / OS max
Standard 32-bit	512MB / 2GB / OS max
Workgroup 32-bit	512MB / 2GB / OS max
Express 32-bit	256MB / 1GB / 1GB
Web 32-bit	512MB / 2GB / OS max

TIP Don't expect more memory utilization than the operating system version will allow. While there are some configuration options that allow you to access additional memory on a 32-bit system, the general behavior is that 32-bit systems provide significantly less memory access than 64-bit systems. We will discuss how to configure additional memory access for 32-bit version in Chapter 2, "Configuring SQL Server 2008."

Table 1.6: Hard Disk Requirements by Feature

Feature	Disk Space Required
Database engine Replication Full-text indexing	280MB
Analysis Services	90MB
Reporting Services	120MB
Client components and tools	850MB
SQL Server Books Online	240MB

> **WARNING**   Be careful and do not rely on these tables as your production limits. The bigger your databases, the more disk space you will need to store them. You should also plan on being very generous with your memory allocations. These tables tell you what you need to get going, not necessarily what you will need in a true production environment. In Chapter 3, "Creating Databases, Files, and Tables," we will discuss reliable capacity planning in more detail.

Software Requirements

The SQL Server setup process will handle the task of preparing the server with the majority of software requirements. Although you do not have to perform this task separately, you should still know what those requirements are and specifically what the SQL Server setup will install. This will enable you to have an accurate record of what is on every server so that you can better troubleshoot and manage potential upgrades, conflicts, and incompatibilities. SQL Server setup will perform these installations only if the server is not already compliant. These requirements are as follows:

- Microsoft .NET Framework components
  - .NET Framework 3.5 SP1
  - SQL Server Native Client
  - SQL Server Setup support files
- Microsoft Windows Installer 4.5 or later
- Network software
  - Shared Memory (not supported on failover clusters)
  - Named Pipes
  - TCP/IP
  - VIA (not supported on failover clusters)
- Microsoft Internet Explorer 6 SP1 or later

Service Account Requirements

Each SQL Server service requires an authentication account to start. You will specify these accounts when you perform the initial installation. You can also modify these accounts later if your needs change or if the initial installation does not meet your requirements. Your account options are as follows:

Domain user accounts   Use this option if the server must interact with other servers on the network, such as in a linked server environment.

Local user accounts   Use this option if the server is not part of a domain. Use the least permissions possible to allow SQL Server to interact as necessary with the local operating system.

Network Service account   This is a built-in account with permissions equivalent to the local Users group. This account has authenticated access to network resources. Use this option for services where you desire a tightly restricted interaction between SQL Server and local/network resources.

Local System account   This is a built-in account that is more privileged than the network service account. This is a common default choice for SQL Server services when the service does not require domain authentication.

If you choose to use a local or domain user account, you should plan the account permissions and create the account in advance. Also remember that each service (Data Engine, SQL Agent, and other services) can use its own account. This may help you plan the granularity of permissions.

Install SQL Server 2008

The SQL Server installation process is organized into three primary phases. Performing a standard installation, a wizard will guide you through each of these phases.

1. Compatibility check

2. Data gathering

3. Software installation

In this section, we will walk through each of these phases as part of a standard installation. Then we will look at the process of performing an unattended installation. Finally, we will show you how to validate the installation before you rely on it for your production data.

Performing a Standard Installation

Most of the installations that you will perform will fall into this category. The SQL Server installer will guide you through each phase of the installation process.

NOTE   The figures and steps in this section illustrate the installation of SQL Server 2008 Developer Edition, which provides a very good representation of the installation process that you will see with the other editions. There is a remote possibility that Microsoft may alter the installation process in later releases of the software, but these examples should be indicative of your overall experience.

Let's begin by starting the standard installation:

1. Inserting the CD or DVD media into the drive should trigger an autostart, which will present you with the screen in Figure 1.1.

Figure 1.1: The SQL Server 2008 Installation Center

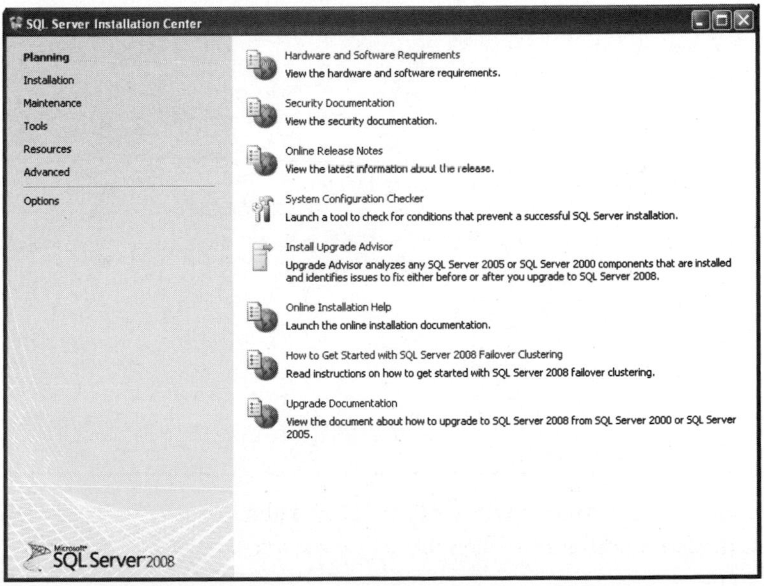

2. You will notice that this screen presents you will all of the options for installing and maintaining SQL Server. From here, you can get additional information about the installation process as well as perform installations, upgrades, and diagnostics. In this example, we will perform a standard installation, so from the menu on the left of the dialog, select Installation. This provides you with the available installation options in the right portion of the dialog. To perform a standard installation, click the "New SQL Server stand-alone installation or add features to an existing installation" link.

3. The next thing that you will see is a compatibility check window. Set up checks to ensure that your server has met the basic system requirements. If you click the Show Details button underneath the green progress bar, you will see a window that looks like the one pictured in Figure 1.2 upon successful completion of the checks. Note that passing these checks does not guarantee a successful installation. Only obvious things that will prevent the installation from successfully starting are checked.

Figure 1.2: Setup Support Rules screen

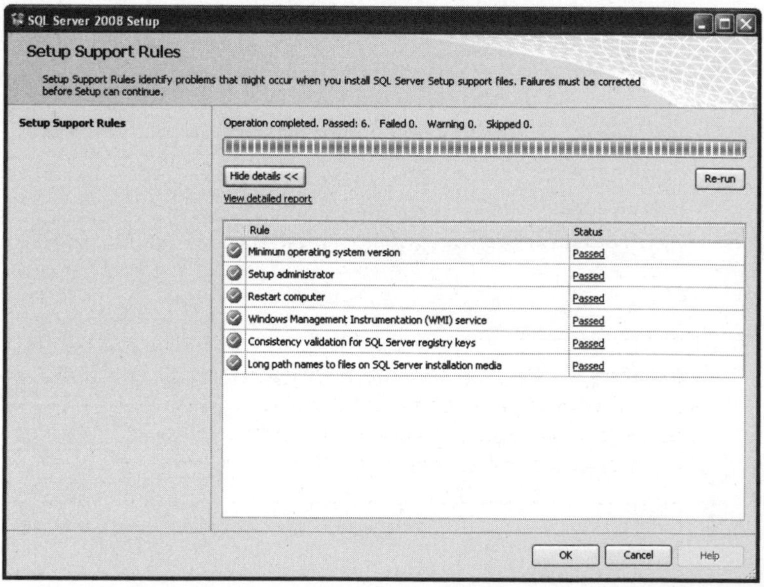

4. Click the OK button to close this window and proceed with the actual installation. The first installation screen you see will ask you to enter the product key. You can either do this or choose one of the free editions, which include the Express editions and an evaluation version of the Enterprise Edition. If you have a key at this point, go ahead and enter it. If not, you can use the Enterprise Edition evaluation version to get a good feel for the installation process. This screen is pictured in Figure 1.3.

Figure 1.3: Entering the product key

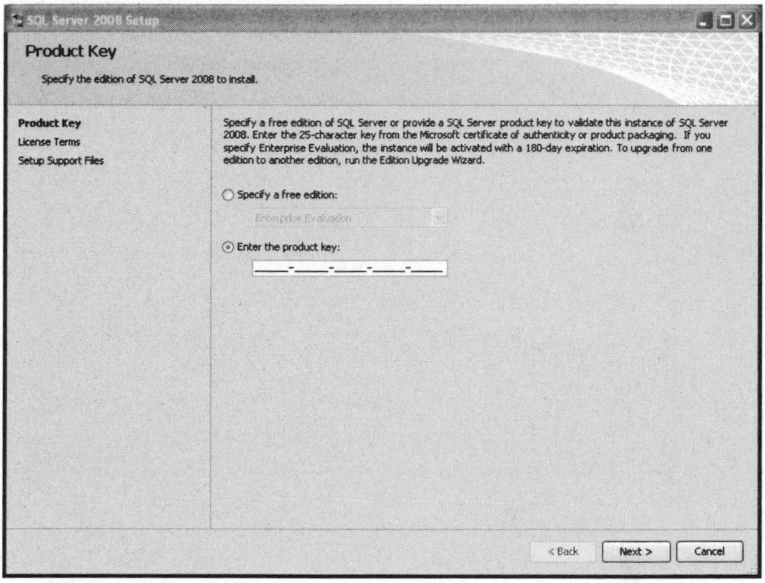

WARNING   Remember that the Enterprise Edition evaluation version is only upgradeable to the full enterprise license. If you plan to use a non-enterprise license, install it now. You will not be able to upgrade the license later.

5. Clicking the Next button will take you to the license agreement screen. This screen, pictured in Figure 1.4, allows you to read,

print, and agree to the license terms. You will notice that this installation is using the Developer Edition, so the license terms in the figure are specific to that edition. Click the check box on the bottom left of the dialog to agree to the license terms and click Next to continue.

Figure 1.4: Agreeing to the license terms

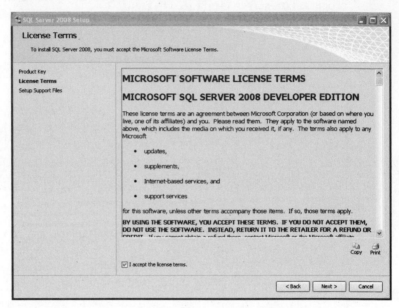

6. The next dialog presents the installer for the setup support files. Click the Install button on the bottom right of the dialog to begin the installation. These files are necessary to perform the actual installation, and you must install them first. This is a simple dialog and it is not illustrated here. Following the installation of the setup support files, you will be presented with another compatibility check. Once you successfully pass these checks, a dialog like the one pictured in Figure 1.5 appears. Again, click the Show Details button under the green progress bar if you want to see the individual checks listed.

Figure 1.5: Installation compatibility check

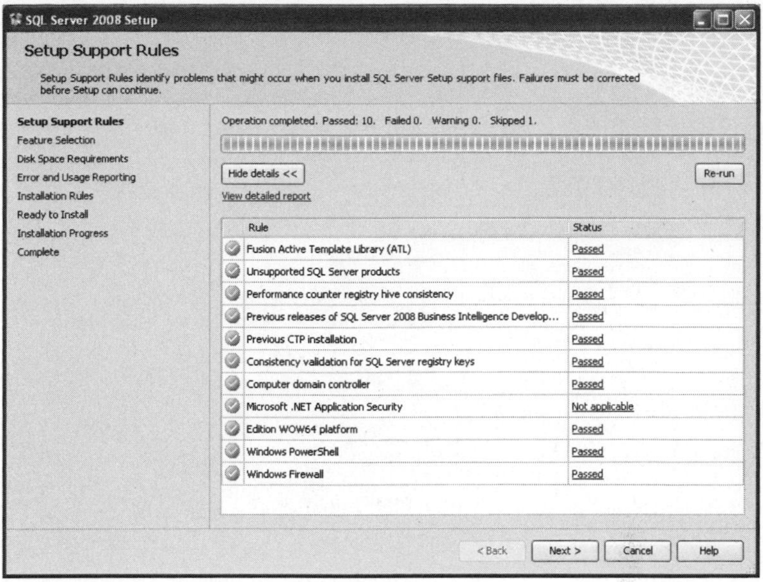

7. Click the Next button and the Feature Selection screen appears (Figure 1.6). This is the first step in the data gathering phase of the installation. We will select all of the features so that we can walk through a complete installation process. To do so, click the Select All button under the feature list. This will install the Database Engine Services, Analysis Services, Reporting Services, and a number of shared features including SQL Server Books Online, which we will refer to frequently in this book, so it is good to have this installed.

8. Click the Next button to go to the Instance Configuration dialog pictured in Figure 1.7. Each server machine can host one default instance of SQL Server, which resolves to the server name, and multiple named instances, which resolve to the pattern server-Name\instanceName. In this example, we will install a default instance. This screen will also report the other installed instances for your information.

Figure 1.6: Feature Selection dialog

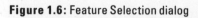

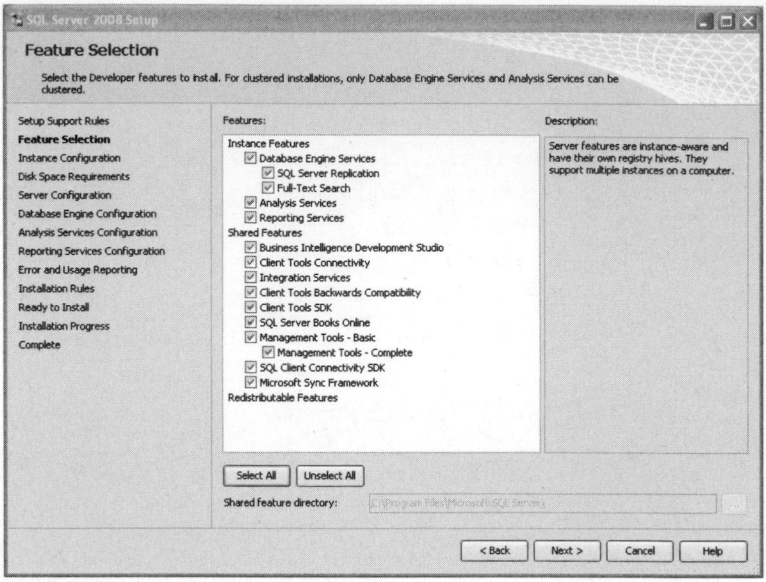

Figure 1.7: Instance Configuration screen

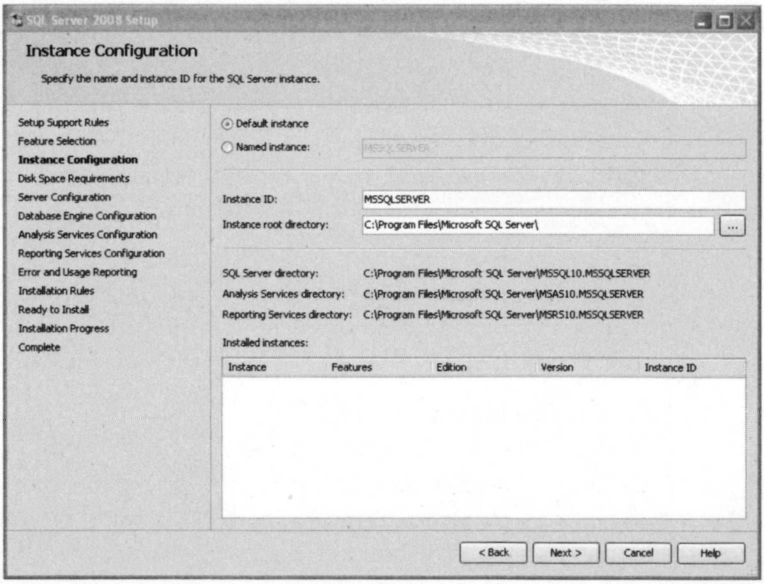

9. Click the Next button and the Disk Space Requirements dialog appears. This dialog will report the disk space needed and available for the installation. You will be informed of any insufficient disk space at this time. This is an informational dialog that does not require you to make any choices, so it is not pictured here.

10. Click the Next button again to advance to the Server Configuration dialog, pictured in Figure 1.8. This dialog allows you to specify service startup behaviors and authentication. In this example, we will authenticate all services using the local system account, but if you had previously created user accounts for service authentication, you would configure those here.

Figure 1.8: Service Configuration screen

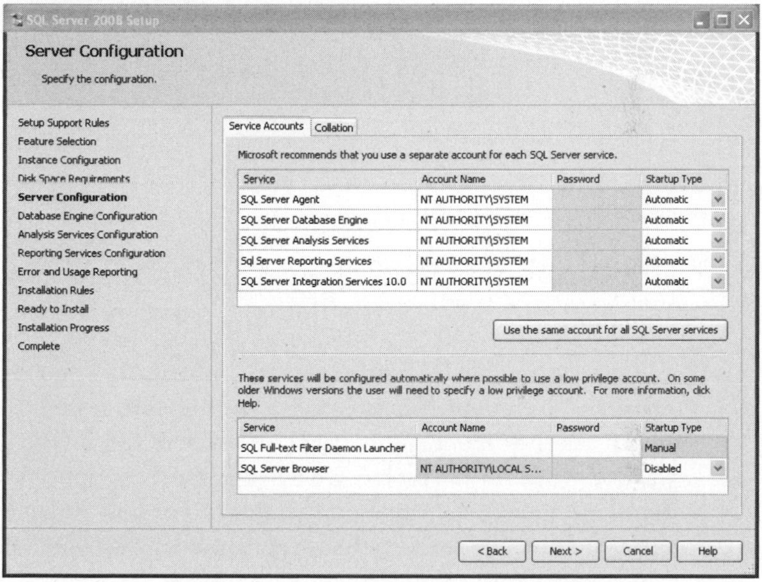

11. You will also notice a tab called Collation in the dialog called Collation. On this tab, pictured in Figure 1.9, you can set a default collation (character set and sort order) for the server. Although you can override these settings later when you create databases and even individual tables, you should choose the option that best matches the majority of your database

structures. Click the Customize button to select a new collation for the Database Engine and/or Analysis Services. In this example, we will leave the defaults.

Figure 1.9: Selecting server collations

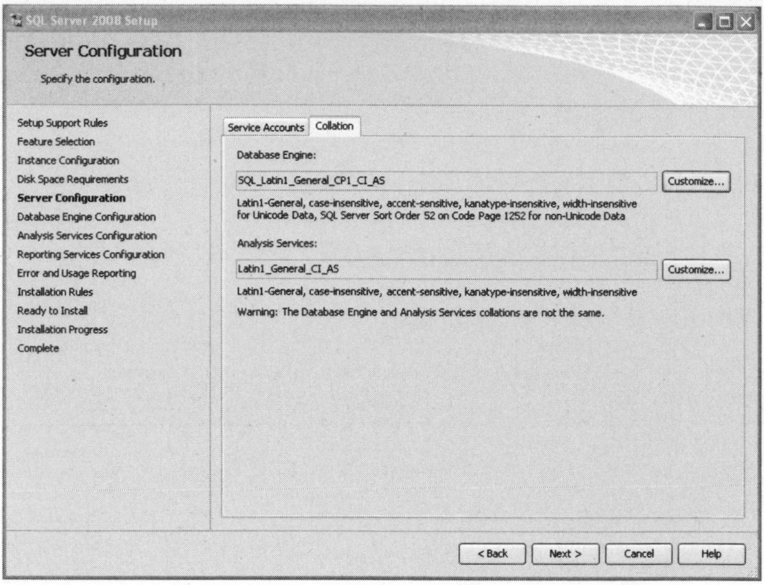

12. Click Next and the Database Engine Configuration dialog appears. This dialog has three tabs. The first tab, Account Provisioning, is shown in Figure 1.10. This is where you set the authentication mode for the server. We will discuss these options in more detail in Chapter 7, "Managing Security." For now, we will leave the default of Windows Authentication mode. This will require you to select at least one Windows account to act as a SQL Server administrator. The buttons at the bottom of the tab allow you to add and remove Windows accounts from the administrators list. In addition, you can easily add the account of the installer user by clicking the Add Current User button. This will add your current logon account to the administrators list. In this example, click this button to add yourself to the list.

Figure 1.10: Account Provisioning

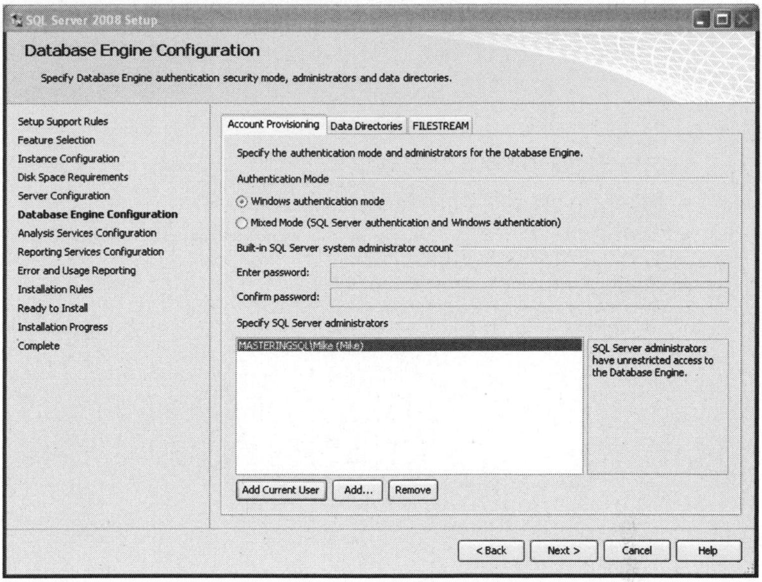

13. The Data Directories tab provides you with the options to set default database, log, backup, and tempdb locations. Set these options to the most common locations for your data, log, and backup files. Finally, on the FILESTREAM tab you can enable a new feature of SQL Server, which is the ability to store data in an unstructured file as opposed to a table. This can be very useful when storing binaries or other data that does not fit neatly in a table structure. We will leave the Data Directories tab at its defaults; however, you should configure the FILESTREAM tab as illustrated in Figure 1.11.

14. Click the Next button to advance to the Analysis Services Configuration dialog. This dialog is similar to the last one, with both an Account Provisioning tab and a Data Directories tab. Once again, click the Add Current User button on the Account Provisioning tab to add yourself to the list. We will again leave the Data Directories tab at its defaults.

Figure 1.11: FILESTREAM configuration

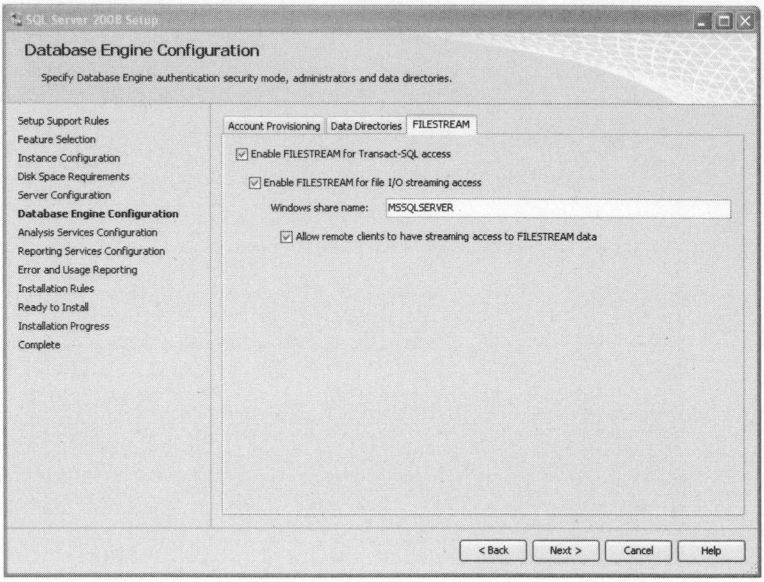

15. Click the Next button and the Reporting Services Configuration dialog appears. This is a simple dialog with three choices:

Native Mode Configuration This is the standard configuration mode, similar to prior versions of Reporting Services. The Report Manager is served out directly through Internet Information Services (IIS), and users can select and run reports from that web-based location.

SharePoint Integrated Configuration Using this option, you must install Windows SharePoint Services or the Microsoft SharePoint Server before you will be able to access the reporting capabilities. This option makes the reporting options available through a SharePoint portal, which can be very convenient for control and organization, but it takes more effort to configure and maintain than native mode.

Do Not Configure In this mode, the wizard will install the services but leave them unconfigured. You will then have to configure the services later using the Configuration Manager utility included with SQL Server. Use this option if you are unsure about which configuration option is best suited for your needs.

16. In our sample installation, we will leave the Reporting Services at the default value of a native mode configuration. When you click on the Next button, you will have the opportunity to provide usage and error information directly to Microsoft as part of its quality improvement program. If you wish to participate, select the appropriate check box; otherwise, just click Next. None of the options on this screen will affect your installation.

Figure 1.12: Install configuration check

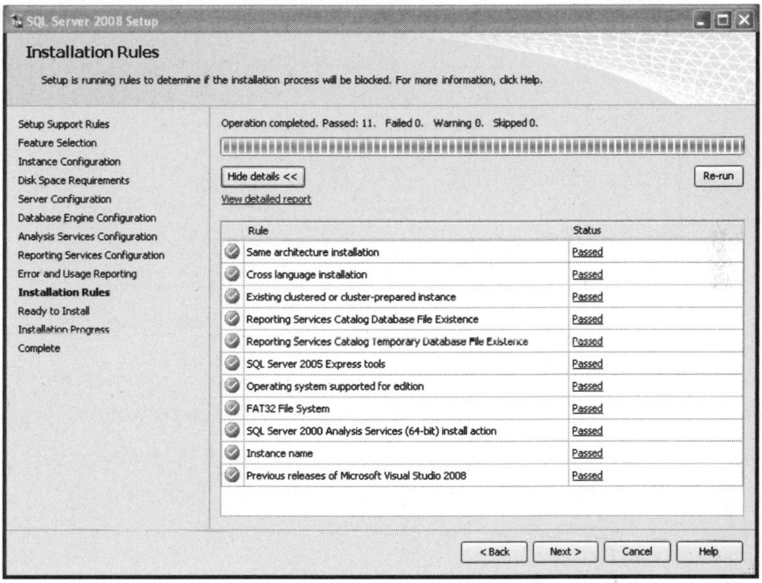

17. Finally, there is one last compatibility check to make sure that none of your selected options conflict with the existing server configuration. Figure 1.12 illustrates a successful execution of this check. If the progress bar and the check marks are green, you are ready to start the final phase, the actual software installation. Click Next to review your options and then Install to begin the installation.

18. While the installation is taking place, you will see an installation progress dialog. Wait for the dialog to show a complete and successful installation before attempting to access any of the SQL Server services. When the installation is completed, the dialog will look like the one pictured in Figure 1.13.

Figure 1.13: Successful installation

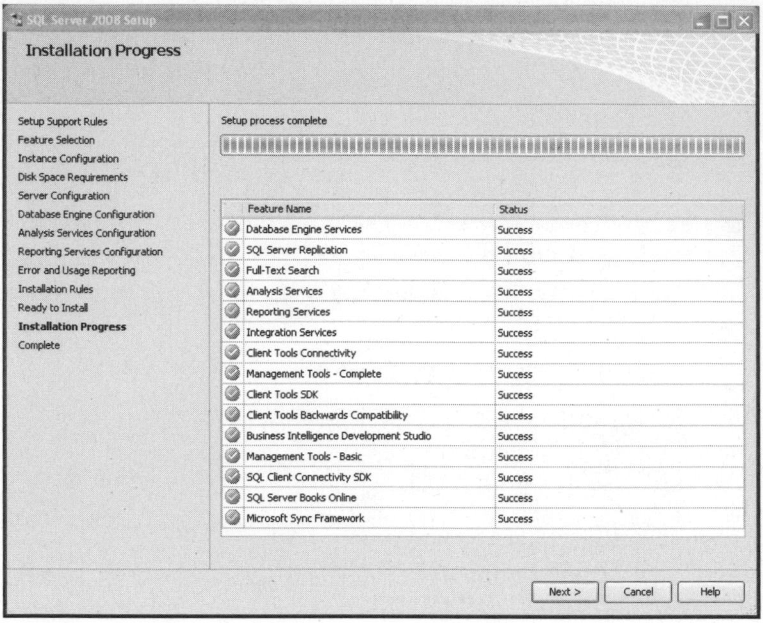

19. Click the Next button to advance to the final screen and then click the Close button to end the process. You have now successfully installed SQL Server 2008 as a default instance.

Verifying a Standard Installation

Now that you have installed SQL Server, it is worth taking a few moments to verify the installation. You will want to ensure that the server is behaving correctly before you declare success. You must first make sure that you can connect to the server and execute some simple queries. Then you can install some sample databases to test the installation further.

Connecting to the Server

Follow these steps to connect to the server:

1. The first step is to make sure that you can connect to the server. To do this, you will use a tool called the SQL Server Management

Studio (SSMS). To open it, click the Windows Start button and choose All Programs ≻ SQL Server 2008 ≻ SQL Server Management Studio.

2. The first thing you will see when you start the SSMS is a Connect to Server dialog. This dialog, pictured in Figure 1.14, allows you to connect the utility to any server that you can see on your network. In this case, you configured the server to authenticate users in a Windows Authentication mode. You also added your own account to the administrator list, so you should be able to connect to the local server simply by clicking the Connect button.

Figure 1.14: The Connect to Server dialog

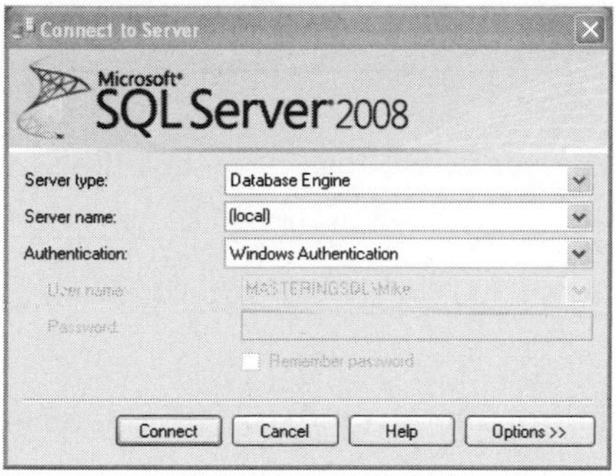

3. You should now see the Object Explorer on the left of the screen. This gives you a tree view of the currently connected resources. You will notice that next to the server name, local in this case, is a green circle with a white triangle. This indicates that the service is running and you have an active connection to it. This dialog is illustrated in Figure 1.15.

Figure 1.15: The Object Explorer

Object Explorer

Connect ▾

⊟ (local) (SQL Server 10.0.1600 - MASTERINGSQL\Mike)
   ⊞ Databases
   ⊞ Security
   ⊞ Server Objects
   ⊞ Replication
   ⊞ Management
   ⊞ SQL Server Agent

Now let's see if we can execute a query against the server. We will start with something simple and have the server respond with its currently installed version, build, and service pack level.

1. To open a query window, click the New Query button immediately above the Object Explorer or select File ➢ New ➢ Database Engine Query.

WARNING   If you use the New Query button, your query window will automatically be connected to the service currently selected in the Object Explorer. If you use the menu instead, you must connect to the query window yourself through the Connect to Server dialog. Look at the status bar at the bottom of the query window to identify the connection status. It is important to always be sure that you are connected to the right service.

---

2. Once you have opened the query window, type the following statement:

```
SELECT @@Version;
GO
```

3. Now click the Execute button on the toolbar. This is the button with the red exclamation point on its face. A results pane appears providing you with the information that you are looking for. This is SQL Server 2008 RTM build 10.0.1600.22, or in other words, the final RTM build with no service packs installed.

4. If it is a bit difficult to read this information in the grid cell, you can have SQL Server output the results to a text format as well by selecting Query ➢ Results To ➢ Results to Text or using the Ctl+T keystroke shortcut and then executing your query again.

NOTE   You will notice a semicolon at the end of the first line in the code in step 2. If you played around with this code, you may also have noticed that this semicolon is not required to run the query. The ANSI convention for SQL includes this marker as an "end of line" identifier. Although SQL Server does not require this marker, it certainly does support it. We feel that using this marker is a good habit to get into, and we will be using it in all of the code examples in this book.

Configuring Services

Another smart validation step is to consult the SQL Server Configuration Manager utility to ensure that everything is configured the way you want it. If you followed our instructions in the setup, the Full-Text Search service will be installed but disabled. In a later step, you will need to use this service for a sample database, so you need to turn it on now and change its startup behavior to automatic by following these steps:

1. To start the SQL Server Configuration Manager, select Start ➤ All Programs ➤ Microsoft SQL Server 2008➤ Configuration Tools ➤ SQL Server Configuration Manager.

2. In the Configuration Manager dialog, locate the SQL full-text filter daemon launcher in the list and double-click the entry to open a configuration dialog.

3. Click the Service tab to see the service configuration. The only option enabled right now should be Start Mode. Click Disabled next to Start Mode to open a drop-down list and select Automatic. Then click the Apply button. This enables the service.

4. Now you have to start the service. Click the Log On tab in the dialog. Click the Start button in the Service status section.

5. Click OK to close the dialog and close the Configuration Manager.

You can configure other services in much the same way from the Configuration Manager. Getting familiar with the options in this dialog will pay later.

Installing a Test Database

The good news here is that we have been able to successfully connect to and select from the server. There are no user databases currently available to test, so that will be our next step. There are sample databases available for download that we will be using in this book. These can be found on the CodePlex.com website. To access the downloads, go to www.codeplex.com/MSFTDBProdSamples and click on the link for SQL Server 2008 product sample databases.

You will be presented with four options, depending on your installation. You can download the appropriate samples for your platform by clicking on the MSI file link at the top of the page. In our case, we would select the SQL2008.AdventureWorks_All_Databases.x86.msi link because that is our currently installed platform. You can either save the file locally and run it later or run it in place now. It doesn't matter which you choose.

WARNING We have no control over the CodePlex website, so the available options may change at any time without notice. If the options that we describe here are no longer available, try navigating to the root of the CodePlex site and drill into the SQL Server section. You should be able to locate the correct download without too much trouble.

Run through the installation, accepting all of the defaults. When you get to the Database Setup dialog asking you which instance to use for the installation, select your preferred instance from the drop-down list. We installed a default instance of SQL Server, so the Instance ID for that instance should be MSSQLSERVER, as illustrated in Figure 1.16. Then complete the installation.

Figure 1.16: Selecting an installation instance

After the installation is complete, go back to the SSMS and look again at the Object Explorer. In the Databases node, you should now see six databases whose names begin with *AdventureWorks*. You may need to right-click the Databases node and choose Refresh if you do not see them. These databases use almost all of the services that we installed, including FILESTREAM storage and the Full-Text Search services, so if they successfully install, you can be very comfortable in the success of your setup. In addition, now you have all of this sample data to play with! Now you can test a database query. Go back to a query window and enter the following code. This should return a total of 12 rows.

```
USE AdventureWorksDW2008;
SELECT FirstName, LastName, EmailAddress
FROM DimEmployee
WHERE BirthDate > '1/1/1980';
GO
```

Performing an Unattended Installation

There may be occasions when you need to install multiple instances of SQL Server and want to do so as quickly and consistently as possible. When this is the case, you may choose to do a silent installation. This approach uses a command prompt to perform the installation. You have two choices when installing from the command prompt:

- Provide all installation details as parameters of the command prompt execution.

- Create a configuration file that the installer will use to answer all installation questions in a silent mode.

The second option is the simplest and most reliable, so we will walk through that approach to install a second instance of SQL Server called Silent. The process begins much like a standard installation. When you walk through the installation using the wizard, it records your selections in a configuration file. You can therefore use the wizard to create the configuration file and simply cancel the installation at the last step.

Creating the Configuration File

Follow these steps to create the configuration file.

1. Start the installer by inserting or auto-playing the media.

2. Click Installation in the Installation Center dialog and click the top option for a new stand-alone installation.

3. Click OK after the first configuration check.

4. Click Install to install the support files.

5. Click Next after the second configuration check.

6. Click Next to perform a new installation of SQL Server 2008.

7. Specify your edition and click Next.

8. Accept the license agreement and click Next.

9. Select Database Engine Services only on the features screen and click the Next button.

10. Specify a named instance called Silent and click Next.

11. Review the disk space requirements and click Next.

12. Set all services to use the Local System account. Leave the Collation option at the default and click Next.

13. Leave the authentication mode as Windows Authentication mode. Add the current user to the administrators list. Click Next to continue.

14. Click Next on the reporting screen.

15. Click Next after the last configuration check.

16. Make a note of the configuration file path on this final screen. This is the file that we are interested in. Click the Cancel button to cancel the installation. Close the Installation Center screen.

Now that you have the configuration file, you can open it up in a text editor and look it over. You will see that there are answers in this file for any installation questions that differ from the defaults. If you wanted to edit this file directly, you could. Copy this file to a convenient location. We will use it in the next step.

Executing the Silent Setup

The next step is to use the configuration file with the command prompt to perform an installation of SQL Server. If the configuration file is correct, this part is very simple. Open a command prompt and navigate to the location of the setup media. Assuming that the media is on the D: drive, you would use the following command line, substituting the location and name of the configuration file as appropriate:

```
D:\>Setup.exe /ConfigurationFile=<ConfigFilelocation> /Q
```

TIP The /Q switch at the end is important. This is what makes it a silent install. If you remove this switch, you will see the installer UI as normal, but the configuration file settings will override the natural defaults. This can sometimes be very handy if you want to create an installer routine that allows input but uses a different set of configurations for the installation base.

After the install is complete, you will want to verify that the server exists. One approach is to check the service list. If you open the SQL Server Configuration Manager, you should now see your new service in the list of available services. You will notice that in Figure 1.17, the instance called Silent has been added to the bottom of the list. This also shows that the Database Engine instance is running.

Figure 1.17: Verifying the silent installation

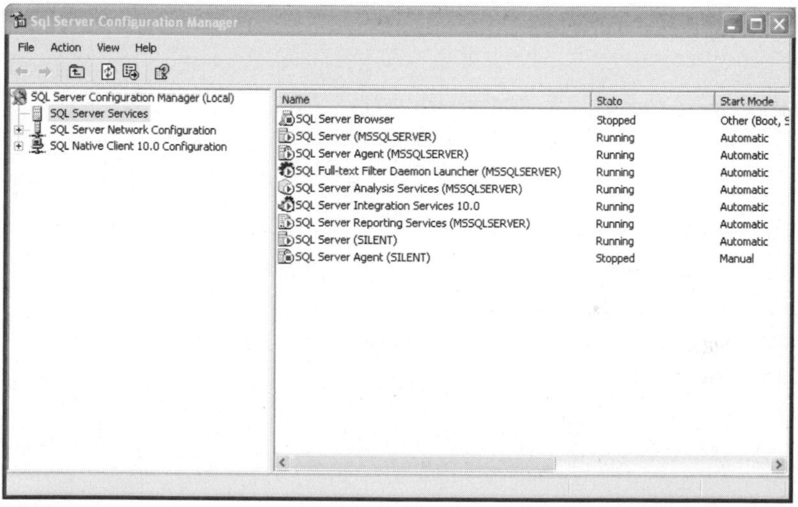

Since the instance is running, you should be able to connect to it and query it. Start the SSMS, and when you see the Connect to Server dialog, use the server name (local)\Silent. Connect using Windows Authentication. You should now see your new server in the Object Explorer window. If you want to try using executing a query, you can use the version example that we used in the previous example.

2

Configuring SQL Server 2008

IN THIS CHAPTER, YOU WILL LEARN TO DO THE FOLLOWING:

O ne of the strengths of SQL Server 2008 is that it can be adapted for numerous implementation scenarios. In a way, that is also one of the greatest frustrations for a database administrator (DBA). In the old days when there were few, if any, alternate configurations that SQL Server could reasonably support, it was much easier to configure the server platform and the SQL Server software that runs on top of it. In those days you had very few choices. Configuring a server was basically just following a recipe.

With SQL Server 2008, we have a highly flexible and adaptable system. Whether your goal is support for a small workgroup environment or for a large enterprise, SQL Server is up to the task, provided the hardware, operating system, and SQL Server services are properly selected and configured. In this chapter we will look at some of the more important configurations. We will begin by looking at the system and hardware configuration and then at the configuration of SQL Server itself.

Configure the Server Platform

SQL Server does not exist in a vacuum. It obviously needs hardware and operating system resources to run. The proper configuration of these resources is essential to the performance of a SQL Server enterprise environment. Since SQL Server is a substantial consumer of disk and memory resources, these should be your primary area of focus. Ensuring that SQL Server has adequate resources that are properly tuned for performance and fault tolerance will provide the foundation for a better-performing data platform.

Configuring System Memory

Data is stored durably in files, but generally SQL Server must read data into memory to be used by client applications. Having sufficient memory is vital to SQL Server's performance; however, the proper configuration to make maximum use of that memory is even more critical. In this section, we will look at the role memory plays and how to properly configure it for maximum impact.

If there is insufficient memory to store the most commonly used data, swapping must occur. This means that data must be continually moved back and forth between memory and disk. Although common in SQL Server, swapping is a time-consuming process that you should try to minimize as much as possible.

So how much memory can SQL Server actually use? That depends on a variety of factors. The primary factors are the CPU architecture of the server and the version of SQL Server that is running on that server. A 64-bit processor can address more memory than a 32-bit processor, but a 32-bit version of SQL Server running on a 64-bit architecture does not fully utilize the capacity of the hardware. When properly coerced through configuration settings, a 32-bit processor can use memory not normally accessible. Table 2.1 lists the user-addressable memory capacity of SQL Server in a variety of typical configurations. Unless otherwise specified, it is assumed that a 32-bit version of SQL Server is running on a 32-bit Windows version. The parallel assumption applies to 64-bit implementations.

Table 2.1: SQL Server Memory Configurations

Configuration	32-bit	64-bit
Conventional	2GB	Up to OS maximum limit
/3GB boot parameter	3GB	Option not supported
/PAE boot parameter	2GB per instance	Option not supported
WOW64	4GB	Option not supported
AWE	OS version dependent	Option not supported

Conventional 32-bit Configuration

In a 32-bit environment, SQL Server is limited to 2GB of physical addressable memory under conventional circumstances. Due to the limitations of the Windows 32-bit memory architecture, only a total of 4GB of physical memory are addressable by the operating system. By default, 2GB of memory are reserved for operating system use only, and the remaining 2GB of memory are available for application use. Even in the most rudimentary of production scenarios, 2GB of memory are insufficient for most SQL Server applications. This is the default and requires no special configuration

/3GB Boot Parameter

Starting with Windows Server 2000 Advanced Server, the server administrator can add the /3GB switch to the boot.ini file to reallocate server memory. Using this option, the 4GB of addressable memory are redistributed such that the operating system is granted access to 1GB of memory while applications can address 3GB. This extra gigabyte of memory can make a significant difference in some applications.

/PAE Boot Parameter

Consider another situation, one in which you may have multiple SQL Server instances running on the same physical server. Each instance is responsible for maintaining its own memory pool; however, with no special memory options enabled, those instances must compete for the same 2GB of available application memory. Although SQL Server will dynamically allocate memory as needed, the multiple SQL Server instances will essentially starve each other's memory needs.

The solution is to use the /PAE switch in the boot.ini file. This switch controls the Physical Address Extensions (PAEs) that allow more than one application to use aggregate memory beyond the 4GB limit. In such cases, each SQL Server instance would get its own 2GB block of memory, assuming physical memory is available, and would not compete with the other instance of SQL Server for memory resources. If the /PAE switch is used in conjunction with the /3GB switch, each instance would have access to 3GB of physical memory.

The Perils of the /3GB Switch

Although it is very useful, the /3GB switch can cause problems. First, you must make sure that it is compatible with your version of Windows. This is an operating system option, not a SQL Server option. It is not supported on the standard version of Windows 2000 Server; it is supported only on Advanced Server and higher. It is fully supported on Windows Server 2003 and Windows Server 2008.

Another problem occurs when you use the /3GB switch in conjunction with the /PAE option. If the /3GB switch is used when the machine has more than 16GB of physical memory, the server will not be able to access any memory over the 16GB threshold. This is because the operating system needs the full 2GB of memory to be able to address any memory over the 16GB threshold.

Address Windowing Extensions (AWE)

Another extended memory configuration option is Address Windowing Extensions (AWE). This option can significantly increase access to extended memory above the standard 2GB application limit. The amount of increase depends on which Windows version you are using. Windows 2003 Server can use up to 4GB of application memory under AWE. Windows 2003 Enterprise supports up to 32GB of application memory, and Windows 2003 Datacenter increases this limit to 64GB.

Configuring AWE in SQL Server requires that you first set the Lock Pages in Memory policy in Windows to prevent extended memory from being paged to disk. The steps to do this differ slightly depending on your operating system, but this is the general process:

1. On the Start menu and click Run. In the Open box, type **gpedit.msc** to open the Group Policy window.

2. In the tree view on the left, expand Computer Configuration, and then expand Windows Settings.

3. Expand Security Settings, and then expand Local Policies.

4. Select the User Rights Assignment folder. This will display the policies in the details pane.

5. In the pane, double-click Lock Pages in Memory to open the configuration window.

6. In the Local Security Policy Setting dialog box, click Add User or Group.

7. In the Select Users or Groups dialog box, add the SQL Server service account and click OK.

8. Click OK to close the policy configuration window.

9. Close the Group Policy Editor.

To configure AWE in SQL Server, set the advanced option, AWE Enabled, to 1. This option allows SQL Server to use physical memory up to the operating system limit. You should also consider configuring the SQL Server option Max Server Memory to an appropriate value. This is especially important if you have more than one instance of SQL Server running. In this case, each instance should have a Max Server Memory setting configured such that the total of all Max Server Memory values does not exceed the physical memory amount that will be made available to applications. Follow these steps to configure these settings.

1. Open the SQL Server Management Studio (SSMS) and connect to the server that you want to configure. In our case, that is the local server.

2. In the Object Explorer, right-click on the server node and select Properties.

3. Click the Memory page of the dialog and enable the option to use AWE to allocate memory. This page is illustrated later in this chapter in Figure 2.2.

4. Set the Maximum Server Memory value on this page if needed to ensure that one server does not starve out others for resources.

5. Click OK to confirm your changes.

64-bit Memory Access

When SQL Server is running on a 64-bit processor architecture, the rules change. If you are running a 32-bit version of SQL Server on a 64-bit platform, SQL Server can use up to 4GB of memory using WOW64 (64-bit Windows on Windows). WOW64 is nothing more than 32-bit applications running on a 64-bit platform. The platform itself, however, provides access to 4GB of memory without any special configuration.

The easiest option is to run a full 64-bit architecture. Although 64-bit architecture is capable of addressing over 18 exabytes (one quintillion bytes) of memory, this is not practical, and lower limits are utilized based on processor type. X64 processors can handle up to 8TB of memory, and IA64 processors can handle up to 7TB of memory—all without any special configuration.

Planning System Redundancy

Redundancy is critical in enterprise systems. Your data is the lifeblood of your company. Any data loss, no matter how seemingly insignificant, can end up having far-reaching effects on the company and its bottom line. You must also ensure that data is always available to the consumers who need it. Two of the most popular ways to provide this redundancy are using RAID and clustering.

Redundant Array of Independent Disks (RAID)

Also called Redundant Array of Inexpensive Disks (the original term for the technology), RAID is a technique in which an operating system or hardware I/O system uses multiple hard drives to distribute data across multiple disks in an effort to provide fault tolerance and/or performance benefits. An administrator can employ various RAID strategies. The following are the most common.

RAID-0: Stripe set without parity   This option is primarily intended to optimize performance. In this scenario, the RAID controller spreads the data stream across two or more physical disks. The objective is to improve performance by placing data on multiple disks simultaneously, thereby eliminating the potential I/O bottleneck of writing to a single physical disk. This option provides no fault tolerance because a single disk failure destroys the entire array and there is no parity information stored on the other disks that you can use to regenerate the lost drive.

RAID-1: Mirrored set   Level 1 provides fault tolerance by duplicating all data writes to a mirror disk. If the data device is lost, the mirror provides a copy of the lost data and thereby minimizes downtime. A good RAID controller will use both disks for read operations, therefore increasing the performance for read operations; however, doing this adversely affects write operations due to the increased write activity.

RAID-5: Striped set with parity   This solution stripes data access across three or more physical disks up to 32 disks, similar to the RAID-0 solution. Unlike RAID-0, however, the controller also writes distributed parity data across the stripe set so that the loss of a drive would not result in the loss of the database. The controller can use the parity information to respond to requests until an administrator is able to regenerate a new disk based on the parity data. In this configuration, the array is still vulnerable to the loss of a second drive. This solution also can adversely affect write performance because of the extra I/O required to calculate and write the parity data, although this can be offset somewhat by the distribution of data across multiple physical disks.

You can also combine these levels to provide options that are more complex.

- RAID-01 (0 + 1): Mirror of striped sets
- RAID-10 (1 + 0): Striped mirror sets
- RAID-50 (5 + 0): Parity striped mirror sets

There are other RAID options, but these are the most common. Always remember that the goal is to ensure adequate availability without compromising performance beyond acceptable levels. Fault tolerance always comes at a cost. The administrator's job is to find the right balance.

All Parity Is Not Created Equal

Although the Windows operating system supports various software-based RAID solutions, they are not reasonable performance alternatives to a hardware-based solution. A variety of vendors support RAID at the hardware level. Do your research and find the vendor that offers a solution that provides the balance of cost, features, and manageability that makes sense for your environment. Since the configuration of these solutions depends on the specific hardware used, this section will not cover the actual configuration of disk systems.

Clustering

While RAID provides fault tolerance from disk failure, it provides no protection against other faults, such as memory, CPU, or I/O controller failures. By contrast, clustering can provide effective protection from hardware failures other than disk failures. As with RAID, many different configuration options are available for clustering. The features and benefits of a particular implementation become selling points for the hardware or software vendor that provides the solution.

In SQL Server terminology, the term *cluster* refers to a failover cluster only. This means that SQL Server cannot use the cluster for load-balancing-only redundancy. The general approach to setting up clustering is to create a two-node active/passive cluster. This requires two servers connected to a single array of disks. Clients direct activity to a "virtual" address, which represents the cluster rather than any individual server in the cluster. Only one of the servers will actively respond to requests. The other server, which is the passive node, monitors the "heartbeat" of the active node so that it can detect if the active node fails to respond. This would trigger an automatic failover, redirecting activity to the second node. Failover clustering provides the following benefits:

- Automatic detection and failover
- Ability to perform manual failover
- Transparency to the client of failover redirection

There are constraints when using clustering, however. You must license at least the Standard Edition of SQL Server, which supports two-node clusters. The Enterprise Edition allows additional nodes as configured by the operating system. Additionally, you must work within the following limitations.

- Clustering operates at the server level of scope. You cannot fail over an individual database.
- There is no protection against disk failure. You should continue to use RAID for disk fault tolerance.
- The cluster performs no load balancing. Only the active node can be queried.
- The cluster requires signed hardware capable of working with the Windows version that you are targeting.
- Each group of clustering resources (for example, disk arrays and processors) can serve only one instance of SQL Server 2008.

When clustering in Windows Server 2008, there are a few new features that can benefit SQL Server. If you're using the Enterprise versions of Windows and SQL Server, you can support up to 16 nodes in your cluster. In addition, Windows Server 2008 removes the requirement that all cluster nodes reside in the same subnet, opening the door to increased geographical distribution of cluster nodes. In a fully geographically dispersed architecture, nodes complete with arrays can be configured in different geographical locations, thereby creating full server redundancy, including array redundancy.

TIP   The configuration of clustering in Windows Server 2008 is beyond the scope of this discussion, but if you are looking for a really good walkthrough, we recommend that you check out Microsoft's virtual lab on Windows 2008 clustering. At this writing, that lab is located at `http://msevents.microsoft.com/CUI/WebCastEventDetails.aspx?EventID=1032345932&EventCategory=3&culture=en-US&CountryCode=US`. Of course, the URL could change, so you could also look up "Windows Server 2008 Enterprise Failover Clustering Lab" on the Microsoft website.

Configure SQL Server 2008

In addition to making sure that you have successfully planned the operating platform for SQL Server, you must ensure that you have configured SQL Server appropriately for your enterprise environment. In the following sections, we will look at the server configuration options in the SSMS and explore the SQL Server Configuration Manager, the tool that you will use for service configuration.

Configuring the Server with the SSMS

Most of the standard server configuration options are available from the Properties window on the server node of the Object Explorer. This is a multipage dialog that organizes all configurations by category. We will take a closer look at the dialog to see the options available.

Accessing the Server Properties Dialog

To open the Server Properties window, follow these steps:

1. Start the SSMS and connect to the server that you want to configure. Remember that you must connect using an account that has SQL Server administrative rights or server configuration permissions.

2. Locate the Object Explorer in the SSMS. If it is not visible, select View ➢ Object Explorer from the SSMS menu or press the F8 key on the keyboard.

3. In the Object Explorer, locate and right-click the server node. Select Properties from the bottom of the pop-up menu. The General page of the Server Properties dialog appears (Figure 2.1).

Figure 2.1: The General page of the Server Properties dialog

SQL Server Basics

PART I

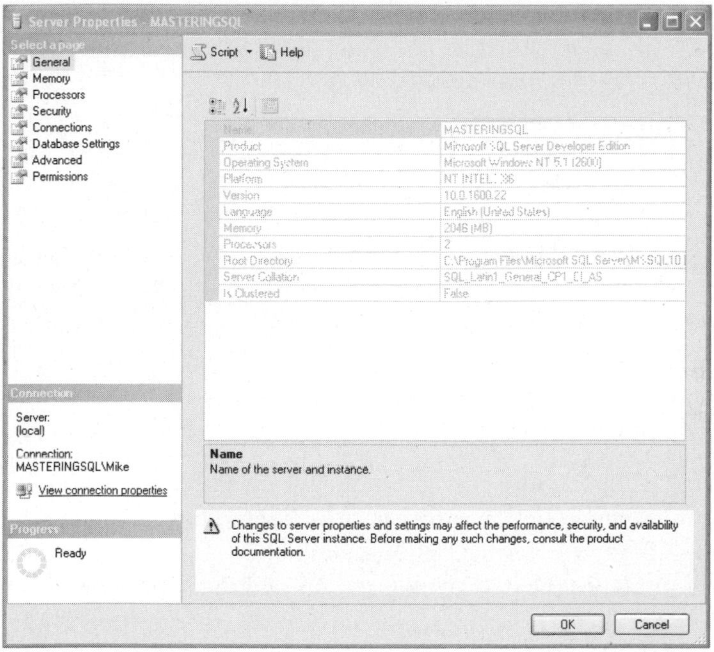

The General page is information only. There are no user-modifiable elements on this page; however, it is a convenient location to access basic system information. Most of this information is also available using a Transact SQL (TSQL) script. To execute a script that retrieves similar information, follow these steps.

1. From the SSMS menu, select File ➤ New ➤ Database Engine Query. Connect to the target server when prompted. This opens a new query window.

2. To send the results to a text output rather than a grid, select Query ➤ Results To ➤ Results to Text from the SSMS menu.

3. Type the following statement in the query window:

```
SELECT @@VERSION;
```

4. Press the F5 key on the keyboard to execute the query. The output will look something like this:

```
Microsoft SQL Server 2008 (RTM) - 10.0.1600.22
(Intel X86)
  Jul  9 2008 14:43:34
  Copyright (c) 1988-2008 Microsoft Corporation
  Developer Edition on Windows NT 5.1 <X86>
(Build 2600: Service Pack 2)
```

You should be able to see that this same information is available on the General tab of the dialog, but the dialog also contains additional information. One advantage of the user interface (UI) provided by the SSMS is that it collects information and settings that are available from a wide variety of other sources and commands. However, you can still access these features using TSQL code, which you will see later in this chapter.

The Memory Page

This tab is for memory configuration. We discussed the Use AWE to Allocate Memory option earlier in this chapter, but as you will see from Figure 2.2, there are other options available.

In addition to the AWE configuration and the Minimum and Maximum server memory settings, you have some other options available. Generally, the default values for these other options will be adequate.

Index Creation Memory   This option allows you to configure the amount of memory reserved for an index creation task. The default is 0, which means that memory will be dynamically allocated for index creation. While this is usually optimal, you may need to alter this if you are concerned that creating indexes on large tables may starve out memory requirements for other server-based activities.

Minimum Memory per Query   When SQL Server executes queries, it must have some memory available for the query execution context and results buffering. This option allows this value to be configured for special execution scenarios.

Running vs. Configured Values   The option buttons at the bottom of the screen allow you to switch the view back and forth between the currently configured options and the currently running options.

Sometimes these options can be different if you make configuration changes but those changes have not yet taken effect. Most of the pages in this dialog include these option buttons. Their behavior is the same on every page.

Figure 2.2: The Memory page

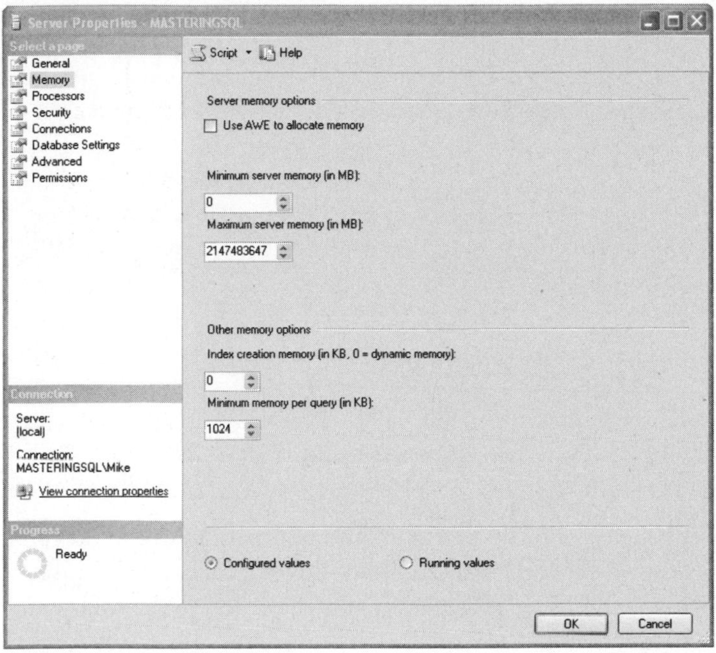

The Processors Page

It is unlikely that you will see a SQL Server operating platform with only one processor these days. With multiprocessor boards and multi-core processors now the norm, the number of processors available to SQL Server and its supporting services is significantly greater than even just a few years ago. Since there are so many services competing for these processor resources now, it is more important than ever to ensure that they are properly configured. Figure 2.3 provides an illustration of this dialog.

Figure 2.3: The Processors page

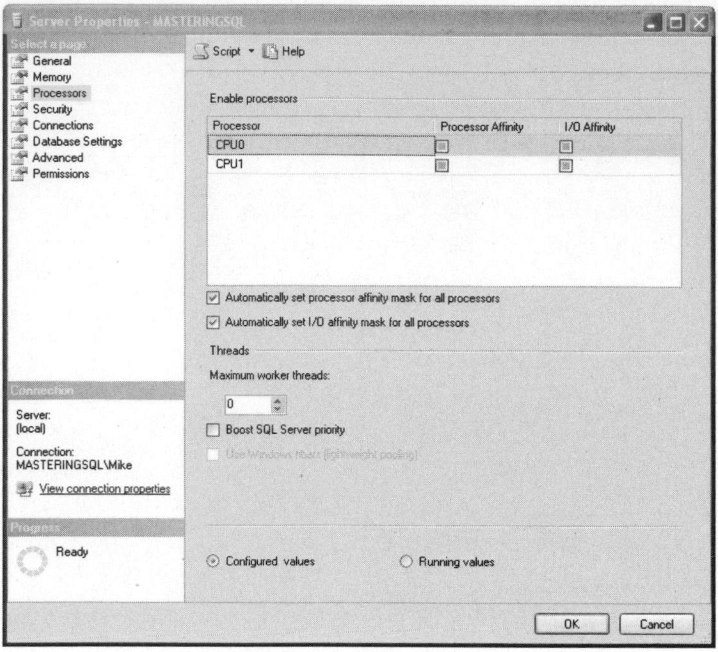

The two check marks below the grid automatically enable all affinity for all processors. By unchecking these two boxes, you can manually set the desired affinity. This page allows you to configure the following options:

Automatically Set Processor Affinity Mask for All Processors This option determines which processors SQL Server is allowed to use. By default, all servers and instances are allowed to use all processors. You can restrict certain processors if you wish to ensure that processor resources will be available to a server instance. This is particularly useful when you have very active instances that may starve other instances for resources.

Automatically Set I/O Affinity Mask for All Processors I/O activities also take processor power. The I/O behavior of SQL Server is managed by Windows, so SQL Server allows for separate configuration for I/O processor resources.

Maximum Worker Threads   Much of a thread's lifetime is spent idle. As a result, its existence consumes resources but provides no functional benefit most the time. To conserve resources, SQL Server can allocate many requests to a pool of threads, thus allowing a single thread to handle multiple requests concurrently. This reduces thread idle time and conserves resources. Table 2.2 illustrates the default number of worker threads SQL Server will assume. If the transaction and extraction activity on your server requires larger or smaller pools, change the worker thread pool maximum size by using this setting.

Table 2.2: Default Worker Thread Pool Maximums

Number of CPUs	32-bit Platform	64-bit Platform
1–4	256	512
8	288	576
16	352	704
32	480	960

Boost SQL Server Priority   SQL Server executes as a Windows service. As a result, it has a lower processor priority for thread scheduling than foreground applications. It also competes with other services for the same processor resources. This option allows the Windows thread scheduling algorithm to give SQL Server a higher priority for scheduled time slices. This can boost SQL Server's responsiveness, but it can also starve out other services, so you must use this option carefully.

Use Windows Fibers   Windows Server 2003 and higher has the ability to perform lightweight pooling using an internal structure called a fiber. This mode is useful primarily when the worker threads perform a significant amount of context switching, which can cause significant overhead. This is unusual, however, especially in Windows Server 2008 due to its improved context management. This option is set to 0 by default and should be modified only after you have verified context-based bottlenecks. SQL Server does not support this option on Windows XP or Windows 2000.

The Security Page

The Security page of the dialog, shown in Figure 2.4, allows you to specify the security settings that SQL Server will assume for authentication and logging. We will discuss the specifics of authentication in more detail in Chapter 7, "Managing Security."

Figure 2.4: The Security page

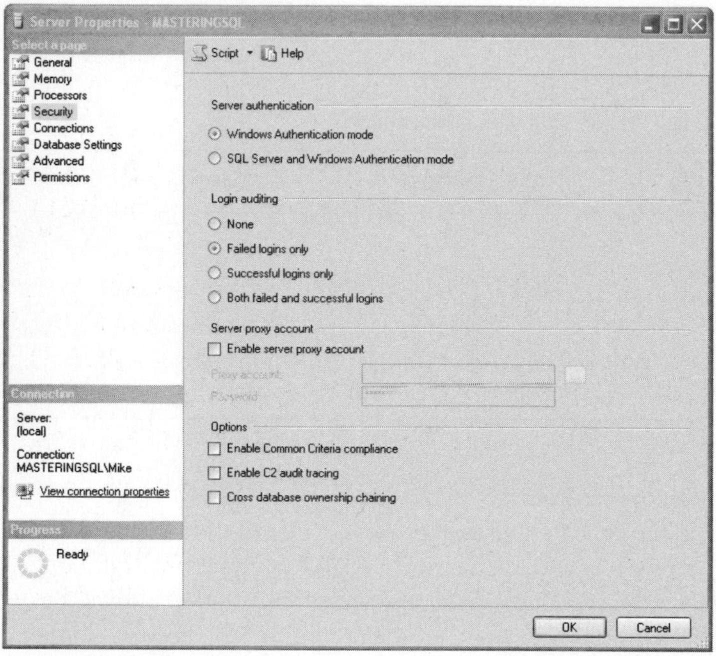

This dialog allows you to specify the most common server-level security settings:

Server Authentication   SQL Server supports two options for authentication. Windows Authentication mode requires that Windows manage all authentication and that logins are trusted by SQL Server. Mixed authentication allows for both SQL Server and Windows authentication. This option allows SQL Server to maintain a login list with passwords and authenticates logins independently from Windows. The latter option is less secure, but it supports connections from clients that do not allow Windows pass-through authentication.

Login Auditing SQL Server can audit login activity. By default, only failed logins are recorded. If you wish, you can audit all login activity or none at all. Remember that login auditing may add to the overall overhead of the solution.

Server Proxy Account SQL Server supports interacting with the operating system shell through an extended stored procedure called xp_cmdshell. To facilitate this interaction you can designate a proxy account that the xp_cmdshell stored procedure will use to interact with the OS shell. If you choose to use this option, you should ensure that the proxy account has the least necessary permissions to perform the required tasks.

Enable Common Criteria Compliance SQL Server 2005 SP2 has been certified as compliant with Common Criteria evaluation assurance level 4 when configured. Enabling this option will enforce the following behaviors:

- Residual Information Protection (RIP) is enforced, which requires memory to be overwritten with a bit pattern before it is reallocated to a new resource. This prevents old data from being accessible in newly allocated resources.

- This option enables logging and auditing and will record the time of the last successful and unsuccessful login and the number of unsuccessful attempts.

- Finally, this option specifies that a table-level DENY will take priority over a column-level GRANT permission. When this option is not enabled, the reverse is true.

Enable C2 Audit Tracing This option has been superseded by Common Criteria, but it is still available for compatibility. C2 audit mode saves a significant amount of data. You should use this option with caution at this time, and only if required.

Cross Database Ownership Chaining This option allows the ownership chaining behavior that exists within a database to be extended across databases. For example, if a SQL Server stored procedure interacts with the table, there is no need to check the permissions on the table as long as there is no break in ownership between the stored procedure and the table. This helps to facilitate database security by minimizing explicitly assigned permissions. You should enable this option only if your application requires this behavior and you are fully aware of the security implications.

SQL Server Basics

PART I

The Connections Page

The Connections page of the dialog allows you to configure connection behavior and the maximum number of connections that SQL Server will permit. It is important to manage connections as well as the behavior and properties of those connections to ensure that resources are managed appropriately and application behavior is as expected. This dialog is illustrated in Figure 2.5.

Figure 2.5: The Connections page

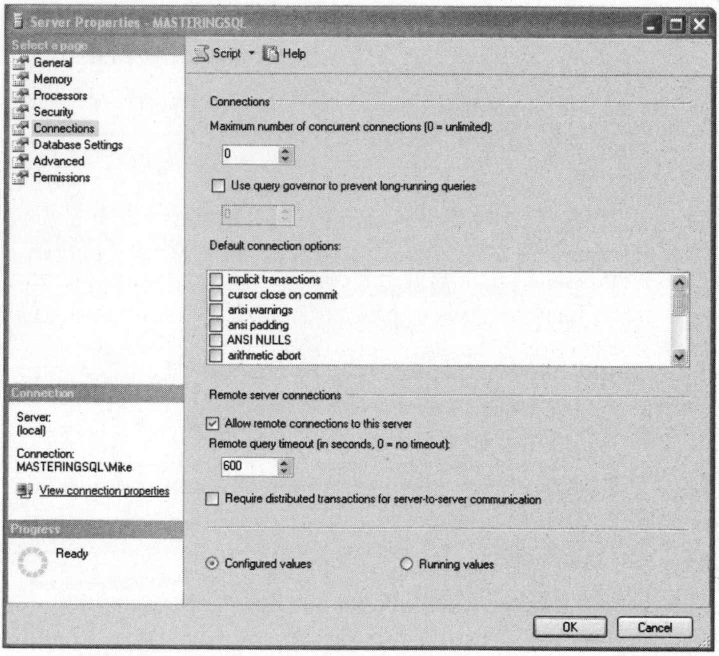

The following options can be configured from the Connections page:

Maximum Number of Concurrent Connections   To prevent too many users from accessing SQL Server concurrently, which can have an adverse effect on system performance, you can configure this option to indicate the maximum number of user connections that will be allowed at any given time. Note that if you must use this option, it usually means that you should investigate the resource bottlenecks that may be contributing to the lack of scalability that caused you to take this action. Also note that this option is not related to licensing. This is a connection throttle only, not a license enforcement mechanism. A value of 0 means that SQL Server allows unlimited connections.

Use Query Governor to Prevent Long-Running Queries   The query governor is a tool that allows SQL Server to prevent the execution of any query when it estimates that the total cost of that query will exceed a configured cost level. Enabling this option and setting a value will prevent some queries from executing. The value, according to the Microsoft documentation, is expressed in seconds. Therefore, if you set this value to 60, any query that the query governor estimates will take longer than one minute to execute will be prevented from executing. The query governor makes this estimate based on the execution plan provided by the query optimizer. You will want to experiment with this before you depend on it; our observation is that the cutoff value is approximate at best.

Default Connection Options   There are numerous options that are configurable at the connection level. You commonly set these options through code, but you can also define the default connection behavior as a server configuration. Be careful about changing the default connection behavior unless you have confirmed that your applications will execute as designed with the changes enabled.

Implicit Transactions   Enabling this option forces a transaction to begin when you use certain Transact SQL statements, such as INSERT, UPDATE, and DELETE.

Cursor Close on Commit   Enabling this option forces a cursor to close whenever a transaction on the same connection commits or rolls back.

ANSI Warnings   This option controls whether you will get warnings when executing a TSQL statement that truncates data or eliminates NULLs from aggregate operations. It also determines if NULL return values exist when arithmetic errors occur.

ANSI Padding   This option controls the padding of fixed-length strings. If the option is on, SQL Server will add trailing blanks and will not trim these blanks from variable data types.

ANSI Nulls   When this option is on, any comparison with a NULL will result in a false return. This is the SQL-92 standard. When this option is off, you can test for the value of NULL in an expression.

Arithmetic Abort   When this option is on, SQL Server terminates a query when a divide-by-zero or overflow error occurs. These errors cause a batch to terminate and a transaction to roll back.

Arithmetic Ignore   When this option is off, SQL Server returns a message when a divide-by-zero or overflow error occurs. These errors do not cause a batch to terminate or a transaction to roll back.

Quoted Identifier   When this option is on, identifiers such as column and variable names can be delimited by double quotes. SQL Server treats any quoted data as an identifier.

No Count   When this option is enabled, SQL Server suppresses the statement that a query returns indicating the number of data rows affected.

ANSI NULL Default ON   This option affects the behavior of the CREATE TABLE statement. If this option is on and the CREATE TABLE statement does not define the column nullability, SQL Server assumes that the column will allow nulls.

ANSI NULL Default OFF   This option affects the behavior of the CREATE TABLE statement. If this option is on and the CREATE TABLE statement does not define the column nullability, SQL Server assumes that the column will not allow nulls.

Concat NULL Yields NULL   When this option is enabled, SQL Server will return a NULL value whenever a query attempts to concatenate a NULL to any other value. If the option is of, the query will return the non-NULL values.

Numeric Round Abort   The effect of this option depends on the setting of the Arithmetic Abort option. Table 2.3 describes the interaction between these two settings.

Table 2.3: Numeric Round Abort Behavior

	Numeric Round Abort ON	Numeric Round Abort OFF
Arithmetic Abort ON	Error; no return	No errors or warnings, rounding occurs if loss of precision
Arithmetic Abort OFF	Warning; returns NULL	No errors or warnings, rounding occurs if loss of precision

XACT Abort   When this option is enabled, SQL Server will roll back an open transaction if any error occurs. If this option is off, only the most severe errors will result in a transaction rollback.

Remote Server Connections   This option allows you to specify if SQL Server will allow connections from locations other than the machine on which the server instance is located. If you disable this option, remote clients will not be able to connect. You can also specify the query time-out for remote connections expressed in seconds.

The final check box in this section, if selected, requires all interaction between this server and another server to be wrapped into a distributed transaction. The SQL Server Distributed Transaction Coordinator will manage this transaction.

The Database Settings Page

The Database Settings page contains a number of general database configurations. They range from data storage to backup and restore configuration. The dialog is illustrated in Figure 2.6.

Figure 2.6: The Database Settings page

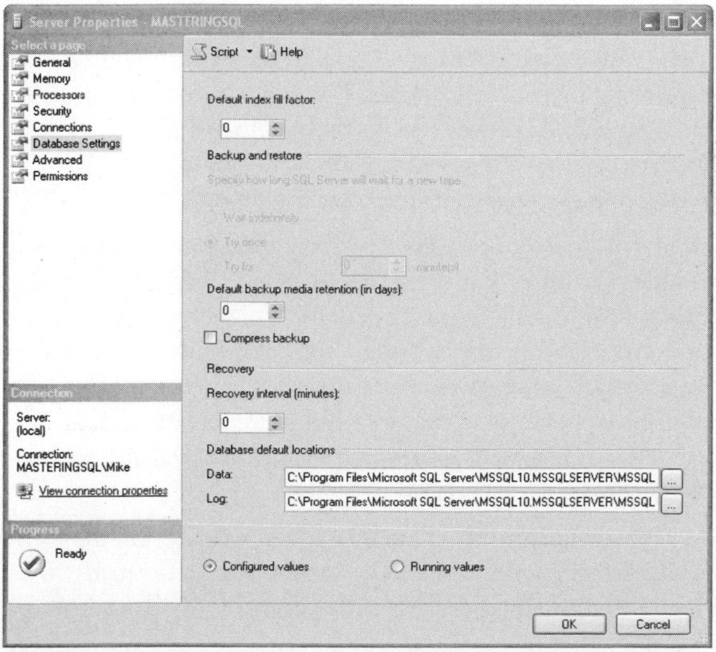

The following options are on this page:

Default Index Fill Factor   When SQL Server creates indexes, the default behavior is that it packs the index pages almost completely full. This also applies to data pages when you create clustered indexes. The result is that when you add new rows to a table, the pages that are full must split and reallocate space within the database. This is time-consuming and causes fragmentation. Setting a default fill factor will allow a percentage of the data or index page to remain empty for new additions. The value is the percentage of the page that you want to fill.

Backup and Restore   This section of the dialog provides three general settings. The first is the treatment of the tape and how long SQL Server will pause a backup operation if an operator must insert a tape. Note that this section is not enabled if there is no tape device available to the server. You can also specify the backup retention period. This setting will write an expiration to the media header on the backup to ensure that you do not overwrite it prematurely. Finally, you can enable the option to compress the backup. This option results in a longer backup process to perform the compression, but the result is a more efficiently stored backup.

Recovery   The recovery setting allows you to specify a recovery interval. This is a value (in minutes) that specifies how long an auto-recovery on each database will take in the event of a non-media-affecting failure. For example, if you lose power to the server and there is no backup power supply, the server will lose the data in memory cache. This value will specify how long it will take to recover that from the flushed transaction log on disk.

This option can significantly affect performance because a long recovery interval means that the server will go longer between checkpoints. This usually results in less I/O unless the interval is so long that you have no available buffers for data. However, a long interval also means a longer recovery time in the event of failure. Shorter intervals mean faster recovery but more frequent batch checkpoint I/O. The default is 0, which means that SQL Server manages this balance.

Database Default Locations   This was actually an option that you specified when you installed SQL Server. You can identify the default location for data and log files. If you want to change this setting after performing the server install, you would come to this dialog and make the change here. Note that this does not change the location of any already existing files. It merely identifies the default location for future files if you do not specify the location in the CREATE DATABASE statement.

The Advanced Page

The Advanced page of the dialog provides a list of miscellaneous and advanced options. This page, pictured in Figure 2.7, looks like a traditional properties list. Simply find the property that you want to alter in the list and change the value in the cell to the right of the property name.

Most of the items in this list are actually self-explanatory. However, if you need additional information, you will notice that you can select the item in the properties list and a brief explanation will appear at the bottom of the dialog in the status area. For now, just acquaint yourself with the items in the list so that you will know where to find them again later.

Figure 2.7: Advanced properties

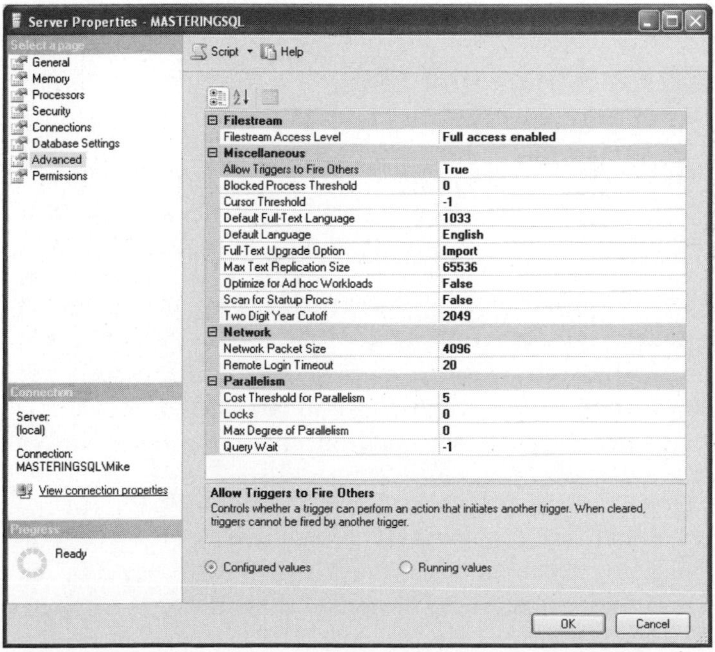

A few of these items are worth noting here. First, you will notice that the first item in the list specifies the level of filestream access. This is one of the options that you specified on installation. This option allows developers to store data in the file system outside of the database. As an administrator, you must know where to access this setting.

You will also notice a section at the bottom labeled Parallelism. The concept behind query parallelism is that if you have multiple processors that can execute a query in parallel, you can increase the performance of the overall result. However, in some cases this may also cause a query to deadlock with itself. If you have this problem, simply change the Max Degree of Parallelism option to 1, indicating that only one processor will execute a plan and it will never run in parallel. Please note that this is not the same thing as processor affinity. Affinity defines the number of processors available to the server, while parallelism defines the number of concurrent processors executing a single plan.

NOTE   The last page, labeled Permissions, allows you to set server-level permissions to logins. We will address this concept in Chapter 7.

Configuring the Server with TSQL

Although you can perform most configurations by using the SSMS interface, there are often occasions when you will want to include configuration changes in administrative scripts. The TSQL language supports this process with the system stored procedure `sp_configure` and the TSQL command `RECONFIGURE`.

The `sp_configure` procedure performs all standard configurations. The general syntax looks like this:

```
sp_configure [ [ @configname = ] 'option_name'
    [ , [ @configvalue = ] 'value' ] ]
```

Following the call to `sp_configure`, you must call the `RECONFIGURE` command to "install" the configuration. Also, many if not most of the configurations that you can modify through the SSMS Server Properties dialog are considered advanced options. An extra step is required to enable the advanced options. For example, if you wanted to modify the number of user connections to 50, you would use the following code:

```
USE master;
GO

EXEC sys.sp_configure 'show advanced options', '1';
RECONFIGURE;
GO
EXEC sys.sp_configure 'user connections', '50';
GO
RECONFIGURE;
GO
EXEC sys.sp_configure 'show advanced options', '0';
RECONFIGURE;
GO
```

You will notice that after each configuration change, the script calls the RECONFIGURE statement to install the configuration. For any configuration involving an advanced option, you must execute the "show advanced options" configuration first before making the change. We recommend that you immediately disable the show advanced options configuration after installing the change. This will ensure a greater level of consistency.

If you do not know the name of the option that you want to change, or if you're not familiar with the syntax, you can script the change from the SSMS interface. For example, to script this user connections configuration change from the SSMS, you would use these steps:

1. Start the SSMS and connect to the target server.

2. Open the Server Properties dialog from the server node in the Object Explorer.

3. Navigate to the Connections page of the dialog.

4. Modify the maximum number of concurrent settings option to 50.

5. At the top of the dialog, locate the button labeled Script. Click the down-pointing triangle next to the button to open the button menu, pictured in Figure 2.8.

6. Select the option to script the action to a new query window.

Figure 2.8: Scripting a configuration change

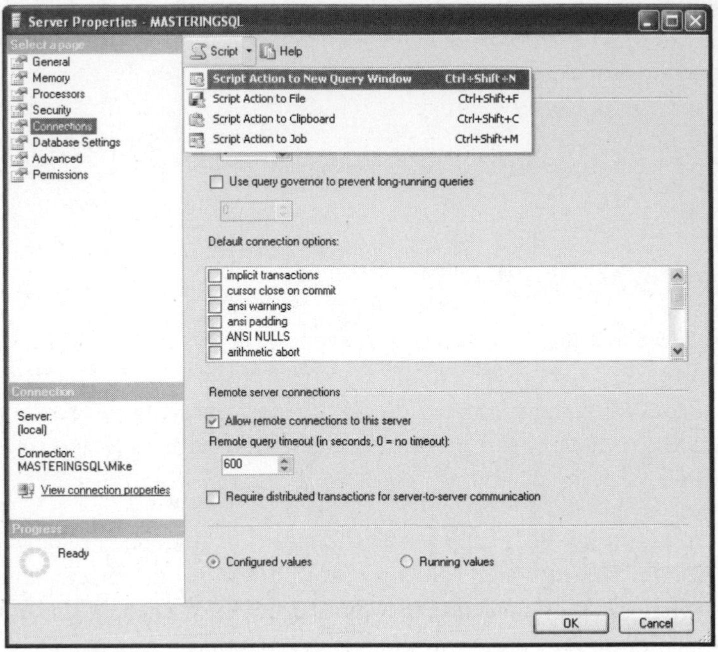

7. Click Cancel on the dialog to close the dialog without making the change.

8. Look at the code in the new query window. It should look similar to the previous code snippet, which we used to make this same change.

You will notice that the code generated by the SSMS uses a RECONFIGURE WITH OVERRIDE statement that the previous script did not contain. The override option disables value checking for the configuration. Since the UI will allow only valid values, there is no need to check those values again when scripting. You could have invalid settings, though, if you are not careful. Although it speeds up the configuration process slightly, there is usually no need to use this option.

Configuring the Services

In addition to the SQL Server configuration options, there are options for configuring the SQL Server services themselves. You can think of these as external configurations as opposed to the internal configurations that you just read about in this chapter. These are the configurations that specify how the services behave and how they interact with the outside world. The primary tool that you will use for this configuration is the SQL Server Configuration Manager. To start this tool, from the Windows Start menu select Start ≻ All Programs ≻ Microsoft SQL Server 2008 ≻ Configurations Tools ≻ SQL Server Configuration Manager.

Service Configuration

There are three primary nodes in the tree view on the left of the Configuration Manager window. The SQL Server Services node presents configuration options for each of the services currently installed on this server. Click this node in the tree view on the left and you will see a list of services in the list view on the right, as pictured in Figure 2.9.

Figure 2.9: Service configuration

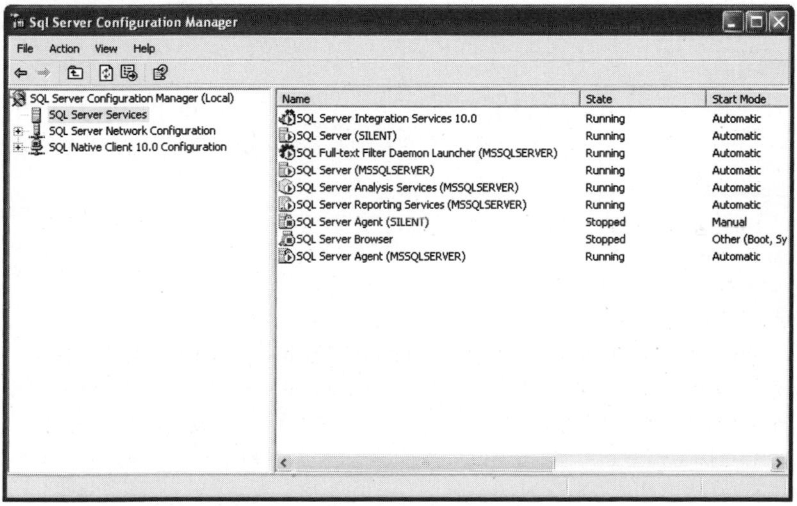

You can start, stop, pause, and restart any service in the list by right-clicking on the service name and selecting the appropriate action from the menu. Notice that there are two instances on the SQL Server service in this dialog. The service labeled MSSQLSERVER is the default instance. SILENT is the named instance that we created in Chapter 1 using the unattended installation options.

Each service also supports properties that are specific to it. To access this properties list, right-click on the service name in the list on the left and select Properties from the menu. Figure 2.10 shows the properties window for the default SQL Server instance (MSSQLSERVER).

Log On The Log On tab (Figure 2.10) of this dialog provides you with an interface to change the service login account and to stop and start the service. You can also change the service login account using the Services applet in the Windows Control Panel.

Figure 2.10: The Log On tab

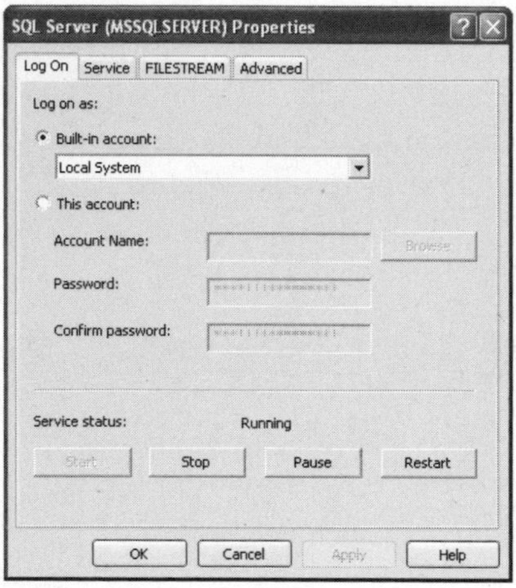

Service The Service tab of the dialog is mostly informational. It provides useful information such as the instance name, hostname, and current service state. The one configurable option is the Start Mode option. This allows you to decide if the service will automatically start when the server is booted or if the startup will be manual. You can also disable a service completely from this tab. Figure 2.11 illustrates this tab for your reference.

FILESTREAM This tab allows you to configure the FILESTREAM behavior at the service level. These are the same settings that you configured when installing the server. You will only find this tab on the SQL Server service properties window because it is not relevant to any other services. Figure 2.12 illustrates this tab for your reference.

Figure 2.11: The Service tab

Figure 2.12: The FILESTREAM tab

Advanced   The contents of the Advanced tab of the dialog will differ slightly depending on the service that you are configuring. Typically, this tab will contain numerous nonmodifiable values for your reference. One of the important advanced settings for the SQL Server service, however, is the Startup Parameters setting. Suppose, for example, that you move the location of the master database files. SQL Server will not start because the startup setting will still be looking to the old location. You would come to this setting and change the value of the -d parameter to indicate the new location. Figure 2.13 illustrates this tab for your reference.

Figure 2.13: The Advanced tab

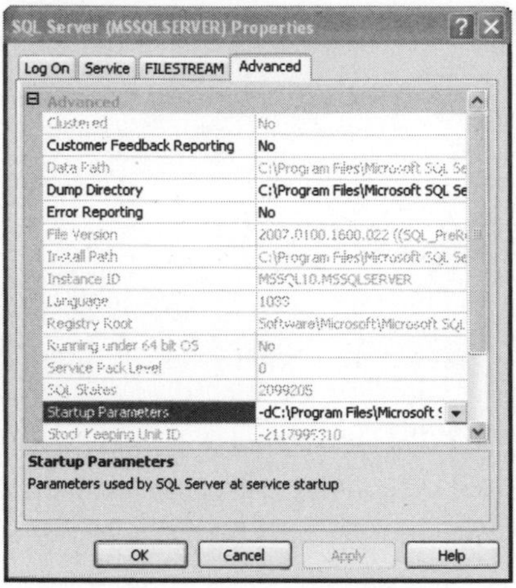

Network Configuration

The second node in the tree view is for network configuration. This is where you will configure the network libraries that the SQL Server instances will use to listen for incoming connections. SQL Server installs four network libraries, which you can enable or disable as needed. For example, if you are using a TCP/IP network and you have already installed the appropriate network software, SQL Server can use the TCP/IP network library to carry information on this protocol.

Figure 2.14 illustrates the network configuration node. You will notice in this example that the network library for TCP/IP is enabled but the library for VIA is not. This means that the default server instance will listen for connection requests only on TCP/IP. This example also shows that the local connection can be resolved using a shared memory connection.

Figure 2.14: Network configuration

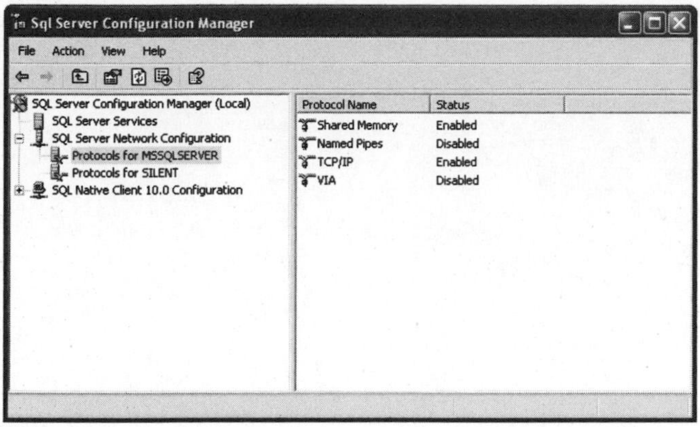

Client Configuration

The SQL Native Client provides the client connectivity layer that any service or client application uses to connect to SQL Server. There are two nodes in this section, one for client protocol bindings and another to create client aliases.

Client Protocols   This configuration allows you to specify the preferred network libraries, in order of preference, that it will use for client connections. In this example, pictured in Figure 2.15, the first attempt for a connection uses the Shared Memory library. If that library cannot create a valid connection, it will fall through to the TCP/IP library.

To enable, disable, or change the order of the client libraries, right-click the Client Protocols node and select Properties. Figure 2.16 illustrates this dialog. Using this dialog, you can move libraries back and forth from the disabled list to the enabled list. You can also use the up and down arrows on the right of the enabled list to change the priority of the libraries. Generally, you should put the libraries in the order of their frequency of use and remove those from the list that you do not need. Note that if shared memory is enabled by using the check box below the two lists, it will always have the highest binding priority because it is the most efficient.

Figure 2.15: Configuring client libraries

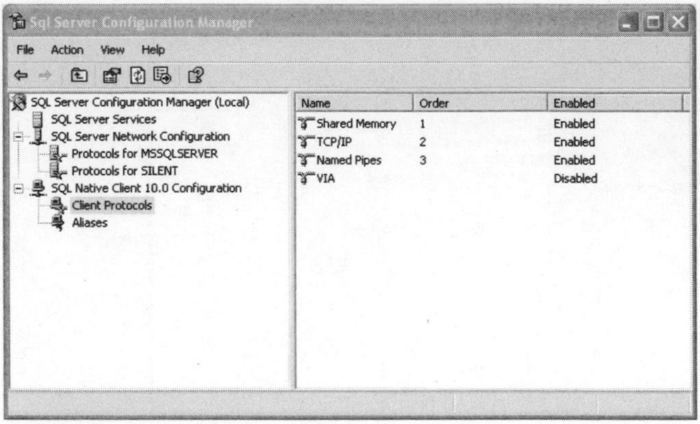

Figure 2.16: Changing client bindings

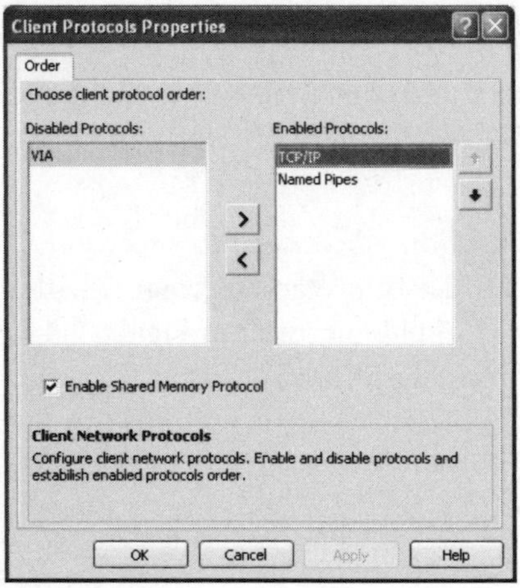

Aliases When you want to connect to SQL Server, you usually specify the name of the server or instance to connect to. This technique requires the SQL Browser to be running. The browser service tracks the SQL Server services by name and facilitates the connection. There may be times that you do not want to publish server names through the browser but you still want to be able to connect to a server using a name instead of an IP address. In these cases, you can create an alias. Open this dialog by right-clicking the Aliases node in the tree view and selecting Properties. Figure 12.17 illustrates this dialog.

Figure 2.17: Configuring a server alias

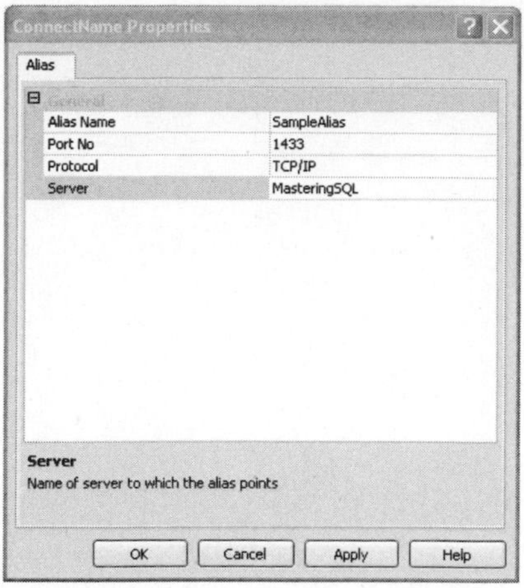

This can also be very useful if you have an application that is expecting to connect to a certain named server but that server does not exist. By creating an alias, you can redirect the client to the desired server without having to make modifications to the application.

3

Creating Databases, Files, and Tables

IN THIS CHAPTER, YOU WILL LEARN TO DO THE FOLLOWING:

All the work to install and configure a server platform isn't much good if you don't have data, and that data has to be stored somewhere. This chapter is all about data storage. Defining data storage in SQL Server requires some planning as well as a thorough understanding of the organization and structure of your data. A well-designed and well-planned data structure can be extensible and efficient, while a poorly planned structure is going to have performance problems and be very brittle to maintain. Making the right choices now can make all the difference later.

SQL Server organizes data storage into three basic structures:

- Databases
- Files
- Tables

In this chapter we will look at these different structures and see how you can leverage them to get the best data storage for your data needs, performance requirements, and fault tolerance.

Perform Capacity Planning

SQL Server requires resources to function efficiently. There are four primary resources that SQL Server will consume to do its job:

- Disk and the I/O subsystem
- Memory
- CPU
- Network

When planning for capacity, it is especially important to pay attention to disk and memory resources. These are the resources most likely to be in short supply as most applications that are resource constrained tend to be constrained by these specific resources. Understanding how SQL Server uses them is critical to creating an effective database environment. Figure 3.1 illustrates the relationship between SQL Server memory and disk resources.

In the figure, you will notice the interplay between SQL Server disk and memory. The disk acts as the permanent storage of data. SQL Server organizes this data storage in files associated with the database, and specifically into 8KB data structures called pages. Although the disk is the permanent record of data storage, data reads and writes requested by a client application do not happen directly on disk but rather in memory.

Figure 3.1: SQL Server disk and memory

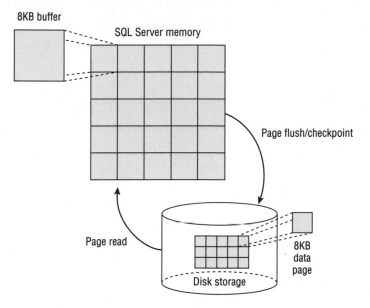

8KB buffer

SQL Server memory

Page flush/checkpoint

Page read

Disk storage

8KB data page

SQL Server I/O Processes

The exchange of data between memory and disk is a critical part of the SQL Server Data Engine's basic processing. Understanding this relationship will help you design the optimal resource structure and tune the relationship between memory and disk. Let's look at some of the typical scenarios where SQL Server exchanges data between cache (memory) and disk.

> **NOTE** This discussion is a very simplified view and does not consider all of the possible variations on these processes. Please be aware that a variety of special processing mechanisms handle these special situations. Understanding the standard mechanisms, however, is sufficient at this point to provide a basis for our discussion.

Reading Data from Disk

Assume that a user wants to read data from a particular data page on disk. The following steps would take place:

1. SQL Server receives the request from the client application and searches cache memory for an 8KB data buffer that contains the data page with the desired information.

2. If SQL Server locates the desired buffer in memory, it returns the data from that buffer. There is no need to request disk resources in this situation.

   If SQL Server cannot find the desired buffer in memory, it locates the data page containing the desired information on the disk.

3. SQL Server reads the page from disk into cache memory, populating an empty cache buffer with information.

4. SQL Server reads the buffer to return the desired information to the client.

Writing Cache Buffers to Disk

The logic behind reading pages into memory is that access to memory is much faster than access to disk. Therefore, we can improve overall performance by using memory as the "live" version of the database. If cache buffers remain in memory for an extended period of time, they can receive multiple data modifications, and therefore we have to write the buffers to disk only periodically instead of with each modification. This batching of buffer writes will also improve performance.

The process of writing this collection of modified (dirty) buffers to disk is called a checkpoint. When the database checkpoints, SQL Server performs the following tasks:

1. SQL Server determines when it should perform the checkpoint. Although you can configure this behavior, SQL Server uses an algorithm that determines the optimal timing for a checkpoint. This includes variables such as these:

   - The amount of SQL Server memory

   - The number of currently available buffers

   - The volume of transaction activity since the last checkpoint

- The amount of time that it would take to recover that transaction activity back to disk

2. At a time that SQL Server determines, it will flush all dirty buffers from cache to disk. SQL Server does this on a database-by-database basis.

3. SQL Server marks all flushed buffers as available for page reads. It does not clear the buffers because it may use the data again in the future.

4. Using a least recently used (LRU) algorithm, it can then read pages from disk into cache buffers by writing to empty buffers first and then to buffers that it has not referenced for the longest period of time.

Although there are a variety of special cases and situations that do not fall into these processes, these are the most common mechanisms that SQL Server will use to manage data.

Disk Capacity Planning

Now that you have a feel for how disk and memory work together to satisfy client requests, we need to look at how to ensure that you will have the required disk space for your SQL Server data. Although you can add more disk space later if your server requirements increase, it is important to get a feel for how to calculate these requirements.

Databases require disk space. Although a well-normalized database will have lower disk requirements than a denormalized one, there is still a significant disk need for any production system. Data warehousing might require significant disk resources, not only to handle the volume of gathered data, but also to perform the multidimensional data modeling that is typical of data warehousing. It is also essential that the I/O subsystem be able to keep up with requests to read and write to disk or the overall performance of the system will suffer.

Disk storage requirements may depend on a number of factors. You have to consider the current data that the business needs to function as well as archival requirements caused by regulatory concerns, data warehousing/mining strategies, encryption requirements, and data growth estimates. Some of these issues, specifically warehousing and archiving, may necessitate additional servers—not just more disk space.

Determining Data Storage Requirements

There is no definite formula for determining exactly how much space a single data row will take on disk. There are a lot of variables:

- The variability of non-fixed-length data storage types such as varchar and nvarchar data structures

- The use of varchar(max) and nvarchar(max) data types and the amount of data that is stored on the row versus off the row

- The presence of features such as replication and row versioning that cause additional overhead on the data row

As a standard rule of thumb, you can use the following process for estimating the size of a single data row in a user table in SQL Server:

1. Add up the bytes needed for each fixed data type (such as 4 bytes for an int) in the data row.

2. Determine the average projected data storage in bytes for each variable-length data type (such as a varchar) in the data row and add those values to the previous figure.

3. Add 6 bytes of overhead for the row and an average of 1 byte per column.

WARNING   This is a very approximate calculation, but it is somewhat difficult to get reliable metrics before you actually create the data structure. For a more accurate value, go ahead and create the table that you will use to store the data, populate the table with some representative data, and then use the sp_spaceused stored procedure to determine the actual data storage.

Planning for Data Growth

Data growth is one of the most complex issues. You need to consider not only how much data you have now, but also how much you will have in the future. There are three basic growth models, each of which has numerous variations. You can probably evaluate your growth patterns according to one or more of these models.

Linear growth   This is the simplest growth model. It assumes that the database will grow at a constant rate over time. For example, assume a 400MB database will grow at a constant rate of 50MB per month. One year from now, therefore, the database will be 1GB in size. Use the following formula to calculate linear growth:

$$FDisk = CDisk + (GAmt \times NPer)$$

In this formula, the terms are defined as follows:

FDisk = future disk space required

CDisk = current disk space used

GAmt = amount of disk growth per period

NPer = number of periods

Compound growth   This model assumes that the growth rate is based on a percentage growth rate rather than a fixed growth amount. As the size of the database increases, so will its future growth amount because each increment is a percentage of the current database size. A database of 100MB that grows 10 percent per year would be 110MB at the end of the first year but 121MB at the end of the second year. Use the following formula to calculate compound growth:

$$FDisk = CDisk \times (1 + Rate)N$$

In this formula, the terms are defined as follows:

FDisk = future disk space required

CDisk = current disk space used

Rate = percentage growth rate per period

N = number of periods

Compound growth with compounding growth rate   This model assumes that as the database grows, so does the growth rate. For example, suppose we expect the database to grow by 10 percent this year but we expect that the growth rate itself will also increase every year by 20 percent. That means that next year, the growth rate will be 12 percent. The first year, therefore, a 100MB database will grow by 10MB. In this case, the 10MB is called the *initial increment* and the 20 percent is called the *incremental rate of growth*. Use the following formula to calculate this model:

$$FDisk = CDisk + (Init \times (1 - IncRate)^{(N+1)}) , (1 - IncRate)$$

In this formula, the terms are defined as follows:

FDisk = future disk space required

CDisk = current disk space used

N = number of periods

Init = initial increment of growth

IncRate = incremental rate of growth per period

Memory Capacity Planning

The short answer for memory capacity is simply this: Add more memory. As simple as it sounds, a SQL Server database needs a lot of memory to be able to function correctly. Of course, the amount of memory that SQL Server can actually use will depend on the edition of SQL Server and the processor architecture that you are using, but the general recommendation is to max out your memory capacity based on these factors. We have never seen a degradation of SQL Server performance by providing more memory to the server, so our preference is to configure the server with as much memory as is possible and/or feasible.

The long answer for memory capacity planning is a little different. You should consider how much data is typically in your working set. If there is a set of data to which your client applications are commonly reading and writing, you should have enough memory to store that working dataset. Add to that additional memory to accommodate the following:

- Relevant index structures
- Stored procedure cache space
- SQL Server program code
- Operating system and networking requirements

WARNING   The most important thing you can do is to be careful you don't starve SQL Server for resources by running on your SQL Server machines other systems or services that might also require significant memory resources. This can be as obvious as a primary domain controller or as seemingly innocuous as a screen saver. The import thing is that you must consider the resource ramification of every service that you run on a SQL Server and consider the probability that it will cause a SQL Server resource problem. We will discuss how to find these kinds of problems in Chapter 11, "Monitoring and Tuning SQL Server."

Create and Alter Databases

SQL Server stores almost all of its data, indexes, and configurations in databases. When you install a SQL Server instance, you get four systems databases by default. The installer creates these for you automatically.

master   The master database is essentially the master catalog for the entire server instance. It stores all instance-level configuration information and instance-level artifacts such as server logins. You can think of the master database as everything that SQL Server knows about itself.

model   The model database serves as the template for all new user databases that you will create on an instance. When you create a new database, you get a copy of the model database. Adding artifacts such as tables or data types to the model database will ensure that those artifacts are present in any databases that you create from that point forward on that instance.

msdb   The msdb database primarily supports the SQL Server Agent Service. This service is the automation engine for SQL Server, so the msdb database is the repository for automation artifacts such as job specifications, schedules, and notifications. It also stores information related to the replication services and provides additional extended repository services.

tempdb   The tempdb database is the repository for temporary storage in SQL Server. When a SQL Server application uses resources such as temporary tables, server-side cursors, and internal work-tables, SQL Server uses tempdb space for that storage. This storage space is very volatile and will usually benefit from being placed on faster physical media. It is also the only system database that you do not need to worry about backing up if it's altered.

In addition to these system databases, you can create user databases for your data-storage needs. You can create, alter, and drop databases in two different ways:

- Use the SQL Server Management Studio (SSMS) user interface.
- Write a Transact SQL (TSQL) script.

> **TIP** When you are working with databases, you will get the same results no matter which option you choose (using the SSMS or writing TSQL scripts). However, you may want to consider the advantages of scripting. You ultimately have more control in many cases when you write your own scripts. Although you can generate scripts from SQL Server for many artifacts that you create in the SSMS, the scripts tend to be very verbose and may not follow your internal coding standard. Having scripts you write yourself is also nice when you want to re-create the artifacts. You can also store the scripts in a source-code repository such as Microsoft Visual Source Safe or Team System Foundation Server, which will allow you to version the scripts, making it easier to roll back to earlier versions of artifacts if necessary.

Create a Database

To create a database, you must provide a database name and file-storage information. When you create the database, SQL Server will organize the database files into 8KB data pages. Additionally, it will create structures called *extents*, which are sets of eight pages. The page is the basic unit of I/O in SQL Server. When SQL Server reads or writes data to or from disk, it generally does so in 8KB page blocks. The extent is the basic unit of allocation in SQL Server. When SQL Server allocates disk space to a table or index, it generally does so in extents.

> **NOTE** The operations referenced in this chapter require elevated permission beyond that of a normal user account. We are assuming that you are authenticating under administrative authority. In Chapter 7, "Managing Security," we will discuss the specific permissions that SQL Server requires for these and other operations.

Creating a Database Using the SSMS

The SSMS provides numerous dialogs for executing administrative tasks. This includes creating a database. Follow these steps to create a database with the SSMS:

1. Start the SSMS from the Windows Start menu by clicking Start ➤ All Programs ➤ SQL Server 2008 ➤ SQL Server Management Studio.

2. When prompted to connect to a database, use the settings pictured in Figure 3.2. This will connect to the default instance that you installed in Chapter 1, "Installing SQL Server 2008." If you are using a different instance, specify the appropriate connection parameters. Click the Connect button to make the connection.

Figure 3.2: Connecting to the default instance

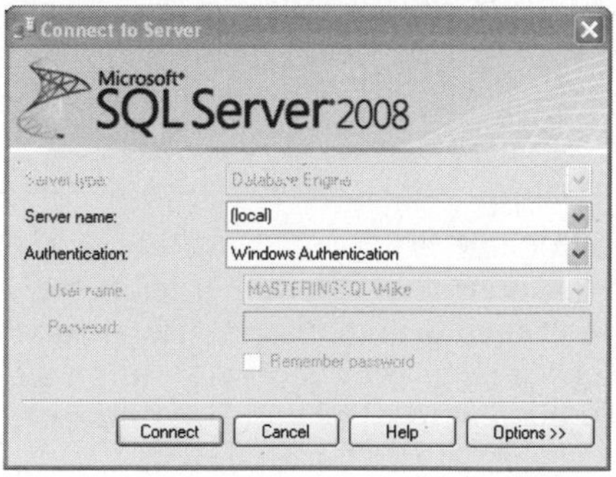

3. To open the New Database dialog, locate the Object Explorer in the upper-left area of the SSMS. Right-click the Databases folder and select New Database from the menu, as pictured in Figure 3.3.

4. When the New Database dialog opens, select the General dialog page. Enter **demo** in the Database Name text box.

Figure 3.3: Opening the New Database dialog

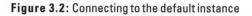

5. You will notice that there are two files listed by default. The file named demo is for data storage, while the file named demo_log is for transaction log storage. Set the initial size of the data file to 10MB and change the Autogrowth setting to 5MB with unrestricted growth by clicking the build button next to the cell value and setting the desired configuration.

6. Set the initial size of the log file to 5MB with an Autogrowth increment of 2MB and unrestricted growth.

7. If you wanted to add additional files to your database, you could add them to this list at this time.

NOTE An Autogrowth setting that is too small will lead to disk fragmentation. You should use Autogrowth for emergency file growth. You should be more proactive in managing growth so that you can control your resources to a greater degree. Unlimited file growth will ultimately allow the file to fill the entire partition on which you have placed it.

---

8. You can change the location of the file by modifying the Path setting. If you are not using a RAID array, you should place the data files and log files on two separate physical disks. This is for recoverability, which we will discuss in Chapter 10, "Managing Data Recovery." The completed General page will look like Figure 3.4.

Figure 3.4: The General page of the New Database dialog

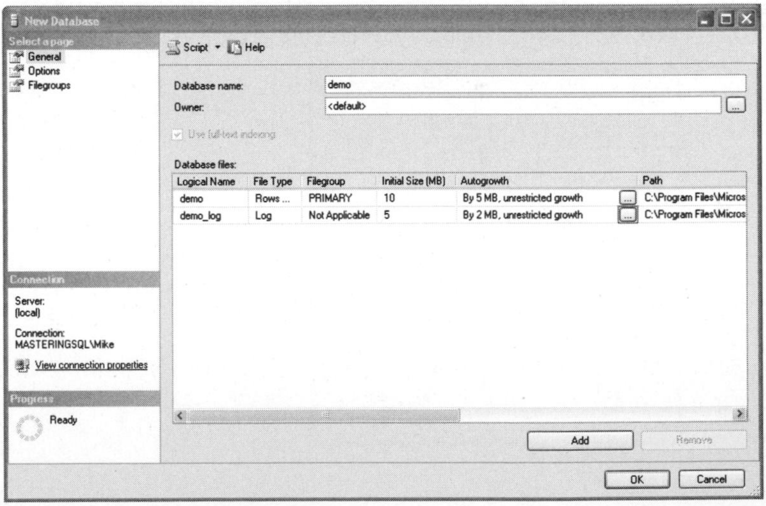

9. Select the Options page to view the database options. Most of these options can be set at this time. Table 3.1 provides a list of the most common database options and the effect they will have on the database. For a complete list, see SQL Server Books Online.

Table 3.1: Common Database Options

Option Name	Description
Collation	Indicates the character set and sort order for the database. This defaults to the server default that you provided on installation.
Recovery Model	Defines the transaction logging and checkpoint behavior. This option affects database recoverability. Simple recovery model does not provide for transaction log backups.
Compatibility Level	Enforces language compatibility with specific versions of SQL Server. This option is useful for providing backward compatibility.
Auto Close	Forces the database to free all resources when the last user logs off.
Auto Create Statistics	Provides for the background generation of distribution statistics used by the query optimizer.
Auto Shrink	Forces the database files to shrink when data usage falls significantly below the size of the file. This is a background operation.
Auto Update Statistics	Provides for the background update of distribution statistics used by the query optimizer.
ANSI NULL Default	Determines whether columns will allow NULL if the CREATE TABLE script does not specifically state that a column allows NULL. A value of true indicates that NULL is allowed by default.
ANSI NULLS Enabled	Indicates the result of a comparison between a NULL and another value. If the value is false, comparing two non-Unicode NULL values will return true. If the value is true, all comparisons to a NULL will provide an undefined return.
Concat NULL Yields NULL	Determines the behavior of concatenating NULL values. If it's false, string+NULL returns the string. If it's true, concatenation of a NULL returns NULL.

SQL Server Basics

PART I

Table 3.1: Common Database Options *(continued)*

Option Name	Description
Quoted Identifiers Enabled	Defines the functionality of the double quote character. If the value is true, the double quote can be used to specify a delimited identifier (an artifact name with an internal space). If the value is false, you must use the square bracket for delimited identifiers.
Database Read Only	Specifies if you are allowed to make modifications to a database. If the value is true, the database cannot be modified.
Restrict Access	Provides access control, primarily for conducting administrative functionality. The default value is MULTI_USER, which allows multiple users in the database concurrently. Other options are SINGLE_USER, which provides for only one user at a time, and RESTRICTED_USER, which allows for only administrative users.

10. The Filegroups page of the dialog shows you the current filegroup structure. You can organize files into groups to better manage administrative tasks such as backups. Currently, there should be only one filegroup, called PRIMARY.

11. Click on the OK button to create the database. If you look at the Object Explorer window, you should now see the new demo database that you just created.

TIP   Look at the New Database dialog in Figure 3.4. You will notice that there is a Script button at the top of the dialog. This button allows you to generate a TSQL script from the dialog if you chose. To use this button, enter the desired data in all pages of the dialog, but do not click the OK button. Instead, click the Script button. This will present you with a list of options for scripting the task in the dialog. In addition to its productivity benefits, this is also a great training tool. If you need to know how to script a task, you can complete the task in the dialog and then examine the corresponding script without actually performing the operation. Look for this button on other dialogs as well.

Creating a Database Using a TSQL Script

Although you can easily create a database using the graphical user interface (GUI) provided by the SSMS, you may choose to use a TSQL script instead. Although there are a variety of tools that you can use to execute SQL scripts against SQL Server, we will use the tool built into the SSMS.

The syntax of the CREATE DATABASE statement allows you to provide the same information that you entered into the General page of the New Database dialog. The basic syntax looks like this:

```
CREATE DATABASE database_name
  [ ON
    [ PRIMARY ] [ <filespec> [ ,...n ]
    [ LOG ON { <filespec> [ ,...n ] } ]
    ]
    [ COLLATE collation_name ]
  ]
  [;]

<filespec> ::=
  {
  (
    NAME = logical_file_name ,
      FILENAME = { 'os_file_name' | 'filestream_path' }
      [ , SIZE = size [ KB | MB | GB | TB ] ]
      [ , MAXSIZE = { max_size
        [ KB | MB | GB | TB ] | UNLIMITED } ]
      [ , FILEGROWTH = growth_increment
        [ KB | MB | GB | TB | % ] ]
  )[ ,...n ]
  }
```

TIP   When reading these syntax examples, remember that anything that is presented in square brackets is optional in the syntax. For these options, there are defaults that the system will use if you do not provide specific instructions. Anything presented in angle brackets—for example, <filespec>—is replaced by a block of code defined later in the sample syntax. The "pipe," or vertical bar, represents a choice, as in the format {option 1 | option 2}.

NOTE We are firm believers in "coding by example." Although the syntax patterns are often a useful reference, you can get these in SQL Server Books Online, so there is no need to duplicate them here. Our theory is that the best way to learn to code something is to see an example of real code that actually runs. For that reason, you will notice that most of the code in this book will be executable samples as opposed to syntax models.

To create a database called demoscript using the same setting as the previous example, you would follow these steps:

1. In the SSMS, select File ➤ New ➤ Database Engine Query. When prompted, connect to the server where you would like to create the database. In our case, that is the default instance.

2. In the query window that opened, enter the following code, replacing the physical path in the FILENAME section with a path of your choosing that exists on your server:

```
USE master;

CREATE DATABASE demoscript
ON (
  NAME = demoscript_data,
  FILENAME = 'C:\SQLData\Data\demoscript_data.mdf',
  SIZE = 10MB,
  MAXSIZE = UNLIMITED,
  FILEGROWTH = 5MB
)
LOG ON (
  NAME = demoscript_log,
  FILENAME = 'C:\SQLData\Log\demoscript_log.mdf',
  SIZE = 5MB,
  MAXSIZE = UNLIMITED,
  FILEGROWTH = 2MB
);
GO
```

3. Press the F5 key on your keyboard to execute the query. If the query returns errors, double-check your TSQL syntax.

4. After the query executes successfully, go back to the Object Explorer window. Right-click the Databases folder and click Refresh. You should see your new database in the list.

If you need a larger database, you can reserve more space in two different ways. You can either define larger files, or you can create multiple files as part of your database. For example, suppose you want a database that is spread across two physical files. You could use the code in Listing 3.1. Notice how this script defines multiple data files, using the filename extension .ndf for the extended data files. You could also add multiple log files with similar syntax in the log section.

Listing 3.1: Creating a Database with Multiple Data Files

```
USE master;

CREATE DATABASE demoscript
ON (
  NAME = demoscript_data,
  FILENAME = 'C:\SQLData\Data\demoscript_data.mdf',
  SIZE = 10MB,
  MAXSIZE = UNLIMITED,
  FILEGROWTH = 5MB
)
, (
  NAME = demoscript_data2,
  FILENAME = 'C:\SQLData\Data\demoscript_data2.ndf',
  SIZE = 10MB,
  MAXSIZE = UNLIMITED,
  FILEGROWTH = 5MB
)
LOG ON (
  NAME = demoscript_log,
  FILENAME = 'C:\SQLData\Log\demoscript_log.mdf',
  SIZE = 5MB,
  MAXSIZE = UNLIMITED,
  FILEGROWTH = 2MB
);
GO
```

> **TIP**　If you are going to use multiple data or log files, it usually makes sense to place these files on separate physical disks or arrays. There is little to can gain by placing multiple files in the same partition or physical disk.

Alter a Database

Once you have created the database and used it in development or put it into production, you may find out that you need to make some changes to database options or other structural elements of the database. Some of these changes require modifications to the underlying database files. We will discuss those changes later in this chapter. There are other alterations, however, that we can make to the database directly. Again, you can make these changes either through the SSMS interface or using TSQL code.

Altering a Database with the SSMS

To modify an existing database from the SSMS, you will use the Database Properties dialog. You can conveniently open this dialog from the Object Explorer. Use the following steps to alter database settings:

1. Locate the Object Explorer window in the SSMS. Find the database that you wish to alter in the Databases list.

2. Right-click the demo database in the list and select Properties from the shortcut menu.

3. You will notice that the items on the General page are grayed out, meaning that they are not modifiable in this dialog. Table 3.2 provides a list of the pages in this dialog and their descriptions.

Table 3.2: Database Properties Dialog Pages

Page Name	Description
General	Provides a noneditable list of general database properties.
Files	Displays the owner and the file structure of the database. You can add files to the database on this page.

Table 3.2: Database Properties Dialog Pages *(continued)*

Page Name	Description
Filegroups	Displays the filegroup structure of the database. You can add filegroups to the database on this page.
Options	Displays and allows modification of the database options. This page is identical to the Options page in the New Database dialog.
Change Tracking	Provides configuration of the change-tracking functionality.
Permissions	Provides a mechanism for setting permissions to database-level securables.
Extended Properties	Allows the administrator to define custom metadata properties for the database. You can find a similar tab on the properties dialog box for most SQL Server artifacts.
Mirroring	Provides a location for configuring database mirroring. We will discuss this availability feature in Chapter 8, "Implementing Availability and Replication."
Transaction Log Shipping	Provides a location for configuring transaction log shipping. We will discuss this availability feature in Chapter 8.

4. Select the Options page to access the modifiable database options. Locate the option that you wish to modify. Change the option value in the dialog. For this example, change the Recovery Model setting to Simple by opening the list next to Recovery Model and selecting Simple.

5. Click the OK button on the dialog to save the change.

Altering a Database with a TSQL Script

You can also modify these same options by using TSQL code. The command to modify database settings with TSQL is ALTER DATABASE. You can change any of the modifiable options by using the following general syntax:

```
ALTER DATABASE database_name
SET
{
    { <optionspec> [ ,...n ] [ WITH <termination> ] }
```

```
}

<optionspec>::=
{
  <auto_option>
| <change_tracking_option>
| <cursor_option>
| <database_mirroring_option>
| <date_correlation_optimization_option>
| <db_encryption_option>
| <db_state_option>
| <db_update_option>
| <db_user_access_option>
| <external_access_option>
| <parameterization_option>
| <recovery_option>
| <service_broker_option>
| <snapshot_option>
| <sql_option>
}

<termination> ::=
{
 ROLLBACK AFTER integer [ SECONDS ]
| ROLLBACK IMMEDIATE
| NO_WAIT
}
```

The <termination> option allows you to specify rollback behavior if there are incomplete transactions registered when the ALTER DATABASE statement is executed. The default is to wait indefinitely for transactions to commit before the statement moves forward. The <termination> options are described in Table 3.3.

Table 3.3: Termination Options

Option	Description
ROLLBACK AFTER *integer*	Indicates the number of seconds to wait before rolling back incomplete transactions when the database state changes.

Table 3.3: Termination Options *(continued)*

Option	Description
ROLLBACK IMMEDIATE	Indicates that incomplete transactions will immediately roll back when the database state changes.
NO_WAIT	Fails the ALTER DATABASE statement if it cannot commit immediately without waiting.

The format is the same regardless of the option that you want to set. As long as you know the possible values for the option setting, simply use that option with a SET statement. For example, execute the following steps to change the recovery model of the demoscript database to Simple.

1. Open a new database engine query window and connect to the default SQL Server instance on the server.

2. Enter the following code in the query window:

```
USE master;

ALTER DATABASE demoscript
SET RECOVERY SIMPLE;
GO
```

3. Press the F5 button to execute the query.

In some cases, you can execute multiple alterations in one statement. For example, if you wanted to change the recovery model and the Auto Create Statistics option in one statement, you would use this code:

```
USE master;

ALTER DATABASE demoscript
SET
  RECOVERY SIMPLE,
  AUTO_CREATE_STATISTICS ON;
GO
```

SQL Server does not allow you to batch all options in an ALTER DATABASE statement. Similarly, you cannot use the <termination> option for all of the database options. Table 3.4 provides a list of option categories and indicates whether you are allowed to batch or use the <termination> option with each category.

Table 3.4: Database-Option Features

Option Category	Can Be Batched	Can Use *<termination>*
<db_state_option>	X	X
<db_user_access_option>	X	X
<db_update_option>	X	X
<external_access_option>	X	
<cursor_option>	X	
<auto_option>	X	
<sql_option>	X	
<recovery_option>	X	
<database_mirroring_option>		
<service_broker_option>	X	
<parameterization_option>	X	X
<change_tracking_option>	X	X
<db_encryption>	X	

Drop a Database

If you no longer need a database on a particular server, you can drop it. If you drop a database from a server, you are removing all of the catalog data that reference the database as well as the user data and other artifacts that the database might store. Be sure that you really want to drop a database before you execute this procedure. Once it's dropped, the only way to recover the database is to restore it from a backup.

NOTE   In the database administration world, we have historically used the term *drop* to refer to removing an object and *delete*
to refer to removing data. The different terminology allows us to
make a firm distinction between data and objects in a database.
Although the SSMS uses the term *delete* in its command menus,
we will continue with the age-old practice of using the term *drop*.
This is partly out of habit and partly because we believe that it is
important for us to preserve this differentiation.

Dropping a Database Using the SSMS

This is a simple operation that only requires a few clicks. As an example,
we will drop the demo database from the default server instance.

WARNING   If you follow these instructions and actually drop
the database, you will have to re-create it before you will be able to
follow any of the other examples in this section because we will
continue to use the same database. This is your choice. You will not
loose any important data if you choose to drop it, but please
remember to create it again according the instructions provided
earlier in this chapter before you continue on to the next section.

Follow these steps to drop the demo database:

1. In the Object Explorer window, locate the demo database.

2. Right-click the database and select Delete. The Delete Object
   dialog opens. The demo database should be the only item listed in
   the dialog.

3. You cannot delete a database if there are any existing connections
   to it, so if you need to force all existing connections to close, select
   the check box at the bottom of the dialog labeled Close Existing
   Connections.

4. If you also wish to delete the backup and restore history (stored in
   the msdb database) for this database, select the corresponding
   check box at the bottom of the dialog.

5. Click the OK button to commit the drop operation.

Dropping a Database Using a TSQL Script

This process is also very simple. The DROP DATABASE statement will drop the named database form the server. In this example, we will drop the demoscript database from the default instance using the following steps:

1. Open a new database engine query window and connect to the default SQL Server instance on the server.

2. Enter the following code in the query window:

   ```
   USE master;

   DROP DATABASE demoscript;
   GO
   ```

3. Press the F5 button to execute the query.

Once the query is completed, the database will be permanently dropped from the server instance. Again, to recover this database, you must restore it from a backup.

Manage Database Files

Data in a database is ultimately stored in a file, so if you want to manipulate database size and storage, you are going to have to deal with the file structure at some level. In the following sections, we are going to look at the database operations that involve files.

First of all, we will look at increasing a database size. There are two ways to do this, either by adding new files to a database or increasing the size of existing files. If you add additional files, you can also choose to organize those files into sets called filegroups. Finally, you will learn how to decrease a database size, which you can do either by decreasing a file size or by deallocating a file.

Add Files to a Database

One way to increase a database's size is to add files to it. There are a couple of reasons you might consider this approach:

- The partition or array that contains the current data file(s) is full and you must extend the database on a separate partition or array.

- You wish to segment the database across partitions or arrays for performance reasons. For example, you may want to divide tables across physical data devices to allow parallel access to data and indexes.

You can add a file to a database by either using the SSMS or writing a TSQL script. We will look at both options.

Adding a File Using the SSMS

You will use the Database Properties dialog to add a file to a database. In this example, we will add a 10MB data file to the database. Follow these steps to complete this task:

1. Locate the demo database in the Object Explorer. Right-click the database and select Properties from the shortcut menu to open the Database Properties dialog.

2. Select the Files tab of the dialog. The database should currently consist of two files, one for the data structures and one for the transaction log.

3. To add a new data file to the database, click the Add button at the bottom of the dialog. This adds a new row to the grid.

4. Under the Logical Name column in the grid, enter the name **demo2** as the new logical filename.

5. Set the initial size at 20MB with no autogrowth.

6. Scroll the grid all the way to the right to see the File Name column. Name the file `demo2.ndf`. The completed dialog will look like the one pictured in Figure 3.5.

7. Click the OK button to confirm the action. Using these steps, you have just added 20MB total disk space to the database by adding a new 20MB file to the database.

Figure 3.5: Adding a new database file

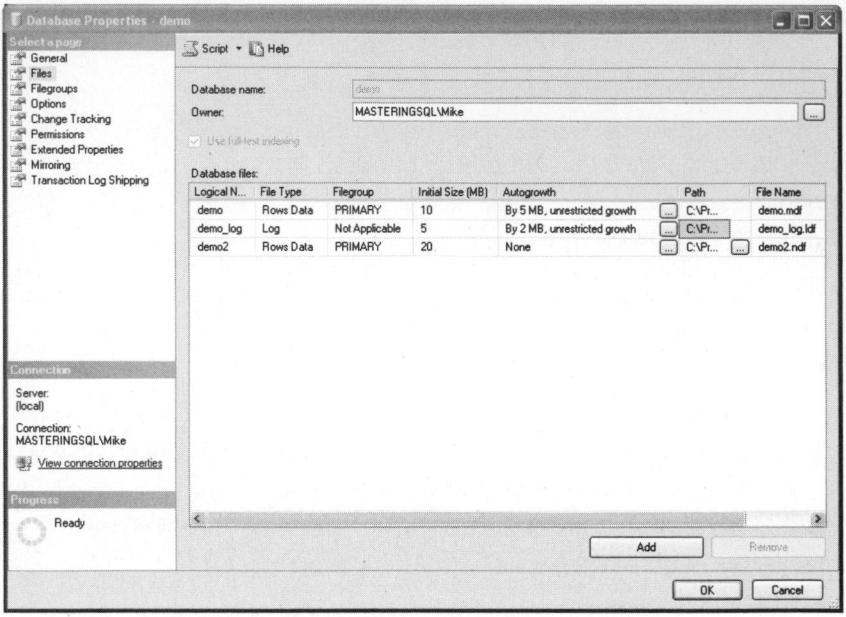

Adding a File Using a TSQL Script

The TSQL code to add a file to a database looks very similar to the script that you used to create a database. When you add a file, you will need to provide all relevant information about it, including its logical name, physical path, and size properties. The difference is that you will embed this information in an ALTER DATABASE statement instead of a CREATE DATABASE statement.

NOTE At this point, you should be very comfortable with the process of opening a new database engine query window and executing the query. Therefore, when discussing TSQL code examples from this point on, I will simply provide the code. You can refer to the instructions earlier in this chapter if you need a refresher on executing a query.

To add a 20MB file to the demoscript database similar to the one that we added in the SSMS, use the following code:

```
USE master;

ALTER DATABASE demoscript
ADD FILE
(
  NAME = demoscript2,
  FILENAME = 'C:\SqlData\Data\demoscript2.ndf',
  SIZE = 20MB,
  FILEGROWTH = 0MB
);
GO
```

WARNING   Although you can add many files to a database, SQL Server does not immediately use a file until the files that precede it in the file list are full. For example, if you had a 10MB data file and then added another 20MB data file, SQL Server would allocate data space to the second file until the first one was full. The exception to this is if you explicitly place an object such as a table or an index on a specific filegroup. You have this option when creating a new database object, and this technique is a common practice for physical database segmentation.

Add Files to a Filegroup

Administrators primarily use filegroups to ease administration for very large databases. For example, if you have a database that is too large to back up in one session, you could break the database into filegroups and back up the filegroups separately on a rotating basis. You would then explicitly place artifacts like tables and indexes into certain filegroups so that they are logically organized and so that related elements such as a table and its indexes could be backed up together.

You can also use filegroups to manually segment your database. Suppose you wanted to place a table on one physical disk and its indexes on another physical disk. The server could be performing a data operation and an index scan at the same time, which could improve performance. To do this, you would create two filegroups, one for the tables and one for the indexes.

Adding Files to Filegroups Using the SSMS

Again, we will go back to the Database Properties window to complete this step. Also note that when you create your database, you can add the filegroups and place the files into those filegroups at that time. Follow these steps to add a filegroup to the demo database and place a new file into that filegroup:

1. Locate the demo database in the Object Explorer. Right-click the database and select Properties from the shortcut menu to open the Database Properties dialog.

2. Select the Filegroups tab of the dialog. Click the Add button associated with the top section of the dialog (which is labeled Rows), as illustrated in Figure 3.6.

3. In the Name column of the top grid, enter **FG2** as the name of the new filegroup. Note that you do not specify a location for a filegroup. Filegroups are logical sets, not physical locations.

Figure 3.6: Adding a filegroup

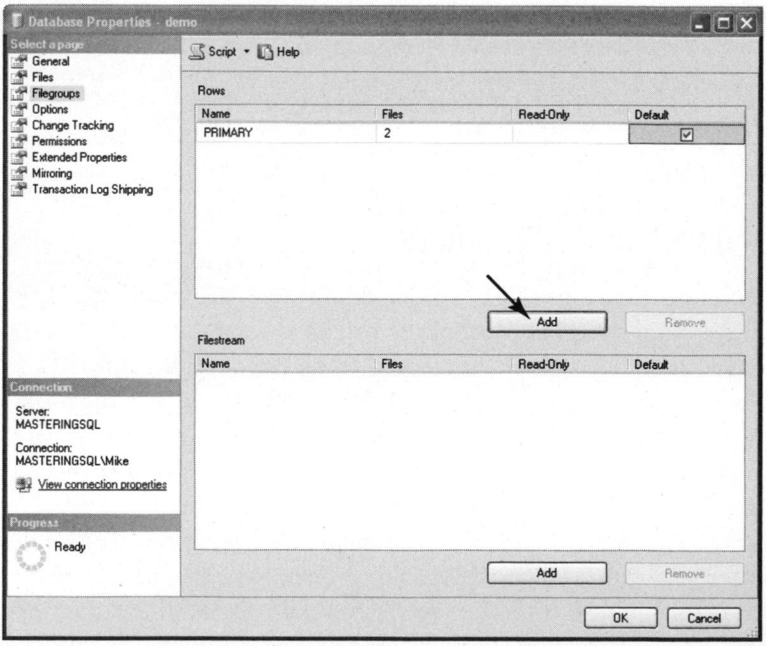

4. Select the Files page and then click the Add button to add a new file. Set the logical name as demo_fg1. Use a size of 5MB with no file growth. Use demo_fg1.ndf as the filename.

5. Click on the Filegroup cell for the new file to activate the filegroup list box. Select FG2 from the list.

6. Repeat steps 4 and 5 to add another file, identical to the last one but with a name of demo_fg2 for the logical name and demo_fg2.ndf for the filename. Figure 3.7 illustrates what the grid should look like at this point.

Figure 3.7: File list for the demo database

Logical N...	File Type	Filegroup	Initial Size (MB)	Autogrowth		Path		File Name
demo	Rows Data	PRIMARY	10	By 5 MB, unrestricte...	[...]	C:\Program...		demo.mdf
demo_log	Log	Not Applicable	5	By 2 MB, restricted g...	[...]	C:\Program...		demo_log.ldf
demo2	Rows Data	PRIMARY	20	None	[...]	C:\Program...	[...]	demo2.ndf
demo_fg1	Rows Data	FG2	5	None	[...]	C:\Program...	[...]	demo_fg1.ndf
demo_fg2	Rows Data	FG2	5	None	[...]	C:\Program...	[...]	demo_fg2.ndf

Database name: demo
Owner: MASTERINGSQL\Mike
Use full-text indexing
Database files:

[Add]   [Remove]

7. Click the OK button to commit the changes.

Adding Files to Filegroups Using a TSQL Script

Since the addition of both files and filegroups represents a database modification, you will use the ALTER DATABASE statement to make the change. You have already seen how to add a file. To add a filegroup, you use very similar syntax. To place the files on a specific filegroup, you will indicate the filegroup by name when you add the file. Listing 3.2

illustrates the complete process of adding the FG2 filegroup to the demoscript database and adding the two new files to that filegroup.

Listing 3.2: Adding a Filegroup and Files to the Demoscript Database

```
USE master;
GO

ALTER DATABASE demoscript
ADD FILEGROUP FG2;

ALTER DATABASE demoscript
ADD FILE
(
  NAME = demoscript_fg1,
  FILENAME = 'C:\SqlData\Data\demoscript_fg1.ndf',
  SIZE = 5MB,
  FILEGROWTH = 0MB
)
,(
  NAME = demoscript_fg2,
  FILENAME = 'C:\SqlData\Data\demoscript_fg2.ndf',
  SIZE = 5MB,
  FILEGROWTH = 0MB
)
TO FILEGROUP FG2;
GO
```

Modify Database File Size

Your other option to expand a database is to increase the size of the existing files. If you have the autogrowth options turned on, this can happen automatically. It is more desirable, however, to manage file growth yourself. This will ensure not only that file growth happens in an orderly fashion, but also that you are aware of the file growth behavior. We strongly recommend that you use autogrowth as an emergency mechanism only, not as your standard file management technique.

> **WARNING**   One of the reasons autogrowth is problematic is
> that databases that grow in this fashion tend to grow frequently in
> small increments. This behavior can cause physical file fragmenta-
> tion, which can degrade performance for some kinds of SQL
> Server operations like sequential access operations like table
> scans. You will be better off if you plan your file growth and explic-
> itly increase file size less frequently but in larger increments. If you
> take this approach, you should also ensure that the Auto Shrink
> database option is disabled.

You can also decrease the size of a database file if you wish to recover
disk space that you are not using. For example, if you have expanded
a database file to accommodate new data that is eventually deleted or
archived, the size of the database does not change. You must reduce the
size of the database file to recover that space.

Modifying Database File Size Using the SSMS

You can both increase and decrease a file's size by using the Database
Properties window. To make the modification, change the value in the
Initial Size column. For example, if you wanted to expand the demo2
file to 30MB, you would use the following steps:

1. Locate the demo database in the Object Explorer. Right-click the
   database and select Properties from the shortcut menu to open the
   Database Properties dialog.

2. Select the Files tab of the dialog. Locate the demo2 file.

3. In the Initial Size column, change the value for the demo2 file to
   30MB.

4. Click the OK button to commit the change.

To reduce the file size, you use essentially the same process, but an
extra step is required. You can't remove more space from a file than the
file has available, so you must first get some usage statistics on the database file. The easiest way to do this is by using a TSQL query. Executing
the following script will provide the file usage information for the demo
database:

```
USE demo;

SELECT file_id, name, size FROM sys.database_files;
```

```
SELECT file_id, unallocated_extent_page_count
FROM sys.dm_db_file_space_usage;

GO
```

This query returns two result sets. The first result lists the files that make up the current database. The size column is measured in extents, which is an 8KB block. The second result shows the file usage of any data file that has any space used. Executing this script on our sample database provides the following results (your results may vary):

```
file_id      name              size
-----------  ----------------  -----------
1            demo              1280
2            demo_log          640
3            demo_fg1          640
4            demo_fg2          640
5            demo2             2560

(5 row(s) affected)

file_id unallocated_extent_page_count
------- -----------------------------
1       848

(1 row(s) affected)
```

In this case, you will see that the demo file (file_id = 1) is currently 1280 extents in size, which equates to 10MB. However, according to the second result set, 848 of those extents are currently unallocated. This means that you can shrink your database by approximately 848 extents. If you remember that each extent is 8KB, you can calculate the amount of free space in MB and round down to the nearest MB. Of course, you do not have to shrink the database to its smallest possible size, but you can now at least calculate this value if necessary.

To shrink the database file, simply follow the steps listed earlier for increasing a file size, except use a smaller size for the file instead of a larger size. As long as you do not try to shrink the file beyond its capacity, it should be fine.

Modifying Database File Size Using a TSQL Script

A database file is also expanded through the ALTER DATABASE statement.
You must use a different code technique to shrink a database file, which
we will discuss later. To expand a database file size, use the MODIFY FILE
command in the ALTER DATABASE statement as shown in this snippet:

```
USE master;


ALTER DATABASE demoscript
MODIFY FILE
(
  NAME = demoscript2,
  SIZE = 30MB
);
```

To shrink a database file with a TSQL script, we will use a special
command called DBCC, which stands for database console command.
This command has a variety of options used for internal structure
manipulation, verification, and maintenance. In our case, we will use
the DBCC SHRINKFILE command to reduce the file size. This statement
gives you significant control over how the file will shrink.

For example, if you have a 30MB file, but the data would fit into a
15MB file, you can use the following statement. This code will rear-
range the data in the file so that all data is moved to the portion of the
file to be retained. SQL Server can then reduce the file size. If you try to
shrink the file more than possible, the code will return an error:

```
USE demoscript;


DBCC SHRINKFILE (demoscript2, 15);
GO
```

Deallocate Database Files

If you have previously added a file to the database but no longer need
the file, you can remove it. As long as the file is empty, you can remove
it using the SSMS. If the file is not empty, you will not be able to drop
the file until you move the data to another file or drop the objects on the
file from the database.

To empty the file of data, you will use the DBCC SHRINKFILE command
again but with slightly different parameters. If you use the EMPTYFILE

flag instead of indicating the target size of the file, the system will move the data on the file to another file in the same filegroup. There must be space on another file in the filegroup to accommodate the data, so this is not an option if this is the only file in the filegroup. To empty the file, use this code:

```
USE demo;


DBCC SHRINKFILE (demo_fg2, EMPTYFILE)
GO
```

TIP   If you want to remove a file from a database but it has a table in it and it is the only file in the filegroup, you will have to move the table to another filegroup before you can proceed. Use the ALTER TABLETSQL statement with the MOVE TO command to identify the filegroup to which you want to move the table.

Deallocating a Database File Using the SSMS

Going back to the Database Properties dialog, you will be able to remove an empty file from the database by dropping it directly from the grid in the Files page. Use the following steps to drop the demo_fg2 file from the database:

1. Locate the demo database in the Object Explorer. Right-click the database and select Properties from the shortcut menu to open the Database Properties dialog.

2. Select the Files tab of the dialog. Click in the Logical Name cell for the demo_fg2 file to identify this as the file that you wish to drop.

3. Click the Remove button to remove the file from the grid.

4. Click the OK button to commit this action. If the file is not empty or you cannot remove it for any other reason, you would get an error at this point.

Deallocating a Database File Using a TSQL Script

As in the previous example, if the file that you want to deallocate is not empty, you must move the data from that file to another file in the filegroup before you will be able to remove the file. Simply follow the previous instructions for emptying the file. To remove a file using a TSQL script, use code like this:

```
USE master;

ALTER DATABASE demoscript
REMOVE FILE demoscript_fg2;
GO
```

Create and Alter Tables

Most SQL Server data exists in data tables. Each table is a collection of data elements called fields or columns. When you define a table in SQL Server, you specify information like the following for each column:

- Column name
- Data type
- Nullability

To begin this discussion, therefore, we must look at our data type options. Then we will see how to take a table through its life cycle, namely create, alter, and drop.

TIP   There are also many other table features that we just don't have the room to address in this guide. The intent of this book is to provide a quick reference for the most common tasks. For more advanced operations such as table partitioning, using calculated expressions in tables, and other similar operations, please refer to SQL Server Books Online or take a look at the Sybex book *Mastering SQL Server 2008* (Sybex, 2008).

Understand SQL Server Data Types

SQL Server provides a comprehensive set of built-in data types that define most storage structures that you will need for your table and other data types artifacts. This list of data types is documented on SQL Server Books Online, but is also provided in Table 3.5 for your convenience.

Table 3.5: SQL Server Data Types

Category	Type Name	Description
Exact Numeric	bigint	8-byte integer (-2^{63} to $2^{63}-1$)
	bit	Up to 8 bits can store in 1 byte—stores 0, 1, or null
	decimal	Fixed precision and scale from -10^{38} to $10^{38}-1$
	int	4-byte integer (-2^{31} to $2^{31}-1$)
	money	8-byte scaled integer (scaled to four decimal places)
	numeric	Equivalent to decimal
	smallint	2-byte integer (-2^{15} to $2^{15}-1$)
	smallmoney	4-byte scaled integer (scaled to four decimal places)
	tinyint	Integer from 0 to 255
Approximate Numeric	float	Floating point storage—4 bytes up to 7 digits precision, 8 bytes from 8–15 digits precision
	real	4-byte floating point storage
Date and Time	date	3-byte date storage (no time)
	datetime	8-byte date and time storage from 1/1/1753 to 12/31/9999, accuracy to 3.33 ms
	datetime2	Extension of the **datetime** type with a large date range and user-defined precision
	datetimeoffset	Datetime storage with time zone awareness
	smalldatetime	4-byte date and time storage from 1/1/1900 to 6/6/2079, accuracy to the minute
	time	5-byte time storage, time zone aware and accurate to 100 ns
Character Strings	char	Fixed-length ANSI character storage to 8,000 characters on row and 2GB max off-row storage
	varchar	Variable-length ANSI character storage to 8,000 characters on row and 2GB max off-row storage

Table 3.5: SQL Server Data Types *(continued)*

Category	Type Name	Description
	`text`	ANSI Character Large Object (CLOB) storage; will not be supported in future releases
Unicode Character Strings	`nchar`	Fixed-length Unicode character storage to 4,000 characters on row and 2GB max off-row storage
	`nvarchar`	Variable-length Unicode character storage to 4,000 characters on row and 2GB max off-row storage
	`ntext`	Unicode Character Large Object (CLOB) storage; will not be supported in future releases
Binary Strings	`binary`	Fixed-length binary character storage to 8,000 bytes on row and 2GB max off-row storage
	`varbinary`	Variable-length binary character storage to 8,000 bytes on row and 2GB max off-row storage
	`image`	Binary Large Object (BLOB) storage; will not be supported in future releases
Misc. Data Types	`cursor`	A reference to an ANSI cursor
	`timestamp`	ANSI rowversion value
	`hierarchyid`	Variable-length value representing a position in a hierarchy
	`uniqueidentifier`	128-bit GUID guaranteed unique within a database
	`sql_variant`	Abstract storage; can contain most standard data types
	`xml`	Equivalent to `nvarchar(max)`; enforces well-formed XML document or fragment structure
	`table`	Stores a table structure

Create a Table

Using the data types presented in Table 3.5, you can create tables that define storage to meet your specific needs. As with other operations, you can do this either using the SSMS or with a TSQL script.

Creating a Table Using the SSMS

Suppose that you wanted to create a Customer table in the demo database with the following characteristics:

- An auto-incrementing ID value, entry required

- A customer name with a maximum of 25 characters, entry required

- A customer state code fixed to two characters, entry required

- A customer credit limit that could potentially accept decimals, entry optional

The following steps walk you through the process of adding this Customer table to the demo database:

1. Locate the demo database in the Object Explorer and click the plus sign next to the database name to expand the node.

2. Locate and expand the Tables node inside the demo database. This will provide a list of all of the user tables currently in the database. This list should now be empty except for the nested node that contains the system tables.

3. Right-click on the Tables node and select New Table from the shortcut menu. This will open the table design screen.

4. In the Column Name cell, type **CustomerID**.

5. In the Data Type cell, type **int,** or select it from the list.

6. Clear the Allow Nulls check box to make an entry required.

7. Look at the Column Properties window at the bottom of the screen. Note that the General section of the properties list contains the same elements that you just defined for the column.

8. In the Table Designer section of the properties list, locate the item Identity Specification and click the plus sign next to it to expand its settings.

9. Change the value of the Is Identity property to Yes. This should enable the Identity Increment and Identity Seed properties. Leave these at their default values of 1.

10. Click in the Column Name cell underneath the CustomerID value. Type **CustomerName** into this cell. Enter **varchar(25)** for the data type and clear the Allow Nulls check box.

11. For the third row in the grid, enter **StateCode** as the column name and **char(2)** as the data type, and clear the Allow Nulls check box.

12. Finally, in the fourth row of the grid, set the column name to CreditLimit with a Data Type of money. Leave the Allow Nulls box checked. The completed screen should look like Figure 3.8.

13. To save the table, choose File ➤ Save Table_1. This will give you the opportunity to save the table with a name of your choosing.

Figure 3.8: Creating a table in the SSMS

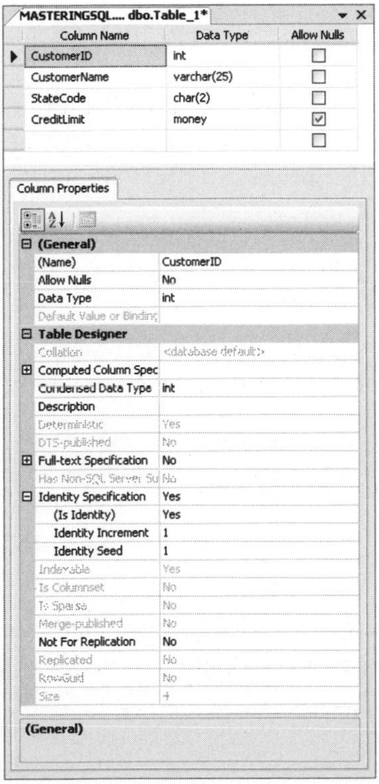

14. Enter **Customer** for the table name and click OK. Close the screen by selecting File ➤ Close. You should see the new table in the table list for the demo database in the Object Explorer window.

NOTE   You may notice that the actual name of the table in the tables list is dbo.Customer. The dbo identifier refers to the dbo schema. A schema is simply a namespace for organizing database objects. You will learn more about schemas in Chapter 4, "Executing Basic Queries."

Creating a Table Using a TSQL Script

The simple form of the CREATE TABLE statement looks like this:

```
CREATE TABLE
    [ database_name . schema_name  . table_name
        ( <column_definition> [ ,...n ] )
    [ ; ]
```

This syntax allows the developer to identify the table by name and by schema. Following the name of the table is a list of column properties placed in parentheses. The column definition can contain the following:

Data type   You must specify a data type for each table column. These data types define storage requirements of each column in the table.

Collation: You can optionally define collations for each individual column that differ from the table collation or the server default collation.

Nullability: You can explicitly specify every column as to whether it will allow null values. If you do not provide this value when you create the table, SQL Server will use the database option ANSI NULL DEFAULT.

Identity: This auto-number property allows automatically incrementing integer values for the indicated column.

To create a table like the one you made using the SSMS, you could use the SQL statement illustrated in Listing 3.3. Note that the formatting in this listing is not required but is included for readability. You should follow your own organization's standards for code formatting. If there is no standard, maybe it's time to create one.

Listing 3.3: Creating a Customer Table

```
USE demoscript;
GO

CREATE TABLE dbo.Customer
(
  CustomerID    int           NOT NULL  IDENTITY(1,1),
  CustomerName  varchar(25)   NOT NULL,
  StateCode     char(2)       NOT NULL,
  CreditLimit   money         NULL
);
GO
```

Alter a Table

You can also make modifications to an already existing table. If your needs change, you can make structural alterations such as these to a table:

- Adding columns
- Dropping columns
- Changing a column data type

WARNING   Be very careful before you make structural altera-tions to tables that contain data. The alterations may result in data loss. For example, if a column in a table has data in it and you remove the column, you will lose the data. The only recovery option once you have committed this action is to restore from a database backup.

Altering a Table Using the SSMS

The same table design screen that you used to create a table will be the tool for altering a table in the SSMS. Assume that you wanted to modify the Customer table to include an email address and to lengthen the CustomerName column to 30 characters. Use the following steps to complete this task:

1. Locate the Customer table item in the Tables node of the demo database in the Object Explorer window. Right-click on the Customer table and select Design from the shortcut menu.

2. The design screen opens. In the Data Type cell for the Customer-Name item, change the Data Type entry to varchar(30).

3. In the empty fifth row in the grid, add a new column specification for an email address using EmailAddress for the column name and varchar(50) for the data type. Select the Allow Nulls check box if it is not already checked.

4. Select File ➤ Save Customer to save your work and File ➤ Close to close the table design screen.

Altering a Table Using a TSQL Script

The ALTER TABLE statement supports numerous options to manipulate many aspects of a file, including constraints, indexing, and structural elements. At this point, we will concern ourselves with only the statements that we use to make structural changes to the table. To make these changes, you can use the ADD and DROP commands to add and drop columns. You can also use the ALTER COLUMN command to make changes to an existing column.

In this case, if we wanted to make the same changes to the Customer table in the demoscript database that we just made to the demo database, we could use the following script:

```
USE demoscript;

ALTER TABLE Customer
ADD
  EmailAddress varchar(50)  NULL;

ALTER TABLE Customer
ALTER COLUMN
  CustomerName varchar(30)  NOT NULL;
GO
```

Drop a Table

If you no longer need a table in your database, you can drop it. As
mentioned earlier, in the discussion of altering tables, however, make
sure you don't need that table before you drop it. Once the action is
committed, you will only be able to recover the data by restoring from
a backup. Also, dropping a table removes all of the indexes associated
with that table. While you can re-create indexes if necessary, it can be a
time-consuming process.

Dropping a Table Using the SSMS

It seems that the most destructive operations are always the easiest to
execute. Dropping a table is no exception. If you wanted to drop the
Customer table from the database, it would require only these few
short steps:

1. Locate the Customer table item in the Tables node of the demo
   database in the Object Explorer window.

2. Right-click the Customer table and select Delete. This will open
   the Delete Object dialog.

3. In the lower-right portion of the dialog, you will see a button
   labeled Show Dependencies. This allows you to see objects such
   as views and procedures that depend on the table as well as the
   objects upon which the table depends.

4. Click the OK button to commit the operation.

Dropping a Table Using a TSQL Script

Dropping a table with a script is equally easy. Use the following script
to drop the Customer table from the demoscript database:

```
USE demoscript;

DROP TABLE Customer;
GO
```

TIP There is no convenient Show Dependencies button when you are using TSQL code, but there are two dynamic system views that can come in handy to give you the same information. If you wanted to see all of the objects that depend on the Customer table as well as the objects upon which the table depends, you can use the following code. This will return two result sets with the desired information:

```
USE demoscript;

SELECT *
FROM sys.dm_sql_referencing_entities
  ('dbo.Customer', 'OBJECT');

SELECT *
FROM sys.dm_sql_referenced_entities
  ('dbo.Customer', 'OBJECT');
GO
```

Although in this example the results are empty because there are no dependent objects at this point, this is definitely a useful tool to add to your toolbelt.

4

Executing Basic Queries

IN THIS CHAPTER, YOU WILL LEARN TO DO THE FOLLOWING:

W e know that the intention of this book is to provide a reference for the SQL Server administrator; however, even administrators need to interact with the actual data from time to time. It is not just all about configuration and maintenance. If you have a good understanding of how the SQL developer or client programmer goes about working with the data, it unlocks some secrets that can certainly help as you approach your database administration tasks. Giving you that understanding is the goal of this chapter.

In this chapter you will learn about SQL Server schemas and how they affect object resolution when you execute queries in a database. We will then explore basic SQL statements, first learning how to retrieve data from a database and then learning how to modify data. Finally, we will see how to apply this knowledge of SQL code to administrative tasks by learning more about the SQL system catalog, including system views, system stored procedures, and DBCC statements.

Use SQL Server Schemas

SQL Server supports many different kinds of objects, such as tables, views, stored procedures, and functions. One of the most important tasks that an administrator does is to manage and secure these objects. These objects are the building blocks of a server-side database application. To simplify the process management and securing them, SQL Server 2008 allows you to organize objects into schemas.

Understand Schemas

A schema is a logical container for SQL objects. When you create objects in Microsoft SQL Server, you can organize them into schema containers. In SQL Server 2008, you can use schemas for the following:

- Name resolution
- Object organization
- Security management

For example, assume you were working with a very large database with hundreds of objects. You have tables, views, and stored procedures that encompass a broad array of business processes. Without a schema there would be no way to differentiate the functionality or security of these different objects into sets, but with a schema you can define functional areas in your business such as human resources, accounting, production, and so forth. Associating objects with the appropriate schema gives you an organizational benefit as well as a resource management benefit.

In addition to objects, you can also associate database users with schemas. Every database user can have a default schema. By default, each user's default schema is dbo, but you can assign another default schema at any time. Refer to Figure 4.1 as we discuss the relationship between users and schemas.

SQL Server Basics

PART I

Figure 4.1: Schemas, objects, and users

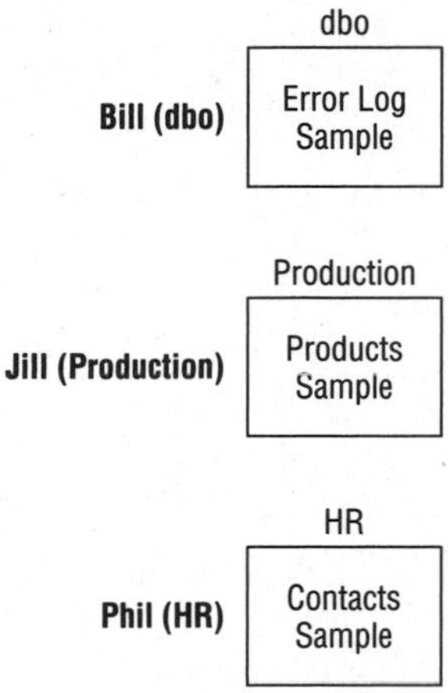

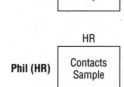

In this figure, you will see three schemas, namely dbo, Production, and HR. Each schema contains tables. Notice that there is a table called Sample in each schema. Your code would refer to these tables as dbo.Sample, Production.Sample, and HR.Sample. Notice that the fully qualified name of the table includes the schema name.

You will also notice three users. The user name Bill is associated with the dbo schema by default. Jill and Phil each also have a default schema. The default schema for a user does not affect security for that user, but it does affect object resolution. The resolution rules for schemas are as follows:

- If a user fully qualifies an object reference, such as dbo.Sample, it will resolve to that specific object regardless of their default schema.

- If a user provides only an object name as a reference without a schema, the following will occur:
  - SQL Server will first attempt to resolve the object reference to the user's default schema.
  - If the object cannot be resolved to the user's default schema, SQL Server will then attempt to resolve the reference to the dbo schema.
  - If the object cannot be resolved to the dbo schema, SQL Server will return an error.

Applying these rules will provide the results illustrated in Table 4.1. These examples assume the organization structure illustrated in Figure 4.1.

Table 4.1: Object Resolution Examples

User	Reference	Result
Bill	Sample	Resolves to dbo.Sample
Bill	Production.Sample	Resolves to Production.Sample
Jill	Sample	Resolves to Production.Sample
Jill	Products	Resolves to Production.Products
Phil	Sample	Resolves to HR.Sample
Phil	Contacts	Resolves to HR.Contacts
Phil	ErrorLog	Resolves to dbo.ErrorLog
Phil	Production.Products	Resolves to Production.Products
Phil	Products	Cannot be resolved; returns an error

NOTE Do not associate resolution with security. Schema resolution rules do not imply permissions of any kind. Schemas can, however, be extremely useful for managing permissions because an administrator can assign permissions at the schema level as opposed to the individual object level. We will address the security implications of schemas in more detail in Chapter 7, "Managing Security." For now, just focus on the resolution rules.

Create Schemas

As with most objects in SQL Server, either you can create schemas in the SQL Server Management Studio (SSMS) visual interface or you can use a Transact SQL (TSQL) script. We will walk you though both approaches here, starting with the SSMS. We will use the demo and demo script databases that we used in Chapter 3, "Creating Databases, Files, and Tables." If you do not have these databases, please create them according to the instructions in the previous chapter. They do not have to be large.

Creating a Schema Using the SSMS

Schemas in SQL Server are database-specific artifacts, so to create a schema, we must navigate to the database node in the SSMS. To begin, start the SSMS utility by selecting Start ➢ All Programs ➢ Microsoft SQL Server 2008 ➢ SQL Server Management Studio. In the Connect to Server dialog, connect to the local instance. This should be populated in the connection dialog by default. If not, you can always type (**local**) in the Server Name text box of the connection dialog, as illustrated in Figure 3.2 in Chapter 3. Now follow these steps to create the schema:

1. Expand the Databases node and locate the demo database.

2. Expand the demo database node and locate the Security node.

3. Expand the Security node and locate the Schemas node.

4. Expand the Schemas node to see a list of current schemas. The list should include the system-defined schemas. Verify that the dbo schema is in the list. This is the default schema for all objects and users if you do not define specific schemas.

5. Right-click the Schemas node and select New Schema. This will open the Schema - New dialog.

6. To create a schema called Sample, enter the schema name in the appropriate text box.

7. You can also enter a database user as the owner of the schema. The owner of a schema will own all of the objects in the schema. The default owner is dbo. In this example, enter **dbo** explicitly in the Schema Owner text box. The complete dialog should look like the example in Figure 4.2.

Figure 4.2: Creating a schema

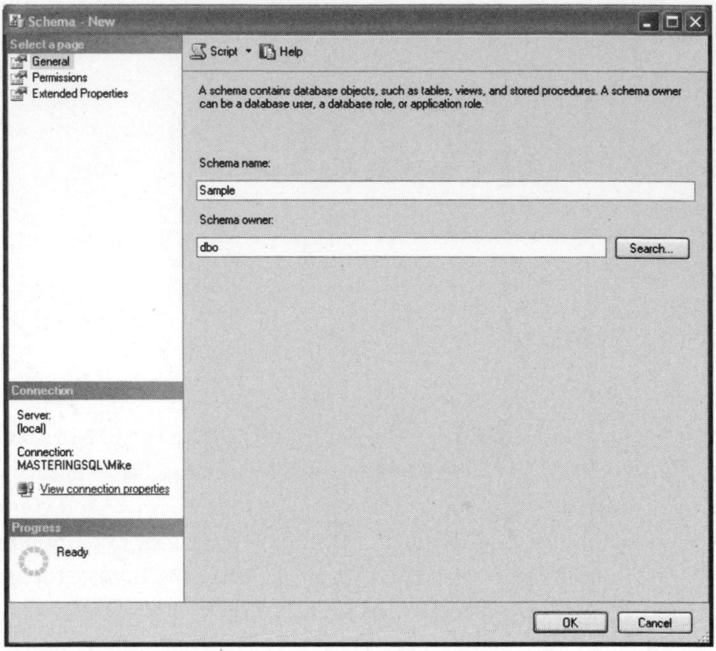

8. Click the OK button to confirm your choices. Your new schema should now appear in the list.

Creating a Schema Using a TSQL Script

The TSQL script that you will use to create a schema is a simple definition statement. You will need to open a query window to type in and execute your script. From this point forward in this chapter, use these steps to open the query window every time you need to execute a SQL script:

1. In the SSMS, choose File ➤ New ➤ Database Engine Query.

2. In the Connect to Server dialog, provide the connection information. In our case, we will connect to the local server using Windows authentication.

3. Click the Connect button to connect the query window to the target database.

The syntax to create a schema requires the same information as the SSMS interface. You will need the new schema name and the owner of the schema. The AUTHORIZATION section on the syntax identifies the owner. This section is optional, and if you do not include it, the owner will be the dbo user. Enter the following code to create an identical schema in the demoscript database.

```
USE demoscript;
GO

CREATE SCHEMA Sample
  AUTHORIZATION dbo;
GO
```

You will notice that there is a GO statement after the USE statement in this script that you did not see in scripts in prior chapters. This is because the GO statement is a batch separator in TSQL. All the code between the GO statements executes as a single batch. TSQL requires a CREATE SCHEMA statement to be in its own batch, so we have to trigger the batch both before and after the statement.

NOTE   Batches are not the same as transactions. Batches are not atomic, meaning that they do not execute as an all-or-nothing set of actions. Batches are for execution efficiency while transactions are for ensuring data integrity.

Associate Objects with Schemas

Objects such as tables, views, or stored procedures are associated with schemas. By default, that schema is dbo, but you can override that when you create the object. You can also move the object to another schema later if you wish, although this action will result in SQL Server dropping all permissions on the object. The following topics show you how to create a table in a schema other than dbo and to change the schema association at a later time.

Applying Schemas Using the SSMS

The first steps in creating a table in an alternate schema are identical to those described in Chapter 3. Assuming that you are creating a sample table with two integer columns, you would have a Create New Table dialog that looks like Figure 4.3. This will be our starting point. This example assumes that you have already created the schema.

Figure 4.3: Creating the sample table

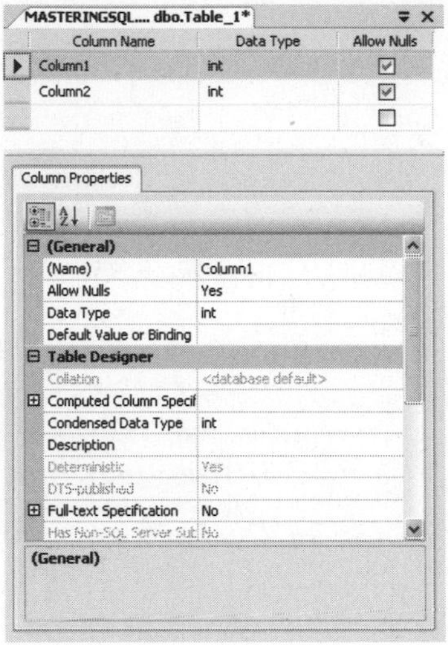

The following steps illustrate how to create a table and associate it with a schema.

1. With the table designer open, access the Properties window in the SSMS. This should already be visible on the right side of the screen, but if it is not, simply press the F4 key on your keyboard to open it. You can also select View ➢ Properties Window. Please note that this is a different window from the Column Properties window at the bottom of the screen.

2. In the Properties window, locate the Schema property. The value should be set to dbo by default.

3. Click on the value in the right column next to the Schema property to open the list selector. Locate and select the Sample schema in the list.

4. Select File ➢ Save Table_1. Enter **SampleTable** as the table name and then close the designer.

5. You should now see Sample.SampleTable in the tables list in the Object Explorer.

If you want to change the schema association of an object, you will use a similar process. These steps walk you through the process of switching SampleTable to the dbo schema:

1. Locate the table in the Tables node of the Object Explorer.

2. Right-click SampleTable and click Design to access the Table Designer.

3. Locate the Schema property in the Properties window and change the property value from Sample to dbo.

4. If you get a warning stating that the permissions will be dropped, click Yes to proceed. Be aware that you will have to reset permissions on objects every time you change their schema association.

5. Save the table design and close the table designer.

6. To see the change, you will probably have to refresh the Tables node in the Object Explorer. Right-click the Tables node and click Refresh. You should now see the new schema association in the list.

Applying Schemas Using a TSQL Script

To create a table associated with a specific schema, you will use exactly the same code that you used to create the table. The only difference will be that you will qualify the name of the table in the script with the schema that you wish to use. To create the SampleTable table in the demoscript database that is associated with the Sample schema, you would use the following code:

```
USE demoscript;

CREATE TABLE Sample.SampleTable
(
  Column1 int NULL,
  Column2 int NULL
);
GO
```

Notice that when you fully qualify the table name to include the schema, SQL Server automatically associates the table with that schema upon creation. This assumes that the schema already exists. If it does not, you will get an error upon script execution. You will need to refresh the Tables node in the Object Explorer before you will see your new table.

SQL Server considers the relocation of an object from one schema to another to be a modification to the schema and not to the object. Therefore, to move the SampleTable object from the Sample schema to the dbo schema, we will use the ALTER SCHEMA statement. The following code moves the SampleTable object from the Sample schema to the dbo schema:

```
USE demoscript;
GO

ALTER SCHEMA dbo
  TRANSFER Sample.SampleTable;
GO
```

Select Data from a Database

Now that you have seen the basics of schemas, we are ready to move into the central theme of this chapter: using basic Transact SQL statements. Transact SQL is generally divided into three categories:

Data Definition Language (DDL)   DDL is the language of object creation. We have already used DDL to create tables and schemas. There are three standard Transact SQL statements associated with DDL. They are CREATE, ALTER, and DELETE.

Data Control Language (DCL)   DCL is the language of object security. When you want to control permissions and access to objects in SQL Server, you will use the primary DCL statements, which are GRANT, DENY, and REVOKE.

Data Manipulation Language (DML)   DML is the language of data interaction. Whenever you want to extract or modify data from a database, you will use DML statements, which include SELECT, INSERT, UPDATE, DELETE, and MERGE.

Use Basic Select Syntax

Selecting data from a database is a simple process. The intention is for the SELECT statement to be as much like a natural English statement as possible. The basic select syntax consists of three primary sections:

- SELECT
- FROM
- WHERE

The SELECT section provides a list of columns or expressions that you wish to return from the database. The FROM section defines a list of tables from which SQL Server will extract the data. Finally, the WHERE section provides criteria that filter the data that SQL Server returns.

> **NOTE**   The following examples of the SELECT statement use the AdventureWorksDW2008 and AdventureWorks2008 databases that you can download from http://msftdbprodsamples.codeplex.com. You may want to do that now before you proceed. Navigate to the SQL Server 2008 product sample database page. From there, you can download and install the MSI that is appropriate for your platform, either 32 bit or 64 bit.

For example, suppose that you wanted to create a list of your customers and their email addresses from the database. The AdventureWorksDW2008 database contains a table called dbo.DimCustomer, which provides this customer information. To view the list of available tables and columns, simply expand the appropriate nodes in the Object Explorer.

Selecting All Data from a Table

To return all of the information from this table, you could use the following code:

```
USE AdventureWorksDW2008;

SELECT *
FROM dbo.DimCustomer;
GO
```

In this example we use the * to represent all columns in the table, so we are not choosing specific columns to return. We are choosing to return all of the columns that the table has available. Notice that the

FROM clause provides the name of the table from which you are selecting the data. Note that if we were to add columns to the table later and execute the statement again, we would see the new columns on the subsequent execution.

Selecting Specific Columns

Although it is simple to use the * to return data, it is very inefficient. It is unlikely that you will need all of the data in every column to satisfy your business requirements. Returning more data than you need wastes network bandwidth and SQL throughput. You should avoid this. Instead, we will provide specific columns in the SELECT list to reduce the unnecessary data that the query returns.

In our example if you simply want the customer first name, last name, and email address, then you should ask for only that information. Using the * in this case is very wasteful. We could easily reconstruct the query to return only the desired information. That query would look like this:

```
USE AdventureWorksDW2008;

SELECT
   FirstName,
   LastName,
   EmailAddress
FROM
   dbo.DimCustomer;
GO
```

TIP You do not have to format your code the way we have formatted this example. Putting each column name on its own line is for readability; it does not affect the way the code executes. SQL Server ignores white space and hard returns, so it is up to you how you organize your code. Most organizations have existing standards regarding code formatting. You should follow those standards. Consistency is critical in an organization, and even if you personally dislike the way the code is formatted according to your organization's standard, that consistency provides a benefit beyond the actual style.

Manipulating Columns

You can also manipulate data as you extract it by defining expressions in your select list. For example, we are extracting the first name and last name of the customer from the table, but suppose you want to assemble these two names into a single field for use on a report. While a good reporting tool can perform that action in the report, you have the option of concatenating the names in the query as well. That code would look like this:

```
USE AdventureWorksDW2008;

SELECT
  FirstName + ' ' + LastName as FullName,
  EmailAddress
FROM
  dbo.DimCustomer;
GO
```

Notice that the + is used as an operator to indicate concatenation. To insert a space between the first name and last name, we used a space enclosed in single quotation marks. Finally, you will notice that we have named the newly concatenated column. The as operator allows you to name a selected expression or even rename an existing column as you extract it from the database.

You can also use other mathematical operators such as +, - , *, and / to create mathematical expressions when selecting numeric data as opposed to character data. This provides significant flexibility when extracting data.

Filtering Data

You have already seen that you can filter columns by providing a select list. However, you can also filter rows from your result set by using a WHERE clause in your query. This clause provides criteria for row-based extraction. You can define criteria in a WHERE clause by using the following pattern:

```
column operator expression
```

For example, suppose you want to select customers that are located only in the state of California. If state is one of the columns in the table, you can use that column as an extraction criterion. Using the previous pattern, the expression in the WHERE clause would look like this:

```
state = 'CA'
```

In our example, suppose you wanted to select female customers having a yearly income greater than $75,000. As before, you want to return only the first name, last name, and email address. You would use the following code to satisfy this requirement:

```
USE AdventureWorksDW2008;

SELECT
  FirstName,
  LastName,
  EmailAddress
FROM
  dbo.DimCustomer
WHERE
  Gender = 'F' AND
  YearlyIncome > 75000;
GO
```

Using Wildcards

Sometimes you may need to filter data based on a pattern rather than on a specific value. For example, if you wanted only customers with a first name that begins with the letter *J*, it is unreasonable to write a query by providing a list of specific names. There is no way you could get them all, and it would be far too much effort. Instead, we will use the wildcard character % to represent zero or more replacement characters in an expression. If we wanted to filter the "greater than $75,000" query additionally to return only customers with a first name beginning with the letter *J*, we would use the following code:

```
USE AdventureWorksDW2008;

SELECT
  FirstName,
  LastName,
  EmailAddress
```

```
FROM
    dbo.DimCustomer
WHERE
    Gender = 'F' AND
    YearlyIncome > 75000 AND
    FirstName LIKE 'J%';
GO
```

> **TIP** This book does not provide exhaustive coverage of SQL struc-
> ture and syntax. We are illustrating only the highlights. You may need
> some additional information depending on your job responsibility.
> There are plenty of resources online that cover the basics of SQL
> syntax. A search should return numerous resources. You might also
> want to look at the book *SQL for Dummies* (John Wiley & Sons, Inc.,
> 2006), which has a great overview of basic SQL syntax.

Group and Aggregate Data

You will often need to consolidate and aggregate data as you extract
it from the database. This allows you to get subtotals and counts from
the database based on grouping criteria that you will provide. You will
use aggregate functions and the GROUP BY clause in TSQL to satisfy these
requirements.

Simple Aggregation

Now look at the AdventureWorks2008 sample database. Let's suppose
that you want to return a list of contacts from the Person.Person table
in ascending order by last name. You could use the following query:

```
USE AdventureWorks2008;

SELECT FirstName, MiddleName, LastName
FROM Person.Person
ORDER BY LastName ASC;
GO
```

This query will give you the list of people sorted in the order you
specified. But what if you need to know the total number of people

who have the same last name? For example, how many Adamses do we have? How many Robinsons are there? SQL supports numerous aggregate functions to summarize information. You use these functions in conjunction with the GROUP BY clause in the SQL syntax. This statement groups data for aggregation, as you will see in the sample code that follows Table 4.2. This table provides a list of standard aggregate functions in SQL Server 2008, along with a description of each.

Table 4.2: Aggregate Functions in SQL Server 2008

Function	Description
AVG	Returns the average value in the set. Ignores null values; can be configured to average all values (the default) or only distinct values in the set
CHECKSUM_AGG	Returns the checksum of the values in the group, either all or distinct, ignoring null values
COUNT	Returns the number of rows, all or distinct, based on an expression or (optionally) a simple row count
COUNT_BIG	Executes like COUNT, except that it returns a **bigint** rather than an **int** data type
GROUPING	Indicates if a specified column in a GROUP BY list is aggregate. Returns 0 or 1
MAX	Returns the maximum value in the set based on the provided column name
MIN	Returns the minimum value in the set based on the provided column name
SUM	Returns the sum of values in the set based on the provided column name
STDEV	Returns the statistical standard deviation of all values based on the provided column name
STDEVP	Returns the statistical population standard deviation of all values based on the provided column name
VAR	Returns the statistical variance of all values based on the provided column name
VARP	Returns the statistical population variance of all values based on the provided column name

In this example, we are interested in a COUNT aggregate. Because the value returned for each breakpoint will not be larger than an int (a 4-byte integer), we will use the COUNT function rather than the COUNT_BIG function, which would return an 8-byte integer value. The resulting query would look like this:

```
USE AdventureWorks2008;
SELECT LastName, COUNT(LastName) as CountOfNames
FROM Person.Person
GROUP BY LastName
ORDER BY LastName ASC;
```

This query produces a new column called CountOfNames that contains the total number of entries in the table for any specific last name. Notice how the query is grouped by last name. This is very important because the syntax rule requires that any SELECT list that contains both aggregated and nonaggregated data must be grouped by the nonaggregated content. Notice how the GROUP BY clause provides breakpoints for the aggregate.

Filtering Groups

Another useful technique when executing aggregates is to use a HAVING clause. Unlike a WHERE clause in a query, which filters out individual rows before the result set is created, a HAVING clause filters out groups that do not meet specific conditions. For example, assume you want to get a result that provides a count of all persons whose last name starts with the letter *A*. Assume further that you want the query to return only the groups that have at least 10 last names.

Your query will actually perform two different operations. The first operation filters out the data to create the groups. Only people with a last name starting with the letter *A* will be counted. The second operation eliminates any group that does not produce a count of at least 10 persons. Look at the following query as an example:

```
USE AdventureWorks2008;

SELECT LastName, COUNT(LastName) as CountOfNames
FROM Person.Person
WHERE LastName LIKE 'A%'
GROUP BY LastName
HAVING COUNT(LastName) >= 10;
GO
```

One somewhat frustrating feature of this type of query is that you can't use the column alias as an identifier in the HAVING clause. Notice that we had to use the syntax HAVING COUNT(LastName) >= 10 and not HAVING CountOfNames >= 10. Be aware of this quirk so you don't drive yourself nuts trying to figure out what's wrong with your query.

Join Data Tables

In a relational data model, you will often have to join tables to extract relevant information. The type of JOIN statement you use, the join fields that you choose, and the order of the tables that you provide in your JOIN statement can all have an impact on both the data that the query will return and the performance of the query. In fact, the I/O cost resulting from join operations in queries is frequently the most resource-consuming and performance-affecting part of the query process.

Let's begin by considering a simple join operation. Suppose that you wanted to get a list of all of the people in your database who have a phone number in the 702 area code. You are planning a trip to Las Vegas and you want a place to stay. The problem is that the names of the people are in the Person.Person table but their phone numbers are in the Person.PersonPhone table. There is a common column between the two tables. That column is BusinessEntityID. To correlate the date between the two tables, use the following query:

```
USE AdventureWorks2008;

SELECT p.FirstName, p.LastName, pp.PhoneNumber
FROM Person.Person as p
INNER JOIN Person.PersonPhone as pp
  ON p.BusinessEntityID = pp.BusinessEntityID
WHERE pp.PhoneNumber LIKE '702%';
GO
```

Depending on how you want to correlate the data, you can use a variety of different JOIN types. Joins work in pairs, from left to right. Remember that the *first* table listed in the join clause is the Left table. These different options determine whether SQL Server will return non-matching data in the results and, if so, from which table(s). Table 4.3 discusses these options.

Table 4.3: SQL Server 2008 Join Types

Join Type	Alias	Description
INNER JOIN	JOIN	Returns requested data for every row in each table only where there is an exact match on the join field
LEFT OUTER JOIN	LEFT JOIN	Returns requested data for all rows from the first table stated in the join operation; only returns data for rows from the second stated table where there is a matching value. This can result in null values in the result when the first stated table in the join has a row with no matching row(s) in the second stated table.
RIGHT OUTER JOIN	RIGHT JOIN	Returns requested data for all rows from the second table stated in the join operation; only returns data for rows from the first stated table where there is a matching value. This can result in null values in the result when the second stated table in the join has a row with no matching row(s) in the first stated table.
FULL OUTER JOIN	FULL JOIN	Returns requested data for all rows in both correlated tables, but the result will contain null values for rows with no matching join value on the other side
CROSS JOIN	—	Returns a Cartesian (Cross) product; in other words, all possible combinations of rows between the two tables

In our previous query example, what would happen if someone in the Person.Person table did not have a phone number provided in the Person.PersonPhone table? Because the query is written using the INNER JOIN operator, it would return only people with at least one matching record in the PersonPhone table.

What if you were to write the query like this?

```
USE AdventureWorks2008;
SELECT p.FirstName, p.LastName, pp.PhoneNumber
FROM Person.Person as p
LEFT OUTER JOIN Person.PersonPhone as pp
  ON p.BusinessEntityID = pp.BusinessEntityID
WHERE pp.PhoneNumber LIKE '702%';
```

SQL Server Basics

PART I

In this case, the JOIN operator is LEFT OUTER JOIN, meaning that all rows will be returned from the Person table but only matching rows will be returned from the PersonPhone table. This means that some people may be returned in the results without a registered phone number. In this example, all people in the list have a registered phone number, but if they did not, the PhoneNumber column would contain the value of NULL.

A null value will appear in the PhoneNumber column for these rows, because the value is unknown for that person. Note that in the AdventureWorks 2008 database, every person in the Person.Person table has a corresponding entry on the Person.PersonPhone table, so in this case, all Person rows have matching rows in PersonPhone, and the results of the two queries will be the same.

Use Subqueries, Table Variables, Temporary Tables, and Derived Tables

Subqueries and derived tables are nothing more than nested SELECT statements. These tools are used to dynamically pull data from the tables so that it can be used to resolve another query. By allowing the query logic to get all of its data from the database (having data-driven logic) instead of hard-coding values (which gives you brittle fixed logic), you increase your ability to maintain the code.

Subqueries can be scalar or can return a list of values. When a subquery returns both columns and rows, it is often referred to as a *derived table*. Derived tables can be a useful way to avoid using temporary tables.

Scalar Subqueries

When a subquery returns exactly one row and one column of data, it is considered a scalar subquery. A scalar subquery is typically constructed either as a query that selects a single column based on a unique key or as an aggregate value with no grouping. In either case, the result of the query is used in place of the value in the containing query. Consider the following query:

```
USE AdventureWorks2008;

SELECT
   SalesOrderID,
   OrderQty,
   UnitPrice
```

SQL Server Basics

PART I

```
FROM
  Sales.SalesOrderDetail
WHERE UnitPrice > (
  SELECT AVG(UnitPrice)
  FROM Sales.SalesOrderDetail
)
AND OrderQty > (
  SELECT AVG(OrderQty)
  FROM Sales.SalesOrderDetail
);
GO
```

This query will return a list of sales orders that meet the conditions of having a higher-than-average unit price and higher-than-average order quantity. In other words, it returns your highest value orders. The great thing about a query like this is that even if the data changes, this query will always return accurate results.

Subqueries that Return Lists

When a subquery returns a list of values, it can be used after an IN operator in a query. When a query returns more than one value, it can't be used as a scalar subquery would. Instead, this query provides a set of possible values that the outer query can use as a filter. Think of it as advanced OR logic.

What if you want to return a list of customer IDs and account numbers of all of your customers in North America? One way to write this query would be like this:

```
USE AdventureWorks2008;

SELECT CustomerID, AccountNumber
FROM Sales.Customer
WHERE TerritoryID IN (
  SELECT TerritoryID
  FROM Sales.SalesTerritory
  WHERE [Group] = 'North America'
);
GO
```

This is not the only way to write this query. You can often rewrite subqueries as join operations and get the same results. For example, the next query will give you exactly the same results as the previous one. Your decision to use one or the other will depend on your performance metrics and maintenance requirements.

```
USE AdventureWorks2008;

SELECT c.CustomerID, c.AccountNumber
FROM Sales.Customer as c
INNER JOIN Sales.SalesTerritory as st
  ON c.TerritoryID = st.TerritoryID
WHERE st.[Group] = 'North America';
GO
```

Derived Tables

You may want to create a temporary table structure, such as a work table, to process intermediate results in your procedure. There are a number of ways to do this. You can use temp tables, table variables, or derived tables. Each approach has its own pros and cons. Listing 4.1 illustrates the use of a table variable to temporarily store data. Although we have not looked at the INSERT statement yet, you should be able to get a feel for the technique from this example.

Listing 4.1: Using Table Variables

```
USE AdventureWorks2008;

DECLARE @NameAndRole table
(
ContactName            nvarchar(101),
BusinessRole nvarchar(50),
ModifiedDate datetime
);

INSERT INTO @NameAndRole
SELECT Name, 'Vendor', ModifiedDate
FROM Purchasing.Vendor;

INSERT INTO @NameAndRole
SELECT p.FirstName + ' ' + p.LastName,
```

Listing 4.1: Using Table Variables *(continued)*

```
        e.JobTitle,
        p.ModifiedDate
    FROM Person.Person as p
    INNER JOIN HumanResources.Employee as e
        ON p.BusinessEntityID = e.BusinessEntityID;

    SELECT ContactName, BusinessRole
    FROM @NameAndRole
    WHERE ModifiedDate > '20010101';
    GO
```

Now look at Listing 4.2, which achieves the same result using a temporary table.

Listing 4.2: Using Temporary Tables

```
    USE AdventureWorks2008;

    CREATE TABLE #NameAndRole
    (
    ContactName             nvarchar(101),
    BusinessRole nvarchar(50),
    ModifiedDate datetime
    );

    INSERT INTO #NameAndRole
    SELECT Name, 'Vendor', ModifiedDate
    FROM Purchasing.Vendor;

    INSERT INTO #NameAndRole
    SELECT p.FirstName + ' ' + p.LastName,
        e.JobTitle,
        p.ModifiedDate
    FROM Person.Person as p
    INNER JOIN HumanResources.Employee as e
            ON p.BusinessEntityID = e.BusinessEntityID;

    SELECT ContactName, BusinessRole
    FROM #NameAndRole
    WHERE ModifiedDate > '20010101';
    GO
```

The primary difference between these two listings is the duration of the temporary structure. Because declared variables are removed from memory after the batch that defines them is complete, the table variables are out of scope as soon as the GO statement executes. Temporary tables, on the other hand, will remain in scope until the connection that creates them is closed.

Another alternative is to use a derived table, which you create by using a subquery. They are "derived" because the tables do not actually exist in the system. Rather, they are derived from other data through the use of a subquery. In the case of a derived table, the scope is limited to the query itself. It is not available anywhere else in the batch or within the current connection scope. Due to this limited scope, using derived tables is often the best way to resolve this type of query when the limited scope is acceptable. Listing 4.3 provides the same results as Listings 4.1 and 4.2 by using a derived table.

Listing 4.3: Using Derived Table Subqueries

```
USE AdventureWorks2008;

SELECT ContactName, BusinessRole
FROM (
  SELECT Name as ContactName,'Vendor' as BusinessRole,
ModifiedDate
  FROM Purchasing.Vendor

      UNION ALL

  SELECT p.FirstName + ' ' + p.LastName,e.JobTitle,p.
ModifiedDate
  FROM Person.Person as p
  INNER JOIN HumanResources.Employee as e
    ON p.BusinessEntityID = e.BusinessEntityID
  ) as ContactList

WHERE ModifiedDate > '20010101';
GO
```

Correlated Subqueries

Sometimes, a subquery cannot process without information from the outer query. In these cases, table aliases are used to define the scope of the query arguments and allow the subquery to be parameterized from the outer query. The inner query is, therefore, *correlated* to the outer query. The net effect is a back-and-forth execution where a single row from the result of the outer query passes parameters to the inner query. This example illustrates a correlated subquery:

```
USE AdventureWorks2008;

SELECT    p.FirstName + ' ' + p.LastName as FullName,
           e.JobTitle,
            (SELECT Name
             FROM HumanResources.Department as d
             WHERE d.DepartmentID = edh.DepartmentID) as
             DepartmentName
FROM Person.Person as p
INNER JOIN HumanResources.Employee as e
  ON p.BusinessEntityID = e.BusinessEntityID
INNER JOIN HumanResources.EmployeeDepartmentHistory as edh
  ON e.BusinessEntityID = edh.BusinessEntityID
WHERE edh.EndDate IS NULL;
GO
```

Because of the way the database is normalized, returning a list of employees with their job titles and current department names is not an easy task. The name information is stored in the Person.Person table, while the job title is in the HumanResources.Employee table. This is a simple join. However, getting the current department name is a little trickier. The HumanResources.Department table has the name of the department along with a DepartmentID key. However, the Human-Resources.Employee table does not contain the DepartmentID foreign key. This is because it is possible that a single employee has worked in many departments in their career. To maintain this historical data, an EmployeeDepartmentHistory table is created.

This table contains one row for every department assignment that an employee has had, along with the DepartmentID and the start and end dates of service with that department. If the entry in the EmployeeDepartmentHistory table has a NULL value for end date, that means that the row represents the employee's current department assignment. After filtering out for only NULL values in the end date column, we can turn our attention to getting the department name.

You will see that the SELECT list contains a subquery, but this subquery uses edh.DepartmentID in its WHERE clause. This value is not defined in the subquery; it comes from the WHERE clause in the outer query. The result is that the subquery is correlated to the outer query. For each row produced by the outer query, the edh.DepartmentID value for that row is passed to the inner query and executed to return the appropriate department name for the SELECT list. This is repeated for every row produced by the outer query. Because the outer query in this example produced 290 rows, the inner query must be executed 290 times to return the appropriate data.

Modify Data

SQL Server 2008 supports four primary data modification keywords: INSERT, DELETE, UPDATE, and MERGE. As their names imply, each modification statement is targeted to a specific modification activity. Let's look at each of them in turn and see how to apply them.

NOTE The MERGE keyword is useful when you want to perform multiple operations such as INSERT and DELETE operations concurrently. However, since it requires more advanced knowledge of TSQL code, we have left it out of this discussion. If you are interested in this feature, it is well documented in SQL Server Books Online.

Insert Data

You use the INSERT keyword to add data to an already existing table. The simplified syntax looks like this (remember that square brackets in these syntax statements mean optional sections):

```
INSERT
    [ INTO ]
    { <object> }
    [ ( column_list ) ]
    { VALUES ( { DEFAULT | NULL | expression } [ ,...n ] )
```

```
| derived_table
| execute_statement
| DEFAULT VALUES
```

Earlier in this chapter, you created a table called SampleTable in the demoscript database with two integer columns named Column1 and Column2. That table should now be in the dbo schema. If you wanted to insert data into that table, you would use a statement like this:

```
USE demoscript;

INSERT INTO dbo.SampleTable
VALUES (1,1);
GO
```

This is the simplest form of the INSERT statement. You do not have to specify the columns into which you are inserting the data as long as you insert them in the same order as they are listed in the table. If you wanted to explicitly identify columns as you insert, you would use this code:

```
USE demoscript;

INSERT INTO dbo.SampleTable (Column1, Column2)
VALUES (1,1);
GO
```

Performing an insert operation using a VALUES list works just fine, but if you look back at the syntax statement, you will see that you also have the option of using a derived table. This example selects literals as the derived table, but it could also be data from anywhere else. This is a very useful technique for loading a temporary table.

```
USE demoscript;

INSERT INTO dbo.SampleTable(Column1, Column2)
SELECT 1, 1;
GO
```

A corollary of this syntax is that you can also use a stored procedure to provide the data for the insert operation, as long as the procedure returns the data in the correct order and data type as required by the first line of the INSERT statement.

Delete Data

Deleting data from a table is a simple process in Transact SQL. The basic form of the syntax looks like this:

```
DELETE
    [ FROM <table_source> [ ,...n ] ]
    [ WHERE <search_condition> ][;]
```

Suppose that you want to delete all of the rows that you just added to the SampleTable. This simple statement will do the trick:

```
USE demoscript;


DELETE FROM dbo.SampleTable;
GO
```

That's it. It doesn't get much simpler than that, does it? But how often will you want to delete all of the entries in a table? Usually you will only want to delete some of the data in the table. That means your DELETE query must have a WHERE clause to provide criteria. Suppose you only wanted to delete from the table rows that have a Column2 value of 2. You could use this code:

```
USE demoscript;


DELETE FROM dbo.SampleTable
WHERE Column2 = 2;
GO
```

In most cases, you will want to use a WHERE clause in your DELETE statements. On the rare occasions that you want to delete all of the data in the table, you can do that much more efficiently with the TRUNCATE TABLE statement. To execute this statement, you must have ALTER TABLE permissions, but it is much more efficient because it does not write every deleted row to the transaction log. The statement looks like this:

```
TRUNCATE TABLE dbo.SampleTable;
```

Update Data

Although the INSERT and DELETE processes modify entire rows at a time, the UPDATE process modifies columns on an already existing row of data.

This adds a little complexity, but it is still an easy statement to use. The simplified syntax looks like this:

```
UPDATE
{ <object> }
SET
{ column_name = { expression | DEFAULT | NULL } } [ ,...n ]
[ FROM{ <table_source> } [ ,...n ] ]
[ WHERE { <search_condition> ][;]
```

To do full-table updates, you can use an UPDATE statement without a WHERE clause. This will apply the update to every row in the table. For example, to change the value in Column2 to 10 for every row, use this code:

```
USE demoscript;

UPDATE dbo.SampleTable
SET Column2 = 10;
GO
```

You can also make incremental changes to data in the table. For example, what if you wanted to increment every Column2 value in each row by 1? That code would look like this:

```
USE demoscript;

UPDATE dbo.SampleTable
SET Column2 = Column2 + 1;
GO
```

Of course, it is far more likely that you will want to apply these updates selectively. Therefore, you will probably want to use a WHERE clause with your UPDATE statement. If you wanted to do the increment only when the value in Column1 is 5, you would use this code:

```
USE demoscript;

UPDATE dbo.SampleTable
SET Column2 = Column2 + 1
WHERE Column1 = 5;
GO
```

Use the SQL Server System Catalog

In the old days it was simple. SQL Server 4.2 had a handful of system tables. Any information that you needed to extract from the system catalog could be pulled from those tables. Once you learned the organization of the tables, you could get anything that you wanted.

In SQL Server 2008, things are now considerably more complicated. The product has advanced significantly since then. There are more system tables, but they are all abstracted from us through system views and system functions. The catalog is now incredibly large and complex. The goal, therefore, is to know your way around generally and then learn the specifics of each system artifact when you need to consult it.

The goal of this chapter is to provide you with a general road map to the SQL Server 2008 system catalog. We encourage you to spend some time with these artifacts and to learn how they work. Sometimes the easiest way for a database administrator to get information is not to search through the user interface but rather to execute a few well-placed queries against the system catalog.

Use System Views

A view is actually a type of procedure. The intent of a view is to allow the user to get information by using a SELECT statement; however, in most cases the view does not actually store any data. When you execute the SELECT, it simply executes the underlying procedural logic.

This means that when you select from a system view, you are actually selecting data from the system tables and, in some cases, from SQL Server dynamic system data. If you are familiar with the system tables in earlier versions of SQL Server, Tables 4.4 and 4.5 provide a reference guide that correlates the system tables to new system views.

NOTE   Some of the items in the Corresponding System View in SQL Server 2008 column in Tables 4.4 and 4.5 are actually implemented as table-valued functions rather than as views. While you can still use them with a SELECT statement, the functions will usually require you to provide parameters with the call. If you consult SQL Server Books Online for the specific syntax for using each object, it will provide you with any argument that you may need to supply.

Table 4.4: System Views in the Master Database

SQL 2000 System Table	Corresponding System View in SQL Server 2008
sysaltfiles	sys.master_files
syscacheobjects	sys.dm_exec_cached_plans
sysconfigures	sys.configurations
sysdatabases	sys.databases
syslockinfo	sys.dm_tran_locks
syslocks	sys.dm_tran_locks
syslogins	sys.server_principals sys.sql_logins
sysmessages	sys.messages
sysoledbusers	sys.linked_logins
sysperfinfo	sys.dm_os_performance_counters
sysprocesses	sys.dm_exec.connections sys.dm_exec_sessions sys.dm_exec_requests
sysservers	sys.servers

Table 4.5: System Views in All Databases

SQL 2000 Systems Table	Corresponding System View in SQL Server 2008
syscolumns	sys.columns
syscomments	sys.sql_modules
sysconstraints	sys.check_contraints sys.default_constraints sys.key_constraints sys.foreign_keys
sysdepends	sys.sql_expression_dependencies
sysfilegroups	sys.filegroups

Table 4.5: System Views in All Databases *(continued)*

SQL 2000 Systems Table	Corresponding System View in SQL Server 2008
sysfiles	sys.database_files
sysforeignkeys	sys.foreign_key_columns
sysindexes	sys.indexes sys.partitions sys.allocation_units sys.dm_db_partition_stats
sysindexkeys	sys.index_columns
sysmembers	sys.database_role_members
sysobjects	sys.objects
syspermissions	sys.database_permissions sys.server_permissions
sysprotects	sys.database_permissions sys.server_permissions
sysreferences	sys.foreign_keys
systypes	sys.types
sysusers	sys.database_principals

One interesting fact about the system views and functions in Tables 4.4 and 4.5 is that when the name of the object begins with dm_, this implies that the data is not being extracted from a static system table but rather it is dynamically retuned from system data. For example, the sys.database_principals view returns a list of database users. This list is stored in the persisted system catalog in a table structure. However, sys.dm_exec_cached_plans returns information about cached procedure plans currently stored in memory. This is not persisted and is extracted dynamically from memory with each call.

Using these artifacts is just like selecting data from a table. For example, look at this query:

```
use demoscript;

SELECT *
FROM sys.database_principals ;
GO
```

Using this syntax, you are not even aware that there is no actual table called sys.database_principals. The same is true with the dynamic artifacts as well, as you see in this query:

```
use master;

SELECT *
FROM sys.dm_exec_cached_plans;
GO
```

There are far too many system views to cover here, but the good news is that they are fully documented in SQL Server Books Online. At this writing, the URL for the SQL Server 2008 system views in the Books Online is http://msdn.microsoft.com/en-us/library/ms177862.aspx. There you will see that the system views are organized into these different categories:

- Catalog views
- Compatibility views
- Database Mail views
- Data Collector views
- Policy-Based Management views
- Dynamic Management views
- Information Schema views
- Replication views

Our advice is to get familiar with the categories of views in Books Online. Then when you need to get system information, instead of using the SSMS and trying to find the data somewhere in the UI, try using the system view. After a little trial and error, you will learn your way around. Most of the views follow a very intuitive naming scheme.

Use System Stored Procedures

System stored procedures have been around for a very long time, so the concept is nothing new. They are a well-accepted part of the Transact SQL language. There have been some transitions lately in the system procedure catalog, however. For example, some operations have moved from the system procedure catalog to the DDL. One such case is creating user-defined types. Formerly, an administrator or developer would use the system stored procedure sp_addtype, but now they would use the TSQL statement CREATE TYPE.

The easiest way to get a list of system stored procedures is to go to the Object Explorer in the SSMS and do the following:

1. Open the node for your database.

2. Locate and open the Programmability node.

3. Locate and open the Stored Procedures node.

4. Locate and open the System Stored Procedures node.

5. To explore any particular stored procedure, open the procedure node. You will see a Parameters node. Expand this node to view the parameters for the procedure.

6. To view the TSQL code used to create the stored procedure, right-click the procedure node and select Modify from the shortcut menu. This will open the code in a query window.

WARNING When you open this query window, you actually have the ability to modify the system stored procedure. In most cases, we recommend that you do not do this. The integrity of the system depends on the system stored procedure functioning as originally scripted and intended. If you modify one and want to return it to its previous state, you can script it on a different database and execute the script over the modified procedure. With that said, it is very interesting to occasionally look at the code for the system stored procedures. It can be illuminating and a great way to get more familiar with the system catalog.

When executing any stored procedures, including system stored procedures, you should use the EXECUTE keyword. You can also use the abbreviated version, which is EXEC. The following code executes a common catalog stored procedure called sp_helpdb, which returns information about the specified database:

```
EXEC sp_helpdb 'AdventureWorks2008';
```

To get a complete list of these special "help" procedures, simply scroll down in the list of procedures in the Object Explorer. Since these procedures are listed alphabetically, they are all clustered together. Look over the list and try a few out. Remember that you can expand the Parameters node to get the list of parameters that a procedure expects.

Use Database Console Commands

In some cases, getting data about your database and table structures requires a little more brute force. This is also true in cases where you need to make modifications to lower-level data structures that are not generally accessible through the standard database catalog. For these occasions, we have the Database Console Commands (DBCC).

A typical example of the use of DBCC statements is to do a low-level consistency check of on-disk data structures. Let's say that you noticed a problem with a database backup of the AdventureWorks2008 database. You might want to do a check of the database for allocation and consistency problems. You could use the following code:

```
DBCC CHECKDB (AdventureWorks2008);
```

This statement actually executes these three other DBCC statements:

- DBCC CHECKALLOC: Checks the internal allocation consistency of a database
- DBCC CHECKTABLE: Checks the integrity of user table and index structures
- DBCC CHECKCATALOG: Checks the integrity of system table and index structures

The following is a list of documented DBCC statements in SQL Server 2008. There are other statements that are not documented and are not officially supported by Microsoft. A call to Microsoft SQL Server technical support, however, may occasionally end up with you executing a DBCC statement that you have never heard of before.

CHECKALLOC	DROPCLEANBUFFERS
CHECKCATALOG	FREEPROCCACHE
CHECKCONSTRAINTS	FREESESSIONCACHE
CHECKDB	FREESYSTEMCACHE
CHECKFILEGROUP	HELP
CHECKIDENT	INDEXDEFRAG *
CHECKTABLE	INPUTBUFFER
CLEANTABLE	OPENTRAN
DBREINDEX *	OUTPUTBUFFER

PROCCACHE	TRACEON
SHOW_STATISTICS	TRACEOFF
SHOWCONTIG *	TRACESTATUS
SHRINKDATABASE	UPDATEUSAGE
SHRINKFILE	USEROPTIONS
SQLPERF	

Some of these statements are supported in SQL Server 2008 but are scheduled to be removed in the next release of SQL Server. Those statements are marked with an asterisk. For example, in the past it was very common to use the DBCC SHOWCONTIG statement to get information regarding the physical distribution and fragmentation of low-level data structures in SQL Server. However, the output of this statement suffered from some significant limitations because it did not return a standard result set. You should replace this statement now with the sys.dm_db_index_physical_stats system view because the DBCC SHOWCONTIG statement will be removed in the next release.

PART II
Data Integrity and Security

IN THIS PART ▶

Data Integrity and Security

PART II

5

Managing Data Integrity

IN THIS CHAPTER, YOU WILL LEARN TO DO THE FOLLOWING:

Data Integrity and Security

PART II

M aintaining the integrity of your data is critical. In some respects, this might be the most important aspect of a database structure, taking higher priority than features such as functionality and performance. As an old database guru once said years ago, integrity trumps all because it doesn't matter how fast you can get the wrong answer. We will discuss the three primary types of data integrity in a database:

- Entity integrity
- Domain integrity
- Referential integrity

NOTE   We have chosen to organize this chapter a little differently than most writings that you will see on data integrity. Rather than simply providing a list of the constraint types and tools that you can use to enforce integrity, we think it's important to help you understand why we use those tools in the first place. You will notice that this chapter addresses each integrity objective and then discusses the tools that you use to meet each objective. We hope that this will be a useful way for you to approach integrity enforcement.

Implement Entity Integrity

Entity integrity is the guarantee that a single entity in the database represents a single unique entity in the real world. Since databases generally store information about real-world objects, it is important that the relationship between the object and the data about the object is maintained. A database administrator will generally enforce entity integrity through keys. Unique keys in the database will ensure that you do not inadvertently duplicate data about a single real object in the real world.

Each row in a data table represents some real object in the real world. For example, information about a customer in the real world must be tracked in the database. However, we need to make sure that the data about that customer always accurately relates to the actual customer. This is entity integrity. There are a number of ways that you can enforce entity integrity:

- Primary key constraints
- Unique constraints

- Triggers
- Stored procedures

NOTE In theory, you can enforce all data integrity types through procedural means using triggers, stored procedures, and other specialized procedural objects. Although these are often the most flexible ways to enforce integrity, they also have the highest overhead and the highest learning curve. As a database administrator, if you can enforce integrity without the overhead of a procedural object, that would be ideal. Therefore, we will focus this discussion on constraint enforcement as opposed to procedural enforcement. At the end of this chapter, we will discuss procedural enforcement, but a broad discussion of procedural integrity is really a development topic as opposed to an administrative topic and is better left to a book targeted at developers.

Implement Primary Keys

Using a primary key is the most common way to implement a unique identifier for an entity in the database. To ensure that the primary key value corresponds to an actual single entity in the real world, the following rules apply to primary keys:

- Primary key values must be unique within the table for every row in the table.
- You can only have one primary key per table, although the key can be composite (consisting of more than one column).
- You must configure columns marked as primary keys as NOT NULL, meaning that column must have a value for every row.
- Creating a primary key on a column automatically indexes that column. This index is a clustered index by default.

You can configure primary keys on a table when you create the table, or alternatively, you can add the key later as long as there is no data in the table that would violate the conditions of the key. You can also create the primary key, as with all of the other constraint types, either through the SQL Server Management Studio (SSMS) interface or by using a Transact SQL (TSQL) script.

Implement Primary Keys Using the SSMS

Adding a primary key as you create a table is a simple process in the SSMS. If you need a refresher on how to create a table in the SSMS, please refer back to Chapter 3, "Creating Databases, Files, and Tables." Figure 5.1 illustrates the New Table dialog for a new Customer table in the demo database.

Figure 5.1: Creating the Customer table

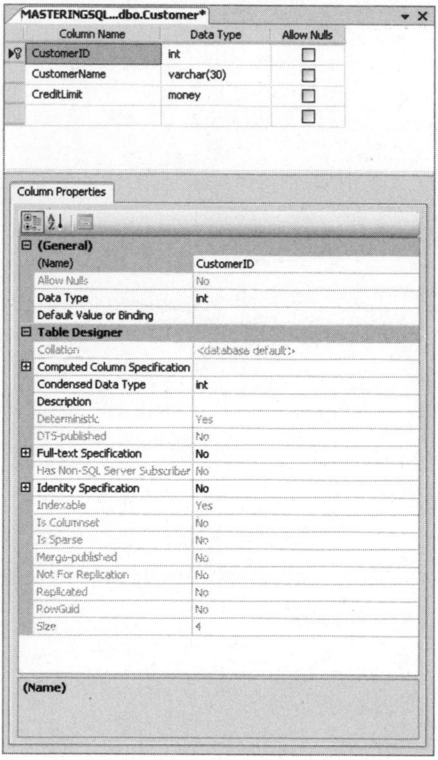

In this example, the CustomerID column will be the most logical choice for a primary key. This column will contain the unique identifier associated with a specific customer. To set the primary key, perform the following steps:

1. Select the CustomerID column as in the illustration. Selecting more than one column using the Shift or Ctrl key would allow you to create a composite primary key.

2. From the SSMS menu bar, click Table Designer ➤ Set Primary Key. This will place a key symbol next to the column name in the designer.

3. To specify the details of the associated index, select Table Designer ➤ Indexes/Keys. You should see a dialog like the one pictured in Figure 5.2.

Figure 5.2: Configuring the primary key

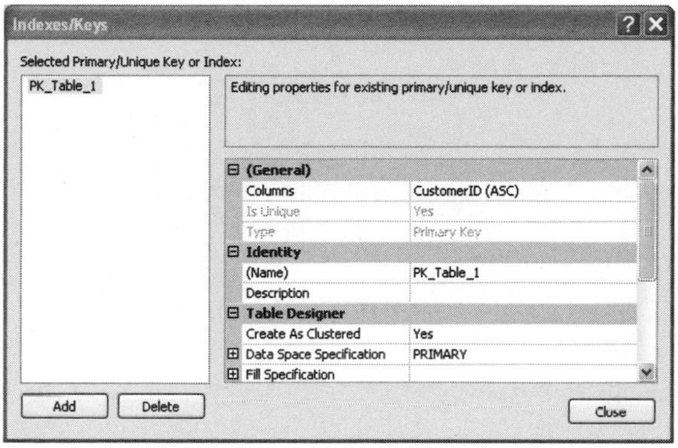

4. In the Indexes/Keys dialog, change the name to something more relevant, such as PK_CustomerID.

5. If you prefer to create a nonclustered index for the key, locate the Create as Clustered property and change the value to No.

6. Click the Close button to close the dialog.

7. From the SSMS menu bar, click File ➤ Save Table_1. Change the name of the table to Customer in the dialog and click OK.

8. Close the Table Designer when you are finished.

At any point, you can return to the table design screen by right-clicking on the table name in the Object Explorer and selecting Design from the shortcut menu. From here you can make modifications to the indexes or remove the primary key entirely by selecting Table Designer ➤ Remove Primary Key. For more details on the difference between clustered and nonclustered indexes, see Chapter 12, "Planning and Creating Indexes."

Implement Primary Keys Using a TSQL Script

Similar to using the SSMS, you can create a primary key when you create
the table or after. When creating the table, you can include the primary
key in the CREATE TABLE statement. After you have created the table, you
can add or drop the primary key by using the ALTER TABLE statement.

To create the primary key, simply include the primary key constraint
in your script. If it is a single column key, the script would look like this:

```
USE demoscript;

CREATE TABLE dbo.Customer
(
  CustomerID    int         NOT NULL   PRIMARY KEY CLUSTERED,
  CustomerName  varchar(30) NOT NULL,
  CreditLimit   int         NOT NULL
);
GO
```

If you prefer a nonclustered index for the primary key, simply replacing the word CLUSTERED with NONCLUSTERED in the script will implement
this change. In this example, the CustomerID column is the primary key
field. If you wanted to create a composite key, it would be a bit different. For example, suppose the primary key is made of a combination of
two columns: a prefix, which is a one-character code, and an ID, which
is an integer. If the business rule is that you identify a customer by the
unique combination of the prefix and the ID, you would use a script
that looks like this:

```
USE demoscript;

CREATE TABLE dbo.Customer
(
  CustomerPrefix  char(1)     NOT NULL,
  CustomerID      int         NOT NULL,
  CustomerName    varchar(30) NOT NULL,
  CreditLimit     int         NOT NULL

  CONSTRAINT PK_Customer
    PRIMARY KEY NONCLUSTERED(CustomerPrefix, CustomerID)
);
GO
```

You can also add and drop the primary key constraint after you create the table. You will do this with the ALTER TABLE statement. For example, assume that you used this script to create the Customer table:

```
USE demoscript;

CREATE TABLE dbo.Customer
(
  CustomerID    int         NOT NULL,
  CustomerName  varchar(30) NOT NULL,
  CreditLimit   int         NOT NULL
);
GO
```

This table currently has no primary key constraint defined. If you want to add a primary key constraint later, you must ensure that doing so will not violate any of the previously stated rules or the CREATE statement will fail. To add the constraint at this point, you would use the following statement:

```
USE demoscript;

ALTER TABLE dbo.Customer
ADD CONSTRAINT PK_Customer
  PRIMARY KEY NONCLUSTERED (CustomerID);
GO
```

You can also drop the primary key constraint using a TSQL script. As before, you will use the ALTER TABLE statement. Here is an example:

```
USE demoscript;

ALTER TABLE dbo.Customer
  DROP CONSTRAINT PK_Customer;
GO
```

Implement Unique Constraints

Sometimes you may have a data point that is not the unique identifier for a record but may still need to be enforced as unique. For example, suppose you have an Employee table in your database. Each employee may have a unique employee number that you use to identify the employee internally, but the Social Security number associated with each employee must also be unique. To enforce this integrity, you can use a unique constraint.

The unique constraint is similar in concept to the primary key constraint except that the rules and requirements are not as strict. The requirements for a unique constraint are as follows:

- Uniquely constrained values must be unique within the table for every row in the table.

- You can have multiple uniquely constrained columns in a table.

- A uniquely constrained column can allow NULL values but will accept only a single NULL for the entire table.

- Creating a unique constraint on a column automatically indexes that column. This index is a nonclustered index by default.

Implement Unique Constraints Using the SSMS

Just like a primary key, you can add a unique constraint to a table in the Table Designer. Figure 5.3 illustrates a Table Designer for a new Employee table. Notice in the figure that the EmployeeID has already been configured as a primary key.

Figure 5.3: Designing the Employee table

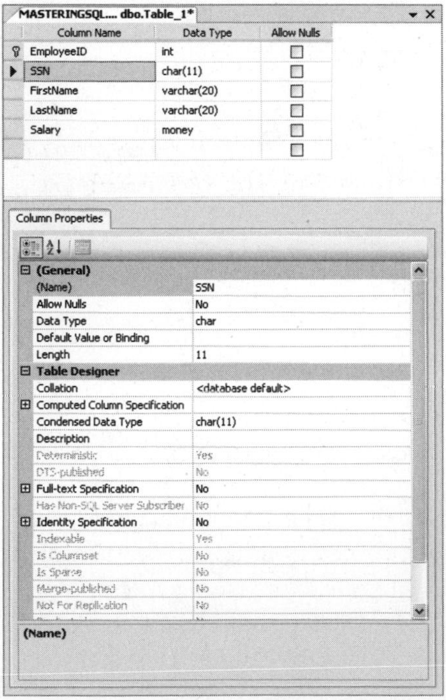

To configure the SSN column in this example as a unique constraint, you would follow these steps:

1. Select Table Designer ➤ Indexes/Keys from the SSMS menu bar to open the Indexes/Keys dialog.

2. Click the Add button to add a new index/key.

3. Configure the Columns, Type, and Name properties for the new key as pictured in Figure 5.4. Changing the type from index to unique key will cause SQL Server to create a unique constraint rather than only an index.

Figure 5.4: Configuring the key

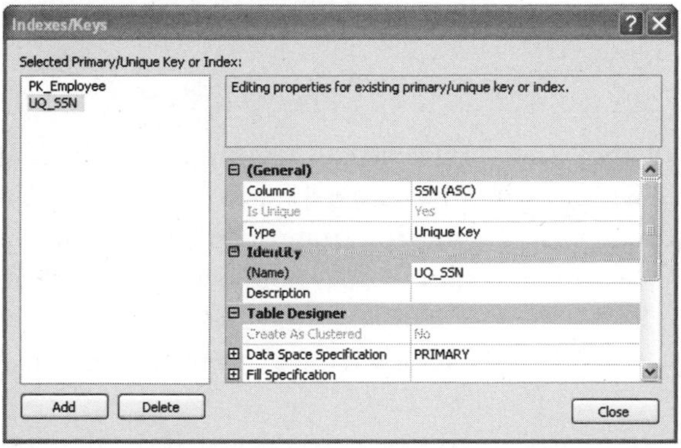

4. Note that the Create as Clustered option is dimmed out but is set to no. Unique constraints always create nonclustered unique indexes.

5. Click the Close button on the dialog.

6. Click File ➤ Save Table_1. Change the name of the table to Employee and click OK.

7. Close the Table Designer.

To remove the unique constraint, you will go back to the Indexes/Keys dialog. Select the index or key that you want to drop and click the Delete button.

Implement Unique Constraints Using a TSQL Script

You can also create the unique constraint using a CREATE TABLE statement. Assuming that you wanted both a primary key on the

EmployeeID column and a unique constraint on the SSN column, the
SQL script would look like this:

```
USE demoscript;
GO

CREATE TABLE dbo.Employee
(
  EmployeeID int NOT NULL,
  SSN char(11) NOT NULL,
  FirstName varchar(20) NOT NULL,
  LastName varchar(20) NOT NULL,
  Salary money NOT NULL,
  CONSTRAINT PK_Employee PRIMARY KEY CLUSTERED (EmployeeID),
  CONSTRAINT UQ_SSN UNIQUE (SSN)
);
GO
```

Notice in this example how multiple constraints are provided in a
comma-separated list following the column list from the table. You will
also notice that this is a slight variation from the previous syntax in that
a constraint based on a single column does not have to be created with
the column. Providing a block of constraints at the bottom of the query
also helps them to stand out visually, which is beneficial when maintaining the code.

To add the unique constraint after you have created the table, you can
again use the ALTER TABLE statement. The code is similar to the example
for primary key constraints. Adding a unique constraint to the Employee
table would look like this:

```
USE demoscript;
GO

ALTER TABLE dbo.Employee
ADD CONSTRAINT UQ_SSN UNIQUE (SSN);
GO
```

Similarly, the code to drop the constraint would look like this:

```
USE demoscript;
GO

ALTER TABLE dbo.Employee
DROP CONSTRAINT UQ_SSN;
GO
```

Implement Domain Integrity

Domain integrity enforces the integrity of the individual data point. Each piece of data about an entity must conform to rules that state acceptable criteria regarding the formats and values of that data. By enforcing such attributes as data types, valid values, and boundary values, a database administrator can ensure that the user does not enter values that are not appropriate for a data point.

Enforcing domain integrity means controlling the values that a user can place into a data point in a database. The collection of database points that share the same rules in a database is called a domain. Column definitions in a table provide the behavioral rules for the domain represented by the column.

There are numerous tools that you can use to enforce domain integrity. One is the data type. By defining a column using a data type, you are placing restrictions on the kind of data that the column can store. This is a form of domain integrity. In the following sections, we will look at the more formal domain integrity tools, specifically the default and check constraints.

Implement Default Constraints

When the user does not provide a value for a particular data point, you must determine what that value will be. The default SQL Server behavior is to insert a NULL value in this case; however, that can cause problems when a NULL is either not allowed by the table definition or not a reasonable substitute based on business rules.

The solution is that you must define a relevant default value. When data is inserted into a table and there is no value for a specific field, that field's default value will be used instead. Defaults must follow these rules:

- The default value must adhere to the data typing restrictions of the column.

- Configured defaults take effect at the point that they are created and do not impact existing data in the table. Previously entered data is not affected.

- A configured default replaces NULL as the SQL Server standard default for a column.

- You can add only one default constraint to any single column.

Implement Defaults Using the SSMS

Setting defaults with the SSMS is very simple process. You can simply go to the Table Designer for the table and set the default value in the properties list. In our example, we will set a default value of 0 for the credit limit on a customer. Follow these steps to set the default:

1. Locate the Customer table node in the Object Explorer for the demo database.

2. Right-click this node and select Design to open the Table Designer.

3. Click on the CreditLimit row in the top pane of the designer; then locate the Default Value or Binding property in the properties grid, as illustrated in Figure 5.5

Figure 5.5: Setting the default

4. Set the value for the default property to 0 as illustrated.

5. Save the table by selecting File ➢ Save Customer.

6. Close the Table Designer.

In this example, we originally configured the CreditLimit column not to allow NULL values. Prior to setting the default, any attempt to add a row to the Customer table without providing a value for CreditLimit would have resulted in an error. Now that the column has a default, an insert without a specific value for the CreditLimit would insert 0 into the column instead of NULL.

In our example, we added the default to an already existing table. Of course, you could have configured this property when you initially created the table. You would configure the property in exactly the same way.

Implement Defaults using a TSQL Script

The TSQL scripting process for defaults is very similar to the one that you used for the keys. You can either configure the default in the CREATE TABLE statement or add the default later using an ALTER TABLE statement. Therefore, the same default for the Customer table in the demoscript database would look like this:

```
USE demoscript;

CREATE TABLE dbo.Customer
(
  CustomerID      int          NOT NULL
    PRIMARY KEY CLUSTERED,
  CustomerName    varchar(30) NOT NULL,
  CreditLimit     int          NOT NULL DEFAULT 0
);
GO
```

Again, you could also use the format that separates the constraints into a separate section at the bottom. If you use that syntax, it will look like this:

```
USE demoscript;

CREATE TABLE dbo.Customer
(
  CustomerID      int          NOT NULL,
  CustomerName    varchar(30) NOT NULL,
  CreditLimit     int          NOT NULL DEFAULT 0,
  CONSTRAINT PK_Customer PRIMARY KEY CLUSTERED (CustomerID)
);
GO
```

You will notice from this example that while the primary key can be separated into the "table constraints" section, the default cannot. Defaults are never relevant to more than one column and are therefore always considered column-level constraints.

You can add the constraint later, however. This technique looks almost identical to the ALTER TABLE statement that you used when working with

Data Integrity and Security

PART II

the keys. Here is an example, assuming that the CreditLimit column did not have a currently configured default:

```
USE demoscript;

ALTER TABLE dbo.Customer
ADD CONSTRAINT DF_CredLim
  DEFAULT 0 for CreditLimit;
GO
```

To drop a default constraint, you use the same syntax you saw earlier. You can drop this constraint with this code:

```
USE demoscript;

ALTER TABLE dbo.Customer
  DROP CONSTRAINT DF_CredLim;
GO
```

Implement Check Constraints

A check constraint is a column-level rule. The purpose is to restrict the values that the user can insert into a column or update. You can base this restriction on constant values, such as a value greater than 0, or you can use another value in the data row as a basis, such as requiring that the value in an EndDate column be later than the value in a StartDate column. You can also use some functions, which allows for a great deal of flexibility on your formula.

You should try to use check constraints rather than procedural tools whenever possible. They are much more efficient. Although you often have much more flexibility when using stored procedures, constraints are definitional at the table level, and as such they avoid all of the procedural overhead. When using check constraints, though, you must follow these rules:

- The check value must adhere to the data type restrictions of the column.

- You can apply check constraints at the table level; multiple check constraints can validate a single column and a single check can reference more than one column.

- All check constraints are Boolean in nature. You can check any expression as long as the test returns TRUE or FALSE.

Implement Check Constraints Using the SSMS

Since check constraints can cross multiple column definitions, they are generally not configured at the column level. The SSMS interface has a special dialog for configuring check constraints. It is easier to think of a check constraint as spanning the entire table rather than targeted to a specific column.

Suppose you want to add a check constraint to the Customer table requiring that the CreditLimit value that you enter into the Customer table be greater than 0. You would use these steps:

1. Open the Table Designer for the Customer table in the demo database.

2. From the SSMS menu bar, select Table Designer ➤ Check Constraints to open the configuration dialog.

3. Click the Add button in the lower-left part of the dialog to add a new check constraint. The dialog should now look like the illustration in Figure 5.6.

Figure 5.6: Creating a check constraint

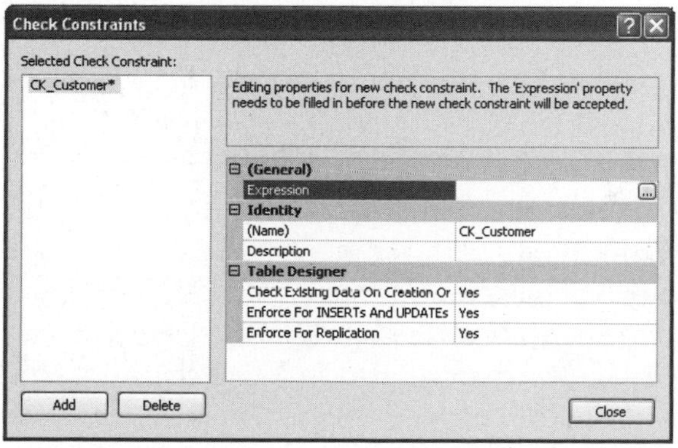

4. Change the Name property to CK_CredLim.

5. Change the Expression to read CreditLimit > 0. You will write the expression like a WHERE clause. Think of it as a Boolean filter expression.

6. Click the Close button on the dialog and then save the table design.

Again, you could have performed these same actions when you created the table, but as you can see from this example, you have the flexibility to add check constraints whenever you want them. You could reference multiple columns as well. For example, if you had both a StartDate and EndDate column in your table, StartDate < EndDate would be a valid expression.

At the bottom of the Check Constraints dialog, you will see some additional properties in the section labeled Table Designer. These properties support some special behaviors of the check constraint that you can control:

Check Existing Data on Create or Re-Enabling   When you add a check constraint to an existing table, you must decide if you want to enforce the expression on all existing data or simply enforce the expression from that point forward. The default value of Yes states that all existing data must adhere to the check constraint condition or the action that places the constraint on the table will fail. If you wish to grandfather data into the table, you must set this option to No. This option will also enforce the constraint when a disabled constraint is reenabled.

Enforce for INSERTs and UPDATEs   This option controls whether the constraint is enabled or disabled. The default value of Yes states that the constraint will be honored. If you set this option to No, you are disabling constraint checking. This means that any data that you insert into the table will not be checked for expression compliance.

Enforce for Replication   SQL Server supports an elaborate replication model that permits the publication of data from one table to another. If the target table in that replication scenario contains a check constraint, you must determine if that check constraint should be honored. The common assumption is that SQL Server will validate all data at the point of publication, meaning that it is not necessary to validate replicated data at the subscriber location. If this is a safe assumption in your architecture, set this value to No. Otherwise, the check constraints will enforce the expression for both standard DML actions and replicated DML actions.

As you can see, you can go back to this dialog at any point in time to perform actions such as enabling or disabling the constraint, dropping the constraint, or modifying the replication behavior.

Implement Check Constraints Using a TSQL Script

Once again, the CREATE TABLE and ALTER TABLE statements are the tools
we will use to create check constraints. Because the check constraint
can reference any column in the table, and even reference multiple
columns in the same expression, we will place the code that creates
the check constraint below the column list with the other table-level
constraints. The following code shows how to create a constraint that
requires data placed in the CreditLimit column to be a numeric value
greater than zero:

```
USE demoscript;

CREATE TABLE dbo.Customer
(
  CustomerID    int          NOT NULL PRIMARY KEY CLUSTERED,
  CustomerName  varchar(30)  NOT NULL,
  CreditLimit   int          NOT NULL DEFAULT 0,
  CONSTRAINT CK_CredLim CHECK (CreditLimit > 0)
);
GO
```

Since this is a brand-new table and there is no existing data in it, there
is no need to defer the constraint checking. SQL Server will create the
constraint with the three special designer properties previously discussed
set to their default values of Yes.

You can also add a constraint to an already existing table; however,
this means that you have to decide how to handle existing data. The
default behavior is that existing data will be checked for compliance
with the constraint expression. You can change this behavior by using
the WITH NOCHECK clause in your script. The following code demonstrates
an example.

```
USE demoscript;

ALTER TABLE dbo.Customer
  WITH NOCHECK
  ADD CONSTRAINT CK_CredLim
    CHECK (CreditLimit > 0);
GO
```

Data Integrity and Security

PART II

Notice that immediately before the ADD statement in the code, the script includes the WITH NOCHECK clause. This clause instructs SQL Server to not check existing data in the table for compliance with the expression. Therefore, existing data that violates the expression will not cause the statement to fail. If you want to check all existing data in the table and fail the expression if the data is not compliant, simply remove the WITH NOCHECK clause.

You can also enable and disable check constraints with the ALTER TABLE statement. Remember that if you created the constraint using the WITH NOCHECK clause, when you reenable the constraint, it will not check existing data for compliance. Use the following code to do disable the check constraint on the table:

```
USE demoscript;

ALTER TABLE dbo.Customer
  NOCHECK CONSTRAINT CK_CredLim;
GO
```

If you replace the NOCHECK keyword in this script with the word CHECK instead, it will reenable the disabled constraint. You can also disable all check and foreign key constraints on a table by using the statement NOCHECK CONSTRAINT ALL.

Finally, you can also drop the check constraint with this statement:

```
USE demoscript;

ALTER TABLE dbo.Customer
  DROP CONSTRAINT CK_CredLim;
GO
```

Implement Referential Integrity

Referential integrity enforces the relationship among entities in the database. Since you will store the data for an individual entity in a table, making sure that entities in one table are appropriately related to entities in another table is critical. For example, having an order in an Order table with no corresponding customer in a Customer table represents a referential integrity failure.

In a relational database environment, data is distributed across many tables. Each table represents a single entity in the real world. Real-world entities have relationships with each other, so it seems logical that entities in the database would also have relationships with each other. It is therefore critical that we maintain the integrity of these relationships. You can think of referential integrity as the integrity of interaction.

In the examples so far, you have seen how to create an entity such as a customer. Customers do not exist in a vacuum. The only reason for a customer to be in our system is that they're going to buy something. Since we also need to keep track of what they order, it seems logical that we would have an Order table as well. As you have seen, there is a critical relationship between customers and their orders. If we do not maintain the relationship, we will have problems billing and shipping those orders.

Consider Figure 5.7. This diagram shows the relationship between the Customer table and an Order table. You will notice that the CustomerID field is repeated in the Order table. This is so that we have a way to relate each customer to one or more rows in the Order table. The Order rows represent the individual orders placed by the Customer. The CustomerID in the Order table is called a foreign key because it provides the point of reference to a foreign table.

Figure 5.7: Relating tables through keys

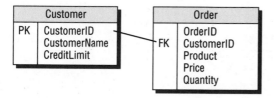

It is very important that you maintain the integrity of this relationship. If you allow an order to exist in the Order table with no corresponding customer in the Customer table, this violates the business rule that states that every order must have a corresponding customer. To guarantee that this will never happen, you will use a constraint called a foreign key constraint.

Implement Foreign Keys

A foreign key is a field (or combination of fields) in one table that references a field (or combination of fields) in another table. The purpose is to correlate entities between tables. Generally this relationship is one-to-many in that a single primary key or uniquely constrained field can relate to one or more foreign key fields in the foreign table. Foreign key constraints on a table must follow these rules:

- You can have only one foreign key constraint per column.

- The data type of the foreign keyed column must be the same or implicitly convertible to the data type of the unique column in the primary table.

Implement Foreign Key Constraints Using the SSMS

In our example, we have a Customer table with a primary key column called CustomerID. Now its time for you to add to the database an Order table that includes a foreign key to the CustomerID. Follow these steps to create the Order table:

1. Locate the Tables node in the demo database. Open a new Table Designer by right-clicking the node and selecting New Table from the shortcut menu.

2. Fill out the Table Designer for the Order table as illustrated in Figure 5.8. Notice that the OrderID column has been marked as the primary key for this table.

Figure 5.8: Adding the Order table

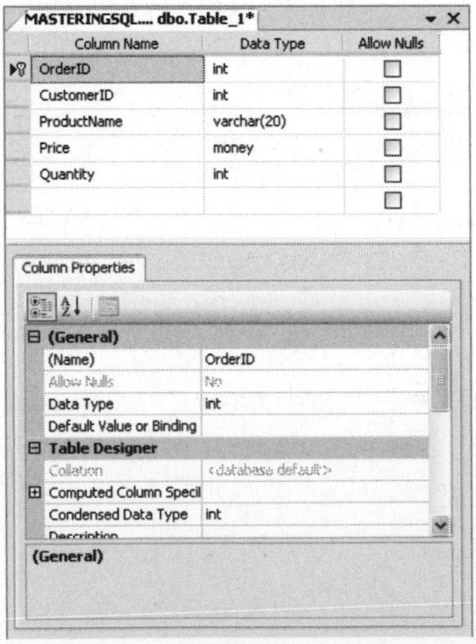

3. From the SSMS menu bar, select Table Designer ➤ Relationships. This will open the Foreign Key Relationships dialog.

4. Change the name to FK_Customer_Order.

5. Select the Tables and Columns Specification property, and click the button with the three dots (...) on the right side. This button is called a builder. This will open the Tables and Columns window.

6. Complete this dialog as pictured in Figure 5.9. Don't worry that the table on the right is still called Table_1. This will update when you save the table later. Click OK to close the dialog.

Figure 5.9: Configuring table relationships

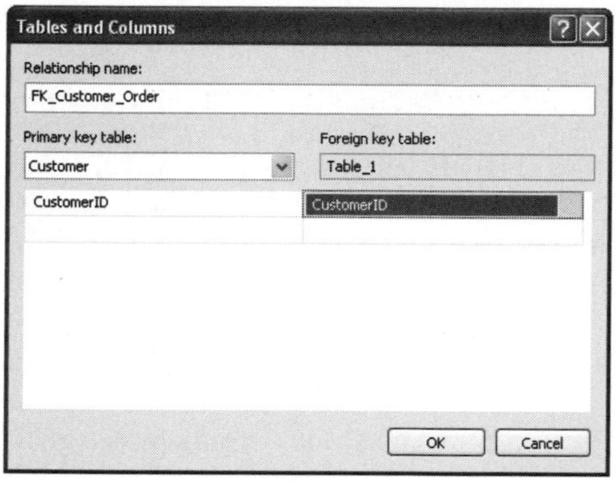

7. Expand the plus (+) sign next to the Tables and Columns specification to see the configuration. Verify that it looks like Figure 5.10.

Figure 5.10: The completed foreign keys dialog

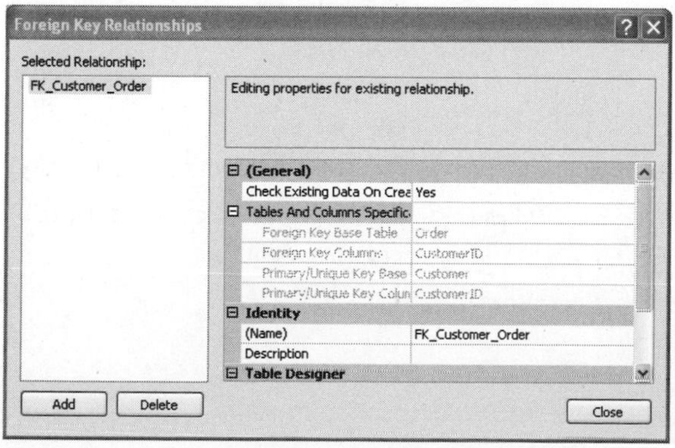

8. Click the Close button to close the window.

9. Save the table as Order and close the Table Designer.

Similar to the check constraint, you can disable the foreign key. You can also defer key checking on tables with already existing data. Look for the properties in the Table Designer properties list that match the three special properties that you saw for the check constraint. They have the same behavior.

Implement Foreign Key Constraints Using a TSQL Script

To create the Order table with a foreign key, you use the same basic structure as the other CREATE TABLE statements. Simply add another constraint definition to the section following the column list.

TIP You will notice that the table name Order is enclosed in brackets in the following code. This is because the word Order is a SQL keyword used to sort data. To tell SQL Server that you want to use Order as an identifier rather than as a keyword, you use the brackets. If the Quoted Identifier option were enabled, you would also be able to use double quotes.

This code illustrates how to create the same foreign key constraint as the one that we previously created in the SSMS.

```
USE demoscript;

CREATE TABLE  dbo.[Order]
(
    OrderID     int          NOT NULL,
    CustomerID  int          NOT NULL,
    ProductName varchar(20)  NOT NULL,
    Price       money        NOT NULL,
    Quantity    int          NOT NULL,
    CONSTRAINT PK_Order PRIMARY KEY CLUSTERED (OrderID),
    CONSTRAINT FK_Customer_Order FOREIGN KEY (CustomerID)
        REFERENCES dbo.Customer (CustomerID)
);
GO
```

Notice that the foreign key constraint statement is divided into two sections. The first piece defines the constraint along with the field(s) that the statement is constraining. Second, a REFERENCES statement, indicates the base or primary table that the foreign table references, and specifically which fields it correlates.

If the table already exists, you will add the foreign key constraint using an ALTER TABLE statement. Like the check constraint, a foreign key can allow existing data to be grandfathered into the table, meaning that you do not have to check existing data. You enable this behavior by using the WITH NOCHECK statement in the query, just as with a check constraint. The following code will add the constraint to an already existing table and allow for existing data to violate the constraint:

```
USE demoscript;

ALTER TABLE dbo.[Order]
  WITH NOCHECK
  ADD CONSTRAINT FK_Customer_Order FOREIGN KEY (CustomerID)
    REFERENCES dbo.Customer (CustomerID);
GO
```

To disable a foreign key constraint, you would use the following code:

```
USE demoscript;

ALTER TABLE dbo.[Order]
  NOCHECK CONSTRAINT FK_Customer_Order;
GO
```

And finally, you would drop the constraint entirely with this command:

```
USE demoscript;

ALTER TABLE dbo.[Order]
  DROP CONSTRAINT FK_Customer_Order;
GO
```

Implement Cascading References

Typically, the motivation behind creating a foreign key is that you want to make sure the foreign table contains no orphaned rows. Every row in the foreign table would have a correlated row in the base table. So what would happen if you tried to delete a row from the base table if it had related rows in the child table? Or what if you tried to update the primary key value in the base table? Would this leave orphaned rows or would it simply fail?

The answer is that it depends on how you have configured the foreign key constraint. There are four special actions that you can take on both DELETE and UPDATE operations. The default behavior is No Action, meaning that there is no special cascading behavior.

No Action   This is the default. It states that there is no special cascading behavior. For example, if you attempted to delete a row from the Customer table that had related rows in the Order table, the delete would fail. Also, if you attempted to modify the CustomerID value in the Customer table on a row where there were related rows in the Order table, the update would fail.

Cascade   This setting tells SQL Server to propagate the action requested to the foreign table. For example, if you were to delete the Customer row, all related foreign rows in the Order table would also be deleted. An update operation would have similar behavior. If you update the CustomerID column on a row in the Customer table, the CustomerID column of all related Order rows would update to the same value.

Set Null   This setting will cause the Foreign Key value to be set to a NULL value if a violating action occurs. For example, if you delete or update a row from the Customer table that has correlated data in the Order table, the CustomerID fields in the Order table would be set to NULL for all correlated rows. For this to work, the foreign key columns must allow nulls.

Set Default   This setting will cause the Foreign Key value to be set to the configured default value if a violating action occurs. For example, if you delete or update a row from the Customer table that has correlated data in the Order table, the related CustomerID fields in the Order table would be set to the configured default for all correlated rows. For this to work, the foreign key columns must have configured default values.

You can configure these special behaviors by using either the SSMS or a TSQL script. Assume that you wanted to perform cascading delete and update actions on the Order table. You would configure that behavior using the following steps.

1. Open the Table Designer for the Order table in the demo database.

2. Open the Foreign Keys window by selecting Table Designer ➤ Relationships from the SSMS menu bar.

3. In the dialog, click the plus sign (+) next to the property called INSERT and DELETE Specification to expand the node.

4. Change the value of the Delete Rule property to Cascade. Note that the other options are listed as well.

5. Change the value of the Update Rule property to Cascade. Your dialog should now look like the example in Figure 5.11.

Figure 5.11: Setting foreign key cascades

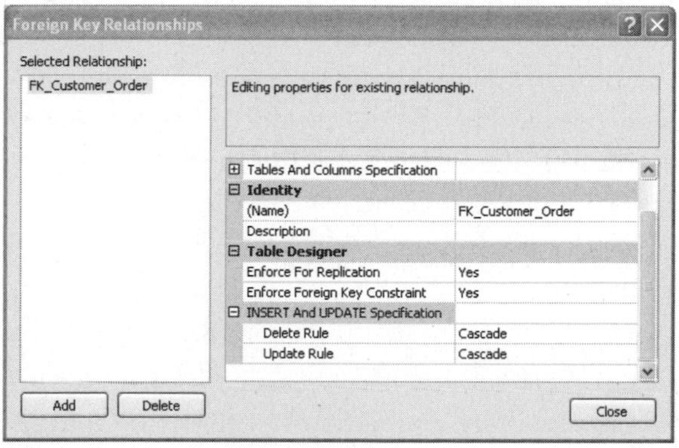

6. Click the Close button to close the dialog.

7. Save the table design and close the designer.

Adding cascading using a TSQL script is also very simple. A small alteration to the script will enforce the cascading behavior. This script uses an ALTER TABLE statement to create a foreign key that performs a cascade on both update and delete operations:

```
USE demoscript;

ALTER TABLE dbo.[Order]
    ADD CONSTRAINT FK_Customer_Order FOREIGN KEY (CustomerID)
```

```
REFERENCES dbo.Customer (CustomerID)
   ON DELETE CASCADE
   ON UPDATE CASCADE;
GO
```

Understand Procedural Integrity

In most cases, procedural integrity should be a last resort. In almost every case, it is higher in overhead than its constraint counterparts There are also a few procedural options, namely rules and defaults that are scheduled to be obsoleted in SQL Server. There are four primary procedural options for implementing integrity:

Rules   The Rule is a special stored procedure that defines a data restriction, much like a check constraint. Microsoft has announced that it plans to remove the Rule procedure type in a future version of SQL Server. It is provided now only for compatibility. It is our strong recommendation that you do not do any new development using the procedural Rule. Instead, use the check constraint. For this reason, we will not address the Rule in this book.

Defaults   The Default is a special stored procedure that defines a default value for a table column or a data type. Microsoft has announced that it plans to remove the Default procedure type in a future version of SQL Server. It is provided now only for compatibility. It is our strong recommendation that you do not do any new development using the procedural Default. Instead, use the default constraint. For this reason, we will not address the Default in this book.

Stored Procedures   Stored procedures are the basic building blocks of a SQL Server application. Since this is a book on the administration of SQL Server, we do not address stored procedures extensively in this book. However, you should be aware that they are often used for managing data integrity. There are both positive and negative aspects of using stored procedures for managing data integrity. While stored procedures are very flexible and give the SQL developer a greater amount of control, the primary problems with this approach are as follows:

- Data integrity logic is distributed throughout the database instead of consolidated at the table definition.

- Stored procedures have a higher overhead and constraints.

- Stored procedures are generally maintained by developers and not by administrators. This can cause problems enforcing data rules if administrators and developers do not communicate.

While we firmly believe that stored procedures are a critical part of any SQL application, we also believe strongly that administrators and developers should strive to enforce as much data integrity at the table level using constraints as they possibly can. This will aid in the maintenance and add to the performance of the application.

Triggers   Triggers are the tools of last resort. They are generally reactive instead of proactive and can cause problems in concurrency by extending transactions for a longer period of time. While earlier versions of SQL Server added proactive triggers called INSTEAD OF triggers, they are generally used as a substitute for stored procedure logic and for managing distributed views.

Although it is not appropriate to do a full discussion of stored procedures and triggers in this book, we will take a quick look at how procedures and triggers enforce integrity. This will better enable you to interact with developers.

Understand Stored Procedure Validation

A stored procedure is a set of Transact SQL statements that are named and stored on the server. The benefit of stored procedures is that you can save commonly used SQL code on the server and reuse it when needed. It is also more efficient to call a stored procedure than it is to pass ad hoc SQL to the server over and over again. There are also security benefits for using stored procedures, which we will discuss in more detail in Chapter 7, "Managing Security."

Because stored procedures are so versatile, they are very commonly used to handle data validation and integrity. While there is nothing inherently wrong with this practice, it is important that the baseline integrity is still implemented using constraints. It is good to see, however, how you might implement some of these rules using stored procedures. For example, we have a check constraint that enforces CreditLimit values to be greater than zero. The following code creates a stored procedure that would perform the same check and insert the data into the Customer table if the test passes. In this code, notice how the procedure returns if the test fails:

```
USE demoscript;
GO

CREATE PROCEDURE dbo.isp_Customer
  @CustID       int,
  @CustName     varchar(20),
  @CreditLimit money
AS
  // Validate the input
  IF @CreditLimit <= 0
  BEGIN
    RAISERROR
      ('Credit Limit must be greater than zero',10,1);
    RETURN;
  END
  // Perform the insert
  INSERT INTO dbo.Customer
    (CustomerID, CustomerName, CreditLimit)
  SELECT @CustID, @CustName, @CreditLimit;
GO
```

Don't worry about all of the details of this code for now. That is not our purpose. If you look at the code you will notice that it is broken into two main pieces. The first piece evaluates the value passed into the procedure in the @CreditLimit parameter. This block performs a test to see if the value is less than or equal to zero. If this statement is true, the procedure raises an error and returns at that point. Nothing below the return statement will run. If the data passes the validation test, the second half of the stored procedure executes and performs the insert operation.

Most stored procedures are much more complex than this, so this example is very simplistic. That said, you should be able to get a basic idea of how validation works in a stored procedure. Generally the technique is to test the data before taking action. That way you'll never have to roll back the transaction. Since it is better to prevent a transaction from ever beginning rather than have to roll it back later, this is a preferred option.

Understand Trigger Validation

A trigger is a special stored procedure that piggybacks onto a called transaction. A trigger is essentially an extension of the transaction that fires it. When you create a trigger for a specific action, the trigger executes before the action fully completes. This gives you the opportunity to perform validation and potentially roll back the entire transaction, including the trigger, if there is a validation problem with the process. Triggers fire in response to the three standard data modification actions, namely INSERT, UPDATE, and DELETE.

To extend our previous example, suppose you want to create a trigger to enforce the credit limit restriction. If this is your goal, you can create a trigger that will react to the insert action and execute after the action completes but before the transaction commits. The following code creates a trigger that meets these qualifications:

```
USE demoscript;
GO


CREATE TRIGGER tr_ins_Customer
ON Customer
FOR INSERT
AS
DECLARE @CredLim money
SELECT @CredLim = CreditLimit from inserted
IF @CredLim <= 0
BEGIN
   ROLLBACK TRAN
   RETURN
END
GO
```

Conceptually, this trigger is very similar to the stored procedure, but you will notice a few differences. First of all, there is no insert code in the trigger. This is because the trigger fires at the end of the insert and is technically an extension of the transaction initiated by the insert.

You will also see a reference to a table called "inserted." No, we did not just pull that out of thin air. That is a special table that SQL Server creates when a trigger executes. All of the data that the user inserts into the Customer table also goes into this special inserted table for the duration of the trigger. After the trigger is finished, the inserted table goes away. This means that you can look at the data that was just inserted by examining the inserted table.

In addition, you will see that the trigger performs a rollback operation if the test fails. It must do a rollback to prevent the insert from taking place. This is inherently less efficient than preventing a transaction in the first place and therefore the reason behind using a trigger only as a last resort.

Now that you have seen the procedural options and can compare them to the constraints, you are better prepared to make a more substantive analysis of your options. The bottom line is that while you must always do whatever is necessary to ensure the integrity of your data, you should also try to do it in the most efficient way possible.

6

Managing Transactions and Locks

I n a shared database environment, it is critical that data access and data modifications happen in an orderly way. To provide this order, SQL Server uses an elaborate system of locks and transactions that can do two things:

- Prevent users from modifying each other's locked resources
- Prevent you from partially executing a multipart operation

In this chapter, we will look at how this infrastructure works, how you can monitor it, and how you can tune it. While SQL Server handles most of the locking and transaction infrastructure for you, there is some control that you can exert to tweak performance and scalability. First, let's define a few terms:

Transaction   A transaction is a statement or set of statements that must all commit together. In SQL Server, transactions conform to the ACID test, meaning that they adhere to these four conditions:

Atomic   An atomic transaction is one that executes in its entirety or not at all. It is already in its smallest stable form and cannot be committed in smaller units without impacting the integrity of the operation. Think of this as the "all or nothing" behavior of a transaction.

Consistent   Every transaction leaves the data in a consistent state. Most transactions perform multiple data modifications. It is important that any inconsistency that may exist during the execution of the transaction be resolved before the transaction completes.

Isolated   A transaction is isolated from other transactions by default. No one transaction can see the data modifications being executed by another transaction until the other transaction is complete. SQL Server enforces this transaction characteristic through locking.

Durable   Once a transaction is committed, SQL Server must record it on durable media to ensure its longevity. SQL Server manages durability through the transaction log.

Lock   A lock is a marker on a resource that identifies it as being used or potentially used by a data operation. There are a variety of lock types that enforce different locking scenarios based on the type of resource and the aggressiveness of the lock. SQL Server uses locks to enforce the integrity of transactional operations and to prevent a certain operation from happening when the resource is in an invalid state for that operation.

Manage SQL Server Locks

SQL Server uses locks to prevent conflicts from multiple operations that are using the same resources. Some concurrent interactions are acceptable. For example, there is no problem if two users are reading the same data from a table at the same time. However, two different users trying to modify the same data at the same time would be a real problem.

Identify Lock Types and Behaviors

Locks in SQL Server are categorized in two different ways. First, locks can be classified based on the objects they affect, such as a data row, a data page, or an entire table. Second, they can be classified by their behavior, such as a shared lock or an exclusive lock. Understanding the different types of locks and how they work is critical to your ability as a database administrator to analyze, tune, and maintain a database environment.

Locked Objects

SQL Server uses a hierarchical locking architecture that allows database resources to be locked at various levels. Since the resources in SQL Server are hierarchical, it makes sense to organize locks this way as well. For example, if a user is editing a specific data row, SQL Server cannot allow another user to get a lock in the page that contains that row or there might be a conflict. The goal is to ensure that the integrity of the data is maintained regardless of where in the hierarchy the user requests the locks. Table 6.1 provides a listing of the object hierarchy in SQL Server and a brief description of each object, sometimes referred to as an artifact.

Data Integrity and Security

PART II

Table 6.1: The SQL Server Lock Hierarchy

Locked Artifact	Description
RID	A single row of data in a table
Key	A single row in an index structure of a table
Page	A block of 8KB in either a table or index
Extent	A block of eight data or index pages (64KB)
Table	An entire table, including all data and index pages
HoBT	A heap or B-tree representing a single index or a heap structure if there is no clustered index
File	A file that hosts database resources
Allocation Unit	A collection of extents that are part of the same file allocation
Database	The entire SQL Server database, including all tables and indexes

The basic lock artifact is the RID, which as you can see in Table 6.1, represents a single row of data in the database. SQL Server uses row-based locking to provide a balance between locking overhead and concurrency.

Lock Modes and Behaviors

Not all objects support all lock modes, but almost all locked objects support some mode that controls the behaviors of the locks, such as their duration and compatibility. Table 6.2 provides a list of lock modes and a description of their behaviors.

Table 6.2: SQL Server Lock Modes

Lock Mode	Description
Shared	Set when performing read operations allowing concurrent reading
Exclusive	Set when performing write operations preventing concurrent writing
Update	Set when updating data; provide a mix of read and write support

Table 6.2: SQL Server Lock Modes *(continued)*

Lock Mode	Description
Intent	Set on objects to protect other objects in the lock hierarchy
Schema	Set on an object definition or schema to protect schema-dependent operations
Key-Range	Set on a range of rows to prevent modification inside the range

The locked objects are fairly self-explanatory, but these modes require a bit more elaboration, so we will address each mode individually and discuss its impacts.

Shared locks   A shared lock is a read lock. These are set when SQL Server performs operations such as SELECT statements or other operations that read but do not modify data. The default behavior is that SQL Server sets these locks when reading the resource, such as a RID or a page, and then releases the lock when the read is complete.

Exclusive locks   As the name implies, only one exclusive lock can exist on a resource at a time at any level in the lock hierarchy. Exclusive locks are generally reserved for data modification activities. If multiple transactions attempt to modify the same resource concurrently, subsequent transactions will queue until SQL Server releases the lock, at which point it is given to the next transaction in the queue.

Update locks   These locks are a hybrid between shared locks and exclusive locks. Operations such as an UPDATE might consist of multiple actions, including a read action to determine the data that it will update and a write action to perform the update. These locks allow SQL Server to maintain read concurrency as long as possible by not exclusively locking resources until it is necessary to do so.

Intent locks   SQL Server uses these locks to mark lock points in the lock hierarchy. For example, if you are reading a data row and have a shared lock on the RID, it would violate data integrity to allow an exclusive lock at the table level. Therefore, if the read operation also places an intent lock at the table level along with the shared lock at the RID level, locks do not have to be checked at every level in the hierarchy. You will find more information about intent locks later in this section.

Schema locks   If an operation is dependent on the schema of a resource, such as modifying a table or index, SQL Server must lock the schema of the resource to prevent multiple concurrent schema alterations. Lightweight versions of these locks, called schema stability locks, prevent schema alterations when queries execute against the schema-defined resources.

Key-range locks   In some cases, you may not want to allow rows to be inserted into or deleted from ranges of data rows that your transaction reads. Most of the time it does not matter, but in these situations you need to have repeatable reads, meaning that if you read the same data again in a transaction, you will get exactly the same rows as before. These situations require that you lock the range of rows in a table or index structure that provides the source for the read. The key-range locks provide this support.

Of these lock modes, the intent lock is the most intricate. In reality, an intent lock is not really a lock at all but a marker in the lock hierarchy that identifies other locked structures. Also, depending on the lock escalation behavior, it can also represent an intent to lock a resource at some point in the future. The specific forms of the intent lock are listed in Table 6.3.

Table 6.3: SQL Server Intent Lock Modes

Intent Lock Mode	Description
Intent shared	Set to mark shared locks on lower-level resources in the hierarchy
Intent exclusive	Set to mark exclusive locks on lower-level resources in the hierarchy
Shared with intent exclusive	Sets an intent shared lock at a higher-level resource such as a table while concurrently setting intent exclusive locks at a lower resource; generally used to protect exclusive locks at the row level
Intent update	Set to mark update locks on lower-level resources; only set at the page level and converted to intent exclusive if/when an update occurs
Shared with intent update	Holds both shared and intent update locks on a page
Update with intent exclusive	Holds both update and intent exclusive locks on a resource

Identify Lock Compatibility

The purpose for locking is to prevent violations of data integrity that occur when transactions are not properly isolated according to the ACID rules of a transaction discussed at the beginning of this chapter. Therefore, you would expect that there are times when locks will conflict with each other, preventing the data operations from continuing until the locks are available.

There are so many lock modes that having a firm grasp on compatibility issues is critical to being able to monitor and troubleshoot database behavior. Table 6.4 provides a summary of the most common modes and their compatibilities. Table 6.5 is the key to Table 6.4.

Data Integrity and Security

PART II

TIP   There is a full compatibility matrix on the Microsoft Developer Network (MSDN) website. You can find it at http://msdn .microsoft.com/en-us/library/ms186396.aspx. We have found it helpful to print this out and have it handy, especially when you are trying to troubleshoot contention issues. Table 6.4 is an abbreviated version of this matrix.

Table 6.4: Lock Compatibility

	NL	S	U	X	IS	IU	IX	SIU	SIX	UIX
NL	N	N	N	N	N	N	N	N	N	N
S	N	N	N	C	N	N	C	N	C	C
U	N	N	C	C	N	C	C	C	C	C
X	N	C	C	C	C	C	C	C	C	C
IS	N	N	N	C	N	N	N	N	N	N
IU	N	N	C	C	N	N	N	N	N	C
IX	N	C	C	C	N	N	N	C	C	C
SIU	N	N	C	C	N	N	C	N	C	C
SIX	N	C	C	C	N	N	C	C	C	C
UIX	N	C	C	C	N	C	C	C	C	C

Table 6.5: Lock Compatibility Key

Key	Description
N	No conflict
C	Conflict
NL	No lock
S	Shared lock
U	Update lock
X	Exclusive lock
IS	Intent shared lock
IU	Intent update lock
IX	Intent exclusive lock
SIU	Shared with intent update
SIX	Shared with intent exclusive
UIX	Update with intent exclusive

Manage Locking Behavior

Just because SQL Server manages most locking automatically does not mean that you do not have any ability to control locking. There are two primary tools that you can use to control the locking infrastructure. First, you can manipulate the default lock escalation behavior if you wish. Second, you can also use Transact SQL query statements to control lock behavior.

Lock Escalation

SQL Server 2008 uses a dynamic locking system. Rather than having a fixed set of locks that is used in every situation, SQL Server has the ability to alter its lock requests based on the number and granularity of existing granted locks. The purpose behind this system is to provide a trade-off between the cost of the locks and the level of concurrency provided by the lock chain.

For example, would it be possible for SQL Server to use byte-level locks and lock only the actual bytes of data that you are modifying? The answer is yes, and it would provide exceptional concurrency, but the overhead costs would be enormous. Conversely, having a single database lock acquired by the transaction that is performing an operation would be a very low-overhead solution, but it would never be acceptable in a multiple-user system.

The goal of dynamic locking is to use the fewest locks possible while still maintaining optimal concurrency. For example, if a transaction is locking a very large number of rows in a table, at some point it will not radically reduce concurrency to simply lock the entire table. The single table lock, however, is a much lower-overhead solution than the large number of RID locks.

Lock escalation settings are controlled at the table level. If you want to change these settings, you will use the ALTER TABLE statement. The basic syntax for this change looks like this:

```
ALTER TABLE database_name.schema_name.table_name
    SET (LOCK_ESCALATION = { AUTO | TABLE | DISABLE })
```

The statement takes the following options:

AUTO   SQL Server selects the best escalation algorithm. This selection is based on the table schema. If the table is partitioned, the lock will never escalate beyond the partition. If not, then table level locks are used.

TABLE   All lock escalation occurs at the table level regardless of the partition status of the table. This means that after SQL Server grants enough lower-level locks, they will escalate to a single table lock.

DISABLE   This setting turns off lock escalation in most cases. Use this option if maintaining concurrency is of primary importance, even at the expense of additional overhead.

As an example, if you wanted to disable lock escalation for the Customer table in the demo database, you would use the following code:

```
USE demo;

ALTER TABLE dbo.Customer
SET (LOCK_ESCALATION = DISABLE);
GO
```

Data Integrity and Security

PART II

Controlling Transaction Isolation

There are two primary ways to control locking with Transact SQL (TSQL) code. Either you can use session-level statements that control transaction isolation for the duration of a user connection or you can use lock hints. The behaviors of these different approaches are essentially identical. The primary difference is the duration.

Remember earlier that we said the way we enforce transaction isolation is through locks? If this is true, any alteration to the transaction isolation settings would then change the locking behavior. SQL Server supports four options for transaction isolation:

Read Committed   This is the default setting. This setting states that one transaction can access only data that is not currently locked by another transaction. For example, if transaction A has page 1 locked and transaction B wants to access the same page, the locks requested by the two transactions must be compatible. If they are not, transaction B will have to wait until transaction A releases its lock, indicating that the operation is complete.

Read Uncommitted   This setting is the least restrictive. When a transaction is running under this setting, it will not place any shared locks on resources and it will not honor any exclusive locks that other transactions own. This means that it is possible that the transaction might read data that may never be committed to the database. This is called "dirty reading."

Although there may be some data integrity issues, this option allows the transaction to access resources without holding locks that might delay or even deadlock other operations. This option can help promote concurrency for some operations.

Repeatable Read   A repeatable read occurs when more than one read operation takes place with a guarantee that the data will be exactly the same for the two reads. This is a more aggressive lock approach than Read Committed and results in more contention. SQL Server uses key-range locks to implement this behavior, ensuring that none of the rows in the range can be updated during the duration of the transaction. Normally, the shared locks would be released as soon as the read is complete, regardless of whether the transaction is still active.

Serializable   This setting also uses a key-range lock, but for a different purpose. Serializable operations are those that guarantee that there are no more or fewer rows between sequential reads. In other words, it guarantees that no INSERT or DELETE operations take place on data that is involved in the Serializable transaction.

Although worded differently, SQL Server implements this in the same way as the Repeatable Read isolation. Therefore, it doesn't matter whether you use Repeatable Read or Serializable as your transaction isolation level. They both do exactly the same thing.

The syntax for implementing transaction isolation uses the SET keyword, meaning that the behavior will remain intact until you close the connection or change the setting to another isolation level. The code is simple. For example, if you wanted to set the transaction isolation level to Read Uncommitted and then select data from the Customer table in the demo database, the script would look like this:

```
USE demo;

SET TRANSACTION ISOLATION LEVEL READ UNCOMMITTED;
GO

SELECT CustomerID
FROM dbo.Customer;
GO
```

Using Optimizer Hints

You can also control locking at the query level using optimizer hints. You can use optimizer hinting for many things other than locking, so for now we will focus on locking hints only. Table 6.6 provides a list of locking hints.

Table 6.6: Locking Hints

Hint	Description
NOLOCK	Specifies that the query should be executed with no locks. Equivalent to Read Uncommitted
HOLDLOCK	Indicates that all locks should be held through the duration of the entire transaction
PAGLOCK	Requests page locks

Table 6.6: Locking Hints *(continued)*

Hint	Description
ROWLOCK	Requests row locks
READCOMMITTED	Requests query behavior consistent with Read Committed transaction isolation
READUNCOMMITTED	Requests query behavior consistent with Read Uncommitted transaction isolation
READPAST	Specifies that the query should skip locked resources during execution. No attempt is made to go back and pick them up later
READCOMMITTEDLOCK	Requests query behavior consistent with Read Uncommitted transaction isolation. Used when the READPAST performance hint is used
REPEATABLEREAD	Requests query behavior consistent with Repeatable Read transaction isolation
SERIALIZABLE	Requests query behavior consistent with Serializable transaction isolation
TABLOCK	Requests table locks
TABLOCKX	Requests exclusive table locks
UPDLOCK	Requests update locks
XLOCK	Requests exclusive locks

To use these optimizer hints, include the hint or combination of hints in the FROM clause of the query. For example, to select from the Customer table using a dirty read, regardless of the session transaction isolation level, you would use this code:

```
USE demo;

SELECT CustomerID
FROM dbo.Customer WITH (NOLOCK);
GO
```

You can also combine hints. This code requests page locks instead of the default RID locks and requests that those locks be held for the duration of the transaction:

```
USE demo;

SELECT CustomerID
FROM dbo.Customer WITH (PAGLOCK, HOLDLOCK);
GO
```

SQL Server does not allow for more than one table hint from each of the following groups for each table in the FROM clause:

- Granularity hints

  - PAGLOCK

  - NOLOCK

  - ROWLOCK

  - TABLOCK

  - TABLOCKX

- Isolation-level hints

  - HOLDLOCK

  - NOLOCK

  - READCOMMITTED

  - REPEATABLEREAD

  - SERIALIZABLE

Manage Transactions

A transaction is a statement or set of statements that commit together as a single unit. Much of the work that you will do in a database is transactional. SQL Server provides full support for transactional operations. In this section we will look at how SQL Server Manages transactions and how you can control transaction behavior.

Data Integrity and Security

PART II

Creating Transactions

SQL Server creates some transactions implicitly. Others you can create explicitly. Either way, they are considered ACID transactions and follow the rules laid out earlier in this chapter. First we will look at how SQL Server manages implicit transactions, and then you will learn how to manage transactional behaviors explicitly.

Implicit Transactions

All data modification statements represent implicit transactional behaviors. If you execute an INSERT, UPDATE, or DELETE statement that affects more than one row, it is important that the transactional integrity of the entire operation is maintained. SQL Server enforces this behavior by treating all individual row operations transactionally.

These operations run in an "auto-commit" mode, meaning that as soon as all of the individual operations complete successfully in an INSERT, UPDATE, or DELETE, the transaction automatically commits. This is true whether the statement affects one row or many.

For example, assume that you have a customer table with 50 customers and you want to increase every customer's credit limit by 10 percent. You would use the following query to affect all 50 customers:

```
USE demo;

UPDATE dbo.Customer
SET CreditLimit = CreditLimit * 1.10;
GO
```

In this case, you are trying to affect 50 customer records. If for some reason even one of those records errors when you are attempting the update, none of the changes will commit. If, however, they can all commit without error, they will commit immediately with no other code needed from the developer. This means that you will also have no opportunity to roll back those operations. This is the meaning of auto-commit.

If you want to change this auto-commit behavior, you can. Using the session option IMPLICIT_TRANSACTIONS, you can require that the transaction be committed explicitly instead of auto-committed. If you turn this option on, any of the statements in the following list will begin a transaction that must be explicitly committed or rolled back:

ALTER TABLE

CREATE

DELETE

DROP

FETCH

GRANT

INSERT

OPEN

REVOKE

SELECT

TRUNCATE TABLE

UPDATE

Normally, executing a statement without error would automatically commit the transaction, but with this statement, you must explicitly commit the transaction before the action will become durable. Notice the difference in this code as compared with the previous version:

```
USE demo;
SET IMPLICIT_TRANSACTIONS ON;
GO

UPDATE dbo.Customer
SET CreditLimit = CreditLimit * 1.10;

COMMIT TRANSACTION;
```

You will learn more about the COMMIT TRANSACTION statement later in this chapter, but what is important to note is that with the implicit transactions mode enabled, this query would have not committed had you not included the COMMIT TRANSACTION statement. Of course, this also means that you can roll back the transaction as well, which is something that you can't do when an operation is running in an auto-commit mode.

WARNING If you use IMPLICIT_TRANSACTIONS ON, be sure to pay special attention to the commit behavior. If you close a connection without committing the transaction, the default behavior is to roll back the transaction and undo the actions. This can result in data loss. You should also remember to commit the transactions as soon as possible so that each transaction is truly atomic.

Data Integrity and Security

PART II

Explicit Transactions

When you have multiple statements that you want to organize as a single transaction, you can include the statements into an explicit transaction block. When you use the BEGIN TRANSACTION statement, everything that follows will be part of the same transaction until you explicitly terminate the transaction using either a COMMIT TRANSACTION statement or a ROLLBACK TRANSACTION statement. Remember that your goal is to create a set of atomic changes, so the transaction should contain only the minimal operations needed to preserve data integrity.

The following code illustrates an explicit transaction. Suppose you want to increase the credit limit for every customer who places an order. If there is an error when the order is placed, you do not want to increase the credit limit. Conversely if there is a problem raising the credit limit, you should not process the order. You can use a transaction to make sure that these two operations happen as a single unit of work. The following code provides an example:

```
USE demo;

BEGIN TRANSACTION;

UPDATE dbo.Customer
SET CreditLimit = CreditLimit * 1.1
WHERE CustomerID =1;

INSERT dbo.[Order](OrderID, CustomerID, ProductName, Price,
Quantity)
SELECT 1, 1,'E34 Muffler Assembly',225, 10;

COMMIT TRANSACTION;

GO
```

You can also force the transaction to roll back if you wish. If you replaced the COMMIT TRANSACTION statement in the previous code with a ROLLBACK TRANSACTION statement, the operations would be undone and no permanent change would be made to the database. In normal circumstances you would want to do that only if some error occurred, so understanding error management in SQL Server is also very important.

Handling Transaction Errors

SQL Server 2008 supports more than one approach for managing errors in transactions. No matter which approach you use, the important thing is that you monitor your application for errors in your code and take corrective action if and when those errors occur. Let's begin by looking at a traditional approach.

Traditional Error Management

Most transactions will take place inside of the stored procedure. Stored procedures support a RETURN keyword that you can use to exit them when something goes wrong. Let's convert the previous code into the stored procedure. Normally we would parameterize all of the information in the procedure, but in this case we will hard-code it just to keep it simple. Listing 6.1 contains the first iteration of this stored procedure.

Listing 6.1: A Transactional Stored Procedure

```
USE demo;
GO

CREATE PROCEDURE dbo.TranTest1
AS
BEGIN TRANSACTION;

UPDATE dbo.Customer
SET CreditLimit = CreditLimit * 1.1
WHERE CustomerID =1;

IF @@ERROR <> 0
BEGIN
  ROLLBACK TRAN;
  PRINT 'Error Updating Credit Limit';
  RETURN;
END

INSERT dbo.[Order]
SELECT
  1,
```

Data Integrity and Security

PART II

Continued

Listing 6.1: A Transactional Stored Procedure *(continued)*

```
1,
'E34 Muffler Assembly',
225,
10;

IF @@ERROR <> 0
BEGIN
  ROLLBACK TRAN;
  PRINT 'Error Adding Order';
  RETURN;
END

COMMIT TRANSACTION;

GO
```

You will notice in the stored procedure that after each operation the procedure tests for an error. This is because the default SQL Server behavior is to commit what it can commit in a transaction even if an error occurs. For example, assume that there was a problem inserting the order row into the table. If the second part of the stored procedure fails, the first part will still commit unless we explicitly tell it to roll back the entire transaction. By checking for an error after every operation, we can roll back the transaction as soon as we discover an error. This will undo any actions that the server has already executed. By following the rollback with the RETURN statement, we are preventing additional actions from executing as well.

Try and Catch Error Handling

Another approach to SQL Server error handling is to use the new "try and catch" system included with SQL Server 2008. If you are familiar with JavaScript or object-oriented languages such as Java or C#, you have probably seen this approach before. The concept is simple. Any code that might cause an error is placed in a TRY block. Following the TRY block is a CATCH block that contains the resolution of the error. As soon as an error occurs in the TRY block, the execution will immediately jump to the CATCH block. Listing 6.2 provides the same functionality as Listing 6.1 but uses this updated error handling approach.

Listing 6.2: Using TRY and CATCH

```
USE demo;
GO

CREATE PROCEDURE dbo.TranTest2
AS
BEGIN TRANSACTION;

BEGIN TRY
  UPDATE dbo.Customer
  SET CreditLimit = CreditLimit * 1.1
  WHERE CustomerID =1;

  INSERT dbo.[Order]
  SELECT
    1,
    1,
    'E34 Muffler Assembly',
    225,
    10;

  COMMIT TRANSACTION;
END TRY
BEGIN CATCH
  ROLLBACK TRANSACTION;
  PRINT 'ERROR IN TRANSACTION';
  RETURN;
END CATCH

GO
```

Using Savepoints in Transactions

Nesting transactions poses some additional challenges. Although nested transactions may make sense to you as "mini" transactions, SQL Server looks at it differently. Its efforts to retain true atomic behavior creates results that you might find surprising at first. As you work through it though, you will see that it makes sense.

Nested Transaction Concepts

It is possible to nest named transactions, but this really buys you nothing because only the outermost transaction is registered with the system for rollback. For example, consider the following code snippet:

```
USE AdventureWorks2008;
BEGIN TRAN T1;
SELECT COUNT(*) FROM Person.Person;
BEGIN TRAN T2;
SELECT COUNT(*) FROM Person.Person;
ROLLBACK TRAN T2;
```

Conceptually, T2 is nested within T1, so a rollback to T2 should only roll back the work that was done from the beginning of T2 to the rollback point. However, if you execute this query, you get an interesting error message that reads like this:

```
Msg 6401, Level 16, State 1, Line 6
Cannot roll back T2.
No transaction or savepoint of that name was found.
```

This is a curious message because we explicitly created a transaction named T2. However, because that transaction was nested inside T1 and only the outer transactions were registered with the system, it is literally as if the transaction point never existed. If you commit or roll back a transaction, it will commit or roll back all the way to the outermost transaction.

This does not mean that nested transactions are not recognized at all. They certainly are. It is just that you cannot roll back or commit to any point other than the outermost transaction point. Consider this code:

```
USE AdventureWorks2008;
BEGIN TRAN T1;
SELECT @@TRANCOUNT;
BEGIN TRAN T2;
SELECT @@TRANCOUNT;
ROLLBACK TRAN T2;
```

The `@@TRANCOUNT` global variable tells us how deeply nested the current transaction is. If you execute this snippet in a fresh connection, the first counter should return 1 and the second should return 2. This means that SQL Server has, in fact, recognized the beginning of the nested transaction but it did not allow roll back or commit to that point in the hierarchy.

What good are nested transactions if you cannot commit or roll back to those points? The real answer is that explicit transaction statements were never meant to be nested within a single script, and this is a misuse (and often a dangerous misunderstanding) of transactional behavior. However, we can simulate this behavior with a savepoint.

Creating Savepoints

Because nested transactions do not give you the ability to partially commit a transaction, there is another option. You can use a savepoint. *Savepoints* are markers in a transaction that represent points of integrity. Using a savepoint indicates that the transaction is potentially safe to commit to that point, even if additional work is pending. Figure 6.1 illustrates the use of savepoints.

Figure 6.1: Using savepoints

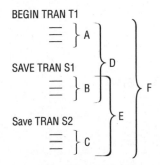

```
BEGIN TRAN T1
   ≡  } A
SAVE TRAN S1         } D
   ≡  } B                  } F
Save TRAN S2         } E
   ≡  } C
--Add End Tran Logic
```

In this diagram, you will see one BEGIN marker with two SAVE markers. At the end of the transaction, the statements you use will determine what SQL Server will commit or roll back. The following is a list of possibilities based on the diagram:

- If you were to use the statement COMMIT TRAN T1, it would commit all of the work indicated by bracket F in the diagram.

- There is a defined a savepoint called S1. Suppose that after executing additional statements, you determine that you cannot commit anything after the savepoint. You might use this logic at the end of the transaction:

```
ROLLBACK TRAN S1;
COMMIT TRAN T1;
```

These statements would roll back all of the work executed in bracket E in the diagram and then subsequently commit the work in bracket A.

- Likewise, if you were to roll back to S2 instead of S1, you could undo the work in bracket C, followed by a commit of the work in bracket D.

Consider a situation in which one stored procedure calls another. If the called stored procedure might need to roll back any of the work that it is doing, it could use a savepoint instead of a nested transaction statement. Then if needed, it could roll back to the savepoint instead of rolling back the entire transaction. Because the called procedure rolls back only its own work, the calling procedure is never even aware that SQL Server had extended and then reversed the transaction. It can continue as if nothing had happened.

Implement Distributed Transactions

SQL Server's standard data engine installation includes a tool called the Distributed Transaction Coordinator (DTC). This utility is responsible for maintaining the integrity of distributed transactions in a SQL Server environment. You can think of the DTC as a "traffic cop," responsible for managing the interaction among the various data engine instances that participate in the transaction. The mechanism that the DTC uses to do this is called a *two-phase commit protocol*. As its name implies, it breaks each distributed transaction into two separate phases called prepare and commit.

The prepare phase The initial phase of the two-phase commit requires each service that participates in the transaction to enlist in the transaction and complete the work assigned to it. The DTC will contact every participating instance, enlist them in the transaction, and verify their ability to participate. Then the DTC will give each instance the work that it must complete. The instance executes the work of the transaction but does not commit the work yet. Each service reports its ability to commit back to the DTC and awaits the second phase.

The commit phase   After enlisting the services in the transaction, the DTC waits for each service to report back its ability to commit. Each service must report back in a timely manner and must indicate that it is able to commit its work. Reporting must be unanimous. If any server does not respond or returns a condition that would prevent the transaction from committing, the DTC sends an abort message to all participants and they all roll back their work. If all participants indicate an ability to commit, the DTC sends a commit message and all services commit together.

Understanding Distributed Queries

Up to this point, the examples have shown queries that execute on a single server and usually in a single database. It is possible, however, to distribute query behavior across multiple databases and even multiple servers. Before we can turn our attention to distributed transactions, however, we must discuss the process of performing server-to-server communications using distributed queries. There are two ways that you can execute distributed queries across servers. One approach is to use the OpenRowset() function and the other is to use linked servers.

NOTE   Before the code examples in this section will work, you must have installed a secondary instance of SQL Server on your computer or have access to another instance. Replace the instance names in the examples with your actual system data. You must also have the AdventureWorks2008 database installed in both the primary and secondary instance.

Using the *OpenRowset()* Function

The OpenRowset() function is primarily a method for performing queries against a target server on an ad hoc basis. Each call using OpenRowset() is self-contained and includes everything the query needs to know to make the connection and execute. The function makes all connectivity through

OLE DB, and therefore, this option is available to all OLE DB–compliant data sources. You are not limited to SQL Server data sources. The basic syntax of the OpenRowset() function looks like this:

```
OPENROWSET
(
{'provider_name',
{'datasource';'user_id';'password'|'provider_string'},
{[ catalog.][schema.]object|'query'}}
)
```

There are three parameters for the function:

- The first is the name of the OLE DB provider that you will use to connect to the remote service. If you are connecting to another SQL Server 2008 service, use SQLNCLI as the provider name. This indicates that you will be using the SQL Server Native Client. Other services have OLE DB providers as well, so you will need to look into the documentation for those services and determine the appropriate name to use.

- The second parameter is a connection string that is provider specific. This contains the information about the target service and database as well as authentication information.

- The final parameter is the object that you wish to access. This could be a stored procedure that you want to execute or a pass-through query that you want to send to the service for execution.

Before you will be able to use the OpenRowset() function, you must first configure the target server to allow ad hoc distributed queries. You can do this by executing the following configuration code on the target server. Note that because the Ad Hoc Distributed Queries option is an advanced Boolean option, you must execute the first statement before you will be able to make the required change. You should then set the option back when complete:

```
EXEC sp_configure 'Show Advanced Options', 1;
RECONFIGURE;
EXEC sp_configure 'Ad Hoc Distributed Queries', 1;
RECONFIGURE;
EXEC sp_configure 'Show Advanced Options', 0;
RECONFIGURE;
```

Now that you have permitted the use of the distributed query on the target server, you are free to execute the query. This example executes a query against an AdventureWorks2008 database on a distributed server instance. Note that you would be executing this query from the context of the server instance called MasteringSQL, but the pass-through query will actually execute on the service instance called MasteringSQL\Silent.

```
SELECT DISTINCT s.FirstName, s.LastName
FROM OpenRowset(
  'SQLNCLI',
  'server=masteringsql\silent;database=AdventureWorks2008;➥
trusted_connection=yes',
  'SELECT FirstName, LastName FROM Person.Person'
) AS s
WHERE s.LastName LIKE 'K%';
```

This example is very selective with regard to the columns that it returns from the target server but not the rows. There are no filter criteria executing on the target server. What you see here is actually two separate queries. One query is the pass-through that executes on the target server, and the other filters out the data on the local server in the outer query. Keep in mind that you are running multiple queries because you will want to tune each one to make sure you are conserving bandwidth and I/O as much as possible.

This example also uses integrated security. The assumption is that the user is logged into the primary server using a Windows account that also has access to the target server. If this is not the case, you may get a login error when attempting to execute the query.

Configuring Linked Servers

The other option for executing a distributed query is to configure a linked server. While an ad hoc query provides authentication information every time a call to OpenRowset() executes, the linked server model will store all authentication and resolution information in the server's configuration data. This facilitates the use of the linked server by allowing a four-part name for the resources that you want to access instead of having to use an ad hoc function with each execution.

You can add a linked server to your configuration by using either a TSQL statement or the Studio interface. The visual interface displays all required and available options, so we will use that approach. You can script the results of the visual configuration, however, if you need to create the same linked server reference on multiple servers in the enterprise. Use these steps:

1. Open the SQL Server Management Studio (SSMS) and expand the node for the server that will be the primary server. This server will host the query that will call the other services.

2. Locate the Server Objects node inside your server list and expand this to find the Linked Servers list. You will also see a Providers list containing the different providers that SQL Server installs by default. You can create a linked server to any of the databases for which there is a provider.

3. To create a linked server, right-click the Linked Servers node in the list on your primary server and select New Linked Server from the menu. This will display a dialog like the one illustrated in Figures 6.2 through 6.4. This dialog has three pages. On the first page, you can do the basic configuration, as shown in Figure 6.2.

Figure 6.2: Configuring linked server connectivity

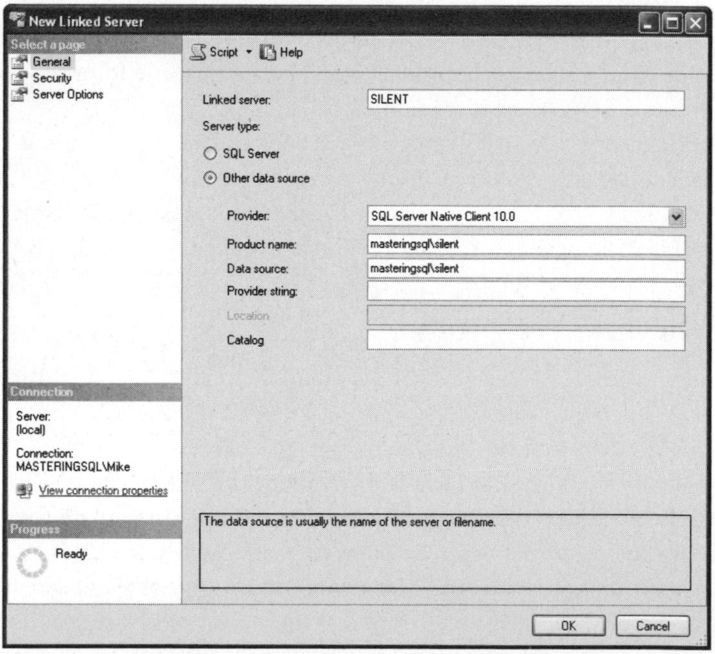

In this dialog, the name of the linked server is SILENT. This is an alias that points to the actual server instance, which is MasteringSQL\Silent. This linked server uses the SQL Native Client interface.

5. Use the next page in the dialog, pictured in Figure 6.3, to configure linked server security.

Figure 6.3: Configuring linked server security

Data Integrity and Security

PART II

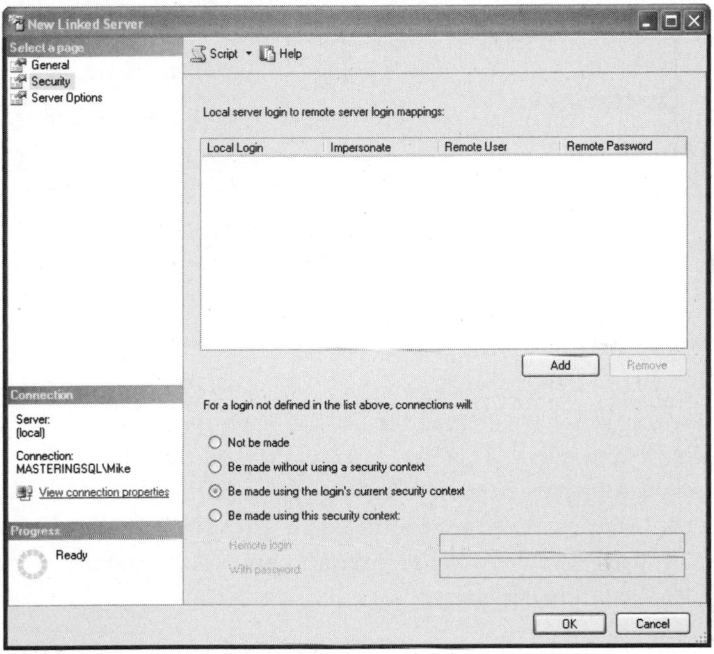

This dialog shows a standard integrated connection. SQL Server will log in to the target server using the same user account you use to log into the primary server. This interface allows a specific login mapping in the top section and other general options below.

6. The final page in the dialog, pictured in Figure 6.4, provides the linked server options. For now, just verify that the Data Access option is set to True. This option must be enabled before you will be allowed to use the linked server in a distributed query. When you are finished with this page, click the OK button to create the linked server.

Figure 6.4: Linked server options

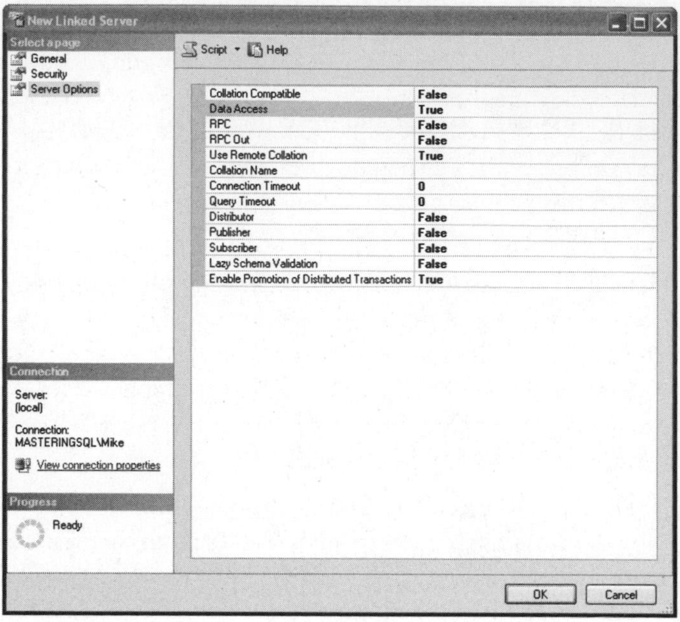

Now that you have created the linked server, you can use that link in a distributed query. There are two ways to do this. The first is to use a standard four-part name in the FROM clause of the query. This will force the target server to return the entire data structure to the primary server, where it can continue to filter and process the data. For example, consider the following query:

```
SELECT * FROM Silent.AdventureWorks2008.Person.EmailAddress
WHERE ModifiedDate >= '01/01/2000 00:00:00.000';
```

This query returns the entire content of the Person.EmailAddress table from the target server to the primary server, which applies the filter criterion and returns the results to the requesting user. This is a very convenient syntax, but if the target table is quite large, or if there are data that cannot be returned to the primary server, such as an XML column, you will need to find an alternative approach. For example, take a look at this query:

```
SELECT FirstName, LastName
FROM Silent.AdventureWorks2008.Person.Person
WHERE LastName LIKE 'K%';
```

If you execute this query, you will get an error message stating that xml data types are not supported in distributed queries. Looking at the query, this seems a little odd because you are returning only FirstName and LastName and neither of these columns is configured as an xml data type. Remember, though, that when you use the four-part name, as in Silent.AdventureWorks2008.Person.Person, in a query, the target server will return the entire data structure to the primary server for processing. You can solve this problem in two different ways:

- One is to use stored procedures or views on the target server instead of accessing the table directly. This will force some execution on the server. Simply use the four-part name of the desired procedural target to access it through the linked server. Use the view name in the FROM clause in place of the table names. Stored procedures will execute as normal with an EXECUTE statement using a four-part name for the procedure.

- The other option is to use the OpenQuery() function. This function provides for a pass-through query to be sent to the target server, much like OpenRowset(), but through the linked server rather than on an ad hoc basis as with the OpenRowset() function. To use the OpenQuery() function, try this syntax:

```
SELECT s.FirstName, s.LastName
FROM OpenQuery(
  Silent,
  'SELECT FirstName, LastName
FROM AdventureWorks2008.Person.Person'
) AS s
WHERE s.LastName LIKE 'K%';
```

Although it is a little more work, you can optimize your linked server queries using this method rather than using a simple four-part name. The performance and security prize still goes to stored procedures in most cases, though, so you should definitely consider that as an option before you default to using OpenQuery().

Defining Distributed Transactions

Once you have created the linked servers, you have completed the real work of configuring distributed transactions. SQL Server handles most of the nuts and bolts of making a distributed transaction work. By defining the linked servers, you have created all the necessary target configurations and set up the required security. Now all you have to do is code the distributed transaction.

Making Distributed Modifications

You can use OpenQuery() to make data modifications as well. By using the OpenQuery() function in place of a table name in an INSERT, UPDATE, or DELETE statement, the data modification will be targeted to the data subset as defined in the OpenQuery() syntax. You can also use this syntax as part of a distributed transaction, making this a very flexible option when needed.

Defining a distributed transaction rather than a standard transaction is a very simple process. Just use the statement BEGIN DISTRIBUTED TRANSACTION to begin the transaction. Everything else will behave normally. Consider the following snippet as an illustration:

```
USE AdventureWorks2008;
BEGIN TRY
BEGIN DISTRIBUTED TRANSACTION;
  UPDATE OpenQuery(
      SILENT,
      'SELECT BusinessEntityID, FirstName
        FROM AdventureWorks2008.Person.Person
        WHERE BusinessEntityID = 1'
      )
  SET FirstName = 'Kenny'
  WHERE BusinessEntityID = 1;

  UPDATE Person.Person
  SET FirstName = 'Kenny'
  WHERE BusinessEntityID = 1;

  COMMIT TRANSACTION;
END TRY
BEGIN CATCH
  ROLLBACK TRANSACTION;
END CATCH
```

This code executes a distributed transaction on the Adventure-Works2008 database on both servers. The goal of this distributed transaction is to keep the two databases in sync by ensuring that any modification made to one database will also be made automatically to the other database. This, of course, requires that the DTC be installed and running because it will act as the transaction manager in this situation, enlisting the SILENT server in the transaction and ensuring that the modification commits to both servers or not at all.

Manage Special Transaction Situations

There are a number of special situations that you will run into when working with transactions in SQL Server as well as important information that you will have to know. In this section, we will address those remaining issues, including performance and concurrency factors, controlling time-outs, and handling deadlocks.

Concurrency and Performance

For all the problems that transactions can solve with regard to data integrity, they can create just as many problems relating to concurrency and performance. It is critical that you consider these issues when planning your transactional strategies as well as your lock isolation and hinting structure. Being aware of the problems is half the battle, though. Here are a few things that you might want to consider as you are designing your transactional infrastructure:

Keep transactions short. The longer the transactions are, the longer you will hold locks and (usually) the more data you will lock. Make sure you do any processing before you start the transaction. Do not start the transaction until you are prepared to execute the operations required by the transaction and then get out as quickly as possible. It is up to you to make sure your locking does not become blocking.

Assume transactions will commit. The performance assumption in SQL Server is that transactions will commit. Once the transaction begins, you are executing work that SQL Server assumes you will want to commit. Before you begin the transaction, do all you can to give the transaction the best chance possible of committing. Then you will not have to deal with rolling back the work that could not commit, which is a very high-overhead process.

Use more concurrent isolation levels.   Don't be afraid of a dirty read. You should assume that transactions will commit; therefore, you should also be able to safely assume that the data that you are reading will ultimately be committed. Although you may run into a few consistency issues from time to time, dealing with those issues often uses less overhead than holding locks and blocking out or deadlocking other users.

Access only necessary data.   Try not to access more data than you really need. This is primarily an issue when selecting data. Use effective WHERE clauses and try to filter out as much of the data as possible. Not only will you improve the select performance and reduce disk and network I/O, you will also be reducing the resources that you have to lock, which will increase concurrency on the server side. This is an easy thing to do that is usually underestimated by most developers. Keep it short and simple.

Eliminate user interaction.   This is a holdover from the old xBase days, but you might be surprised at how much the authors see this issue when tuning applications. Do not begin a transaction and then enter a user interactive mode. You never know what the user is going to do or how long they will take. You lose complete control of transaction duration when the transaction does not commit until the user hits that Save button. Instead, don't even begin the transaction until you have all of the information you need to perform the task at hand.

Use implicit transaction mode with caution.   If you come from another database system that used implicitly started transactions, you might be used to that pattern. If yours is primarily a SQL Server background, be careful. You can get very used to working with auto-commit behaviors, and sometimes you don't remember that when the implicit transaction mode is enabled, once you commit or roll back a transaction, the very next statement probably starts another one. If you do not manage this process, transactions tend to get very long and brittle.

Managing Deadlocks

Deadlocks are the bane of every database professional, but they are difficult to avoid altogether. When you are working in a multiuser environment, you will eventually run into a situation where the users will block each other. Knowing how to handle this is an important part of keeping your database up and responsive to user requests.

Deadlocks occur when two or more users need to use resources that are locked by other users before they can continue with their process. What separates this from simple blocking is its reciprocity. Here is a comparison of blocking and deadlocking:

- Simple Blocking

    - User A has row 1 locked and now needs to access row 2.

    - User B has row 2 locked.

    - User A waits for User B to release the lock; when the lock is released User A's query can continue.

- Deadlocking

    - User A has row 1 locked and now needs to access row 2.

    - User B has row 2 locked and now needs to access row 1.

    - Neither User A nor User B can continue. The only way that User A can continue is if User B completes or rolls back. User B is in exactly the same situation. At this point, neither user can continue and one of transactions must be cancelled.

SQL Server deals with deadlocks in a very heavy-handed manner. It kills whichever connection has done the least amount of work up to that point. This is based on the overhead of undoing the work of the connection. SQL Server does not attempt to predict which connection is closest to completing, but only which one can be cancelled the fastest and with the least overhead. Once the connection is identified, SQL Server will kill it immediately.

There are two ways that you can deal with deadlocking.

Follow a consistent access pattern.   The simplest way is to be disciplined in your code to ensure that all resources are accessed in the same order all the time. For example, if our two users both started by locking row 1 and then requesting the lock for row 2 subsequently, this would merely be a blocking situation rather than a deadlock. One user would never deadlock another because it would never hold a resource lock out of order.

Allow low-priority transactions to be killed.   The other approach is a little more drastic. You can allow a connection to volunteer to be the victim of a deadlock. If you have a very low-priority connection that is deadlocking and causing the cancellation of other, high-priority connections, you can configure the low-priority connection to be killed no matter how much work it has done to that point. You would accomplish this by using a session statement as follows:

```
SET DEADLOCK_PRIORITY LOW;
```

This indicates that the connection has a very low priority to continue when it deadlocks with another connection, essentially volunteering it to be the victim.

Setting Lock Time-Outs

By default, SQL Server will wait forever for a blocked transaction to acquire a lock. This allows SQL Server to defer to a client time-out such as an ODBC time-out or a CommandTimout in ADO.NET. At times, however, you may want to enforce a time-out at the server level. This is a very simple process using a session statement. The following code sets a lock time that will return an error instead of waiting for a 6,000 millisecond wait time to elapse while the subsequent query waits for an available lock:

```
USE demo;
SET LOCK_TIMEOUT 6000;
GO

SELECT CustomerID
FROM dbo.Customer;
GO
```

You can also return the current value of the lock time-out setting by using the following statement. If the lock time-out has not been set, this statement returns a value of –1:

```
SELECT @@LOCK_TIMEOUT;
```

Please note that the query time-out option has no effect on deadlocking because SQL Server does not wait for a time-out to complete before killing the necessary connection. Once SQL Server detects a deadlock situation, it will kill that connection immediately.

7

Managing Security

IN THIS CHAPTER, YOU WILL LEARN TO DO THE FOLLOWING:

D atabases often contain sensitive information, and it is important that you keep unauthorized users from accessing data. Microsoft SQL Server features a robust user security infrastructure that allows the database administrator to control exactly which users get access to specific database objects such as stored procedures, tables, or even data columns within tables. In this chapter, we will walk you through the process of implementing user security, including creating login accounts and database user accounts and managing permissions. We will also look at the SQL Server key infrastructure and discuss how to handle data encryption through keys.

Implement User Security

The security infrastructure in SQL Server 2008 is very similar to the security model used in other Microsoft platforms and products. The good news, then, is that if you are accustomed to the Microsoft way of managing security, you are halfway there. To get the rest of the way requires that you apply the security model to the specific nuances of working in a database environment.

To design a good security model, you must understand how the model is organized and be able to identify its architectural characteristics. Then you can use this information to define and implement a security model that will provide the correct balance of convenience and protection, which is the hallmark of any flexible security model. In the following sections, we will look at the elements of the SQL Server security infrastructure and explain the role they play in a security model.

Understand the Security Architecture

There are many aspects to the SQL Server security architecture, including authentication, validation, and rights management. The functional architecture is based on three basic artifacts:

- Principals: Security accounts
- Securables: Objects to be protected
- Permissions: Rights provided on securables to principals

SQL Server Authentication

SQL Server uses two mechanisms to authenticate users. SQL Server can authenticate logins using its own internal mechanisms, or it can rely on Windows to authenticate logins. Each approach has its advantages and disadvantages.

SQL Server authentication   This was the standard mechanism for authenticating logins in early versions of SQL Server. With this technique, SQL Server stores a login and encrypted password in the SQL Server master catalog. Regardless of how users have authenticated to the operating system, they are required to provide credentials to SQL Server before they are allowed to access server resources.

The primary advantage of using this authentication scheme is that SQL Server can authenticate any login no matter how they may have authenticated to the Windows network. This is the preferred method when Windows authentication is not an option, such as with non-Windows clients. This option is typically less secure, however, because it gives access to anyone who has the SQL Server password, without regard to their Windows identity.

Windows authentication

This authentication method relies on Windows to do all of the work. Windows performs the authentication and SQL Server trusts that authentication and provides access to the Windows accounts as configured. Windows user and group accounts can be mapped to SQL Server, allowing all authentication to be managed at the Windows level. This technique is also called integrated security or trusted security.

We would generally consider this technique more secure than SQL Server authentication because the database administrator (DBA) can configure SQL Server to not recognize any user that has not previously authenticated with Windows under a mapped account. Therefore, the level of SQL Server access is inseparable from the Windows identity of the login. It also provides single sign-on (SSO) support and integrates with all Windows authentication schemes, including Active Directory.

The DBA can configure these authentication schemes in two ways:

- Mixed Security: The login can make either a SQL Server or a Windows Integrated connection.

- Windows Only: The SQL Server does not permit non-Windows authentication.

You can configure the authentication setting by using the SQL Server Management Studio (SSMS). You can access this setting in SSMS by taking the following steps:

1. Open SQL Server Management Studio and connect to the server that you want to configure.

2. Right-click the server name in the Object Explorer window and select Properties from the shortcut menu.

3. Select the Security tab on the left side of the Properties window.

4. In the Server Authentication section of the dialog, you can select either Windows authentication mode or SQL Server and Windows authentication mode.

5. Click OK to accept your change. You will have to restart your SQL Server data engine before this change will take effect.

Understanding Schemas

A SQL Server *schema* is a logical namespace within a database. A DBA can use schemas to organize the large number of objects that a database stores as well as the permissions granted to those objects. A schema both acts as a collection of securable objects and *is* a securable object itself. Schemas provide three basic features in a database application:

Organization   Schemas provide a context of organization so that it is easier to understand larger sets of objects. For example, multiple artifacts that provide support for a specific application or department could be grouped into a single schema. Organizing objects into schemas does not change the behavior of the objects themselves, but it can provide a needed logical layer that makes large server applications understandable.

Resolution   The schema provides a resolution context for objects and users and is part of the full name of an object. For example, a

customer table in the sales schema would have a qualified name of
Sales.customer. Including the schema name in the object reference
is always a best practice in SQL Server 2008 to ensure correct user
context. To select data from the sales table, you would use this query:

```
SELECT * FROM Sales.Customer
```

Permission hierarchy   You can also use schemas to define permissions hierarchically. For example, if you wanted to grant a user permissions to select from every table in a schema, one option would
be to grant the user individual permissions for each table. If there
were 10 tables in the schema, this would require 10 separate grants.
To consolidate this action, you could simply grant the user permission on the entire schema.

You must create the schemas in the database before you can assign
users or objects to those schemas. You can do this in two different ways,
either through SSMS or through Transact SQL. To create a schema in
SSMS, use these steps:

1. Open SSMS and connect to the desired server instance.

2. Open the Databases folder and then open the folder representing
   the database into which you want to create the new schema.

3. Open the Security folder and the Schemas subfolder to display a
   list of schemas. You should see schemas such as *dbo* and *sys* in
   the list.

4. Right-click the Schemas folder and select New Schema from the
   shortcut menu. The resulting dialog provides you with a text box
   that you can use to name the schema as well as to provide for a
   schema owner. We will discuss the effects of schema ownership
   later in this chapter in the section "Permissions."

5. Click OK to create the schema.

You can also create a schema with Transact SQL code. Assuming
that you wanted to create a schema called demo that is owned by the
dbo user, you could use the following statement:

```
CREATE SCHEMA demo AUTHORIZATION dbo;
```

Security Principals

A *principal* is a SQL Server representation of an entity that has the authority to perform some action. You can configure a variety of different entities as principals. Principals exist hierarchically, and the hierarchical level of the principal affects the securables that are visible to that principal.

Windows-level principals   The highest level in the principal hierarchy is the Windows principal. The entities at this level exist as Windows entities as opposed to SQL Server entities. This level consists of the following:

- Windows domain logins/groups
- Windows local logins/groups

For example, configuring a Windows local group as a SQL Server principal provides SQL Server access to any Windows account in the group, including Windows logins, Windows domain groups, and other Windows local groups.

SQL Server–level principals   These are not Windows entities but rather SQL Server logins that are defined and authenticated by SQL Server. They do not map to any specific Windows account, and the identity of the Windows user does not impact the ability of that user to access the server using a SQL Server login.

Database-level principals   Once authenticated to the server, an entity gains access to an individual database through a database principal. These entities exist on individual databases and represent mappings of Windows or SQL Server login accounts to those individual databases. The following list includes database-level principals:

Database user   The *database user* is a mapping of an individual Windows login or group, or a SQL Server login account, to the database. Because the user can represent an authenticated collection, such as a Windows group, the database user can provide a consolidated behavior for the entire collection as well as an individual login. Database users are primarily intended as vehicles for granting database access to login accounts.

Database role   A *database role* represents a functionality or task set in the database that requires specific permissions. The database administrator aggregates permissions to the role and then associates database users with the role. Although you can assign permissions directly to users, roles provide a significantly cleaner approach for managing the permission process.

Application role   Like a database role, the *application role* aggregates permissions. Users cannot be assigned to an application role. The application invokes the role programmatically, which provides a set of permissions specific to the application. They override all user permissions to all users except administrative users.

Special principals   Some principals in each category have some unique characteristics. It is worth mentioning these special cases because you will certainly run into them later in your security designs.

The sa login   This special SQL Server principal, whose name stands for *system administrator*, has full administrative permissions on the server instance. It is automatically created when you perform a new installation of SQL Server. The sa login is usable only when you configure the server to allow SQL Server standard authentication. A new feature of SQL Server 2008 lets you rename the sa account during installation in addition to providing a password. This solves a security problem with the administrative account in prior editions of SQL Server, wherein a known account name existed that a hacker could potentially compromise.

The public role   Every database has a role called public. Every database user is automatically a member of this role, including any guest user you might provide. You can use this role to define a base level of permissions that will apply to all users on the server. This database role is fixed and you cannot remove it.

SQL Server Securables

A *securable* is a SQL Server artifact that provides some functionality to an authenticated user. Securables can exist at different levels called *scopes*, specifically *server*, *database*, and *schema*. Remember that because securables are also organized into a hierarchy, both the database and schema scopes are securables themselves. Typical securables include databases, tables, and schemas.

Permissions

Permissions represent the nexus between a principal and a securable. To provide the ability for a principal to interact with a securable, the principal must have permission for the desired action on the securable. Some securables support a variety of permissions, so each permission granted represents a single action that the principal is authorized to perform on the securable. Table 7.1 provides a list of common permissions assignable to schema scope securables.

Table 7.1: SQL Server Schema Object Permissions List

Permission	Description	Applicable Securables
SELECT	Executes a SELECT query against the securable	Synonyms Tables Views Table-valued functions
INSERT	Executes an INSERT query against the securable	Synonyms Tables Views
UPDATE	Executes an UPDATE query against the securable	Synonyms Tables Views
DELETE	Executes a DELETE query against the securable	Synonyms Tables Views
EXECUTE	Executes a procedural object	Procedures Scalar and aggregate functions Synonyms
CONTROL	Provides all permissions available on the object	Procedures All functions Tables Views Synonyms
TAKE OWNERSHIP	Takes ownership of the object if needed	Procedures All functions Tables Views Synonyms

Table 7.1: SQL Server Schema Object Permissions List *(continued)*

Permission	Description	Applicable Securables
CREATE	Creates an object	Procedures All functions Tables Views Synonyms
ALTER	Modifies an object	Procedures All functions Tables Views Synonyms

Implement Server Logins

The first step in implementing a security infrastructure is to define logins. Because logins can be either SQL Server authenticated or Windows authenticated, you must first determine which authentication scheme you will use and plan accordingly.

If you plan to implement a Windows authentication scheme of any kind, you must first create or identify the Windows accounts you will map to SQL Server. They can be either Windows user accounts or Windows group accounts, and they can include domain and Active Directory accounts. We recommend that you use Windows groups. This gives you the ability to add Windows users to SQL Server by adding them to the Windows group.

Creating Windows and SQL Server Logins

Once you have planned how the login will authenticate, you can create the principal account in SQL Server. To create the account in SSMS, use the following steps:

1. Open SSMS and connect to the server instance in which you want to create the login principal account.

2. Expand the Security folder and locate the Logins subfolder. Open this folder to view all of the current logins. You should see both the sa and the Builtin\Administrators logins in this list.

3. Right-click the Logins folder and select New Login from the shortcut menu. This will open the New Login window pictured in Figure 7.1.

Figure 7.1: The Login - New window

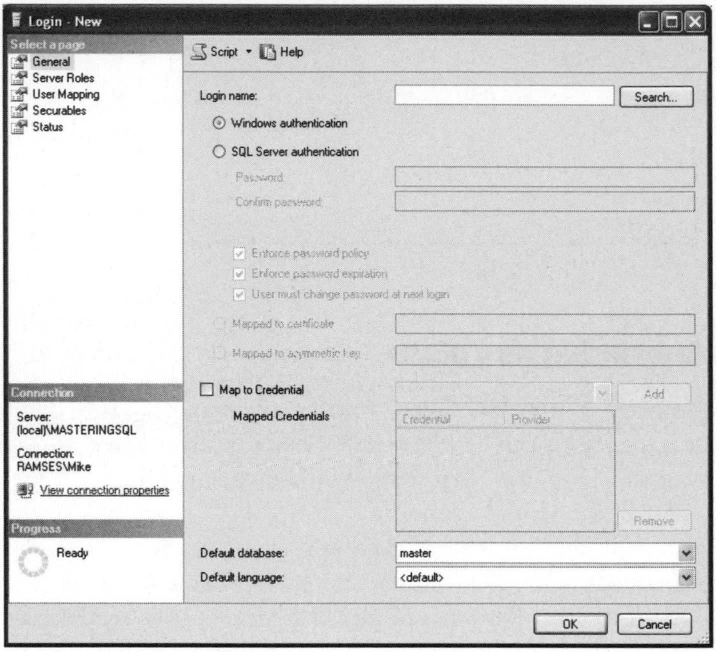

At this point, you will fill out this form in one of two slightly different ways, depending on whether you are creating a SQL Server login or a Windows login. We will look at the Windows login first:

1. In the Login Name text box, enter the full name of the Windows account to which you want to provide SQL Server access. You must enter the full name in the format *Domain\User_or_Group*. If you prefer to search for the name, click the Search button.

2. At the bottom of the screen, you will be able to specify the default database and default language of the login. The default will be the database to which the login is mapped when initially connected.

If you plan to use a SQL Server login instead of a Windows account, you will need to take these steps instead:

1. Click the option button for SQL Server authentication. This will enable the Password text boxes and the check boxes to provide password policies.

2. Enter a login name of your choosing in the Login Name text box. Remember that this name does not map to a Windows account.

3. Enter a password and confirm that password. The checkboxes below the Password text boxes will provide password policy enforcement if desired.

Scripting Login Creation

All of the options provided in SSMS are also available through TSQL code. The dialog does not map to a single TSQL statement, though. There are many TSQL commands that correlate to the functionality of this one tabbed dialog. Again, for a full description of all the options, consult the SQL Server Books Online.

The most important is the CREATE LOGIN statement. The basic syntax of the statement looks like this:

```
CREATE LOGIN loginName { WITH <options> | FROM <sources> }
```

As an example, creating a SQL Server–specific login called DemoLogin that uses a password of Pa$$w0rd would look like this:

```
CREATE LOGIN DemoLogin
WITH PASSWORD='Pa$$w0rd',
DEFAULT_DATABASE=AdventureWorks2008;
```

Alternatively, a Windows login that maps to the Windows local group called DemoUsers on a computer named Testing with the same default database would look like this:

```
CREATE LOGIN [Testing\DemoUsers]
FROM Windows
WITH DEFAULT_DATABASE=AdventureWorks2008;
```

Notice that the login name is enclosed in brackets. This format is required. In addition, there is no password because the login is trusted from Windows.

Data Integrity and Security

PART II

Implement Database Users

Remember that users are database principals. Users are mapped to logins, and as a result, the login executes all operations in a database under the identity of its mapped user account. Just as you did with logins, you can create users either with SSMS or through TSQL code.

Creating Users with SSMS

We have already shown you how to create users with the New Login dialog in SSMS. After you have created the login, you can go back to that dialog at any time by following these steps:

1. Expand the Security node in the target server in SSMS.

2. Expand the Logins node.

3. Right-click the login in the server logins list and select Properties from the shortcut menu. This will bring up the Login Properties window.

4. Click on the User Mapping page to map users directly to logins, as illustrated in Figure 7.2. This is one way to create database users.

Figure 7.2: Mapping logins to users

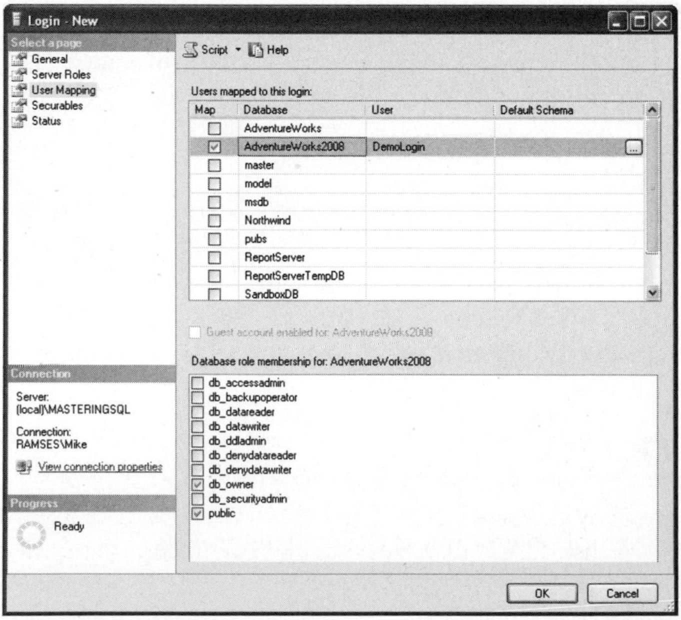

Another approach is to use the User folder within each database. To take this approach, follow these steps:

1. In SSMS, expand the Security folder of the database to which you would like to grant the login access. There you will see the Users folder.

2. Expand this Users folder to see the list of current users.

3. Right-click the Users folder and select New User from the menu. This will bring up a dialog like the one pictured in Figure 7.3.

Figure 7.3: Creating a new user in AdventureWorks2008

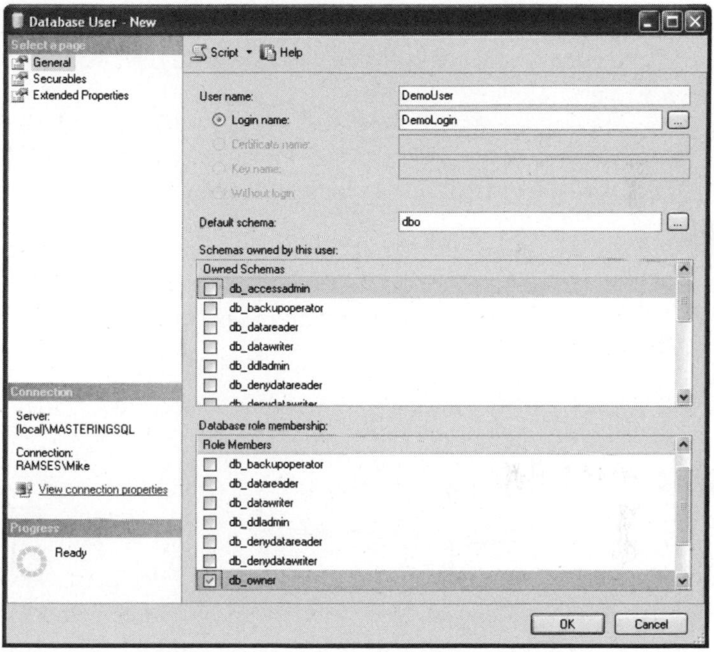

4. Enter the username and select the mapped login, as illustrated in the dialog.

5. Select any schemas that this user owns in the Schemas Owned by This User list. Each schema can be owned by only one user.

6. Select any database role association from the Database Role Membership list. This applies the permission of that rule to the user.

7. Click OK to commit your choices and close the dialog.

Scripting User Creation

To create users with TSQL, we use the CREATE USER statement. The same action illustrated in Figure 7.3 could also be coded with the following statements:

```
USE AdventureWorks2008;
CREATE USER DemoUser FOR LOGIN DemoLogin
  WITH DEFAULT_SCHEMA=dbo;
```

Associating the user with the database role requires the use of another system stored procedure. In this case, it is the sp_addrolemember procedure. This is very similar to the procedure we used to add a login to a server role. The difference with this one is that we use it to associate a database user with a database role instead. The syntax to add the DemoUser to the db_owner role would look like this:

```
USE AdventureWorks2008;
EXEC sp_addrolemember 'db_owner', 'DemoUser';
```

Once you have associated the user with a database role, the user will inherit all the permissions associated with that role. This mechanism allows a high level of flexibility in managing permissions as we will note in the section on implementing permissions.

Implement Roles

Roles are all about permissions—permissions that we don't want to assign specifically to users. With the ability to assign all needed permissions to the roles and simply associate users with roles, you can easily add and drop users from defined functionality through manipulations of role association. Server roles are nonconfigurable collections of server permissions. Configurable roles come in two flavors: database roles and application roles.

Manage Server Roles

You can associate server roles with server logins to grant specific server-level permissions to a login account. To access the server roles configuration, use these steps:

1. Expand the Security node in the target server in SSMS. Then expand the Logins node.

2. Right-click the target login in the server logins list and select Properties from the shortcut menu. This will bring up the Login Properties window.

3. Select the Server Roles page from the list on the left to open a dialog like the one pictured in Figure 7.4.

Figure 7.4: Server roles association

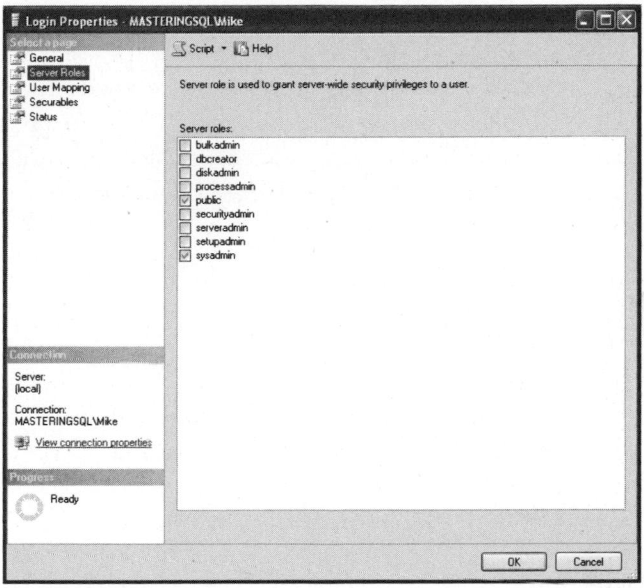

4. Select the roles that you would like to associate with the target login. Then click OK to commit your changes and close the dialog.

Each role represents a collection of permissions. The roles reflect the permissions necessary to perform common server-level tasks. Table 7.2 provides a list of server roles and a brief description of their associated permissions.

Table 7.2: Server Roles

Server Role	Description
bulkadmin	Allows the login to execute the BULK INSERT statement
dbcreator	Allows the login to create, alter, drop, and restore any database

Data Integrity and Security

PART II

Table 7.2: Server Roles *(continued)*

Server Role	Description
diskadmin	Allows the login to manage disk files
processadmin	Allows the login to terminate SQL Server processes
securityadmin	Allows the login to grant, revoke, and deny permissions on all databases as well as to reset passwords
setupadmin	Allows the login to manage linked server relationships
serveradmin	Allows the login to configure and shut down the server
sysadmin	Allows the login full administrative access to the server

Implement Database Roles

The database roles are listed in SSMS under the Security folder. To view the database roles for the AdventureWorks2008 database, use the following folder path in SSMS: `Server\Databases\AdventureWorks2008\Security\Roles\Database Roles`. To add a new custom role, use the following procedure:

1. Right-click the Database Roles folder in SSMS and select New Database Role from the menu. This will display the dialog pictured in Figure 7.5.

2. Enter the role name and owner. The owner can be any database user or another role. The owner is the principal with authority to drop and modify the role. This example uses dbo as the owner.

3. The rest of the dialog should look familiar. You can specify schemas that the role owns and add database users or other roles to the membership of this role. This dialog assigns the DemoUser to the new role.

4. The Securables tab allows the assignment of permissions at the Database and Schema scopes as in other dialogs. The Extended Properties tab also behaves identically to the Extended Properties tab in other dialogs.

You can also create a database role using TSQL code. Use the `CREATE ROLE` statement to do this. The syntax is very simple. Just define the role name and optionally an owner. We could duplicate the dialog in Figure 7.5 by using the following code statements:

```
USE AdventureWorks2008;
CREATE ROLE DemoDBRole AUTHORIZATION dbo;
EXEC sp_addrolemember DemoDBRole, DemoUser;
```

Figure 7.5: Creating a database role

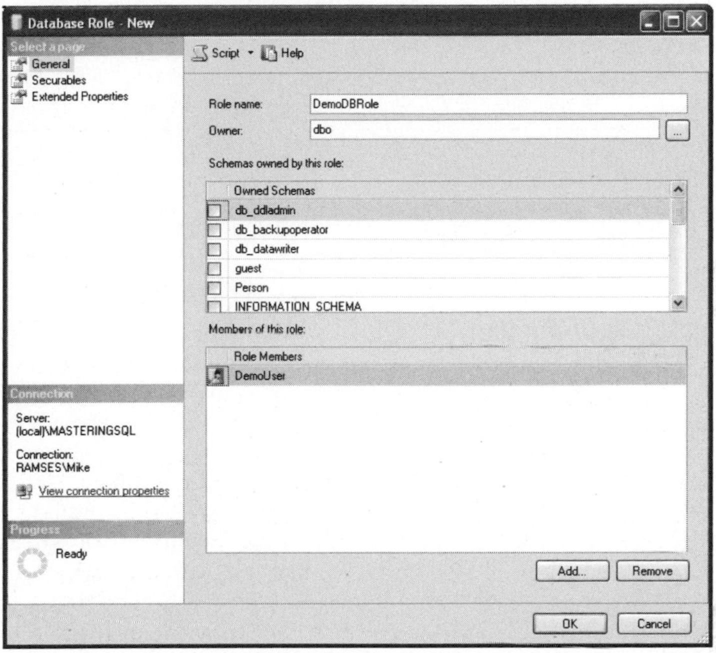

The CREATE ROLE statement generates a new role called DemoDBRole with ownership assigned to the dbo user. The subsequent system stored procedure call associates the DemoUser with the new role. Now any permissions assigned to the role will affect the user's ability to interact with objects in the database.

Implement Application Roles

Application roles differ from database roles in that you cannot assign users to application roles. In fact, SQL Server uses application roles to replace user permissions with the permissions assigned to the application role. The idea is that if you have an application that has specific requirements but you do not want to assign the rights needed by the application to specific users or database roles, you can use the application role instead.

The client application or middle tier component is responsible for activating the application role and its associated permissions. As such, the permissions belong to the application rather than the user. A user with no permissions whatsoever could still access the database through the application role. A user that has been assigned permissions that are more generous than the application role will lose those permissions when accessing through the application. Only administrative users remain unaffected.

There are three steps to using an application role:

1. Create the role.

2. Assign permissions to the role.

3. The application must activate the role to enable the permissions assigned to the role.

Creating the Application Role

An application role is little more than an identity with a password assigned to it. To create the application role, you will provide the name of the role along with a default schema and a password that the application will use to activate the role. To add an application role, use these steps:

1. Right-click the Application Roles folder under Security\Roles in the target database and select New Application Role from the shortcut menu.

2. The dialog looks like the one pictured in Figure 7.6. This example creates a new role called DemoAppRole and defines the dbo schema as its default.

3. The dialog also provides the password and confirmation. The other sections of the dialog are similar to those previously discussed.

You can also create the role using the CREATE APPLICATION ROLE TSQL statement. This statement requires a role name and a password. Optionally, you can define a default schema to the role. The statement to create the role pictured in Figure 7.6 looks like this:

```
USE AdventureWorks2008;
CREATE APPLICATION ROLE DemoAppRole
```

```
WITH PASSWORD = 'Pa$$w0rd',
DEFAULT_SCHEMA=dbo;
```

Figure 7.6: Creating the application role

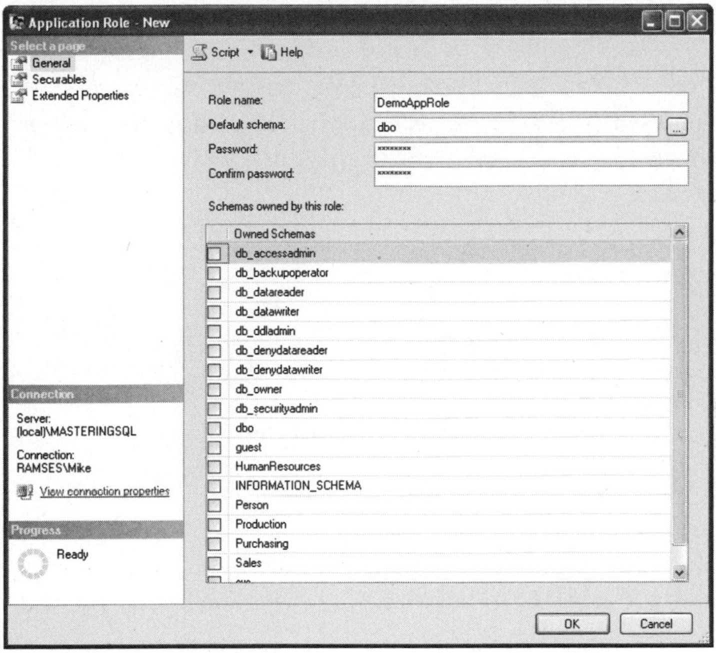

Assigning Role Permissions

You must assign permissions to the role before it is useful. The process of assigning permissions to an application role is identical to permission assignments for any other principal. We will discuss this process in detail in the section on implementing permissions.

Activating the Role

You must activate the role before the permissions associated with the role become active. To activate the application role, the client must execute the sp_setapprole system stored procedure. This call requires the name of the role and the password like this:

```
EXEC sp_setapprole DemoAppRole, 'Pa$$w0rd';
```

Data Integrity and Security

PART II

Optionally, the caller can choose to encrypt the password in transit. The default mechanism is to send the password in clear text, so it is a best practice to encrypt the password. You must meet some conditions before you can encrypt the password:

- The client must connect through ODBC. If connecting through ADO.NET, you cannot use the SQL client. You must use ODBC or the OLE DB provider for SQL Server.

- You must send the password as Unicode. To marshal the password as Unicode, preface the password in the call with the uppercase *N* character.

The following example shows the same call with an encrypted password transmission:

```
EXEC sp_setapprole @rolename = DemoAppRole, @password =
N'Pa$$w0rd', @encrypt = odbc;
```

The application role remains active until the user either closes the connection or executes the sp_unsetapprole stored procedure.

Implement Permissions

It does not do you much good to go through the bother of authenticating someone if you are not going to use that information to restrict or permit their activities. In SQL Server, permissions granted to principals on securables are the basis for all access restrictions. SQL Server manages all permissions at every scope through three TSQL statements:

- GRANT

- DENY

- REVOKE

Understand the Permissions Model

Whether you are using SSMS or TSQL to set permissions, the concepts are all the same. The functional permissions that are assigned to a principal are the aggregate permissions that are based on their association with multiple roles or permissions that may be assigned directly to the account.

The GRANT statement   The default condition for any principal is that unless it has been initially configured as an administrative principal, it has no rights to perform any action. The rights must be granted before the actions are allowed. Granting permissions is an affirmative process that provides authorization to perform an action. To perform a GRANT, you need to know three things.

- The principal
- The securable
- The permission

The principal is the security account. As you have seen in great detail in this chapter, the principal can be a server- or database-level principal. The securable is the artifact for which we are setting access rights. Finally, the permission is the specific access right, such as SELECT or EXECUTE. When you grant a permission, you are explicitly giving the principal the authority to perform an action dictated by the permission.

The DENY statement   If a grant is an affirmative process, a DENY is the polar opposite. It explicitly prevents the principal from acquiring the authority to perform an action, even if that authority is defined somewhere else. The deny is, therefore, used as a negation flag. In other words, all permissions must be unanimous in the affirmative before SQL Server will allow the action. Even one DENY will prevent the action.

The REVOKE statement   The REVOKE statement removes all permissions, including GRANT and DENY, and returns the principal to its original state of having no permissions at all. Think of the REVOKE as a permission eraser. No matter what you have done with permissions, the REVOKE will take you back to square one.

Manage Permissions through SSMS

Because permissions represent many-to-many relationships between principals and securables, you can come at this problem from two different directions. You could start with the principal and configure the access that you want it to have on all available securables. Alternatively, you can start with the securable and decide which permissions you want to assign to it for each principal. It doesn't matter which direction you choose. You will get exactly the same result either way, so it is a matter of preference or convenience.

You can configure permissions on a securable as you create the principal. If you want to go back and modify these permissions later, you will use the same dialog. For example, assume that you wanted to grant the role DemoDBRole in the AdventureWorks2008 database the right to select from the Person.Person table. You would take the following steps:

1. Locate the role in the Database Roles list under the Security\ Roles path in SSMS. Right-click on the role to open the Role Properties dialog.

2. Click the Securables page on the left of the screen to open the securables configuration.

3. To locate the Person.Person table, click the Search button. The dialog allows you to browse all objects, only objects of a specific type, or only objects belonging to a specific schema. You could locate the table using any of these techniques. Select All Objects of the Types ... and click OK.

4. This dialog allows you to select the type of object you want to secure. Note that this list will be different depending on the scope of the principal. Select the Table checkbox and click OK. This will populate the securables list with tables.

5. Locate the Person.Person table in the list and select it. This will activate the bottom pane with permissions for that table. Click the box to grant a SELECT permission, as pictured in Figure 7.7.

6. Click OK to close the dialog. The permission is now set.

You can take a similar approach when configuring permissions through the securable. To perform exactly the same operation through the securable, use these steps instead:

1. Locate the Person.Person table in the tables list in SSMS. Right-click the table and choose Properties. This will open the Table Properties dialog.

2. Click the Permissions page on the left of the screen to open the permissions configuration. You will need to find the role in the top pane by clicking the Search button.

3. Click Browse to open a list of applicable principals at this level of scope and locate the DemoDBRole. Click the check box next to the role and click OK.

4. Click OK in the Select Users or Roles dialog, and this will add the DemoDBRole to the top pane of the Permissions dialog.

5. Select the DemoDBRole in the top pane to activate the permissions for that role in the bottom pane. Click the checkbox to grant SELECT permissions, as pictured in Figure 7.8.

6. Click OK on the Table Properties dialog to close the window. The permissions are now set.

Figure 7.7: Setting permissions through the principal

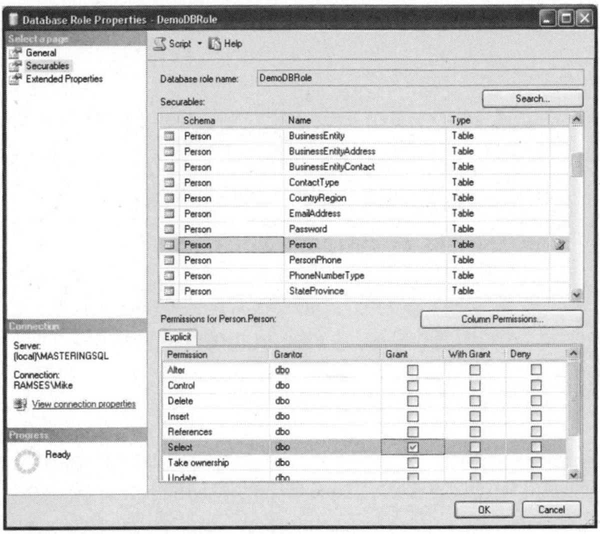

Figure 7.8: Setting permissions through the securable

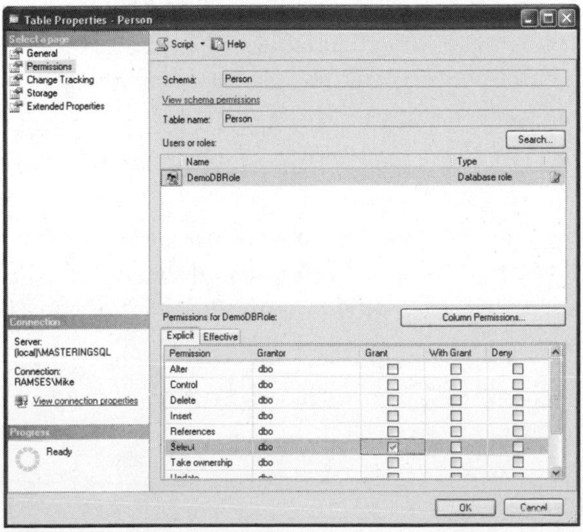

Also, note that at the database scope, there are numerous permissions that we call statement permissions. These are not permissions to access objects but rather to do things such as creating and altering objects. If you look at the Permissions tab of the Database Properties window, you will see numerous statement permissions for the database. These are also important permissions if you want to control who can execute Data Definition Language (DDL) statements.

Manage Permissions through a Transact SQL Script

The whole permissions functionality is primarily provided with three TSQL statements: GRANT, DENY, and REVOKE. All of these statements follow the same general pattern:

```
{GRANT|REVOKE|DENY} <permission>
  ON <Securable> {TO|FROM} <principal>
```

As an example, if you wanted to grant SELECT permissions on the Person.Person table to the DemoDBRole, the code would look like this:

```
GRANT SELECT ON Person.Person TO DemoDBRole;
```

You also have some special options that you can include. If necessary, you can give the grantee the right to grant the same permission to others. This is called a *grant option*. The code is the same; simply reference the grant option at the end of the statement, like this:

```
GRANT SELECT ON Person.Person TO DemoDBRole WITH GRANT OPTION;
```

To explicitly deny SELECT permission on that table to the DemoDBRole principal, the code would be very similar. We just use the command for deny instead of grant, like this:

```
DENY SELECT ON Person.Person TO DemoDBRole;
```

Logically, whatever you grant or deny, you must be able to revoke. If you had either granted or denied SELECT permission on the Person. Person table to the DemoDBRole, you could remove those permissions with the following statement:

```
REVOKE SELECT On Person.Person FROM DemoDBRole;
```

If you have granted the permission with a grant option, you must also decide what to do with the permissions that the principal from whom you are revoking permissions has granted. For example, if you granted Paulette SELECT permissions on Person.Person with a grant option through the DemoDBRole and then she grants the SELECT permission to Bob, what happens when we revoke the permission from the DemoDBRole? Is it still safe for Bob to have those permissions? SQL Server says no, and you must use the CASCADE keyword in the revoke to revoke the permission from Bob as well. The statement looks like this:

```
REVOKE SELECT On Person.Person FROM DemoDBRole CASCADE;
```

You can also revoke just the grant option without actually revoking the permission entirely. If you want to revoke the grant option only from the DemoDBRole and do not want to revoke the actual SELECT permission, you would use this code:

```
REVOKE GRANT OPTION FOR SELECT ON Person.Person
    FROM DemoDBRole Cascade;
```

Statement permissions work a little differently because there is no securable. The permission itself is the securable. If you want to grant the DemoDBRole permissions to create stored procedures, for example, you do not have a target securable. You just want to grant permission to use the statement. The syntax would look like this:

```
GRANT CREATE PROCEDURE TO DemoDBRole;
```

To find the names of the statement permissions that you can use, either look them up in SQL Server Books Online or go to SSMS. The names of the permissions in SSMS dialogs are the same names that you would use in your code.

Encrypt Data with Keys

Although not directly related to user security, it is also important at times that you obfuscate your data. If you are storing very sensitive information such as credit card numbers or security-related data, you have to be concerned about not only who can get access to the data through data database but also the security of the data in transport and in storage.

Microsoft SQL Server 2008 supports a variety of encryption options to further protect your data. These include explicit encryption of data through symmetric and asymmetric keys and certificates, and implicit encryption through the new Transparent Data Encryption (TDE) feature.

Understand SQL Server Keys

SQL Server uses keys to manage its encryption infrastructure. A typical SQL Server key environment might contain the following keys:

Service master key   A service master key is created when you install SQL Server 2008. This key is the "root" key for all other keys on a service instance and ensures that all keys defined in any one service instance are independent from all other service instances. SQL Server manages this key, so you have no particular responsibility with regard to the service master key other than backing it up, but you should be aware that it exists and is the basis for all other keys that you create on the instance.

Database master key   The database master key is the base key for all keys that you create in a database. This key is protected by the service master key. SQL Server does not automatically create the key, so you must create it before you create any other keys or certificates in SQL Server. Once you create it, you must make sure you back it up. You will not be able to regenerate an identical key again, and if you lose this key, all other keys will be useless.

Asymmetric keys   An asymmetric key structure provides a private key/public key infrastructure for encryption. SQL Server makes the public key available to clients but will keep the private key secure. These keys are inverse of each other, so data that the public key encrypts can be decrypted only by the private key. The reverse is also true.

Symmetric keys   Symmetric keys use a common key infrastructure. This means that both the client and the server use the same key, which can both encrypt and decrypt data. This is less secure than an asymmetric key model, but it is simple and easy to implement.

Certificates   SQL Server certificates are valid for both authentication and encryption. One advantage of a certificate is that it stores identifying information about the sender. It is also a highly secure mechanism for encrypting information in transport.

Manage SQL Server Keys

Although the process is simple, you must get in the habit of managing the various keys that are part of this infrastructure. In some cases, you must actually create the keys. In others, you will be responsible for backing up and restoring the keys. Let's look at each of the keys and see what your responsibilities are for each.

The Service Master Key

Your primary responsibility for the service master key will be to back up the key and restore it if necessary. You will do this through TSQL code. When backing up the key, you will specify the location of the backup file and provide a password for the key that you must supply to restore the key. The following code makes a backup of the service master key:

```
USE master;

BACKUP SERVICE MASTER KEY TO FILE = 'C:\Keys\SM.bak'
   ENCRYPTION BY PASSWORD = 'P@ssw0rd';
GO
```

If the service master key becomes corrupt or you must rebuild a service instance, you must restore the service master key for the existing encrypted resources to be available. When you restore a service master key, all of the existing encrypted resources are decrypted with the current key and then encrypted with the restored key. The code looks like this:

```
USE master;

RESTORE SERVICE MASTER KEY FROM FILE = 'C:\Keys\SM.bak'
   DECRYPTION BY PASSWORD = 'P@ssw0rd';
GO
```

If the system cannot locate or decrypt existing resources, the restore fails. To force the new key into place regardless, use the FORCE option immediately after the password in the previous syntax.

The Database Master Key

The first task is to create the database master key because SQL Server does not automatically create this key for you. SQL Server encrypts the database master key and stores it internally, so you do not have to specify a storage location. The syntax looks like this:

```
USE AdventureWorks2008;

CREATE MASTER KEY ENCRYPTION BY PASSWORD = 'P@ssw0rd';
GO
```

Once you create the key, SQL Server will automatically use it to protect all database-level keys and certificates. Without this key, every other key in the database is useless, so you should back up this key as well. The following code backs up the database master key:

```
USE AdventureWorks2008;

BACKUP MASTER KEY TO FILE = 'C:\Keys\DM.bak'
  ENCRYPTION BY PASSWORD = 'P@ssw0rd';
GO
```

NOTE Note that although the password we used to create the key and back up the key in this example are the same, this is not required. The password that you supply when you create the key is used to protect the key internally. The password that you provide when backing up the key protects the backup.

You can drop a database master key from a database at any time, but be aware that if you have created other keys in the database and encrypted data with those keys, you must have the database master key to decrypt the data, so be careful. Dropping a database master key is accomplished using this code:

```
USE AdventureWorks2008;

DROP MASTER KEY;
GO
```

Once you have dropped the key, you can restore it from the backup. The restore syntax is very similar to the code that you used to restore a service master key except that you will provide two passwords. You need the password used to protect the backup as well as the password that you will assign to protect the key in storage. The syntax looks like this:

```
USE AdventureWorks2008;

RESTORE MASTER KEY FROM FILE = 'C:\Keys\DM.bak'
   DECRYPTION BY PASSWORD = 'P@ssw0rd' -- Password of the
backup
   ENCRYPTION BY PASSWORD = 'P@ssw0rd';-- Password in storage
GO
```

Asymmetric Keys

These keys represent a public key/private key pair. You have many options for creating the key. The key pair can be imported from a file or from a signed assembly. Alternatively, you can generate a new key pair and protect it with a password. If you already had the key pair stored in a file, you could use code like the following. Please note that this code will not work unless there is a valid key pair stored in the target file. This example creates a key that is owned by the dbo user:

```
USE AdventureWorks2008;

CREATE ASYMMETRIC KEY AsmDemo AUTHORIZATION dbo
   FROM FILE = 'c:\Keys\Asm.key'
   ENCRYPTION BY PASSWORD = 'P@ssw0rd';
GO
```

The advantage of creating a key from an existing stored key pair is that you can easily re-create the key again at any time should you need to. You also have more control over the generation of the key.

The other option is to generate a new key pair by executing the statement without the FROM clause. If you use this approach, you must provide the encryption algorithm in the code. You can use 512-, 1024-, or 2048-bit RSA encryption. This code demonstrates a new key pair using a 2048-bit RSA encryption:

```
USE AdventureWorks2008;

CREATE ASYMMETRIC KEY AsmDemo
   WITH ALGORITHM = RSA_2048
```

```
        ENCRYPTION BY PASSWORD = 'P@ssw0rd';
    GO
```

Once you add the key, you should be able to see the key in the Object Explorer window in SSMS, as pictured in Figure 7.9. Note that you will see folders for asymmetric keys, symmetric keys, and certificates, so you can repeat this step for every key type.

Figure 7.9: Viewing the asymmetric key

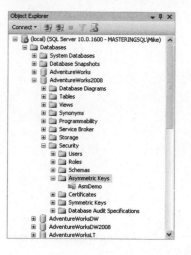

You can also drop the key from the SSMS using these steps:

1. Locate the key you wish to drop in the Server Explorer window.

2. Right-click the desired key and select Delete.

3. Click OK in the dialog to commit the action and close the dialog.

As an alternative, you can also use this code to drop a key:

```
    USE AdventureWorks2008;

    DROP ASYMMETRIC KEY AsmDemo;
    GO
```

Symmetric Keys

You can create a symmetric key by specifying a pass phrase from which the key will be derived, or you can simply indicate the algorithm and let SQL Server generate a key for you. If you want to be able to re-create the key again later, you should use a pass phrase; however, the syntax is simpler if you let SQL Server generate the key for you. You can use a variety of different encryption algorithms. The most popular are listed here:

- TRIPLE_DES (128-bit key)
- TRIPLE_DES_3KEY (192-bit key)
- AES_128
- AES_192
- AES_256

The following code creates a symmetric key using a 256-bit AES encryption algorithm. This example is protected with a password, but it could also be protected with a certificate or asymmetric key:

```
USE AdventureWorks2008;

CREATE SYMMETRIC KEY SymDemo
  WITH ALGORITHM = AES_256
  ENCRYPTION BY PASSWORD = 'P@ssw0rd';
GO
```

If you choose to use a pass phrase, SQL Server will build the key based on it. This will allow you to re-create the key again at any time as needed. The following code illustrates this approach:

```
USE AdventureWorks2008;

CREATE SYMMETRIC KEY SymDemoPass
    WITH ALGORITHM = AES_128,
    KEY_SOURCE = 'Sample encryption passphrase',
    IDENTITY_VALUE = 'Typing_101'
    ENCRYPTION BY PASSWORD = 'P@ssw0rd';
GO
```

To drop the key, you can either use the SSMS as previously described in the previous section or execute a TSQL statement. A symmetric key must be closed before you can drop it, so you might need to close the key before executing the DROP statement as in the following example. However, if the key is not open, this statement will return an error:

```
CLOSE SYMMETRIC KEY SymDemo;
DROP SYMMETRIC KEY SymDemo;
GO
```

Certificates

Certificates are asymmetric in nature and can be either generated by SQL Server or imported from an external file or a signed SQL Server assembly. In addition to the keys, certificates contain other metadata and can be used for authentication as well as encryption. To create a self-signed certificate, use code like the following:

```
USE AdventureWorks2008;

CREATE CERTIFICATE CertDemo
  ENCRYPTION BY PASSWORD = 'P@ssw0rd'
  WITH SUBJECT = 'Demo Certificate',
  START_DATE = '1/1/2009',
  EXPIRY_DATE = '10/31/2009';
GO
```

As with an asymmetric key, you can load the certificate from an external file. For example, assume that you had a certificate file from a valid certification agency and you wanted to create a SQL Server certificate using that content. You would use code like the following example. Again, this code will work only if you have a valid certificate file and a corresponding private key file. The password included is the password that the certification agency gave you to open and install the certificate:

```
USE AdventureWorks2008;

CREATE CERTIFICATE CertDemoFile
    FROM FILE = 'c:\Certs\DemoCertFile.cer'
    WITH PRIVATE KEY (FILE = 'c:\Certs\DemoCertFile.pvk',
    DECRYPTION BY PASSWORD = 'P@ssw0rd');
GO
```

As before, you either drop a certificate using the SSMS as previously described or use TSQL code. The code to drop a certificate looks like this:

```
USE AdventureWorks2008;

DROP CERTIFICATE CertDemoFile;
GO
```

Encrypt and Decrypt Data with Keys

Once you have created the key, using it to encrypt data is a very simple process. SQL Server supports functions that you can use to perform the encryption and decryption. All you need to know is the ID of the key that you plan to use for the process.

Encrypting and Decrypting with Asymmetric Keys

You will use the function `EncryptByAsymKey` to perform the encryption. Likewise, the `DecryptByAsymKey` function provides the support for description. Before using these functions, you must know the SQL Server ID of the desired key. The easiest way to get that information is by using the `sys.asymmetric_keys` system view like this:

```
USE AdventureWorks2008;

SELECT asymmetric_key_id
FROM sys.asymmetric_keys
WHERE name = 'AsmDemo';
GO
```

You will use the ID number that this query returns to perform the encryption. If you gave your asymmetric key a different name than the one in our example, replace the name with your name in the preceding code.

The following code demonstrates a complete encryption and decryption loop. This code performs the following tasks:

- Extracts the key ID number from the `sys.asymmetric_keys` system view

- Uses the key to encrypt a string and store it in the `@encData` variable

- Decrypts the value in the `@encData` variable and stores it in the `@clearData` variable

- Selects both variables so that you can see the effect of the encryption process

Here is the code:

```
USE AdventureWorks2008;
```

```
DECLARE @encData varchar(8000);
DECLARE @clearData varchar(8000);
DECLARE @id int;

SELECT @id = asymmetric_key_id
FROM sys.asymmetric_keys
WHERE name = 'AsmDemo';

SET @encData = ENCRYPTBYASYMKEY (@id, 'Hello World');
SET @clearData = DECRYPTBYASYMKEY(@id, @encData, N'P@ssw0rd')

SELECT @encData;
SELECT @clearData;
GO
```

In this example, you will notice that the decryption routine requires a password. This is the same password that you used when you created the key. You must provide this password when explicitly decrypting data. For this reason, this process is usually encapsulated into an encrypted stored procedure.

Encrypting and Decrypting with Symmetric Keys

Symmetric keys work a little differently because they use a common key infrastructure. One difference is that you must open the key before you can use it; therefore, you should always get in the habit of closing the key when you are done with it. Another difference is that the symmetric keys are identified internally using a globally unique identifier (GUID), so we have a function called KEY_GUID to identify the key by name.

The following code illustrates a similar "round trip" using the symmetric key instead of the asymmetric key to perform the encryption:

```
USE AdventureWorks2008;

DECLARE @encData varchar(8000);
DECLARE @clearData varchar(8000);

OPEN SYMMETRIC KEY SymDemoPass
  DECRYPTION BY PASSWORD = 'P@ssw0rd';

SET @encData = ENCRYPTBYKEY
  (Key_GUID('SymDemoPass'), 'Hello World');
```

```
SET @clearData = DECRYPTBYKEY(@encData);

SELECT @encData;
SELECT @clearData;

CLOSE SYMMETRIC KEY SymDemoPass
GO
```

Encrypting and Decrypting with Certificates

Since a certificate is an asymmetric mechanism, the syntax to encrypt and decrypt data with a certificate is very similar to using the asymmetric key. Although this option provides for the highest level of security, it also requires the highest overhead, so use it with caution.

In the following code, the same "round trip" is demonstrated with the CertDemo certificate that we created in the previous code examples. Notice the similarity to the asymmetric encryption:

```
USE AdventureWorks2008;

DECLARE @encData varchar(8000);
DECLARE @clearData varchar(8000);
DECLARE @id int;

SELECT @id = certificate_id
FROM sys.certificates
WHERE name = 'CertDemo';

SET @encData = ENCRYPTBYCERT (@id, 'Hello World');
SET @clearData = DECRYPTBYCERT(@id, @encData, N'P@ssw0rd')

SELECT @encData;
SELECT @clearData;
GO
```

Implement Transparent Data Encryption

Although you have seen in the previous examples that you can control encryption and decryption of data as you read and write from a database, it should be obvious that this is a lot of extra code if you want to encrypt and decrypt all data as you move it in and out of the database. Imagine how much work it would be to include encryption and decryption in every single database call.

The solution is Transparent Data Encryption (TDE). This technique allows you to create a database encryption key based on a certificate. SQL Server can then use this key to encrypt and decrypt all data as you read and write from the database with no further action on your part or a database developer's part. To set up this feature, you should do the following (not all of these steps are required, but we recommend that you do all of them):

1. Back up the service master key
2. Create and back up the database master key
3. Create and back up a certificate in the database
4. Create a database encryption key based on the certificate
5. Configure the database to use TDE

The certificate that you use to create the database encryption key must adhere to these requirements:

- The certificate must reside in the master database.
- The certificate must have a configured private key.
- The private key must be encrypted by the database master key in the master database.

The previous CertDemoFile example illustrates how to create the appropriate certificate. When creating the database encryption key, you can choose from any of the following encryption algorithms:

- AES_128
- AES_192
- AES_256
- TRIPLE_DES_3KEY

Assuming that you want to use the AES_256 algorithm and that the database encryption key will be based on the CertDemoFile certificate, you would use this code to create the key in the database. Note that there can be only one database encryption key in each database and

that the certificate must reside in the master database, so create the
certificate in that database if necessary:

```
USE AdventureWorks2008;

CREATE DATABASE ENCRYPTION KEY
WITH ALGORITHM = AES_256
ENCRYPTION BY SERVER CERTIFICATE CertDemoFile
GO
```

Once you have created the database encryption key, you must enable
the database to support TDE. This is a simple query, as follows:

```
ALTER DATABASE AdventureWorks2008
SET ENCRYPTION ON;
GO
```

Once the database is enabled, SQL Server will use the encryption key
to encrypt all data going in and out of it. This sounds like a great thing,
but be careful of the following issues:

- Enabling TDE will result in a performance degradation on all IO.

- If you lose your keys for any reason, you will not be able to recover
  any of the data in the database.

- TDE also encrypts backups, so if you want to restore a backup on
  another server, you must have the appropriate key infrastructure
  in place.

PART III

Data
Administration

Data Administration

PART III

8

Implementing Availability and Replication

IN THIS CHAPTER, YOU WILL LEARN TO DO THE FOLLOWING:

Data Administration

PART III

I t is not just enough to keep your data safe with its integrity intact. You also have to make it available to everyone who needs it, and sometimes that can pose challenges. Making sure you always have data available to your consumers and ensuring that it's distributed to the parties who need it should be central to your planning. In this chapter, we will assume the following definitions to these terms.

Availability *Availability* is the characteristic of a database that relates to its uptime. Losing access to a database can cause significant business problems. Without the database, many business processes cannot continue. An availability solution focuses on the steps necessary to minimize downtime. This might include providing for necessary hardware redundancy as well as data redundancy to guarantee that data systems are available when client applications need them.

Distribution *Data distribution* is the process of placing data geographically based on the data needs or the performance requirements of the application. Distributing data is one way to offload activity from transactional data stores or reduce bandwidth requirements when many applications are interacting with data in a central location.

Data distribution is similar to availability in one respect. Like availability, distribution can also involve data redundancy and therefore requires some mechanism to maintain data synchronization.

Implement Availability Solutions

Any availability solution must provide for both hardware availability and data availability. One is not a replacement for the other any more than a database backup is a replacement for an effective availability strategy. A complete discussion of hardware strategies is beyond the scope of this book, but you should consider hardware-based availability as an important component of any availability architecture.

Data availability requires planning and implementation at the SQL Server configuration level. Common approaches to data availability include log shipping and database mirroring. Both hardware and data availability are critical to an overall availability strategy. In the following sections, we will overview basic concepts of hardware availability and then look in more detail at data availability configuration.

Understand RAID

RAID, or Redundant Array of Independent Disks, also sometimes called Redundant Array of Inexpensive Disks (the original term for the technology), is a technique by which an operating system or hardware IO system uses multiple hard drives to distribute data across multiple disks in an effort to provide fault tolerance and/or performance benefits. An administrator can employ various RAID strategies. The following are the most common:

RAID-0: striped set without parity   This option is primarily intended to optimize performance. In this scenario, the RAID controller spreads the data stream across two or more physical disks. The objective is to improve performance by placing data on multiple disks simultaneously, thus eliminating the potential I/O bottleneck of writing to a single physical disk. This option provides no fault tolerance since a single disk failure destroys the entire array and there is no parity information stored on the other disks that you can use to regenerate the lost drive.

RAID-1: mirrored set   RAID-1 provides fault tolerance by duplicating all data writes to a mirror disk. If the data device is lost, the mirror provides a copy of the lost data and thus minimizes downtime. A good RAID controller will use both disks for read operations, therefore increasing the performance for read operations; however, using both disks adversely affects write operations due to the increased write activity.

RAID-5: striped set with parity   This solution stripes data access across three or more physical disks, similar to the RAID-0 solution. Unlike with RAID-0, however, the controller also writes distributed parity data across the striped set so that the loss of a drive would not result in the loss of the database. The controller can use the parity information to respond to requests until an administrator is able to regenerate a new disk based on the parity data. In this configuration, the array is still vulnerable to the loss of a second drive. This solution also can adversely affect write performance because of the extra I/O required to calculate and write the parity data, though this can be offset somewhat by the distribution of data across multiple physical disks.

Data Administration

PART III

You can also combine these levels to provide options that are more complex.

- RAID-01 (0 + 1): mirror of striped sets
- RAID-10 (1 + 0): striped mirror sets
- RAID-50 (5 + 0): parity striped mirror sets

There are other RAID options, but these are the most common. Always remember that the goal is to ensure adequate availability without compromising performance beyond acceptable levels. Any fault tolerance always comes at a cost. It is the job of the administrator to find the right balance.

NOTE   Although the Windows operating system supports various software-based RAID solutions, they are not reasonable performance alternatives to a hardware-based solution. There are a variety of vendors that support RAID at the hardware level. Do your research and find the vendor that offers a solution that provides the balance of cost, features, and manageability that makes sense for your environment. Since each vendor configuration is different, we will not address the specific configuration in this book, but you should consider it as part of an overall availability strategy.

Understand Clustering

While RAID provides fault tolerance from disk failure, it provides no protection against other faults, such as memory, CPU, or I/O controller failures. By contrast, clustering can provide effective protection from hardware failures other than disk failures. As with RAID, there are many different configuration options available for clustering. The features and benefits of a particular implementation become selling points for the hardware or software vendor that provides the solution.

An in-depth discussion of clustering technology is beyond the scope of this book, but you should be aware of the clustering options that Windows supports as well as how SQL Server behaves on those clusters.

In SQL Server terminology, *cluster* refers to a failover cluster only. This means that SQL Server cannot use the cluster for load balancing—only redundancy. The most common approach is to create a two-node active/passive cluster. This requires two servers connected to a single array of disks. Clients direct activity to a "virtual" address, which represents the cluster rather than any individual server in the cluster.

Only one of the servers will actively respond to requests. The other server, which is the passive node, monitors the "heartbeat" of the active node so that it can detect if the active node fails to respond. This would trigger an automatic failover, redirecting activity to the second node. Failover clustering has the following benefits:

- Automatic detection and failover

- Ability to perform manual failover

- Transparency to the client of failover redirection

There are constraints when using clustering, however. You must license at least the Standard Edition of SQL Server, which supports two-node clusters. The Enterprise Edition allows additional nodes as configured by the operating system. Additionally, you must work within the following limitations:

- Clustering operates at the server level of scope. You cannot fail over an individual database.

- There is no protection against disk failure. You should continue to use RAID for disk fault tolerance.

- The cluster performs no load balancing. Only the active node can be queried.

- The cluster requires signed hardware capable of working with the Windows version that you are targeting.

For clustering in Windows Server 2008, there are a few new features that can benefit SQL Server. If you're using the Enterprise versions of Windows and SQL Server, you can support up to 16 nodes in your cluster. In addition, Windows Server 2008 removes the requirement that all cluster nodes reside in the same subnet, thus opening the door to increased geographical distribution of cluster nodes. In a geographically dispersed architecture, nodes complete with arrays can be configured in different geographical locations, thus creating full server redundancy, including array redundancy.

Implement Log Shipping

The goal of *database log shipping* is to create a warm standby server that you can promote to a primary server upon server failure. As a warm standby, it is not completely current; it's current only to the last transaction log that you have shipped and restored to the server. You can use the warm standby for reporting purposes, but you cannot make any data modification to the server. It is read-only.

One advantage of the log shipping model is that you can configure multiple target servers. Since each server can be used for reporting purposes, this can be an effective technique for both availability and distribution of data. This is also an easy solution to configure and maintain.

The primary disadvantage is the latency between the time that the transaction commits on the master server and the time when the master ships and restores the log to the target server(s). There is also the potential of some data loss.

Configuring log shipping is a simple process. You can easily manage the process through the SQL Server Management Studio (SSMS). The basic steps are as follows:

1. Configure the primary and target servers to support transaction log backups.

2. Take a full database backup on the primary server.

3. Restore the full database backup on the target server with NORECOVERY or STANDBY option selected.

4. Configure the log shipping scenario in the SSMS, which will schedule the backups and log shipping through jobs.

5. Optionally configure a monitor server to record log shipping events and errors.

In the following sections, we will look at each of these steps in more detail. We will begin by performing the server and database configuration. Some of these steps require that you perform backup and restore operations. If you need guidance through theses steps, please consult Chapter 10, "Managing Data Recovery."

This example will also require three server instances. We have created a default instance on a computer called MasteringSQL and installed two named instances called MasteringSQL\PrimaryServer and MasteringSQL\SecondaryServer. The default instance will act as a monitor server. If you need guidance installing instances, please refer to Chapter 1, "Installing SQL Server 2008." You should also create two file shares in advance, one in which to place the backups from the primary database and one to store the copied backups on the secondary server.

Downloading the Pubs Database

To reduce complexity, in our examples of log shipping and database mirroring, we will use the pubs sample database provided by Microsoft. You should be able to find this download at www.microsoft.com/downloads. Search for "Northwind and pubs Sample Databases for SQL Server 2000." Even though the databases are intended for SQL Server 2000, they will install just fine in SQL Server 2008. You will be downloading an MSI file. Executing the MSI will create a folder with the installation scripts at C:\ SQL Server 2000 Sample Databases. Run the instpubs.sql script on your SQL 2008 instance to create the pubs database.

Preparing the Servers and Databases

The master or primary database is your production environment. You will do the initial configuration of each server individually on that server, but you will perform all configuration for the actual log shipping behavior from the SSMS on the primary server. To prepare the servers, perform the following tasks:

1. Connect to the MasteringSQL\PrimaryServer instance in SSMS.

2. Configure the primary database to support the full or bulk logged recovery model by right-clicking the pubs database and selecting Properties.

3. Select the Options page in the dialog and set the Recovery Model option to either Full or Bulk-Logged (see Figure 8.1).

4. Click OK to close the dialog and commit the changes.

5. Perform a full database backup of the pubs database on the primary server. Consult Chapter 10 for specific instructions.

6. Connect to the MasteringSQL\SecondaryServer instance in SSMS.

7. Restore the backup of pubs from the primary instance to the secondary instance. You have two options on the restore, depending on if you want the secondary server to be queryable:

   NORECOVERY Restoring the database with this option allows you to restore additional transaction logs to the database but does not allow client applications to query the database. This is the most efficient approach to log shipping because the database does not have to roll back any uncommitted transactions after loading the database backup or any additional transaction log backups. Using the NORECOVERY option means you cannot use the server for any reporting and it will play no role in a data distribution model. It is strictly for availability only.

Figure 8.1: Setting the recovery model

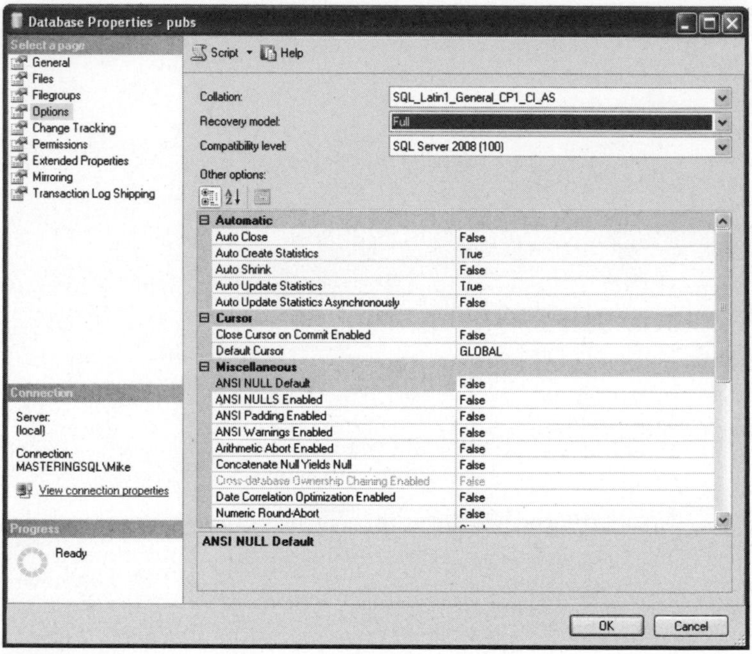

STANDBY When you restore the database with this option, the server rolls back any uncommitted transactions and places them into an "undo" file. These are then saved so that they can be recommitted to the database before any additional transaction log backups are restored. Because all transactions are in a consistent state after the uncommitted transactions are rolled back, the database is available for reporting and querying purposes, making it a potential player in a data distribution strategy. This higher-overhead approach requires additional resources when the log restoration process takes place.

Configuring Log Shipping

To configure log shipping, follow these steps:

1. Open SSMS and connect the Object Explorer to the primary server.

2. Right-click the pubs database in the primary server and select Properties.

3. Select the Transaction Log Shipping page in the menu on the left. This will display the dialog pictured in Figure 8.2.

Figure 8.2: The log shipping dialog

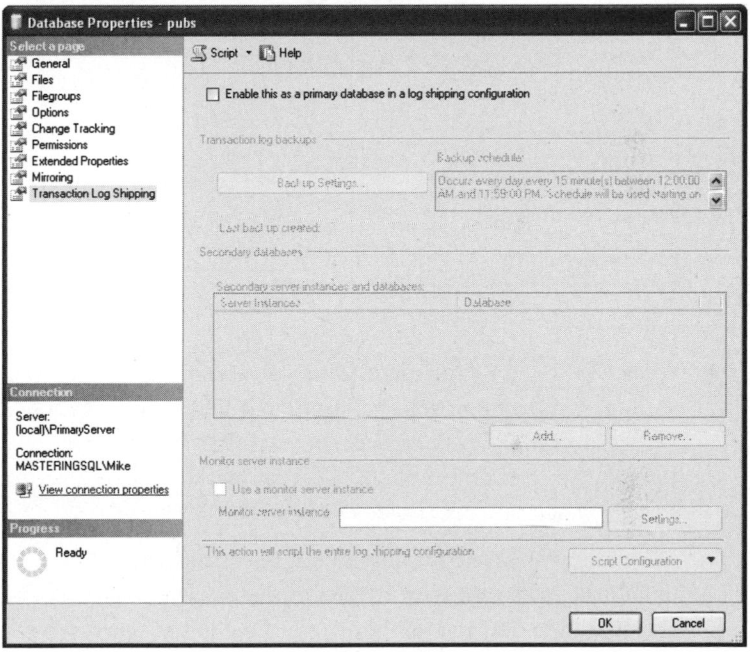

4. Click the check box at the top of the dialog to begin the configuration process and enable the Backup Settings button on the page.

5. Click the Backup Settings button to open the dialog pictured in Figure 8.3. This dialog will provide the information needed to perform the transaction log backups, including the location of the backups and the retention time.

Figure 8.3: Configuring backup settings

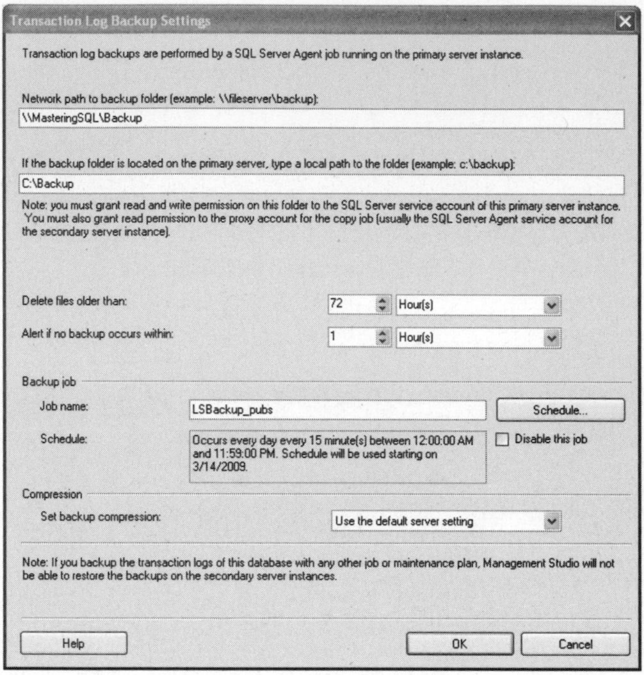

6. Click the Schedule button midway down this dialog to open a standard SQL Agent scheduling dialog where you can specify how often the system will perform the backups. If you want to rename the job, you can do that here. This job will run on the primary server. When you are finished, click OK.

7. Now that you have configured your backup settings, SQL Server will enable the Add button under the Secondary Databases section. Use this button to add and configure all of the target servers to which you will ship and restore the logs. Click the button to present the dialog pictured in Figure 8.4, which defaults to the first of three tabs.

8. Before you will be able to access any of the tabs, you must connect to the target server. Click the Connect button to set the server instance and database that will be the target. The first tab will then allow you to specify how to do the initial synchronization. You have three options:

   ▪ Have the system perform a database backup and restore that backup to the target server.

- Restore an already existing database backup to the target server.

- Do nothing (if you have already synchronized the two servers with a backup).

Figure 8.4: Log shipping initialization

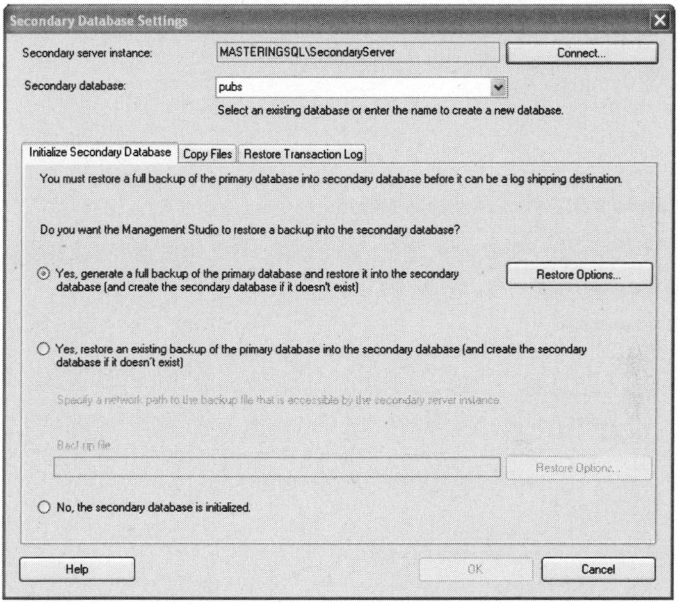

If you did not perform the backup and restore steps before you started the log shipping configuration process, you will choose the first option to perform the synchronization for you. Whether this will be done with the STANDBY or NORECOVERY option will be determined in a later step. If you already performed these tasks, choose the third option.

9. If you plan to sync now, click the Restore Options button to display a dialog, shown in Figure 8.5, that allows you to specify the locations for the data files and log files of the newly restored database.

10. The Copy Files tab of the dialog, pictured in Figure 8.6, requires a URL for the location to which the log files will be copied. Configure the Copy Files job here. This job will run on the target server. (Make sure you specify a reasonable amount of time for deletion of log files.)

Data Administration

PART III

Figure 8.5: Setting restore options

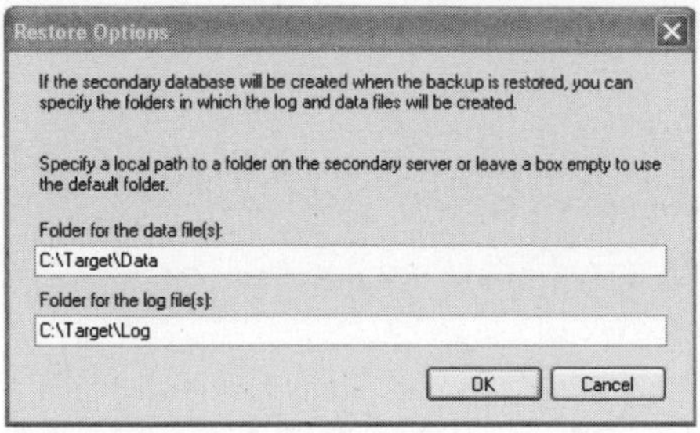

Figure 8.6: Setting file copy options

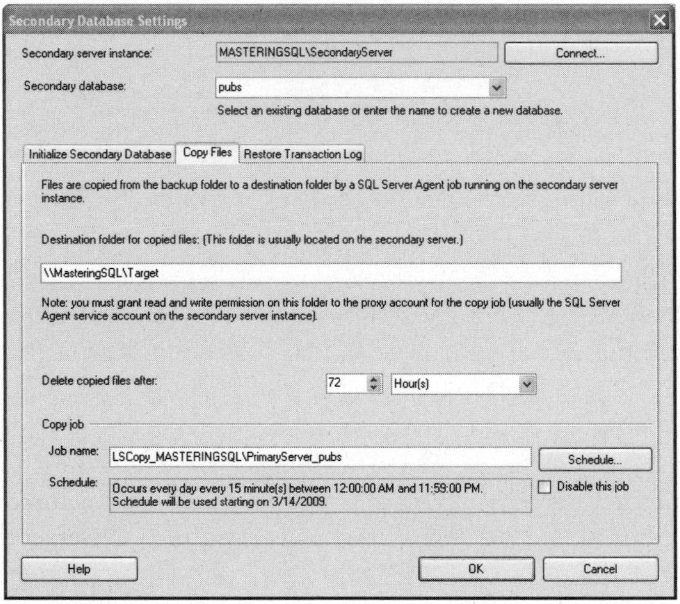

11. On the Restore Transaction Log tab, pictured in Figure 8.7, decide which type of recovery you will use for the log restores. This example shows a STANDBY configuration that creates a queryable server. Note that when you choose the STANDBY option, you will also have the option of disconnecting users when the restore job executes. This is important if you want to make sure the database is as current as possible. If there are users connected, the restore job will fail and will have to be repeated later.

Figure 8.7: Configuring file restore

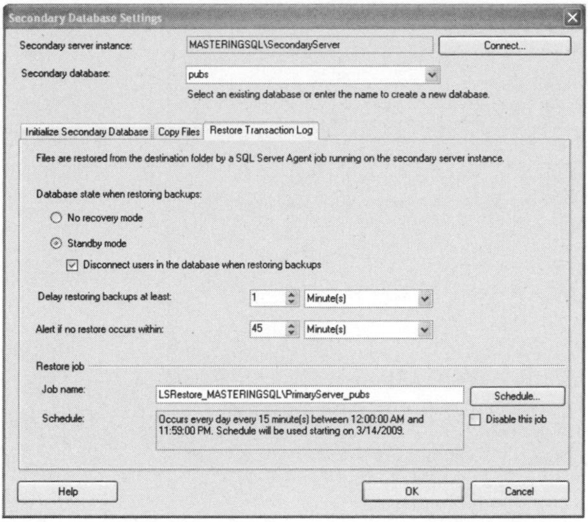

12. Configure a restore delay here, if any, as well as a job name and schedule. This job will execute on the target server.

13. When you are done, click OK on the dialog and it will return you to the log shipping configuration screen. From here you can repeat the process if you want to add additional target servers.

14. If you want to use a monitor server to watch the log shipping activity and raise a centralized alert, do it now. You won't be able to add it later. Click the check box to add the monitor and then click the Settings button. This will open the dialog pictured in Figure 8.8. This dialog allows you to connect to the server that will act as monitor and configure the connection properties and schedule. This job will run on the monitor server.

15. Click OK to close the dialog.

16. You are now ready to start the log shipping scenario that you have just configured. Click the OK button on the Database Properties window and the SSMS will perform the actions that you have requested. A pop-up dialog will indicate if the process was successful. Figure 8.9 illustrates the resulting database in the Object Explorer. Notice that the new pubs database on the secondary server is marked Standby / Read Only. You will also see that new jobs have been configured in each of the SQL Agent service instances.

Data Administration

PART III

Figure 8.8: Configuring the monitor

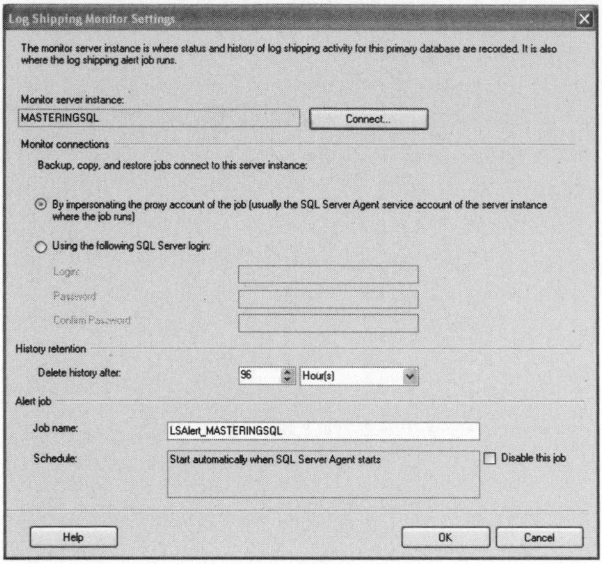

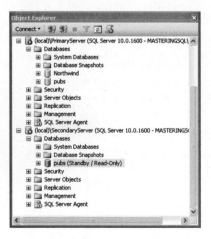

Figure 8.9: A successful configuration

At this point, any data modifications that take place on the primary server will be executed on the secondary server by restoring the primary log to the secondary database. SQL Server Agent will perform this transfer of data based on the schedules that you defined. To change the frequency of data transfer, simply alter the SQL Agent schedules.

> ### Configuring Log Shipping with TSQL
>
> You can configure log shipping with TSQL code, but this is not a common task, so it is usually easier to do it through the SSMS. If you want to create a script of a particular configuration, however, you should use the Script Configuration button located at the bottom of the Transaction Log Shipping page in the Database Properties window. This button will allow you to script the configuration to a new window, to the clipboard, or to a file. Rather than print the content of the script here, we recommend that you set up a log shipping model in the SSMS, script it, and then review it.

Failing Over in a Log Shipping Scenario

In case of failure of the primary server, the secondary server can be brought to a current state. If you wish, you can then switch the roles of the primary and secondary servers. Since the secondary server is only a warm standby, you will usually have to restore all remaining log backups to the server to bring it current. Follow these steps to get to that point:

1. If possible, take a manual transaction log backup of the primary database with NORECOVERY to capture the trailing log and put the primary database in a recovering state. This will be the last log that you restore on the server.

2. Copy all remaining logs from the primary to the secondary server and apply them in order with NORECOVERY, applying the training log last.

3. After applying the last log, recover the secondary database by using this statement:

    ```
    RESTORE DATABASE <dbname> WITH RECOVERY;
    ```

Your secondary server is now recovered and current. Client applications can be directed to use this server instead of the primary server for all database access requirements. If you wish, you can now switch the roles of the server so that the current server (formerly the secondary server) is the new primary. Take the following steps:

1. Remove any existing log shipping configuration. You will replace it with a new one.

Data Administration

PART III

2. If you were able to back up the primary database with recovery, you should be able to restore any transaction log backups taken on the secondary server since recovery back to the original primary server. If not, you will have to resynchronize the databases.

3. Reconfigure the log shipping model using the current server as the primary and the recovered server as the secondary. You will have effectively swapped roles at that point.

One disadvantage of the log shipping solution is that this must all be done manually. Having a warm standby server available can be extremely convenient, and log shipping is an easy way to maintain that server without having to perform a significant amount of configuration and maintenance.

Implement Database Mirroring

Database mirroring provides for either a high-performance (asynchronous) mirror or a high-safety (synchronous) mirror, both of which are detailed later in this section. It is different from log shipping in a number of very important ways:

Transaction-based   Log shipping synchronizes databases by loading log backups on the target server, which means that the target is only a warm standby. The target is only as current as the last log restore. Any transactions that have occurred on the primary server since the last log restore will not be reflected on the target server. Mirroring is different: Transactions commit on the two servers at roughly the same time, with the timing dependent on whether you use a high-safety or high-performance implementation. This means that the mirror target is a true hot standby server.

Auto failover   While the administrator can fail over a log shipping target to the primary role, this is a manual process. In the database mirroring model, it can be an automatic process. A third server called a *witness* monitors the status of each partner server; upon failure of the primary server, the witness forces a failover to the secondary server. This makes database mirroring a much better solution in terms of downtime.

Connections   Log shipping uses simple SQL Agent jobs to execute the backup, copy, and restore process. Database mirroring uses *endpoints*, connection points that allow the partners and the witness to be in constant contact with each other. Part of the process of configuring database mirroring is defining these connection endpoints, which must be active for the database mirroring behavior to function.

There are a number of requirements that you must observe before you will be able to initialize a successful database mirroring configuration. These are all fully documented in the SQL Server Books Online. The most important requirements are as follows:

- All servers in the quorum must be running the same version of SQL Server. For example, a primary server running SQL 2005 Standard cannot be in the same quorum as a mirror running SQL Server 2008 Enterprise.

- Asynchronous (high-performance) mirroring requires an Enterprise Edition of SQL Server.

- The primary server and the mirror server must have the same logins so that if failover occurs, client users will be able to authenticate as necessary.

- System databases such as master, model, and msdb cannot be mirrored.

- Although this is not a hard requirement, Microsoft recommends that both the primary and the mirror server use the same collations and sorts.

Preparing the Servers and Databases

Similar to log shipping, you must perform certain actions to prepare for database mirroring. Specifically, you must do the following:

- You must set the database recovery model to full. Database mirroring uses only a full recovery model. This ensures that the mirror will fully execute all bulk operations.

- You must prepare the mirror server by restoring a full database backup of the primary database to the mirror server along with at least one transaction log backup up to and including the last log. Unlike log shipping, the database mirror configuration will not create the target database for you. It must have the same name as the primary database, which means that the mirrored database must be on a separate SQL Server instance (either on the same server or a different one).

- It is critical that no transactions occur on the primary database between the time when you take the transaction log backup and the time when you restore it to the mirror server.

Once the database and transaction logs have been restored on the mirror instance, you are ready to use the database mirroring wizard to configure the mirroring scenario. Before we begin working with the wizard, we'll quickly review a few terms to make sure you understand them clearly:

Principal database   This is the production database that we will mirror. All transactions take place on this server and are copied to the mirror database for execution. Clients interact exclusively with the principal database.

Mirror database   This is the database copy. It must be on a different SQL Server instance than the principal database, although it can be on the same server. The mirror database is always in a state of recovery and you cannot query or report from it. Clients never interact directly with the mirror unless failover occurs.

Witness   The witness is a server that is responsible for monitoring the state of the two partner databases. If it loses contact with the primary database, it can initiate a failover. The witness is only used in a synchronous (high-safety) mode when the model requires automatic failover.

Synchronous mirroring   Also called high-safety mirroring, transactions are not fully committed on either the principal or mirror database unless there is a guarantee that both servers can commit. This may come at a performance cost as the transactions will be able to commit only as quickly as the slowest server allows. This does, however, provide a reasonable guarantee against data loss.

Synchronous mirroring can be configured with or without a witness, depending on if you want to support auto failover. Even without a witness, you can still fail over manually at any time if needed.

Asynchronous mirroring   Also called high-performance mirroring, transactions are committed to the principal server immediately and then copied to the mirror for execution. There may be a time delay between the commit on the principal and the commit on the mirror. There is a possibility of some data loss if a transaction is unable to commit on the mirror after committing on the principal.

Asynchronous mirroring does not support auto failover and therefore never uses a witness.

Mirroring endpoints   An endpoint is a communications port in SQL Server that allows services to interact with each other. SQL Server 2008 supports numerous endpoint types, including TSQL, Service Broker, and database mirroring endpoints. Mirroring endpoints communicate via TCP using a port number specific to the endpoint. The wizard will configure the endpoints, including granting permissions to a service account to communicate using the endpoint. Note that if the principal, mirror, or witness ever exist on the same server, they will need to use different port numbers on their endpoints.

Using the Database Mirroring Wizard

In the steps that follow, we will illustrate the use of the database mirroring wizard. In this example, we have prepared the server by creating a full database backup followed by a transaction log backup on the principal instance and then restoring those backups in order to the mirror instance with NORECOVERY. Remember that before taking the full database backup in the principal server, you must set the recovery model to full. You should double-check the mirror database to ensure that it is in a "restoring" state. You should also create the Windows accounts that SQL Server will use to communicate through the endpoints. You will configure security for these accounts in the wizard. Follow these steps:

1. To start the wizard, connect to the principal instance in the Object Explorer and open the Databases folder.

2. Right-click the pubs database and select Properties.

3. Click Mirroring on the left of the dialog. This will display the dialog that you see in Figure 8.10.

4. You will begin by creating the endpoints and configuring security. Click the Configure Security button in the dialog to start the security wizard.

5. Click Next on the first page of the wizard.

6. The next page will ask you if you want to configure a witness. You only need a witness if you plan to configure synchronous mirroring with automatic failover. For this exercise, select Yes and click Next.

Figure 8.10: Configuring database mirroring

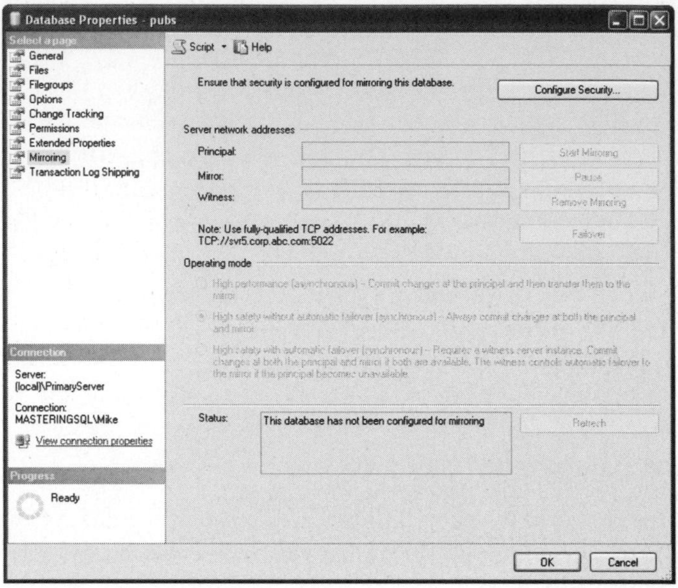

7. The following page will ask you to confirm the configuration locations. All three check boxes should now be selected. Click Next again to move the first configuration page, pictured in Figure 8.11.

Figure 8.11: Configuring the principal endpoint

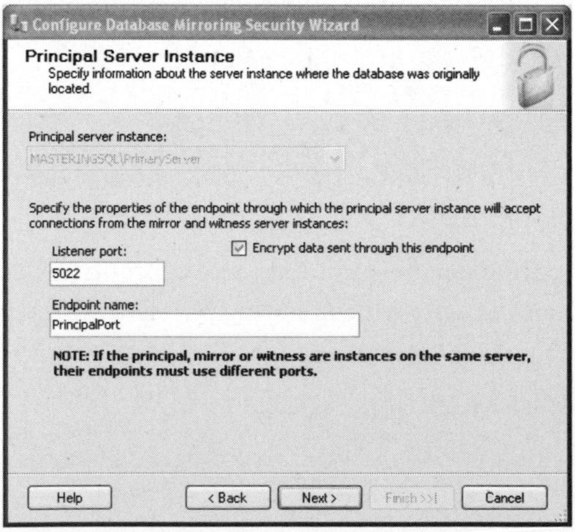

8. The endpoint configuration requires a port number and an endpoint name. In this case, the endpoint name is PrincipalPort and the port number is 5022, which is the default port number for database mirroring endpoints. If you wish all transaction traffic to be encrypted when sent through the port, enable that option here using the check box.

9. Click the Next button to advance to the next page. When you advance to the mirror endpoint configuration page, the dialog may prompt you to connect to the instance, as pictured in Figure 8.12. You will not be able to provide endpoint names or port numbers until you click the Connect button and provide authentication credentials for the mirror server. In our example, the endpoint name will be set to MirrorPort and it will use port number 5023. Note that whenever you have more than one mirroring endpoint on the same server, you must use a unique port number for each.

Figure 8.12: Configuring the mirror endpoint

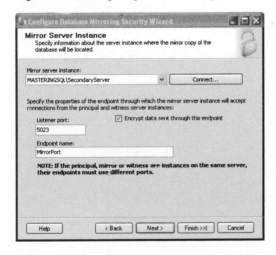

10. Click the Next button to advance to the witness configuration page, which is the same as the previous two pages. You must first connect to the witness instance and then configure the endpoint information. In this example, the endpoint name will be WitnessPort using a port number of 5024, as shown in Figure 8.13.

Figure 8.13: Configuring the witness endpoint

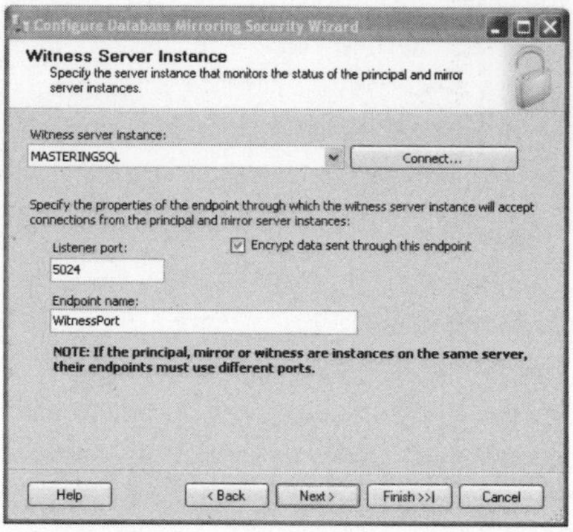

11. Click Next to advance to the service accounts configuration page, pictured in Figure 8.14.

Figure 8.14: Configuring the service accounts

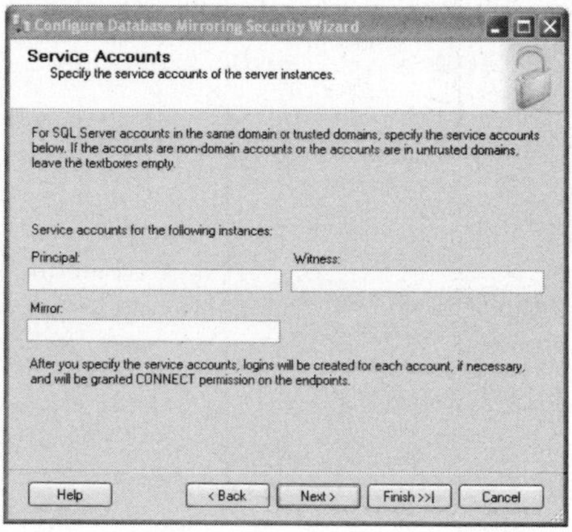

12. If you leave this dialog blank, the wizard will use the existing service accounts. This will work fine if all the instances use the same domain account for their service account. Otherwise, you will need to enter the full domain/account name for the service accounts that the server uses so that they can be granted permission to connect to the endpoints. The wizard will configure this permission for you. Since all of our server instances use the same account, we'll leave this dialog blank and click Next, which will bring up the summary page.

13. Review the summary for accuracy and click Finish to complete the wizard.

14. After the requested configuration is executed, you should get a success message for the three configuration tasks in the next dialog. If there are any errors, review the messages and correct any problems.

15. Close this dialog. A message box like the one pictured in Figure 8.15 appears, asking you if you wish to start mirroring now using the default configuration. (If you select No, you will still be able to start mirroring later in the Database Properties window.)

Figure 8.15: Starting the default configuration

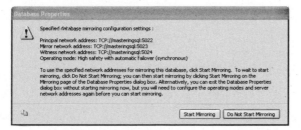

16. Finally, you will see a completed configuration dialog as pictured in Figure 8.16. The wizard has configured each of the endpoints and you now have the option to start, pause, or remove mirroring by clicking the appropriate button. The dialog shows two mirroring options. You can use high-performance mode or high-safety mode with auto failover.

The option to start high-safety mode without auto failover is not selectable because you configured a witness. If you did not want to have the option of auto failover, you would not have configured a witness.

17. Click the Start Mirroring button if you did not start mirroring previously and close the dialog when finished. Now if you look back at the Object Explorer, pictured in Figure 8.17, you will see the pubs databases in the two servers, marked with their current state.

Data Administration

PART III

Figure 8.16: Configuring mirroring

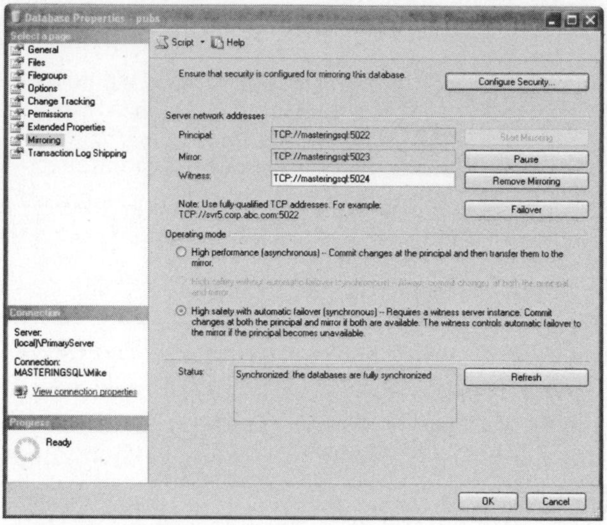

Figure 8.17: Viewing the results

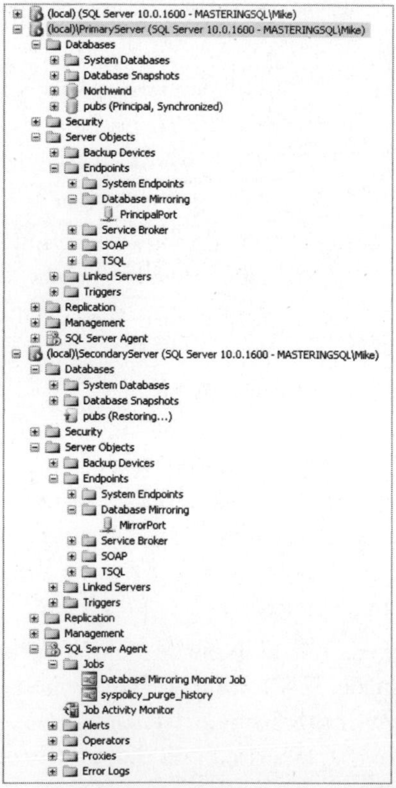

NOTE Since all of the endpoints are running on the same domain on the same server, you will not need to fully qualify the endpoint address. However, if you need to resolve domains in your model, you will have to be more specific. If you have not fully qualified your server names, you will get a message box prompting you to do so before starting mirroring. You can ignore this if all servers are running on the same domain.

Failing Over a Mirroring Solution

If you look at the Object Explorer now, you will see several new artifacts. You may need to refresh the nodes in the Explorer to see them. Look again at Figure 8.17. You will see that the primary database is now marked as Synchronized. You will also see the endpoints along with new SQL Agent jobs that do the monitoring. At this point, any transaction executed against the principal will be synchronously executed against the mirror as well. Feel free to try it out, making some modifications to data on the principal. You will not be able to query the mirror to test for the changes, but you will be able to see the changes after failover occurs. There are now two ways that this scenario can fail over, manually and automatically:

Manual failover If you wish to force a manual failover, go back to the Mirroring page of the database properties dialog on the pubs database in the primary server. Clicking the Failover button on the dialog will reverse the roles of the two databases. If you go back to the Object Explorer, after refreshing the nodes, you will see that the mirror database is now online and marked as the principal. This is your only failover option if you do not have a witness. You can also manually fail over by using this TSQL statement:

```
ALTER DATABASE pubs SET PARTNER FAILOVER;
```

This will break the mirror and set the status of the mirror database as the principal. The former principal will now be marked as disconnected and in recovery. After the former principal server is recovered, manually failing over again on the mirror will swap the roles back so that the model is as it was before.

Automatic failover The other approach is an automatic failover. For example, if you stop the MSSQL Server service on the primary server, the witness will force an automatic failover. That status of the mirror will switch to Principal / Disconnected and that database will now become the principal. After the former principal database comes online again, executing a manual failover will resync the databases and swap the roles back.

Implement Replication

Replication is one of the oldest data distribution techniques supported by SQL Server. The purpose of replication is to copy data or transactions from one server to another. While this can be a very effective distribution technique, there is no support for failover or transparent client redirection, so it is a marginal availability solution in most cases. Replication can still be an excellent data distribution technique, however.

Understand Types of Replication

SQL Server 2008 supports three major varieties of replication:

Snapshot replication   This approach focuses on copying data from one database to another. Entire data pages are copied from the publisher to the subscriber, meaning that the data is aging from the time of the initial copy to that of each subsequent copy. While you can configure the frequency of replication, this approach works best when you have small volumes of data that are either nonvolatile or tolerate data latency.

Transactional replication   This is the standard replication model. In this approach, the publishing server stores transactions in its transaction log for replication. Periodically, a log reader service gathers the transactions and sends them to a distribution server that then executes the transactions on each of the subscribing databases. This process can be scheduled to occur at regular intervals or can be configured to execute whenever transactions commit on the publishing server.

Merge replication   This model values data independence over consistency. Unlike snapshot and transactional models that require the subscribing databases to be treated as read-only, the merge replication model permits changes to the subscribing servers with the ability to merge the changes made in the subscriber with the data on the publishing server. Although this increases the independence of the servers in the replication model, it also increases the probability of data synchronization problems between the publisher and subscriber databases.

There are variations on each of these techniques, including the use of a two-phase commit on the subscriber and numerous topologies such as the central publisher or central subscriber. All three of these models use the database servers participating in the model in slightly different ways:

Publisher   In most replication scenarios, the publisher is the production server that accepts all transaction activity and makes that activity available for replication to other servers. The publisher will generally store transactions to be replicated in its transaction log until the distributor picks them up for delivery.

Distributor   This is the service that is responsible for delivery of replicated data. In a typical mode, the distributor will retrieve data from the log of the publisher and store that data in its own log until it can distribute the data to the subscriber. It is essentially a store-and-forward service.

Subscriber   The subscriber receives the replicated data from the distributor. In most cases this database must be treated as read-only since the transaction activity should occur on the publisher. There are exceptions to this rule, however, including merge replication models and updating subscribers.

Additionally there are some replication-specific terms with which you should be familiar. We will assume that these terms are understood for the remainder of this chapter:

Push subscription   A subscription model in which the distributor services push data to the subscriber. SQL Agent jobs running on the distributor will periodically connect to the subscriber and execute transactions necessary to bring the subscriber current.

Pull subscription   With a pull subscription model, the subscriber services retrieve transactions from the distributor for execution to keep the subscriber current. Pull subscriptions allow some of the overhead of replication to move from the distributor to the subscriber, which may load-balance the model better.

Article   An individual collection of replicated data usually associated with a table. Creating an article from a table allows the administrator to filter out columns or rows that they wish to exclude from the replication scenario.

Publication   A collection of articles usually associated with a database. A subscriber can subscribe to either an individual article or the entire publication.

In addition to these server roles and the replication types previously discussed, it is also possible to combine these components in different ways to create various replication topologies. A *topology* is a collection of replication services that are combined in a specific way to accomplish a desired goal. Some of the more prominent topology patterns are listed here:

Central subscriber   It is possible to have multiple publishers replicate data to a single subscriber. The data for each publisher article may even be published to the same table in the subscriber as long as each publisher's data is distinct. This pattern, illustrated in Figure 8.18, is most common where there is a centralized data need for reporting or decision making.

Figure 8.18: Central subscriber

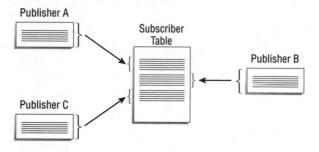

Central publisher   You can also configure a single publisher that can partition data to various subscribers. Assuming that each subscriber needs only a subset of the data, the administrator can create multiple articles, each one filtering out data for a particular subscriber. Each subscriber can then receive the data that's relevant for them. This approach, pictured in Figure 8.19, is useful when data is centrally collected but must be distributed locally for decentralized processing.

Figure 8.19: Central publisher

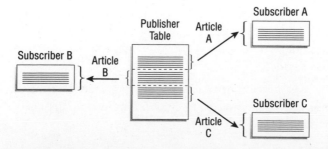

Regional publishers/subscribers It is also possible that each server may need to maintain its own distinct data but also send and receive replicated data from other servers. This approach, pictured in Figure 8.20, supports a highly decentralized environment. One of the problems with this model, however, is its ability to scale. Adding additional nodes to the model will exponentially increase the overhead for each added node.

Figure 8.20: Regional publishers/subscribers

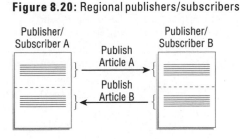

Distributed subscriber/republisher Designers often use this model when data must replicate to more than one subscriber but those subscribers are geographically located where it is either expensive or impractical to perform a direct replication. All data will replicate to a single subscriber that has more convenient access to the ultimate subscribers. The subscriber then republishes the data to the subscribers that need it. In this model, pictured in Figure 8.21, the central server is responsible for both subscription and publication services.

Figure 8.21: Distributed subscriber/republisher

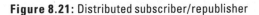
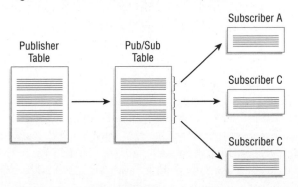

Data Administration

PART III

Of course, there are other patterns that you can use, and almost limitless combinations of these patterns, so be creative. Just be sure to do production-level performance and reliability testing on your models before taking them live. What looks good on paper will not always work so well in the real world.

NOTE   Before you can configure replication, you must install it into the servers that will participate in your replication topology. If you have not already installed replication on all participating servers, go back to the SQL Server Installation Center and add the replication feature to your servers. It will also make the process of configuring replication easier if you connect your Object Explorer in SSMS to all the Data Engine services that will participate in your replication model.

Configure the Replication Distributor

In this example, the PrimaryServer instance will act as publisher, the SecondaryServer instance will act as subscriber, and the MasteringSQL default instance will act as the distributor. Remember that it is possible for a single server to play any combination of roles.

1. Start the replication process by connecting to the distribution server.

2. Right-click the Replication node in the Object Explorer for the target distribution server and select Configure Distribution from the menu. (This replication node will not be present if you have not installed replication.)

3. Advance past the first page of the wizard and you will see a page that asks you to either configure the selected server as a distributor or point this server's publications to another distributor. Since this server will act only as a distributor, you will select the first option, as pictured in Figure 8.22. Click Next.

4. In the next page of the wizard, configure the location of the snapshot folder. Whenever the distributor needs to perform a synchronization between the publisher and subscriber, it will use an article snapshot. In cases where the subscriber will use its own distribution agents (i.e., pull subscriptions), those agents will need access to this folder. You will need to use a network location such as a UNC name before you will be able to support pull subscriptions. The SQL

Agent service account on the subscriber will also need permissions to access this share. In Figure 8.23, this dialog shows the user of a share called ReplSnap. Click Next to continue.

Figure 8.22: Setting the distributor

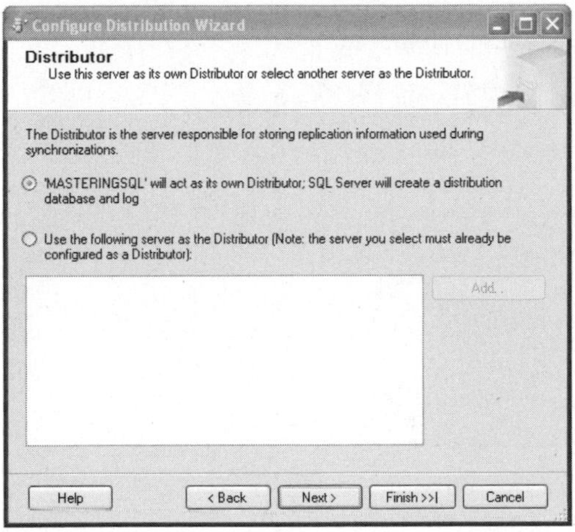

Figure 8.23: The distribution snapshot folder

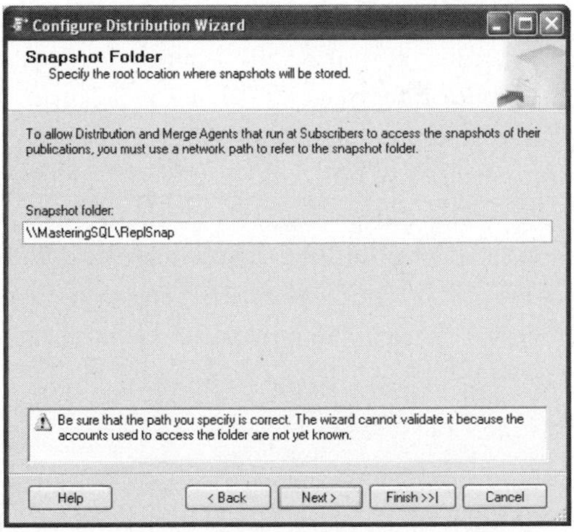

5. The screen that now appears will provide the configuration of this database, specifically the database name and file locations. The default name is distribution, which we will retain for this example

as pictured in Figure 8.24. Note that when you configure distribution, you are creating a database that the distribution agents will use for storing and forward transaction activity. The log is heavily used in this database and should be physically positioned accordingly. Click Next to advance.

Figure 8.24: The distribution database

6. The distribution server must authorize publishers before they will be able to use its distribution services. This next page authorizes publishers to use this distributor. By default, the distribution server can always publish to itself. You must add any other publishers here before they can use this distributor. Click the Add button at the bottom of the dialog to add a publisher. You will see that you can add either a SQL Server or an Oracle publisher. Select SQL Server and connect to the server that you plan to use as the publisher.

7. You should see a configure dialog like that shown in Figure 8.25. Click Next to continue.

8. Enter a strong password and click Next. (This simple dialog is not pictured here.) Publishing servers may occasionally need to connect to the distributor to perform administrative tasks on the distributor configuration. To do this, they will have to provide a distribution password. This is not the password of any existing account but rather an administrative password that the publisher must give to be allowed to access distribution configuration.

Figure 8.25: Configuring publishers

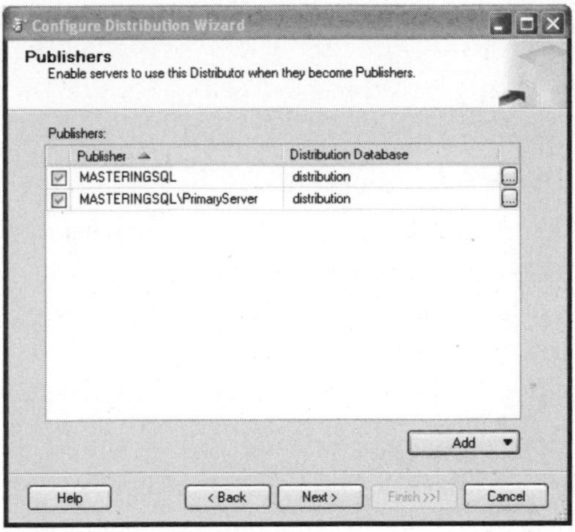

9. The final page in the wizard allows you to immediately configure the distributor or generate a script that you can execute later or on a different server. (You can also do both if you wish.) Select the option to configure the distributor now and click Next, which navigates to the summary page.

10. Review the page for accuracy and click Finish when you're ready to execute the configuration. When the replication is complete, click Close.

Configure the Replication Publisher

Now that you have successfully configured the distributor, it is time to create publications. We will publish articles from the pubs database on the PrimaryServer instance. If you have not set the recovery model of this database to Full or Bulk-Logged, you must do that now before you can configure publishing. Then follow these steps:

1. To begin, expand the Replication node of the server from which you wish to publish. Right-click the Local Publications node and select New Publication. This will start the New Publication Wizard. Click Next to advance past the first page.

2. The next page allows you to set the distributor. This dialog is like the one previously illustrated in Figure 8.22. If this publisher will

act as its own distributor, you can configure the distributor now. In this example, however, you will point to the distributor that we configured in the previous step. Click the second option in the dialog to enable the Add button.

3. Click the Add button and connect to the server previously configured as the distributor. Then click Next to advance.

4. Provide the distributor password that you specified when you configured the distributor. (You will not be able to make an administrative link to the distributor without this resource password.) After providing the password click Next to advance. (This simple page contains only the password prompt and is not pictured here.)

5. Select the database that you wish to publish from the list of databases that are eligible for publication. In this case, only the pubs database is on the list. Data from multiple databases will be published as multiple publications. Click Next to continue.

6. You will now see the page illustrated in Figure 8.26, which lists all publication types previously discussed. Refer to the introductory section of this chapter if you need a refresher on replication types.

Figure 8.26: Selecting a replication model

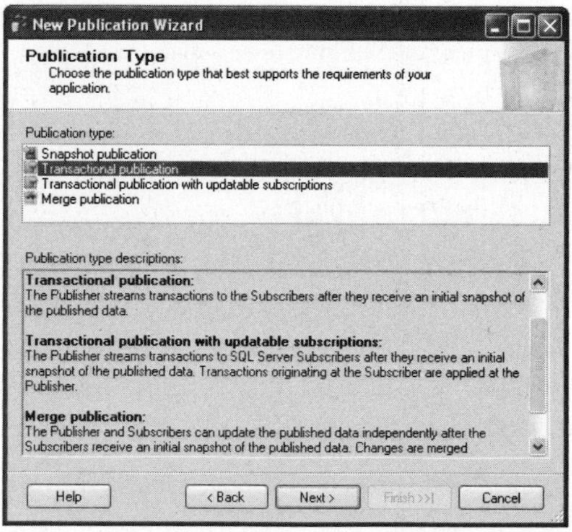

You will see one additional option; that is Transactional publication with updatable subscribers. This option allows data modifications at the subscriber by using a two-phase commit to commit the subscriber change immediately to the publisher to ensure data integrity. Use this

option with caution because it can often result in significant performance degradation.

7. Select the Transactional Publication option and click Next to
advance. In this example, we will use a standard transactional
replication. There are advantages and disadvantages to each
approach, but the transactional method was the first replication
model supported and it is still the most common approach due to
its lower resource consumption and greater flexibility.

NOTE We wish that we had the time and space to cover all of
the replication models more exhaustively, but that is unfortu-
nately not possible. The good news, though, is that this information should be enough to get you going and the replication
process is very well documented in the SQL Server Books Online
when you are ready to dive deeper. Again, don't be afraid to
experiment with the options and be sure to do some testing
before you pull the trigger in production.

Now it is finally time to decide what you are going to publish. You
can publish tables, views, and stored procedures as articles. If you
publish a table, it must have a primary key.

8. On the right side of the dialog pictured in Figure 8.27, you will see
a button with two options, one to set properties for the selected
article and one for all articles. Review these properties carefully
on your own. You will control much of the replication behavior
here, including copying related artifacts, doing type conversions,
and other useful options. In our example, we will replicate only a
limited number of columns in the authors table. Select the check
boxes for the authors table as shown and click Next to advance.

9. The next step is to select articles to filter. The previous dialog
allowed you to filter out any columns that you did not need. The
next dialog provides the ability to do row filtering based on criteria
that you provide. Figure 8.28 illustrates a completed dialog. To add
filtering for an article, click the Add button on the right, which will
be enabled if there are any articles remaining that do not have
filters. This will open the dialog pictured in Figure 8.29, where you
will provide a WHERE clause for the filter statement to indicate which
data you want to include in the article. In our example, we are only
publishing authors that live in the state of California. Click Next on
the dialog to advance.

Figure 8.27: Selecting articles for publication

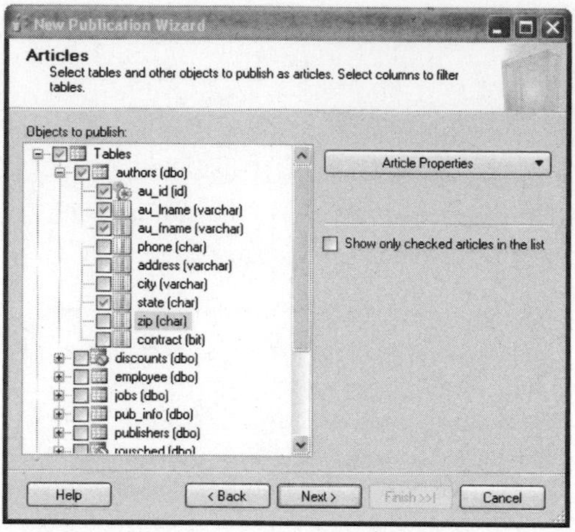

Figure 8.28: Selecting articles to filter

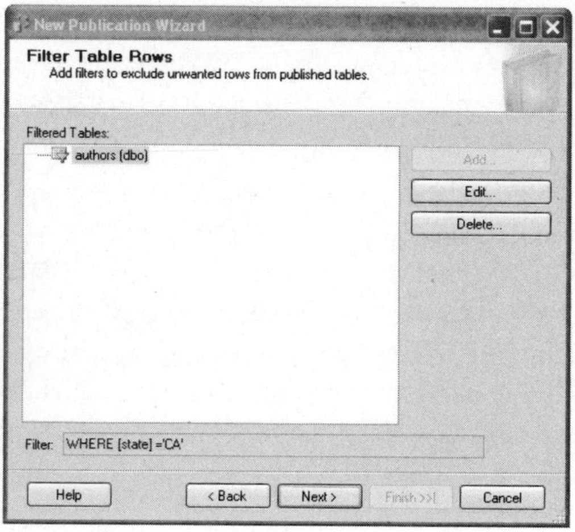

10. The initial synchronization of the articles requires a snapshot distribution to the subscriber. If you would like to generate the initial snapshot immediately upon a new subscriber coming online, select the check box on the next dialog. (This dialog has only these two options and is not pictured.) Otherwise, the snapshot will be generated on a schedule and the subscription will not be available until after the snapshot generates and syncs with the subscriber.

Figure 8.29: Configuring an article filter

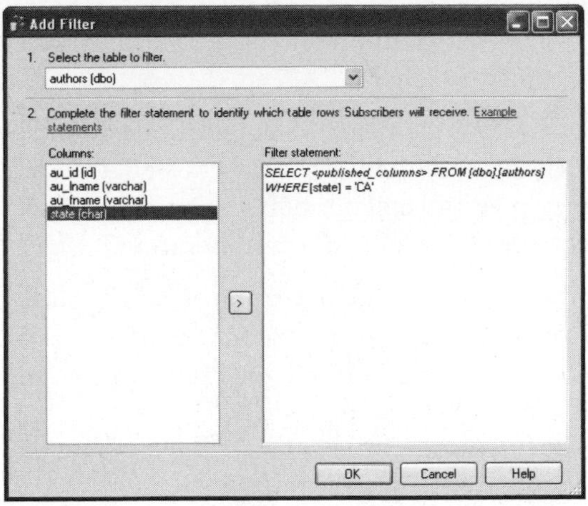

11. Select immediate generation of the snapshot and click Next.

12. The following dialog will request security account information for two agents, the snapshot agent and the log reader agent. The snapshot agent is responsible for doing snapshot syncs and must execute under an account that has permissions to execute the snapshot on the subscriber. The log reader agent is responsible for retrieving transactions from the publishing log. You should use domain accounts with necessary permissions for these agents. This is pictured in Figure 8.30. Click Next to advance.

Figure 8.30: Configuring agent security

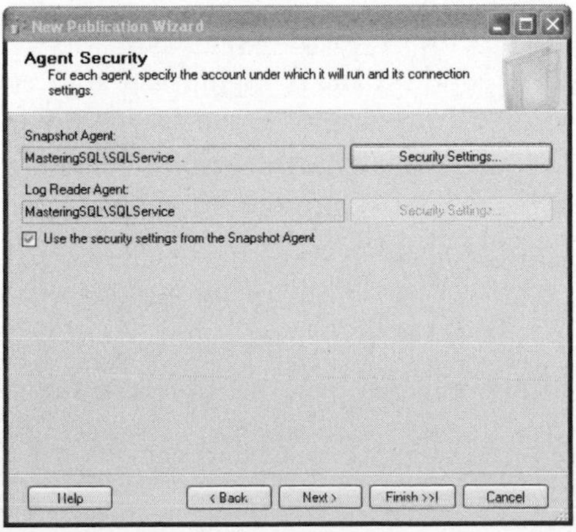

13. Decide if you want to commit the configuration at this time or generate a script to commit the configuration at a later time or place. (This is similar to the distribution configuration.) Click Next and advance to the summary screen.

14. Don't forget to enter the name of the publication at the top of the summary screen. It's easy to miss but the Finish button will not enable without it. We will call our publication pubs. Click Finish when you are ready to commit your configuration.

15. After the wizard reports successful creation of your publication, go back to the Object Explorer. You should now see the pubs publication in the Local Publications folder in the PrimaryServer instance.

Configure the Replication Subscriber

The last step is to configure the subscriber. We will use the SecondaryServer instance as the subscriber in our example:

1. Connect to that server in the Object Explorer and locate the Local Subscriptions folder.

2. Right-click the folder and select New Subscriptions from the menu. Click Next to advance past the first page of the wizard.

3. Point to the publisher. Open the publisher drop-down list at the top of the dialog and choose the option to connect to a SQL Server publisher.

4. Connect to the server that you configured as the publisher. This will list the available publications in the dialog, as illustrated in Figure 8.31. Select the pubs publication and click Next to continue.

5. Choose either a push or a pull subscription and click Next. (This page has only these two options and is not illustrated.) Remember that push subscriptions run the agents on the distributor and pull subscriptions use the resources of the subscriber. You must have configured the distributor to handle pull subscriptions by using a network path for the snapshot folder before this option will execute without error. Select a pull subscription for this example and click Next.

6. The next page, pictured in Figure 8.32, has two functions. First, it allows you to specify the target database for each subscription. If you click in the cell for the subscription database, you can either

select a database from a list or create a new database. If you have not already created the database that will host the subscriptions, this is your opportunity to do so. Second, this dialog also allows you to add subscriptions through the Add Subscriber button at the bottom of the page. This example shows a database named PubsSub. Click Next to continue.

Figure 8.31: Selecting a publication

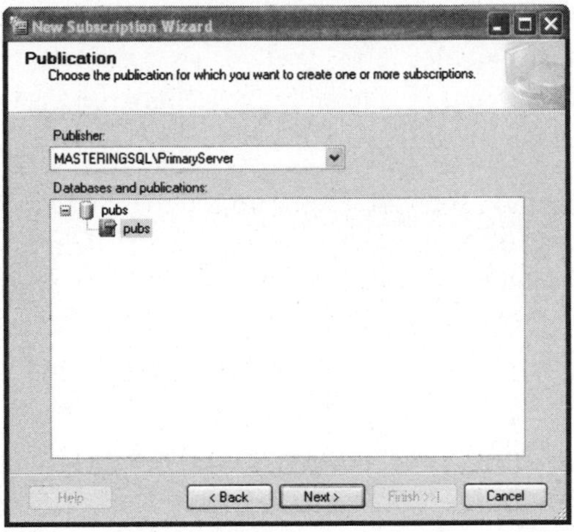

Figure 8.32: Selecting subscribers and databases

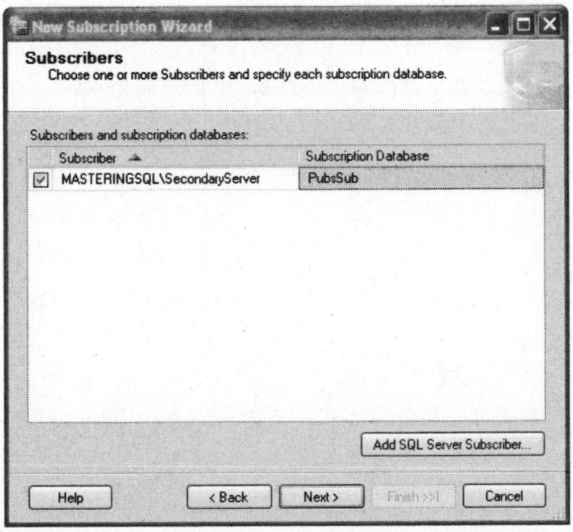

Data Administration

PART III

7. Similar to configuring publishing, the next dialog allows you to specify how the agents will authenticate to the servers upon which they will run. Click the ellipsis on each subscriber row to open the security configuration. These dialogs are similar to those previously shown and are not illustrated here. Click Next to advance.

8. The next dialog provides configuration for the synchronization schedule. You have three options:

   - Run continuously, which will run the agents whenever there is work to do. This will provide the best concurrency, but at a higher resource cost.

   - Run on demand, which will delay execution until manually triggered.

   - Run on a schedule. If you select the option to set a schedule, you will see a standard SQL Agent scheduling screen where you will be able to configure the schedule.

   Figure 8.33 shows these options. Select Run Continuously for this example. Click Next to continue.

Figure 8.33: Setting the synchronization properties

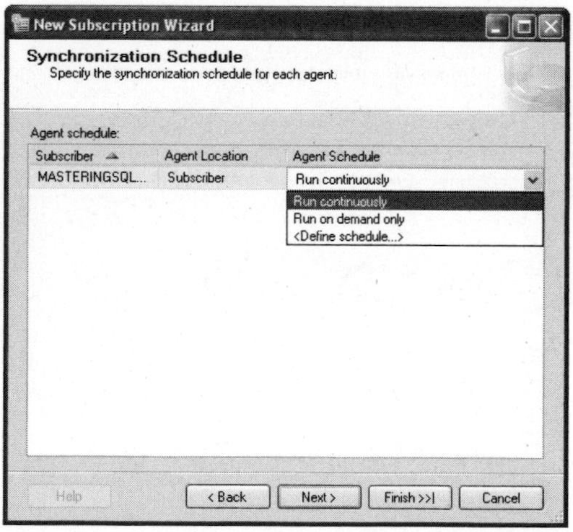

9. The next dialog is similar except that it allows you to specify how the subscription will be initialized, either immediately or on the first sync task. If you choose to wait for the first sync task, you will

not see any data in the article until a database modification occurs on the publisher and that transaction replicates to the subscriber. Choose to initialize immediately. This is a simple dialog and is not pictured here.

10. You are almost done. Click Next and choose the option to create the subscription immediately or generate a script.

11. Click next to review the summary page, and then click Finish to complete the wizard.

Once the wizard reports that you have successfully created the subscription, you can go back to the Object Explorer. You will now see a table in the target database with the same name as the article that you created, in this case authors. Since we configured this to initialize immediately, you should be able to select from the table and see the initial snapshot of data.

Additionally, if you make a modification to the published data on the publishing server, you will be able to select from the subscription table and see the change. Do a couple of experiments with your databases and see how long it takes for the subscriptions to update.

9

Extracting, Transforming, and Loading Data

IN THIS CHAPTER, YOU WILL LEARN TO DO THE FOLLOWING:

Data Administration

PART III

xtracting, transforming, and loading (ETL) are fundamental processes to any data environment. These processes include using the Bulk Copy Program (BCP) utility to import and export large quantities of data and using SQL Server Integration Services (SSIS) for full transformations of many and varied types. ETL operations also provide the foundation for business intelligence, granting the ability to establish effective data mining and data warehouse environments. There are literally hundreds of books and courses on ETL techniques and processes. In this chapter, we will provide an overview of the general processes as well as specific information to perform some of them. We encourage you to pursue further information on these subjects.

Use the Bulk Copy Program Utility

The Bulk Copy Program (BCP) utility is run from the command line, and a version of it is available in many editions of SQL Server. However, there have been enhancements in SQL Server 2008. Any DBA that has used BCP will tell you that it is a valuable and flexible tool. Using it, you can easily import and export large amounts of data. A simple example of the syntax follows:

```
bcp {dbtable | query}
{in | out | queryout | format} datafile
[-n native type] [-c character type]
[-S server name] [-U username]
[-P password] [-T trusted connection]
```

The vertical | symbol inside the curly braces means that you can use only one of the choices listed inside the braces. All of the switches listed in the preceding syntax are case sensitive. Let's step through this syntax:

- dbtable is the name of the destination table when data is being imported into SQL Server and the source table when it's being exported from SQL Server.

- query is a Transact SQL query that returns a result set. Use double quotation marks around the query and single quotation marks around anything embedded in the query. queryout must also be specified if you are bulk copying data from the query. The query can also reference a stored procedure as long as all tables that are referenced exist prior to executing the BCP statement.

- `in| out| queryout| format` is the clause that specifies the direction of the copy as follows:
    - `in` takes a file and brings it into a database table or a view.

    - `out` copies from a database table or view to a file. Note that if you specify an existing file, you will overwrite that file.

    - `queryout` takes data from the query and must be specified only when copying data from a query.

    - `format` will create a format file based on the option you have specified. These options will be explained in the section "Use BCP Format Files" later in this chapter.

- `datafile` is the full path of the data file when data is imported into SQL Server. The data file has the data to be copied into a specific table or view. The data exported from SQL Server table contains the data copied from the table or view.

- `-n` will perform the bulk copy operation using the native or database types of the data.

- `-c` will perform the operation using the character data type. This does not prompt for each field and uses the chart as the storage type without prefixes. The tab character is used as a separator and the new line character as a row terminator.

- `-S` specifies the name of the server or instance to which the utility should connect. If no server is specified, the BCP utility will connect to the default instance of SQL Server on the local computer. This option is required when a BCP command is run from a remote computer to a local or main instance. To connect to the default instance of SQL Server, specify only the server name. To connect to a named instance of SQL Server, specify the server name\instance name.

- `-U` specifies the login ID to be used to connect to the server.

- `-P` specifies the password to be used for the login. If this option is not used, the command will prompt for a password. If this option is used at the end of the command prompt without a password, BCP uses the default password (null).

- `-T` informs the BCP utility to connect to SQL Server or a trusted connection using integrated security. In integrated security, network credentials are not required because they were established when you logged in to the network.

There are several other switches that you can use for the BCP utility, but these are the ones that we will be concerned with in this chapter. For good listings and descriptions of other uses for the BCP utility, refer to the MSDN SQL Server Developer Center at `http://msdn.microsoft.com/en-us/sqlserver/default.aspx`.

Perform a Standard BCP Task

To use the BCP utility, you must first open a command prompt. The command example we are using starts with `bcp` followed by a fully qualified table name. For example, if you were to export the customer table from the demoscript database, you would use demoscript.dbo .customer. Next is the out argument since we plan to export a copy of the table. If we were importing, it would be to an argument to bring the data into the table. The command would need to specify a location of the data file on the server. Please remember that switches and commands in the BCP utility are case sensitive. To achieve what we have just outlined, our command will look like this:

```
bcp demoscript.dbo.customer out c: \NewCopyofCustomer.bcp
```

Now let's add some switches to increase the functionality of our command. Let's use the -S switch to specify a server, the -U switch to log into the sa account with the -P switch for the password, and the -c switch to specify a data type of char so that we may easily open our output file with Excel. Add as well the –e switch to create an error output file. These additions will now make our command look like this:

```
bcp demoscript.dbo.customer out
C: \NewCopyofCustomer.bcp –c
-SMarvinTheGenius\Mikebook –Usa –P
-eC: \expError.txt
```

A command that will take data from a query and write it into a data file would look like this:

```
bcp  "SELECT * FROM demoscript.dbo.Customer"
queryout C:\NewCopyofCustomer.dat -T –c
```

That second command is using a trusted connection with integrated security to the database and is formatting the results in a char data type. If we were to use a specific column name rather than the asterisk (*), it would write only the specified column to the data file.

Use BCP Format Files

As you can see, the BCP tool is very flexible. The switches listed earlier as well as the syntax help should give you all the basic tools required to be effective in your BCP projects. With BCP, you have the ability to output to format file types. The first format file type is a non-XML format. It is useful if you wish to have a file formatted as currency, for example. The code to generate this type of file is as follows:

```
bcp demoscript.dbo.Orders format null -T -c  -f Currency.fmt
```

A non-XML format file is a text file that has a specific structure. It contains information about file storage type, prefix length, and field length and a field terminator of every table column. The code table that follows shows a typical output of a format result. The BCP utility uses the version number of SQL Server to define the source; in this case, it is 10.0 to indicate that we are using SQL Server 2008 (version 10.0). The next number, the 4, shows there are four columns in the output. The first number in each of the four columns is the host file field order. The next number is the prefix length followed by a host file data length. The fifth column of the chart is the terminator. The three possible choices for the terminator are the comma (,), the tab ("\t"), and the end of line ("\r\n"). The sixth column of the chart shows the server column order and the seventh column displays the server column name. Last, the column collation is displayed. Collation specifies the character set and the order of associativity that the data would use and follow. The *column collation* defines how the data is stored in the targeted columns of the data table. Having a " " in this column causes the data to be stored in the format specified in the -c switch option in the BCP command. The non-XML format exists for backward compatibility with SQL 2000. Here is the code table:

```
10.0
4
1 SQLCHAR   0   7     "\,t"    1   DepartmentID      " "
2 SQLCHAR   0   100   "\t"     2   Name              SQL_Latin1_
General_CP1_CI_AS
3 SQLCHAR   0   100   "\t"     3   GroupName         SQL_Latin1_
General_CP1_CI_AS
4 SQLCHAR   0   24    "\r\n"   4   ModifiedDate      " "
```

The XML format file can be used to bulk import data for data tables or views and to bulk export data. XML format files are more powerful and flexible than non-XML format files. They have the advantage of being able to be understood and read by humans, which can assist operators when bulk data processing is occurring. The XML encoding clearly describes the data types and data elements of the data file and also the mapping between the elements and table columns. An XML-formatted file can be enhanced and yet remain compatible with earlier versions of itself. Like a non-XML-formatted file, the XML files have a distinct format and structure of data fields, and in a data file, that maps those fields to a column in a single target table. An XML-formatted file possesses two main components, <RECORD> and <ROW>:

- <RECORD> describes the data as it is stored in the data file. Each <RECORD> element contains a set of one or more <FIELD> elements. These elements correspond to fields in the data file. The basic syntax is as follows:

```
<RECORD>
    <FIELD .../> [ ...n ]
</RECORD>
```

Each <FIELD> element describes the contents of a specific data field. A field can be mapped to only one column in the table. Not all fields need to be mapped to columns. A field in a data file can be either of fixed/variable length or character terminated. A *field value* can be represented as a character (using single-byte representation), a wide character (using Unicode 2-byte representation), native database format, or a filename.

- <ROW> describes how to construct data rows from a data file when the data from the file is imported into a SQL Server table. A <ROW> element contains a set of <COLUMN> elements. These elements correspond to table columns. The basic syntax is as follows:

```
<ROW>
    <COLUMN .../> [ ...n ]
</ROW>
```

Each <COLUMN> element can be mapped to only one field in the data file. The order of the <COLUMN> elements in the <ROW> element defines the order in which they are returned by the bulk operation. The XML format file assigns each <COLUMN> element a local name that has no relationship to the column in the target table of a bulk import operation.

Use Views to Organize Output

Views are often used to receive and provide data in the Bulk Copy Program utility operation. The following code shows how you can output a view from the pubs database to a text file with a simple char format:

```
bcp pubs..titleview out titleview.txt -c
```

To copy data into a view, you use the standard data insertion rules. Note that if you use BCP and do not specify values for columns in which defaults have been defined, those columns will be populated with NULL. Here is an example of the output generated by the preceding query:

Use the SQL Server Import and Export Wizard

SQL Server import and export wizards provide the simplest manner in which to copy data between various data sources and construct basic data transformation packages. There are five ways to launch the SQL Server Import and Export Wizard:

- In a command prompt window, run DTSwizard.exe, located in C:\Program Files\Microsoft SQL Server\100\DTS\binn.

- In SQL Server Management Studio, do the following:

  1. Connect to the Database Engine server type.

  2. Expand Databases.

  3. Right-click a database.

  4. Point to Tasks.

  5. Click Import Data or Export Data.

- In Business Intelligence Development Studio (BIDS), from the Project menu, choose SSIS Import and Export Wizard.

- In Business Intelligence Development Studio, right-click the SSIS Packages folder and select SSIS Import and Export Wizard.

- On the Start menu, point to All Programs and then point to Microsoft SQL Server 2008 and click Import and Export Data.

64-bit and 32-bit Import and Export Wizard

NOTE   On a 64-bit computer, Integration Services will install the 64-bit version of the SQL Server Import and Export Wizard. However, some data sources, such as Access and Excel, only have 32-bit data providers to work with. To be able to use these data sources, you might have to install the 32-bit version of the wizard. To install the 32-bit version, select either client or Business Intelligence Development Studio during setup.

Execute the Import and Export Wizard

When you begin using the Import and Export Wizard, you will see the same welcome screen regardless of how you launched it. Take the following steps:

1. Click Next on the welcome screen to open a dialog to select your data source (Figure 9.1).

Figure 9.1: Choose a data source

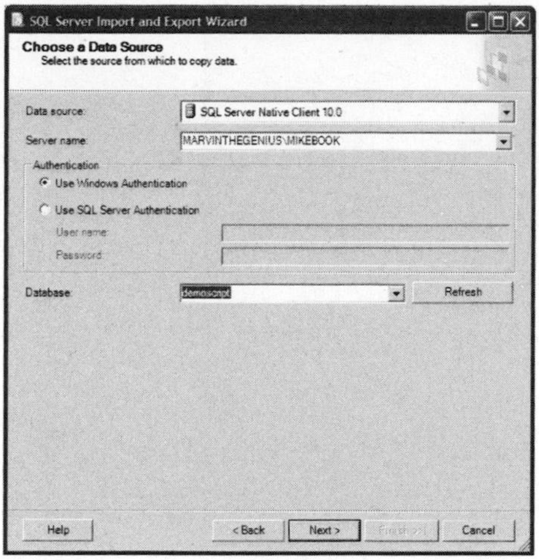

2. Choose your data provider: SQL Server data, Flat File Source, Microsoft Access, or Microsoft Excel.

3. In the Server Name drop-down menu, select the instance of SQL that you wish to use as a data source. The Database drop-down menu in the lower portion of the dialog will populate with a list of databases to select from. The area in the center of the dialog is for authentication choices.

4. Choose a destination for the data that you plan to extract. You can select an existing database or, as illustrated in Figure 9.2, create an entirely new one. When a new database is created, database options are set in the dialog, as seen in the figure. The other options for data destination are .NET Framework data providers, OLE DB providers, SQL Server native client, flat files, and Microsoft Office Access and Excel. Depending upon the option you select, you will be presented with choices to format the data being written to the destination.

5. After you've chosen both the source and the destination for your data, you have to decide which data you wish to extract. From the dialog in Figure 9.3, you will choose whether to use existing tables or views or write a query for data extraction purposes. For this example, select the tables and views option and click Next.

6. In the next screen, select the table or view you wish to use (Figure 9.4).

Data Administration

PART III

Figure 9.2: Creating a new database destination

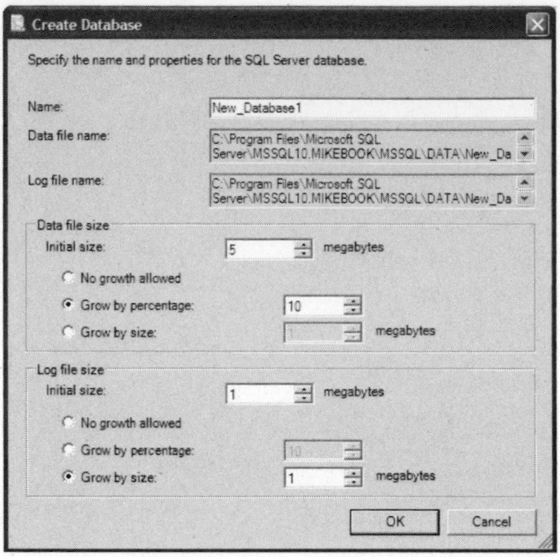

Figure 9.3: Selecting tables and views or a query

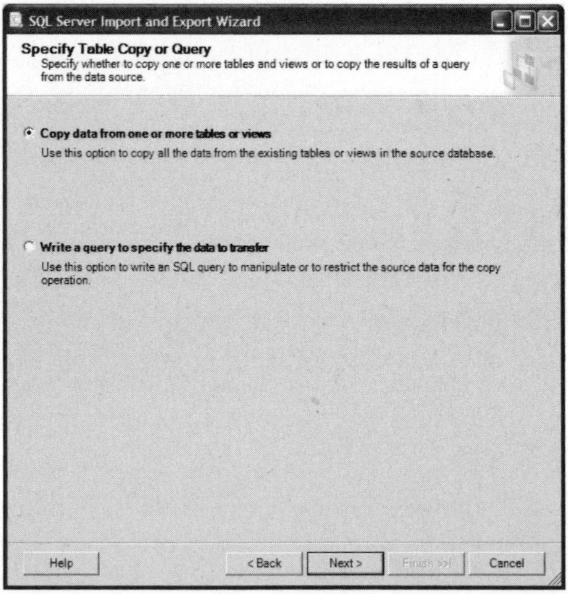

Figure 9.4: Selecting tables and views

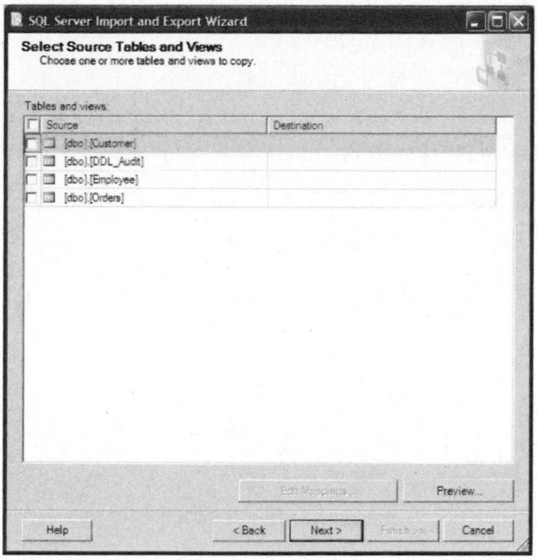

7. If you click the Edit Mappings button, you will see a Transfer Settings dialog. The Edit Mappings button is disabled until you have selected data objects for your source. This gives you the options of dropping and re-creating new destination tables, specifying the destination schema name, deleting existing rows in a destination table, and enabling the identity insert. Figure 9.5 illustrates options that may be selected.

Figure 9.5: The Transfer Settings dialog

Data Administration

PART III

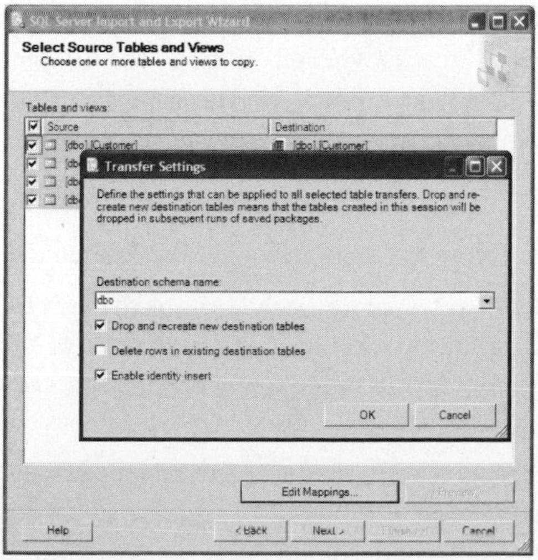

8. Next you will store packages that you will reuse in SQL Server and use SQL Server to manage the security. This is an option presented in by dialog shown in Figure 9.6. Other options presented include running the package immediately, saving the package in SQL Server or the file system, and choosing the package encryption level password if necessary.

Figure 9.6: Saving and running a package

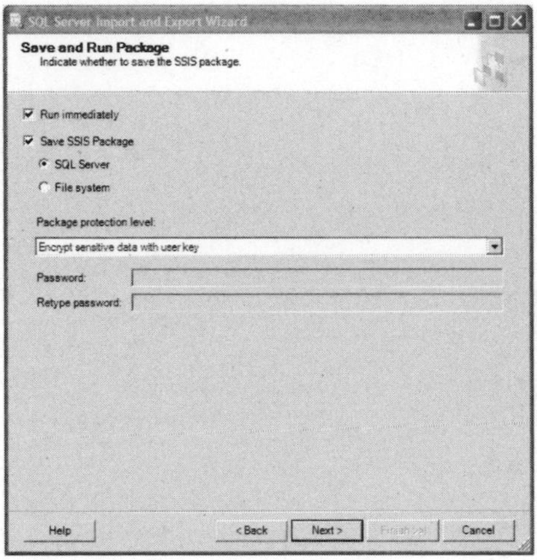

Saving and Scheduling an Import/Export

Once you choose to save a package, you will be presented with the dialog shown in Figure 9.7. Here is where you make the distinct choices to save your SSIS package created via the wizard.

1. Start by naming the package and giving it a description.

2. Select the server on which the package should be saved.

3. Set up the authentication for each package execution in the future.

4. Review all the selections you made in the Complete the Wizard page (Figure 9.8), and then click Finish. If you selected the Run Immediately check box in step 8 in the preceding section (Figure 9.6), the package will now run.

5. Figure 9.9 shows the execution process as the package runs. Notice the error in executing. The error is generated because we attempted to drop a table that did not exist. To see details of the

execution, simply click Report and you are presented with the report (shown in Figure 9.10).

Figure 9.7: Saving an SSIS package

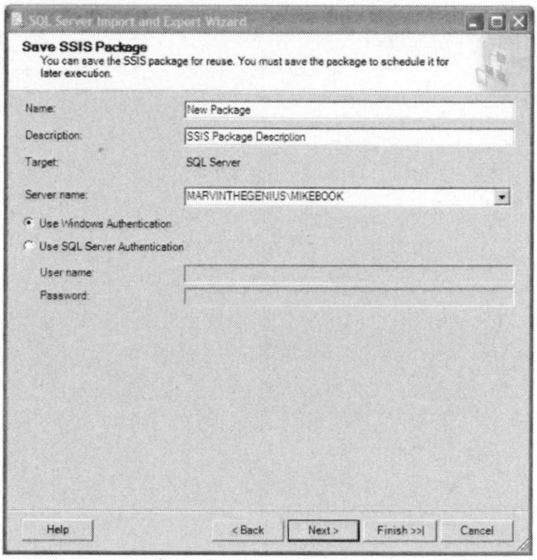

Figure 9.8: Summation screen

This report allows for easy analysis and error correction. Using the SQL Server Import and Export Wizard provides the easiest methods for the ETL process with the database.

Figure 9.9: Package execution

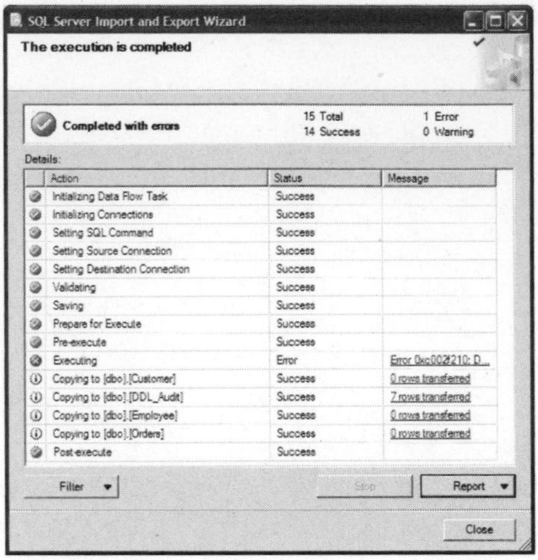

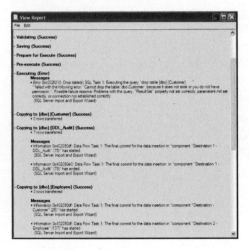

Figure 9.10: Execution report

Create Transformations Using SQL Server Integration Services (SSIS)

SQL Server Integration Services provides nearly everything that you could want for any ETL process. It can be used to move data between SQL Server and a variety of sources or destinations. It can merge, mesh, and combine data from multiple and varied data sources. It can interpret fuzzy logic—for example, the use of the LIKE operator. It can be used to scrub and clean data and then provide extensive support for many business intelligence operations and environments. The broad range involved with SSIS has spawned many books, classes, and white papers. In this book the focus will be more narrow, concerned primarily with the fundamentals of data ETL processes.

The basic parts of SSIS are as follows:

- *Package*: This is a unit of work that is defined, retrieved, and executed. Packages are stored in either the msdb database or an XML file in the filesystem. The filename extension for these XML files is .dtsx.

- *Control flow*: This contains tasks and containers. Tasks aid in performing operations such as preparing and copying data. Containers are used to manage groupings of tasks as logical units. Every package will contain at least one control flow member.

- *Data flow*: The data flow contains sources, transformations, and destinations. Simply put, the data flow is concerned with what happens to the data.

- *Variables*: Variables can be used for more dynamic operations— updating column values and controlling repeated control flows, for example.

- *Event handlers*: These answer conditions established for runtime occurrences to aid in monitoring and responding to the packages.

To open the SQL Server Business Intelligence Development Studio, the program used to define SSIS packages, choose Start ➤ All Programs ➤ SQL Server 2008 ➤ SQL Server Business Intelligence Development Studio. It is also possible to use command-line utilities to run packages or scripts by typing DTExec. Type DTExec/? to learn the switches and syntax of this command. The command line will also allow you to move, check, and verify the packages by using the DTDUTIL utility. Type DTDUTIL /? to gain information about syntax and switches provided by this utility. We will explore a few of these command-line choices later in the chapter.

Once you have the SQL Server Business Intelligence Development Studio (BIDS) open, you will see the screen in Figure 9.11.

From this start page there are several methods you can use to open the dialog to create a new package:

- Select File ➤ New ➤ Project to open a new project template dialog.

- Clicking the first icon on the toolbar will also open a new project template dialog.

- On the bottom of the Recent Projects pane on the left side of the page, click the project link next to the word *Create*.

Figure 9.11: SQL Server Business Intelligence Development Studio start page

Using one of these methods, open the New Project dialog (Figure 9.12) and follow these steps:

1. Click on Business Intelligence Projects in the Project Types list in the left pane of the dialog. The other choices provide groupings of templates for purposes we will not explore in this book, but you will not see the selections in the screenshot unless you have high-lighted the Business Intelligence Projects heading in the left side pane of the dialog.

2. In the pane on the right, choose Integration Services Project from the list of Visual Studio installed templates.

3. In the lower section of the dialog box, enter a name for the project and choose a location from the drop-down list. You can also use the Browse button to choose a location.

4. Select the Create Directory for Solution check box to make a new directory instead of adding the project to an existing directory. As

you type the name, in this case Sample_Package_1, the Solution Name text box is automatically populated with the same values.

5. Click OK to move on to the studio.

Figure 9.12: The New Project dialog

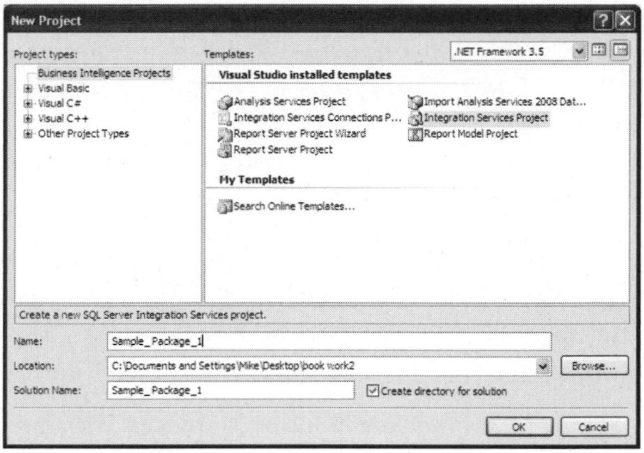

Figure 9.13 shows the main package design interface. Shown initially are the most important components that you will use in package design. Be aware that everything is context sensitive. What you have highlighted or focus on will determine what options you see in the Toolbox and Properties window.

Figure 9.13: SQL Server Business Intelligence Development Studio interface

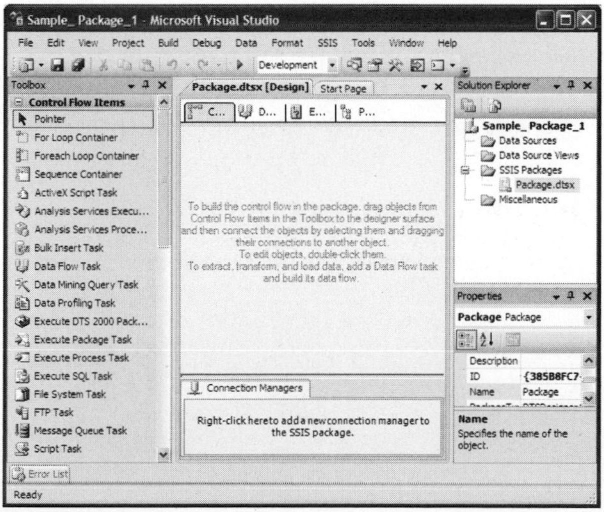

Data Administration

PART III

NOTE If you are looking for a dialog window that is not readily apparent, it can often be found on the View menu.

There are three different sections in the main package design interface:

- The Control Flow Items list shows in the left pane because the highlighted tab in the middle is the Control Flow Designer tab. If we had the data flow designer tab highlighted, we would see the toolbox with data flow objects. We will return to the toolbox as we walk you through package creation later on in the chapter.

- The center area of the screen is for designing packages and is controlled by the tabs across the top of that region. The first tab is for control flow tasks, the second tab is for data flow tasks, the third tab is for events, and the final tab is for the Package Explorer.

- The pane on the right holds the Solution Explorer, which is a container for all objects within the project, including data sources, views, packages, and the miscellaneous folder. Notice that the Solution Explorer contains a default package under the SSIS folder. This will exist every time this particular template is opened. Below the Solution Explorer is the Properties pane. It will display the properties for the highlighted object.

Now that we outlined some of the basic components and identified some of the fundamental items of SSIS, we'll make a package. The process to make a package mirrors in many ways the steps undertaken by the wizard. You perform those same steps manually and in your own design environment. You can launch the Import and Export wizards within the BIDS by choosing Project ➤ SSIS Import and Export Wizard. This will begin the exact process we outlined earlier in the chapter.

Create a Data Connection

Just as the first choice in the wizard is to select the data source, your first job is to create a data connection:

1. Start a New Data Source wizard by right-clicking on the Data Sources folder in Solution Explorer and choosing New Data Source. This will launch a New Data Source Wizard.

2. Click Next on the welcome screen; you'll see a dialog box.

3. Select the radio button to create a data source based on an existing or new connection.

4. Click the New button. The Connection Manager dialog appears, as shown in Figure 9.14.

Figure 9.14: The Connection Manager dialog

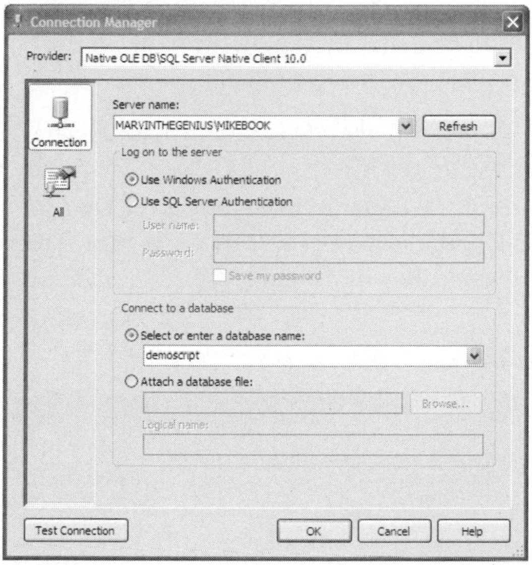

5. Select the type of data source you wish to connect to from the Provider drop-down menu.

6. From the Server Name drop-down menu, select specific servers available to you.

7. In the Connect to a Database section, choose a database in the drop-down that you wish to use.

8. Finally, click the Test Connection button to make sure the Connection Manager is aware of your data source.

A new data source name, in this case Demoscript.ds, will appear in the Solution Explorer under the Data Sources folder when this process is complete.

Implement a Data Flow Task

Now that you have a data connection defined, you are ready to move on to creating your first package:

1. Start by renaming the default package supplied in Solution Explorer. Right-click on Package.dtsx and choose Select Rename ➤ Provide a New Value. You may also rename the package by selecting it and then clicking on it again and typing the new name in the box. You can also use the Properties dialog below the Solution Explorer by typing the name in the File name field. Name this file First_ package.dtsx.

2. When you are prompted to decide if you want to change the package object name as well, select Yes.

3. In the design area in the center of BIDS, select the Data Flow tab and click the link in the center of the Data Flow page. The view will change to the one shown in Figure 9.15.

Figure 9.15: The Data Flow Task design area

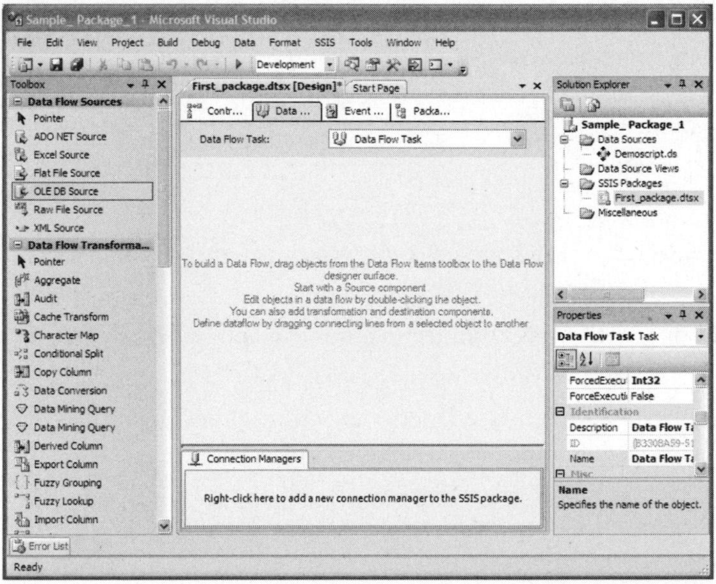

The text in the design area outlines the order in which you should develop a package.

    a. Start with a source component.

    b. Edit objects in the data flow by double-clicking the object.

    c. Lead transformation and destination components.

    d. Define data flow by dragging connecting lines from one selected object to another.

4. Drag OLE DB source from the toolbox to the data design area, as shown in Figure 9.16. If you do not see the toolbox, or any other window you are seeking for that matter, select it from the View menu. To show the toolbox, select View ➢ Toolbox. You can also press Ctrl+Alt+X on your keyboard.

Figure 9.16: The Data Flow Task design area with the OLE DB source

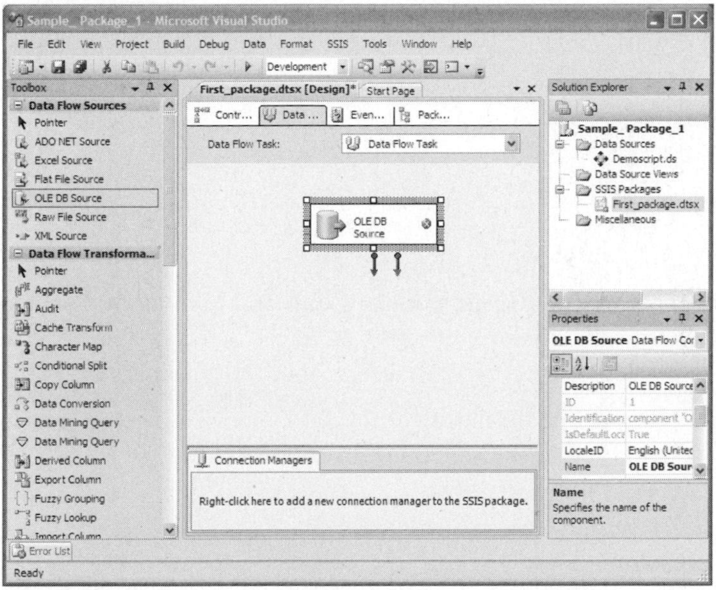

5. When the data source object is highlighted, you'll see a red and a green connector at the bottom of the object. The green connector provides a logical flow to the next object in the package design; the red connector shows how error output should be handled. We will discuss the connectors later on in the chapter.

6. Double-click the OLE DB source object to open the dialog shown in Figure 9.17, the OLE DB Source Editor dialog.

Figure 9.17: The OLE DB Source Editor dialog with the Configure OLE DB Connection Manager

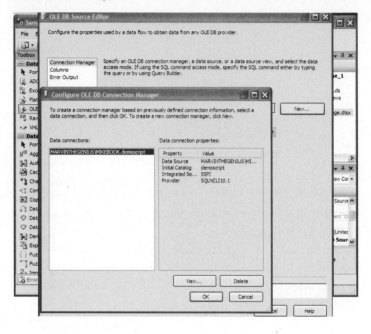

7. The pane on the left has areas that can be configured once you have selected the connection manager. Select one of the available defined connection managers from the drop-down list.

8. Next, define the nature of the data you wish to extract or use from the Data access mode drop-down. Your possible choices are as follows:

   - An existing table or view from the data source.

   - A table name or view name variable. If you select a table name or a view name variable, you will be prompted with a screen asking for the name of the predefined variable.

   - A SQL command. If you choose a SQL command, you will be presented with a text area in which to write your SQL query. SQL syntax is discussed in Chapter 4, "Executing Basic Queries."

- A SQL command from a variable. If you select a SQL command from a variable, you will be prompted for the variable name and the variable values to be supplied in the Variable Value field at the bottom of the dialog.

For this, choose the first selection, an existing table or view, as the data access mode.

The next step is to configure your connection manager. The connection manager is a gateway through which data will enter your SSIS environment from your data source. The data source creates the connection string with a data provider; the data manager tells you what data to bring into our package.

To configure a connection manager:

1. Select Connection Manager in the left pane and click the New button to the right of the drop-down to open the dialog in the forefront of Figure 9.17, Configure OLE DB Connection Manager. Data connections that have been defined for this solution will be shown in the Data Connections pane on the left. The pane on the right shows the properties for the highlighted data connection. At the bottom of this dialog there is a New button to define a new connection and a Delete button to remove a data source. For this example, we will use the default data source for this project, which we defined earlier.

2. Click Columns in the left pane to open the dialog shown in Figure 9.18, in which you can map the external data columns from the data source to output columns for SSIS purposes.

3. Select the available columns from the data source to use within your SSIS package in the center of the dialog. Below the column selection section there are two headings: External Column, in which each field value will provide a drop-down of the available fields to select, and Output Column, which is described in step 4.

4. Choose the name you desire for the column within your SSIS operation in the Output column field.

5. Select Error Output in the left pane to open the dialog shown in Figure 9.19. You'll use this dialog to handle errors that occur with data as it is extracted from its source.

Data Administration

PART III

Figure 9.18: The Columns Editor Screen

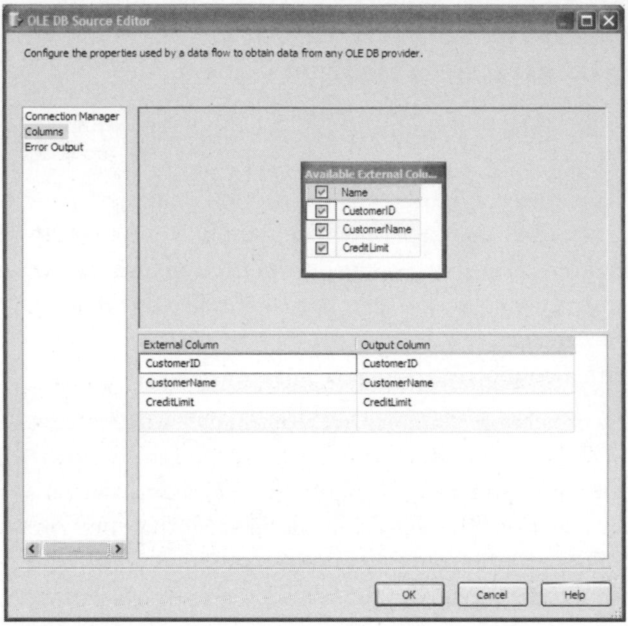

Figure 9.19: Error output

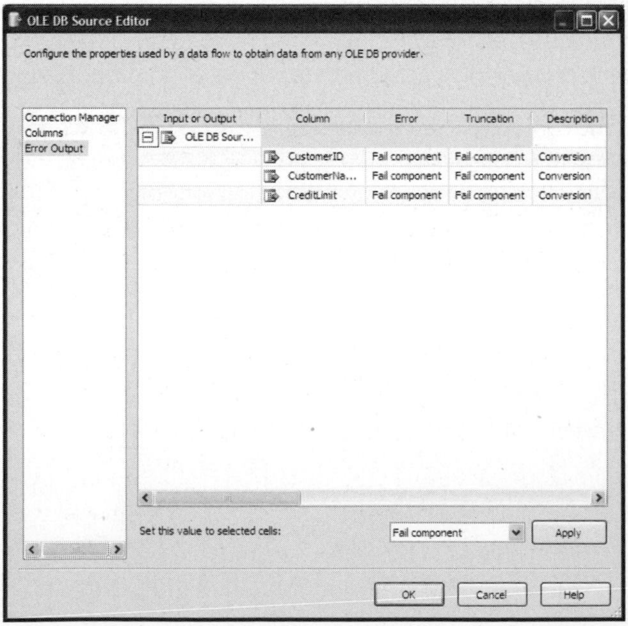

6. Next to each field that is being extracted are two columns. The first one is called Error. Each field under this column is a drop-down menu that allows you to choose an action should a data extraction row fail. There are three options in this column:

   a. The first selection is to fail the component. This means that the OLE DB source that is in the package will be recorded as an error and the package will stop running.

   b. The second choice in the drop-down menu is to redirect the row. Redirecting the row allows you to send the offending rows to a location where they can be collected and dealt with individually.

   c. The last choice is to ignore failure. This choice performs exactly what it says: the package will continue to run an attempt to complete the rest of its process. Do not select this option. If you have several rows that you want to give the same action to at the bottom, there is a Set This Value to Selected Cells drop-down menu from which you can select several cells, choose an action, and have it applied to all the cells you choose. In this exercise, leave the default of failing the component to fail the entire package as a result.

Perform a Transformation

The next step is to perform a data transformation:

1. From the toolbox, drag the conditional split data flow transformation control to the design area below the OLE DB data source.

2. Click the arrowhead on the green arrow under the OLE DB source; it must be highlighted for the arrows to appear. Drag it until it joins the conditional split control you just added. When the + appears, release the mouse button.

3. After you have made the connection, double-click the conditional split transformation control to configure it. The configuration dialog is shown in Figure 9.20.

4. In the Conditional Split Transformation Editor dialog, expand the Columns folder. Select the CreditLimit column and drag it to the condition area in the lower pane.

Figure 9.20: Conditional Split Transformation Editor dialog

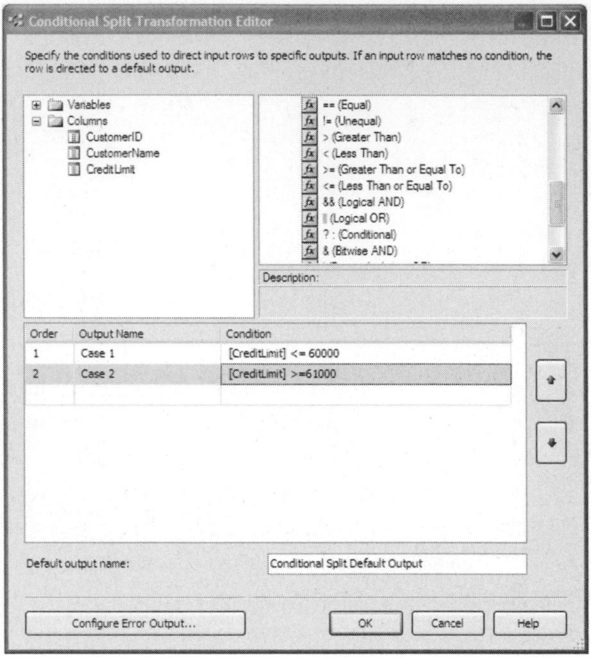

5. In the upper-right portion of the dialog, expand the Operators folder, choose Less Than or Equal To (<=) and drag it into the same condition box where CreditLimit is. This will become case 1 for determining the data split.

6. After the mathematical less than or equal to operator, enter a value of 60000.

7. Now repeat the process with the CreditLimit column, only use the greater than or equal to (>=) operator and enter a value of 61000. This will become case 2 for sorting your values.

8. At the bottom of the dialog, you can choose to give the default output a name and configure the error output as well.

9. After you configure your cases, click OK and return to the data flow designer pane. Add to the designer two flat file destinations from the data flow destination part of the toolbox and place them below the conditional split.

10. Highlight your conditional split control, which will cause the connector arrows to appear.

11. Click on the green arrow and drag it to the first flat file destination. The Input Output Selection dialog appears. The first drop-down will allow you to choose the case on you wish to base the data that will be sent to that destination. Use your drop-down and select case 1. Those customers meeting the condition that you established for case 1 will be sent to that flat file destination. You can see this action completed in Figure 9.21.

Figure 9.21: Conditional Split Transformation Input Output Selection dialog

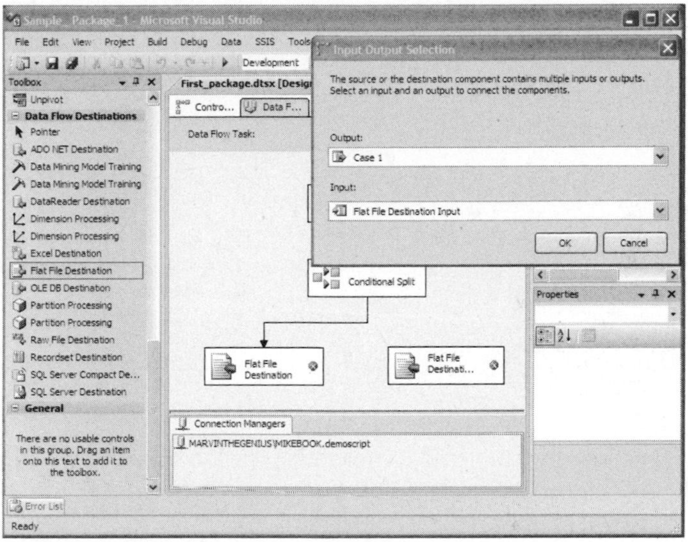

12. Double-click the flat file destination object in the data flow designer, and then configure the flat file destination editor by creating a new connection manager.

13. Once you choose to create a new connection manager, you will be asked what flat file format to you wish to use. Choose the delimited.

14. After you select delimited, you will be presented with a flat file connection manager editor in which the first blank asks for a name, the second line asks for description.

15. Click the Browse button next to the filename.

16. In the open file dialog box that appears, choose a name for the file and a location to save your output. Once you have done so, other options become available, as seen in Figure 9.22

17. Repeat steps 11 through 13 for the other destination, selecting a name that's different than the name you chose for the first destination.

Figure 9.22: Flat File Connection Manager Editor dialog

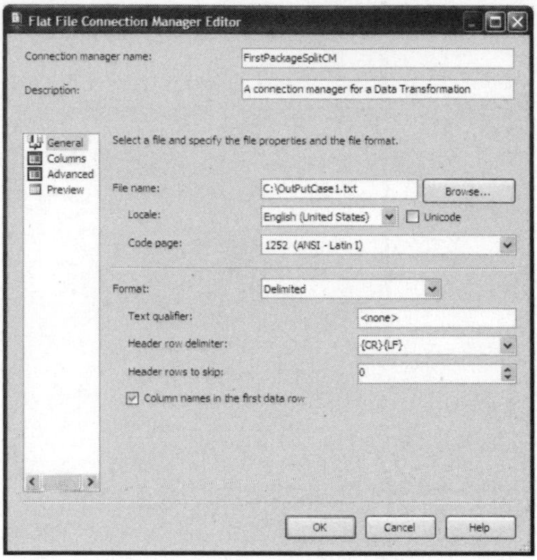

When you have completed these configuration steps, your BIDS should look like it does in Figure 9.23.

Figure 9.23: BIDS configured

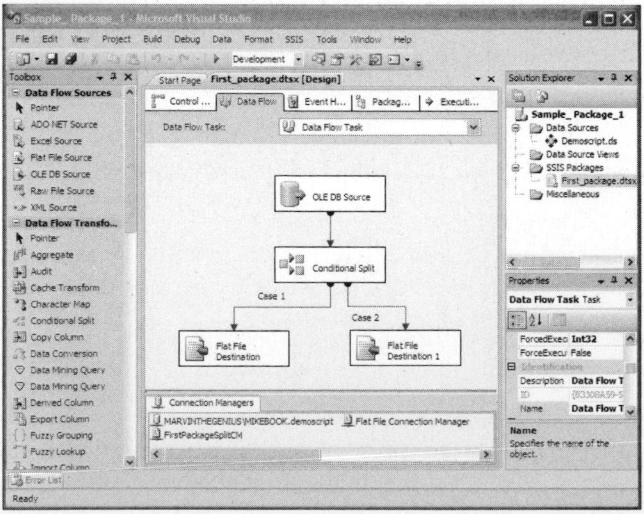

It is time to run the package you created. You can start a package by pressing F5 or clicking the green arrowhead in the toolbar above the design area. As the package runs, each component in its design will turn green. If a component fails, it will turn red. Figure 9.24 shows what BIDS should look like if the package successfully completes.

Figure 9.24: BIDS after a successfully run package

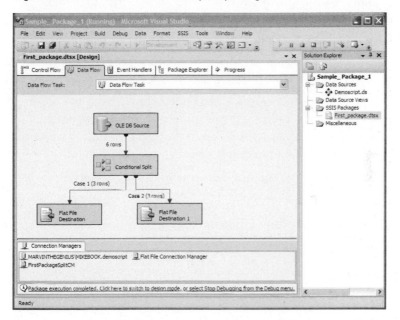

Figure 9.25 shows the output of the package that we just designed in two text files.

Figure 9.25: First_Package sorted output

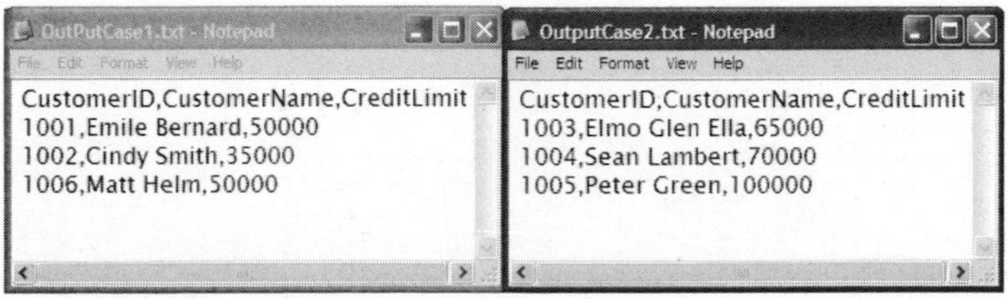

Data Administration

PART III

Implement Control of Flow Logic

In this brief example, we hope it is clear how versatile and valuable the SSIS processes can be. Now let's discuss how to implement the control flow. Control flow provides containers to hold various data flow tasks, loops, and other logical structures that can be used in data processing. It is possible to have a control flow task without a data flow task, but it is not possible to have a data flow task without a control flow task.

To implement a Control Flow section of a package, use the following steps:

1. Once you decide which components you wish to use, drag components to the design surface.

2. Use the precedent constraints to connect the elements of the control flow. The precedent constraints in the control flow design surface are the green arrows that in the data flow task are used to create the records connector between the objects.

3. Configure the properties of the elements of the control flow.

4. Group related tasks in containers.

5. Add comments or annotations to document the control flow.

The basic control flow task groups that can be performed are data tasks, database object transfer tasks, analysis services tasks, file and network protocol tasks, script and program execution tasks, package execution tasks, WMI tasks, maintenance plan database tasks, and other maintenance plan tasks.

When using the precedent constraints in the control flow, you specify not only which tasks are performed in order but also how the success or failure of the tasks involved controls the execution of further operations.

SSIS lends itself to a far greater examination of its topics and abilities. We encourage you to pursue this information in other publications and classes. Here we have presented a fundamental look at the operations of SSIS.

10

Managing Data Recovery

IN THIS CHAPTER, YOU WILL LEARN TO DO THE FOLLOWING:

Data Administration

PART III

O ne of the most critical parts of any database administrator's job description is handling data recovery. There are a variety of things that can go wrong, ranging from device failure to a system overheat. You must have a disaster recovery plan in place. Part of that plan should include a tested and verified backup strategy that allows you to restore your database with minimal exposure to data loss. While the strategies and trade-offs of a complete disaster recovery plan are beyond the scope of this book, the architecture and mechanics of backup and restore operations are fundamental to this process. This chapter presents you with those mechanics as defined by SQL Server 2008.

Understand Recovery Concepts

The entire SQL Server transaction architecture is really designed around the concept of recoverability. As a database administrator, you must be able to guarantee that your data is preserved and recoverable. Since you can't effectively design a recovery architecture without understanding SQL Server recovery concepts, we will begin with a discussion of transaction architecture and how it affects recoverability. Then we can examine different recovery strategies and match them up to your data recovery needs.

Understand Transaction Architecture

Transaction logging is a fundamental feature of SQL Server. It can provide for recoverability from a media-affecting failure as well as be the mechanism that makes common operations functional, such as triggers and the ability to roll back transactions. For this reason, you cannot turn off transaction logging in SQL Server. While you can allow for minimal logging or for certain types of nonlogged operations to occur, transaction logging is always there. Let's take a closer look at how it works.

How Transaction Logging Works

When SQL Server makes a data modification to a data page, it uses a technique called *write-ahead logging*. That is just a fancy way of saying that SQL Server writes any data modification to the transaction log before it writes those changes to the database. Figure 10.1 illustrates how this process executes.

Figure 10.1: The write-ahead log process

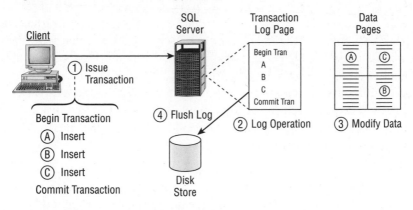

Step 1: Issue the transaction   In this example, the transaction has three INSERT statements, marked A, B, and C. These statements are all enclosed inside a user-defined transaction, meaning that the entire process must commit or fail atomically. The client submits this transaction to the server for processing.

Step 2: Log the operation   SQL Server makes all data modifications in a reserved memory block called the data cache. Both data pages and transaction log pages are part of this cache. Each data modification is first made to a transaction log page. In this example, INSERT A would be entered into a transaction log page.

Step 3: Modify the data   After the transaction log entry, SQL Server inserts the data row onto the appropriate data page. Figure 10.1 shows that the inserts are placed on specific data pages, implying that this data table is organized with a clustered index. This process repeats for all operations that are part of the transaction, with the log entry first and the data modification second.

Step 4: Flush the transaction log   Upon committing the transaction, SQL Server will flush the transaction pages that contain the record of the transaction from cache to disk. This ensures that there is a permanent record of those operations. The data pages do not flush to disk at this time but stay in cache as dirty pages until SQL Server determines that it is the optimal time to save this and any other transactions that have accumulated on these data pages to disk.

Data Administration

PART III

There are some distinct advantages to using this approach. These advantages address all stages of required recoverability:

- Since all operations exist on the transaction log in memory while a transaction is executing, SQL Server can use this log to roll back any transactions that must not commit.

- Since the transaction log record is permanently stored on disk, data cache loss due to a non-media-affecting failure, such as a power disruption, can be recovered automatically from the transaction log record stored on disk.

- If the database administrator takes transaction log backups, data can be recovered after media-affecting failures by restoring database backups and subsequent transaction log backups.

Planning the Physical Transaction Log Architecture

As you can see, the SQL Server transaction log is much more than a convenience. It is a critical part of the stability and recovery architecture. Planning the implementation of the transaction log is critical. As you are setting up your environment, here are some things that you should consider:

- Although you can create multiple transaction log files, there is little if any benefit in doing so. A single file will be easier to manage.

- Place the transaction log on a separate physical structure from the database. For example, if you have two physical disks in your server, you should create the data files on one disk and the transaction log files on the other. That way a loss of the disk containing the data files will not affect the log file.

- If you are using RAID, place your transaction log on a separate array for performance and recoverability. For recoverability, RAID-1 (mirroring) will ensure that the log is available if there is a device loss.

- The log devices tend to be more active than the data devices. There can be some advantage to placing the transaction log on the fastest physical devices.

- Performing regular backups of the database and transaction logs will keep the log from getting too large. Regular truncations can also help the log from getting too fragmented.

Design Backup Strategies

There are a variety of different backup strategies that you can employ to ensure the optimal mix of overhead versus recovery time. You should choose your strategy with the following recoverability needs in mind:

- Database volatility and transaction volume

- Acceptable recovery time for a media-affecting failure

- Acceptable level of potential data loss

- Acceptable size of backups

Types of Backups

Before we get into too much detail, however, we must first discuss the backup options available. There are a variety of different backup processes, each one providing an element of an overall strategy:

Full database backup A full database backup will truncate the transaction log and then copy every remaining data page and transaction log page to the backup media. The transaction log truncation will be non-reorganizing, meaning that no attempt is made to defrag/compact the log. It is simply truncated to the point of the last required transaction. Configured options such as replication can force transaction log pages to be retained even after they are not needed by the database because those transactions may need to be replicated to other servers. Most backup strategies require a full database backup as the baseline for recovery.

Differential backup A differential backup will store all of the database pages that have been modified since the last full database backup. Note that this is a true differential backup and not an incremental backup. This means that each differential backup is inclusive of all transactions executed since the last full database backup and not simply since the last differential backup.

File or filegroup backup If you are dealing with a very large database, you can back up individual files or filegroups. Breaking a large database into files or filegroups for backup allows you to back up portions of it on a rotating schedule when it might be too time-consuming to back up the entire database at once. If there is a failure affecting only one file or filegroup, only that portion and subsequent transaction logs would need to be restored.

Transaction Log Backup   This backup type will perform a non-reorganizing backup of the transaction log and store the transactions to the backup media. The primary difference between this and the other backup types is that while other backups store copies of the data pages, the transaction log backups store the actual transaction statements. This means that while restoring a full or differential backup means copying pages back to the database, restoring a transaction log backup requires reexecuting the transactions on the database. This can affect recovery time because restoring a log can be very time-consuming.

The Recovery Model

Also affecting the recovery strategy is the recovery model of the database. This property dictates the level of logging and log retention. To set this property, follow these steps:

1. Connect the SQL Server Management Studio to the server instance that hosts the database that you wish to configure.

2. Expand the Databases folder and locate the database that you wish to configure.

3. Right-click the database and select Properties from the menu.

4. Click on the Options page on the left side of the dialog. You will see a Recovery Model property with three options, as illustrated in Figure 10.2.

5. Select the desired option and then click OK to confirm and close the dialog.

This setting provides three options, as illustrated in Figure 10.2. It will directly affect which backup options SQL Server makes available to you.

Simple   The simple recovery model does not retain transaction logs for backup. When the database performs a checkpoint—that is, when it flushes all data and log pages to disk—it truncates the transaction log. This option is generally used during development when recoverability is not an issue. It can prevent the transaction log from getting too large when you're developing a database application. It does have some limited production uses.

Figure 10.2: Setting the Recovery Model property

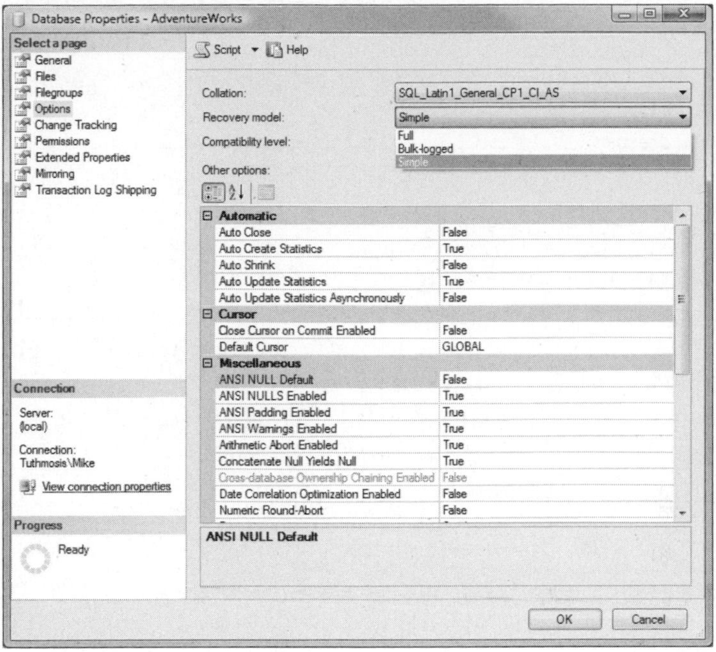

Bulk-logged The bulk-logged recovery model uses less disk space than a full logging solution by performing minimal transaction logging for the following operations:

- `SELECT INTO`
- bulk-load
- `CREATE INDEX`
- All operations involving text and image data types

Under this scenario, these operations are not fully recoverable.

Full The full recovery model is the most appropriate in the majority of situations. While it does require more logging overhead and regular log truncations, the result is a more recoverable database environment. Microsoft recommends that you use this option unless there is a specific justifiable reason not to do so.

Data Administration

PART III

> **NOTE** The following sections describe different recovery strate-
> gies. They do not go into the details of how to execute the steps.
> The mechanics of backup and restore will be addressed later in the
> chapter in the sections "Perform Backup Operations" and "Perform
> Restore Operations."

The Simple Backup Strategy

If you have a small to moderately sized database that is not very volatile,
you may be able to use a simple backup strategy. This approach will help
contain transaction log growth, but it does not allow you to back up
transaction logs. This means that there may be a small amount of data
loss. If this side effect is not acceptable, then this option will not be your
best choice. To use this strategy, follow these steps:

1. Set the Recovery Model option to Simple.

2. Take full database backups based on your preferred schedule.

3. If there is a failure, you will restore the most recent full database
   backup. You will not be able to take transaction log backups with
   Recovery Model set to Simple.

Figure 10.3 illustrates an example scenario using this strategy. In this
example, the database administrator takes a full database backup every
night at 10 p.m. Since the recovery model is set to Simple, there are no
recoverable transaction logs. If there were a disk failure on Thursday at
4 p.m., the DBA would restore the backup from Wednesday at 10 p.m.
Any transactions from that point to the point of the failure would be lost.

Figure 10.3: Using the simple recovery strategy

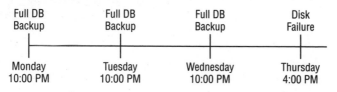

The Database-Only Backup Strategy

This option is similar to the previous strategy with the exception of the
fact that the recovery model is set to Full or Bulk-Logged. Using these

options, SQL Server will not truncate the transaction log on check-points, which means that the DBA can use the full log for recoverability. This option is acceptable only when there is a low transaction volume because the log will be truncated only when the DBA performs a full database backup. This option also requires that the transaction log be on separate physical media from the database so that a database failure will not affect the log. The steps to implement this strategy are as follows:

1. Set the recovery model to Full or Bulk-Logged.

2. Take full database backups on your preferred schedule.

3. If there is a database disk failure, begin by taking a backup of the orphaned log.

4. Restore the most recent full database backup, followed by a restore of the orphaned log.

Figure 10.3 can also illustrate this scenario. In this example, when the failure on the database device occurs Thursday at 4 p.m., the DBA would immediately take a backup of the transaction log to capture the activity from Wednesday at 10 p.m. to the point of the failure. The DBA would then restore the Wednesday 10 p.m. database backup, followed by the backup just taken of the orphaned log. When complete, there should be no data loss whatsoever.

The Transaction Log Backup Strategy

This option is more suitable for environments with higher transaction volumes. Instead of relying on full database backups to handle the transaction log truncations, the DBA will back up the log periodically, capturing all of the transactions and truncating the log. These transaction logs are then restored in the event of a failure. The downside to this option is that while transaction log backups are fast to take, they can be very time-consuming to restore. This option would involve the following steps:

1. Set the recovery model to Full or Bulk-Logged.

2. Take a full database backup that will act as the transaction log baseline.

3. Take regularly scheduled full database backups with periodic log backups in between.

Data Administration

PART III

4. If there is a database disk failure, begin by taking a backup of the orphaned log.

5. Restore the most recent full database backup, followed by each of the subsequent log backups in the order that they were taken.

6. Finally, restore the orphaned log.

Figure 10.4 illustrates an example scenario using this strategy. In this example, you will see that full database backups are interspersed with periodic log backups. If a database disk failure occurs at 5 p.m. on Tuesday, the DBA would immediately take a backup of the orphaned log. The DBA would then restore the following backups in this order:

1. Full DB backup from Tuesday 1 a.m.

2. Transaction log backup from Tuesday at 10 a.m.

3. Transaction log backup from Tuesday at 2 p.m.

4. Orphaned log backup from Tuesday at 5 p.m.

Figure 10.4: Using the transaction log backup strategy

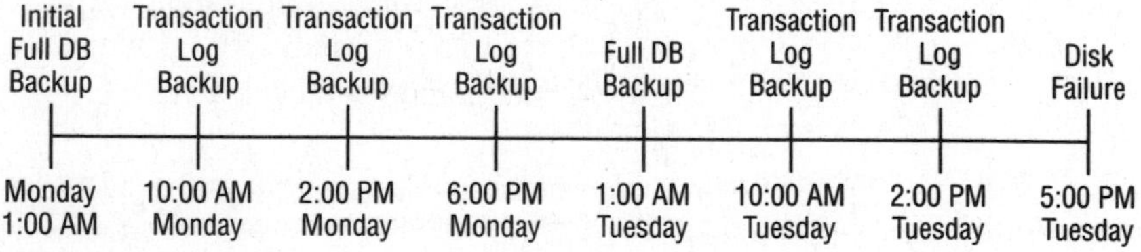

Initial Full DB Backup	Transaction Log Backup	Transaction Log Backup	Transaction Log Backup	Full DB Backup	Transaction Log Backup	Transaction Log Backup	Disk Failure
Monday 1:00 AM	10:00 AM Monday	2:00 PM Monday	6:00 PM Monday	1:00 AM Tuesday	10:00 AM Tuesday	2:00 PM Tuesday	5:00 PM Tuesday

The Differential Backup Strategy

If you have too many transaction log backups to restore, it can be a very time-consuming process. In some cases where most of the data modifications are isolated to a smaller subset of data pages in the database, it can be more efficient to periodically copy only the modified pages into a differential backup. The transaction logs would then need to be restored only from the point of the latest differential backup. You can also use differential backups without transaction log backups, in which case it works like the simple recovery model:

1. Set the recovery model to Full or Bulk-Logged.

2. Take a full database backup that will act as the transaction log baseline.

3. Take periodic full database backups as needed.

4. Take differential backups between the full database backups to record only the data pages that have been modified since the last full database backup.

5. Take transaction log backups between the differential backups to record the individual transactions between each of the differentials.

6. If there is a database disk failure, begin by taking a backup of the orphaned log.

7. Restore the most recent full database backup followed by the most recent differential backup.

8. Restore all transaction log backups taken since the last differential backup in the order that the backups were taken.

9. Finally, restore the orphaned log.

Figure 10.5 illustrates an example scenario using this strategy. You will see in the figure that there is a database backup taken on Monday at 1 a.m. There would be a subsequent full database backup as well—for example, maybe every subsequent Monday at 1 a.m., but these are not on this diagram. If the disk failure occurs on Wednesday at 1:00 p.m., the DBA would immediately take a backup of the orphaned log to capture the transactions from Wednesday at 10 a.m. to the point of the failure. The DBA would then restore the following backups in this order:

1. Full DB backup from Monday at 1 a.m.

2. Differential backup from Tuesday at 6 p.m.

3. Log backup from Wednesday at 10 a.m.

4. Orphaned log from Wednesday at 1 p.m.

Figure 10.5: Using the differential backup strategy

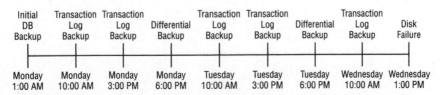

Initial DB Backup	Transaction Log Backup	Transaction Log Backup	Differential Backup	Transaction Log Backup	Transaction Log Backup	Differential Backup	Transaction Log Backup	Disk Failure
Monday 1:00 AM	Monday 10:00 AM	Monday 3:00 PM	Monday 6:00 PM	Tuesday 10:00 AM	Tuesday 3:00 PM	Tuesday 6:00 PM	Wednesday 10:00 AM	Wednesday 1:00 PM

Data Administration

PART III

Perform Backup Operations

As with most tasks in SQL Server, you can do backup and restore operations by using either the SQL Server Management Studio (SSMS) visual interface or Transact SQL (TSQL) code. In the following sections, we will show you both techniques for performing backup operations.

NOTE There are numerous third-party utilities that you can use to assist you in managing SQL Server backups. Most of these have their own tools and interfaces that you would use to take backups and perform restores. The rest of this chapter applies only to the SQL Server built-in toolset for backup and restore and does not directly apply to any of these third-party environments.

Perform Full Database Backups

A full database backup is a page-level copy of the entire database to backup media. You can execute a full database backup using any recovery model. The backup can be executed manually, or you can schedule backup operations using the SQL Server Agent service, which we will discuss in more detail in Chapter 14, "Automating with the SQL Server Agent Service."

Full Database Backups Using SSMS

There are a couple of different ways to drill into these dialogs. This is just one example. Once you get to the database backup configuration dialog, it is all the same. To back up a database using the SSMS, follow these steps. In this example, we will back up the AdventureWorks2008 database.

1. Open SSMS and connect to the server that hosts the target database.

2. Expand the Databases folder and locate the node for the AdventureWorks2008 database.

3. Right-click the AdventureWorks2008 Database node, and select Tasks ➤ Backup from the menu.

4. On the General page of the dialog, ensure that the database is set to AdventureWorks2008.

5. Set the backup type to Full. The Copy Only option will perform the backup without performing any truncations. This is usually done when a database backup needs to be taken for a special purpose outside of normal maintenance.

6. Name the backup set. In this example, we'll use the name AW_Full. Provide a description if desired.

7. Configure the backup to expire if you wish by providing either a number of days that the backup is allowed to age or a specific expiration date and time. You are not allowed to overwrite backups if they have not yet expired. Zero days means the backup expires immediately.

8. Provide a location for the backup. There is a default location provided. If you do not want to use it, click Remove and then Add to specify a new location. The Select Backup Destination dialog is pictured in Figure 10.6.

Figure 10.6: Adding a backup location

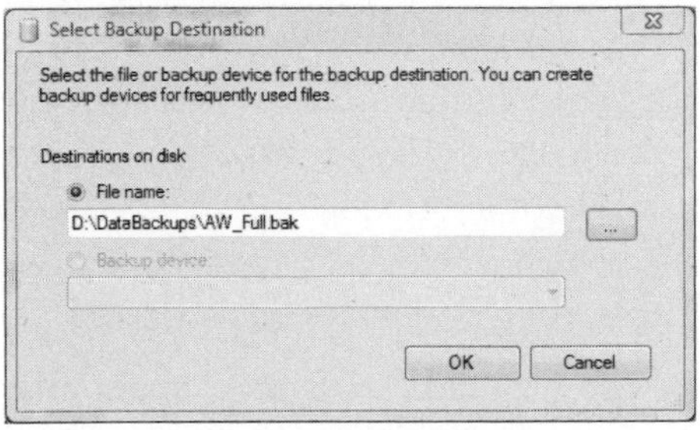

9. This example shows a backup file called AW_Full.bak. The system will not create this file until the backup is actually performed. Note that the Backup Device option is dimmed out. A backup device is a preconfigured backup location, such as a file location or a tape drive. Click OK.

10. You can add multiple locations for a striped backup. This can sometimes improve performance, but all members of the media set must be present to do the restore. The completed General page is illustrated in Figure 10.7.

Figure 10.7: General backup configurations

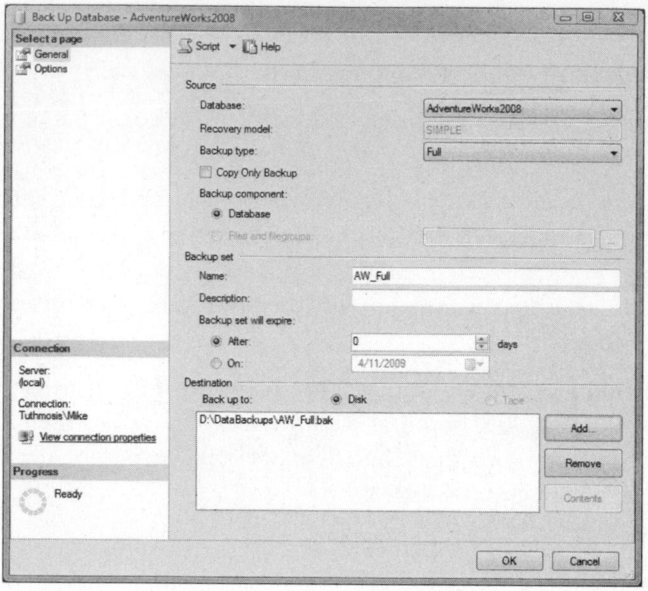

11. Click the Options page. Your first option is to overwrite the media set. You can set this option on or off, and you can also have it check the media expiration for automatic overwrite. You can also overwrite any existing media set with a completely new one. This will destroy all existing backup structures on the media.

12. The reliability options allow you to perform verifications and error checking to ensure that your backups are valid. These options will increase the time requirements and overhead of performing backups.

    Note that the options for transaction logs in this example are dimmed because the Recovery Model property is set to Simple. Also, the options for tape drives are dimmed in this example because there is no tape drive attached and installed on this server.

13. If you wish to compress your backups, you can select a compression option at the bottom. If you choose Use the Default Server Setting, whichever compression setting is currently configured for the backup compression default server option will be used.

14. The completed Options page is illustrated in Figure 10.8. Click OK to start the backup.

Figure 10.8: Backup Options

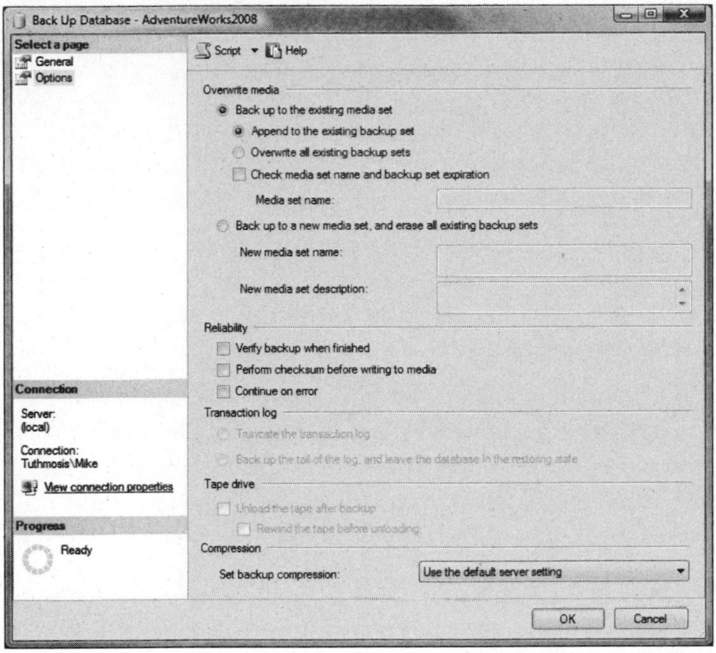

Data Administration

PART III

Full Database Backups Using TSQL

The basic syntax for a database backup operation looks like this:

```
BACKUP DATABASE { database_name | @database_name_var }
 TO DISK = <filename> [ ,...n ]
 [ WITH { DIFFERENTIAL | <general_WITH_options> [ ,...n ] } ]
 [;]
```

The most common general options are as follows:

```
<general_WITH_options> [ ,...n ]::=
--Backup Set Options
 COPY_ONLY
 | { COMPRESSION | NO_COMPRESSION }
 | DESCRIPTION = { 'text' | @text_variable }
 | NAME = { backup_set_name | @backup_set_name_var }
 | { EXPIREDATE = { 'date' | @date_var }
 | RETAINDAYS = { days | @days_var } }
```

```
--Media Set Options
  { NOINIT | INIT }
  | MEDIADESCRIPTION = { 'text' | @text_variable }
  | MEDIANAME = { media_name | @media_name_variable }
```

Most of these options should be clear if you compare them to the SSMS dialogs that we saw previously; however, there are two options that require additional discussion.

INIT   This option indicates that SQL Server will overwrite any existing backups on the target media with new backups. In other words, the backup that you are taking with this statement will be the initial backup on the media.

NOINIT   This option indicates that SQL Server will append this backup to any other backups on the target media. This option allows you to take multiple backups and target them to the same media set. For example, all transaction log backups that might need to be applied in sequence following a full database restore might be placed in the same media set.

The following code shows how to create a simple database backup. This backup will always be the first backup on the target media and will expire after seven days:

```
USE master;
GO

BACKUP DATABASE AdventureWorks2008
TO DISK = 'D:\DataBackups\AW_Full_TQSL.bak'
WITH RETAINDAYS = 7, INIT;
GO
```

The following example shows a backup that is striped across two files. This is most advantageous when the files are on separate devices and, ideally, separate controllers. This example will also compress the backup as it stores it on the media:

```
USE master;
GO

BACKUP DATABASE AdventureWorks2008
```

```
TO DISK = 'D:\DataBackups\AW_Full_TQSL_1.bak',
 DISK = 'D:\DataBackups\AW_Full_TQSL_2.bak'
WITH COMPRESSION, INIT;
GO
```

Perform Differential Backups

A differential backup looks almost identical to a full database backup. When taking a differential backup in the SSMS, you only need to change the Backup Type option to Differential. Figure 10.9 illustrates the General page of the Back Up Database dialog set to take a differential backup.

Figure 10.9: Taking a differential backup

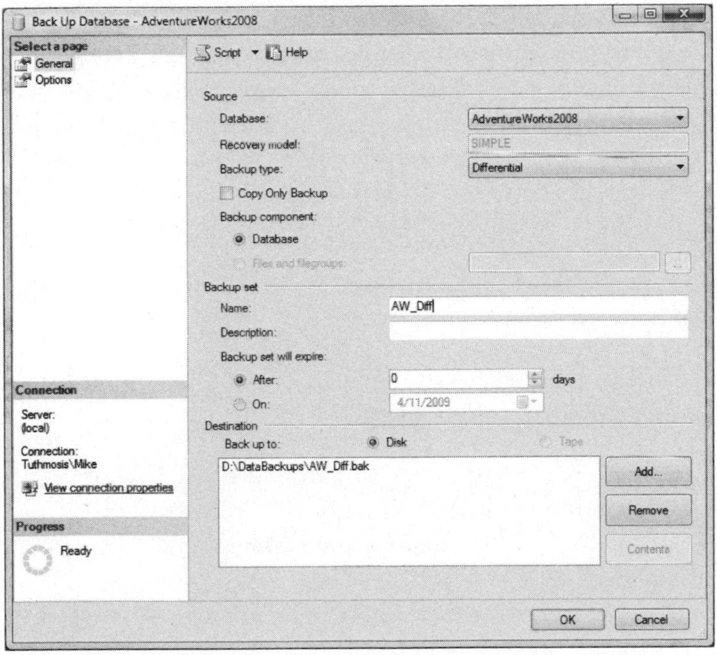

The TSQL code for a differential backup is also virtually identical to a full database backup. All you have to do is to add the WITH DIFFERENTIAL statement in your code. All of the other options are the same. The following code example shows a differential backup appended to a media file that contains the corresponding full database backup. This backup expires in seven days:

```
USE master;
GO


BACKUP DATABASE AdventureWorks2008
TO DISK = 'D:\DataBackups\AW_Full_TQSL.bak'
WITH DIFFERENTIAL,
RETAINDAYS = 7, NOINIT;
GO
```

Perform Transaction Log Backups

Transaction log backups allow the DBA to manage the transaction log size while not requiring the overhead of taking frequent database backups. This is especially useful for large databases that are only moderately volatile. Again, you can execute this process either by using the SSMS or with TSQL code. Before you will be able to take a valid Transaction log backup, you must do two things:

- Ensure that the Recovery model is not set to Simple

- Take a full database backup that will act as the initial point in the recovery process.

Transaction Log Backups with SSMS

Most of the options are the same as with a full database backup. However, there are a few differences. Figure 10.10 illustrates the General page of the Back Up Database dialog when you're taking a transaction log backup.

You will notice the following differences in the dialog:

- The recovery model is set to FULL.

- The Backup Component section is dimmed out. This section is not relevant for transaction log backups.

There are also a few differences in the Options page. Figure 10.11 provides an illustration of this page for a transaction log backup.

Figure 10.10: Transaction log backup General page

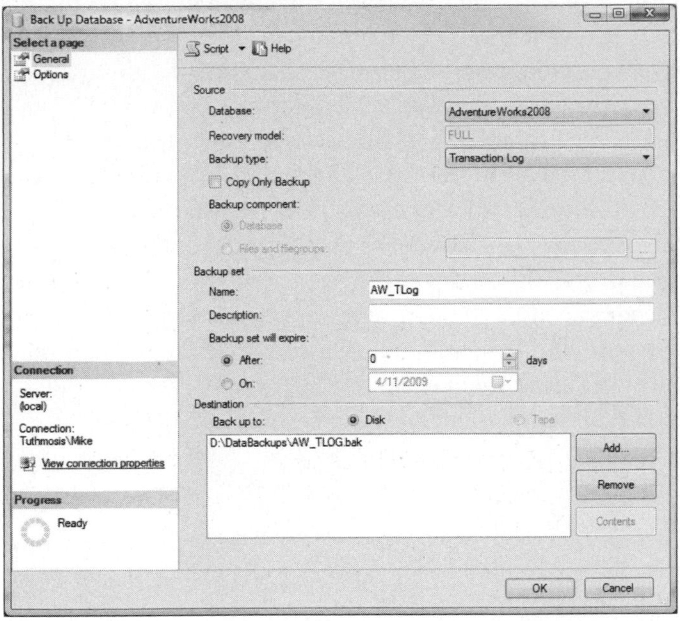

Figure 10.11: Transaction log backup Options page

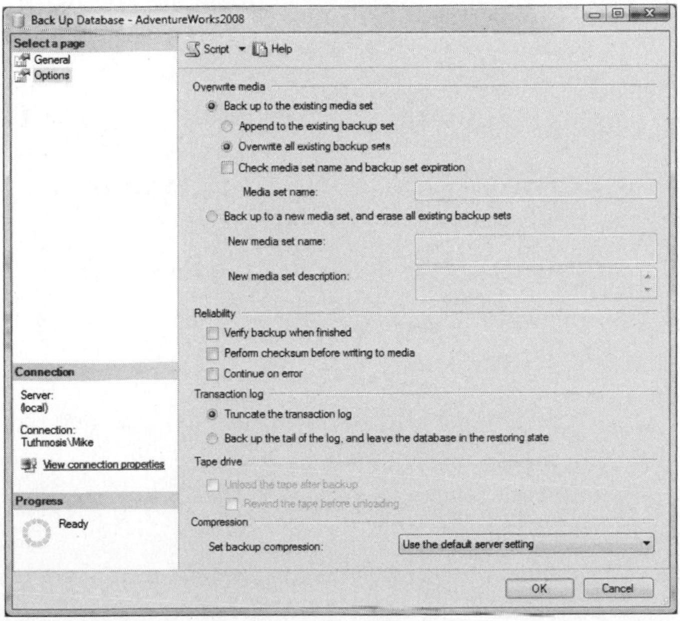

The primary difference in this dialog is the Transaction Log section. The default option is to truncate the transaction log. This would be the desired option for most standard maintenance. However, it is not always the option you should use. Remember that when we discussed backup strategies, we mentioned that at certain times you would need to take a backup of the orphaned log? The second option, "Back up the tail of the log, and leave the database in the restoring state," is the option that you will choose to perform this important task.

The rest of the options are identical to the full database and differential backup behaviors, although generally you will apply them a little differently. For example, if you take a series of transaction log backups between full database backups, you may want to place them all on the same media. This will make them easier to restore later. You should therefore be careful about your use of the overwrite options to ensure that related backups are grouped together on a common media set and that you do not inadvertently destroy backups by initializing the media set out of sequence.

Transaction Log Backups with TSQL

The TSQL syntax for backing up a transaction log is very similar to the database and differential log backup code. The basic syntax looks like this:

```
BACKUP LOG { database_name | @database_name_var }
 TO <backup_device> [ ,...n ]
 [ WITH { <general_WITH_options> | <log-specific_optionspec>
 }
  [ ,...n ] ]
[;]
```

The options are basically the same, except that you have these options as well:

```
{ NORECOVERY | STANDBY = undo_file_name }
| NO_TRUNCATE
```

The default behavior for a transaction log backup is to truncate the log. Using these options will change that behavior. Specifically, these options have the following impact:

NORECOVERY   This option allows the DBA to capture a trailing log prior to a restore. When you use this option, the system does not truncate the log. Following the log backup, the database is set to a restoring state pending recovery from the backup media.

STANDBY   This option allows the DBA to create a standby server. When you take a transaction log backup using this option, the tail portion of the log is backed up and the database is left in a read-only state. The undo file contains any log fragments needed to apply additional transactions.

NO_TRUNCATE   This is a copy-only option for the log that backs up the entire log but does not truncate the log. If the database is damaged, you must use this option to capture the log. If you are attempting to capture an orphaned log after a database device failure, use this option in conjunction with the NORECOVERY option.

As an example, the following code will back up the transaction log and initialize the media. SQL Server will truncate the transaction log as part of the backup process:

```
USE master;
GO


BACKUP LOG AdventureWorks2008
TO DISK = 'D:\DataBackups\AW_LOG_TQSL.bak'
WITH INIT;
GO
```

If you wanted to take a subsequent backup of the transaction log and append it to the existing media, the statement would look like this:

```
USE master;
GO


BACKUP LOG AdventureWorks2008
TO DISK = 'D:\DataBackups\AW_LOG_TQSL.bak'
WITH NOINIT;
GO
```

At this point, if the database were damaged due to a corruption or loss of a data device, you would capture the orphaned log with the following code example. Please note, do *not* execute this statement unless

Data Administration

PART III

you have all backups needed to restore the database. This statement will render the database inaccessible until it is restored:

```
USE master;
GO


BACKUP LOG AdventureWorks2008
TO DISK = 'D:\DataBackups\AW_LOG_TQSL.bak'
WITH NOINIT, NO_TRUNCATE, NORECOVERY;
GO
```

After executing this statement, the system will mark this database as "restoring." If you refresh the database in the Object Explorer window of SSMS, you will see an indication that the database is in a restoring status, as illustrated in Figure 10.12.

Figure 10.12: A database in restoring status

Perform Partial Database Backups

There are some cases when performing a full database backup might be wasteful. For example, suppose you have a large database that stores many static lookup tables. Or maybe the database contains a large set of data that is imported from another database or other data feed. In this case, perhaps only a small portion of the database is ever the target of user transactions. It would be wasteful to continually back up the entire database when only a subset of the data is truly user-affected. This is the perfect scenario for a partial backup.

This is a new feature of SQL Server 2008. For this approach to work, you must plan ahead by taking the following steps:

1. Create the database using multiple data files in filegroups.

2. Separate the nonvolatile data from the user-affected data by placing them into different filegroups.

3. Mark the filegroups that contain the nonvolatile data as read-only.

Now you are ready to perform a partial backup. This option is not supported by the SSMS, so if you want to use this approach, you must do it through TSQL code. In your backup script, include READ_WRITE_ FILEGROUPS to instruct SQL Server to back up only the primary filegroup and any other filegroup that is marked as a read/write filegroup. SQL Server will not back up any filegroups that are marked as read-only. Other than this behavior, the resulting backup is identical to a standard database backup. The following code shows an example:

```
USE master;
GO

BACKUP DATABASE AdventureWorks2008 READ_WRITE_FILEGROUPS
TO DISK = 'D:\DataBackups\AW_Partial_TQSL.bak'
WITH INIT;
GO
```

Perform Restore Operations

The best backup processes in the world will not help you much if you do not have a plan for restoration. The first section of this chapter, "Understand Recovery Concepts," covered backup strategies and also addressed restore options, so you should already be somewhat familiar with how you will approach the restoration of your databases. In fact, it is critical that you consider how you will implement the restore process as this will directly affect the backup strategy that you will select.

SQL Server tracks information about backup processes in two places. First, SQL Server stores a backup history in the system catalog. This can be convenient as you perform restore operations because SQL Server will know through this history which backups you have taken. Second, each

Data Administration

PART III

backup media has a header that keeps track of the specific backups that are on in the media set. This will help you to know if you have the right media in place as you begin a restore operation.

In the following sections, we will look at the different approaches to restoring SQL Server databases and transaction logs. We will also look at some special cases, such as point-in-time recovery.

NOTE   The examples in the following sections will use the old pubs database for simplicity because we will be demonstrating the process of merging backup and restore processes. If you do not have the old SQL Server 2000 pubs database installed in your server, you can download the installation scripts from Microsoft. Navigate to www.microsoft.com and search the website for "Northwind and Pubs Sample." The first hit should be the installation for the sample databases. These work just fine on SQL Server 2008. Download and execute the MSI, which will create a folder with the installation scripts. Then run the instpubs.sql script to install the pubs database.

Perform a Full Database Restore

There may be a variety of reasons why you want to restore a database, including the following:

- You need to restore a backup copy over the top of an existing database on a server to restore it to an earlier point in time.

- You need to restore a database to a server after it has been damaged.

- You want to move or copy an entire database to another server.

To illustrate how to restore a database, we will walk you through the process of taking a backup of the pubs database, modifying data, and performing restores. First, you will need to take a full database backup of pubs, and then we will show you how to execute the restore using both SSMS and TSQL. Follow these steps to prepare the database for a restore.

1. Set the recovery model of the pubs database to Full. Refer to the steps earlier in this chapter if you need help.

2. Take a full database backup of the pubs database. You can either use the SSMS or the following script. If you use this script, replace the filename with an appropriate path and name for your system:

```
USE master;
GO

BACKUP DATABASE pubs
TO DISK = 'D:\DataBackups\pubs_full.bak'
WITH INIT;
GO
```

3. Execute the following query to find out the first name of the author in the database with the last name of White (the name should be Johnson):

```
USE pubs;
GO

SELECT au_fname
FROM authors
WHERE au_lname = 'White';
GO
```

4. Modify the first name of this author to John by executing the following code:

```
USE pubs;
GO

UPDATE authors
SET au_fname = 'John'
WHERE au_lname = 'White';
```

5. Perform a differential backup that captures this change by executing the following code:

```
USE master;
GO
```

```
BACKUP DATABASE pubs
TO DISK = 'D:\DataBackups\pubs_full.bak'
WITH DIFFERENTIAL, NOINIT;
GO
```

Restore a Database and Logs with the SSMS

The following steps will walk you through performing a restore of the full database:

1. Connect the SSMS Object Explorer to the server instance to which you would like to restore the database.

2. Locate the Databases folder and right-click. Select Restore Database from the menu. You should be looking at the General page of the Restore Database dialog.

3. Enter **pubs** in the To Database box. If the database already exists on the server and you are restoring over the top of it, you can select it from the list. Leave the point in time setting at Most Recent Possible.

4. To select the backup source, you have two options. If the database exists on the target server, you can use the backup history to select your source. In the From Database list, select pubs. This will populate the backup sets list with the relevant backups. You should see both the database and differential backups in the list.

5. You can also point to the media to select backups. Select the From Device option and click the ellipses (...) button to the right of the text box. This will open a Specify Backup dialog. Make sure that the media is set to File and click the Add button.

6. Browse to your media file and click OK. Repeat this process if there is more than one file in the media set. The completed dialog should look like Figure 10.13. Click OK to return to the restore dialog.

7. This list in Figure 10.14 shows the same backups that you took previously, but for a different reason. These are the backups that are stored on this media. No matter which approach you use, make sure you click the check box on the row for each backup that you want to restore. In this example, we will restore only the full database backup and not the differential. The completed page should look like Figure 10.14.

Figure 10.13: Adding backup media files

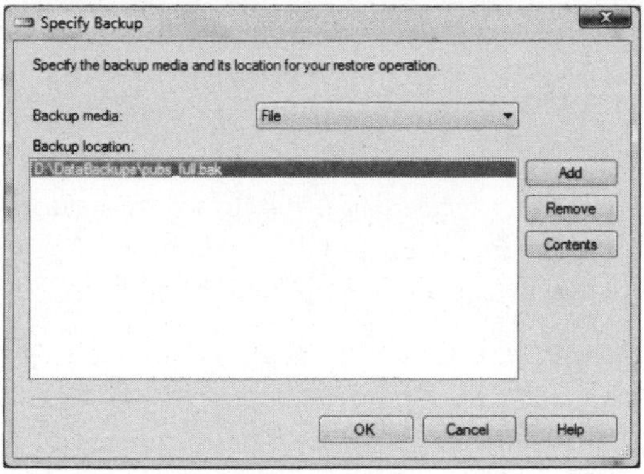

Figure 10.14: The Restore Database General page

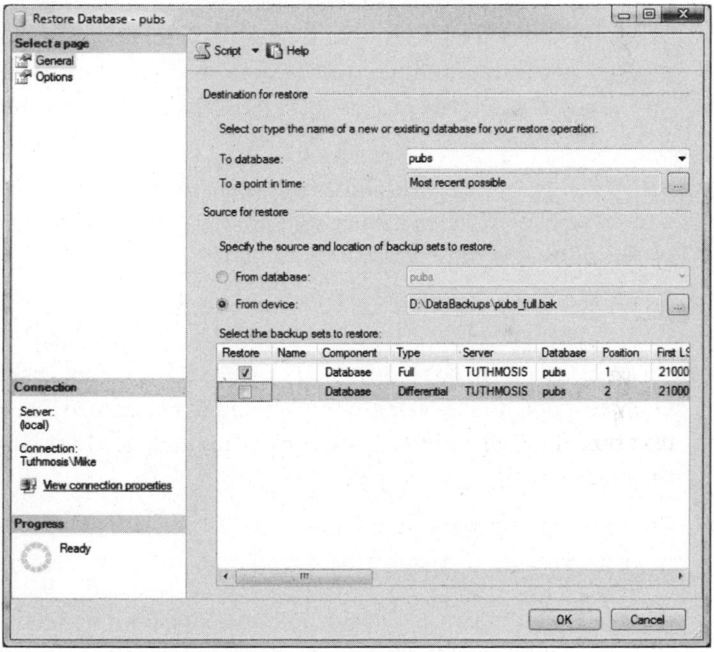

8. Click the Options page to see the restore options. If you are restoring over the top of an already existing database, you must select the Overwrite option. This prevents you from accidentally overwriting a database. The default is off.

9. If the database is originally configured for replication, you can decide if you want to preserve those settings on restore. The default is off.

10. If you are restoring multiple backups at once, you can choose to be prompted for each backup. The default is off.

11. You can choose to restrict access to the database after restore so that admin users can verify the restore and do any other post-restoration tasks necessary before bringing it online. The default is off.

12. If you want to restore the data and log files to a different physical location, you can specify that location here. This is useful when restoring a backup to a different server where you may be using a different physical file organization.

13. The recovery state allows three options, depending on if you plan to restore additional components to the database:

    a. If this is the final restore sequence and you want the database to be operational, then restore with recovery. This means that you will not be able to restore any additional transaction logs to the database.

    b. If you plan to restore additional logs, then restore with no recovery. The database will not be accessible to users at this point.

    c. If you want the database to be in a queryable read-only status but still allow additional logs to be restored, then restore with standby. The standby file will contain the log fragments needed to restore additional logs later. This is very useful for creating a warm standby server.

14. In our example, we will restore with recovery. The completed Options page should look like Figure 10.15. Click the OK button to execute the restore operation.

Because we took the database backup before we modified Mr. White's first name, if you execute the SELECT statement again, it should return the name Johnson. If you run through the process again and restore both the database and the differential backup, you would be able to see the change to the first name that you made earlier.

Remember that when restoring differential backups, you only need to restore the latest differential. For example, if we had taken two differentials after the full database backup and now wanted to restore to the latest point, the restore screen would look like Figure 10.16. Notice how only the last differential is selected for restore.

Figure 10.15: The Restore Database Options page

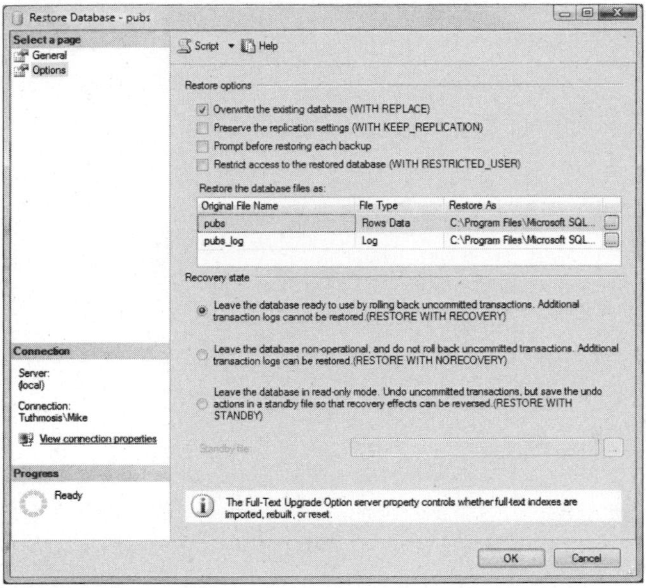

Figure 10.16: Restoring with multiple differentials

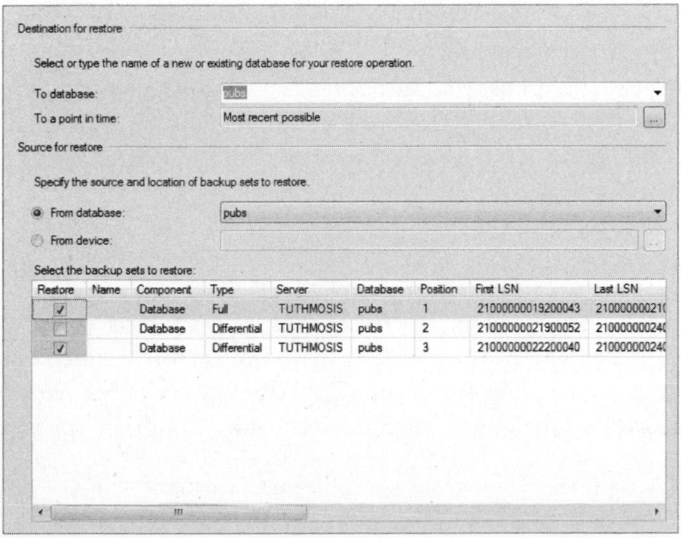

If you have taken transaction log backups, you will see those backups in the history as well. Figure 10.17 illustrates the backup history of pubs with a series of differential and log backups. Notice that when doing the restore, we would ignore all but the last differential and then restore all of the log backups taken since the last differential.

Figure 10.17: Restoring transaction log backups

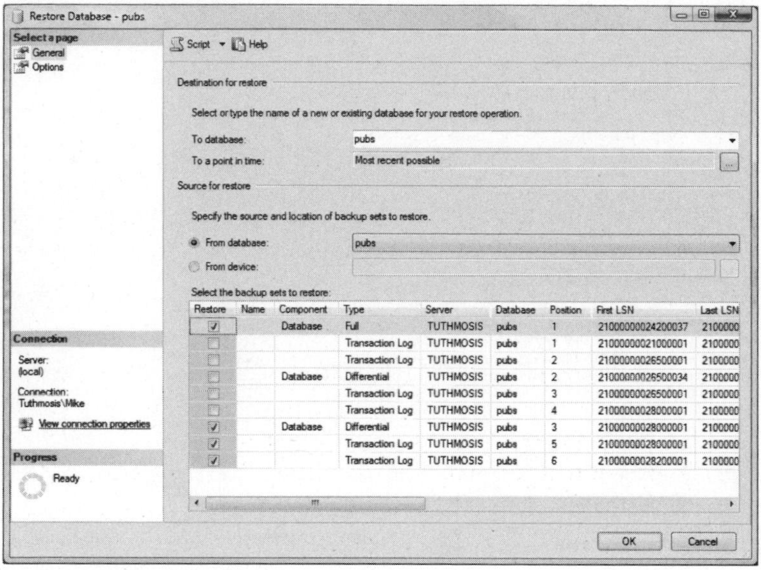

If you are restoring all of the logs, including the orphaned log if necessary, in this single operation, then you can perform the restore with recovery. Otherwise, if you have additional logs to restore, you would want to restore with no recovery until you restore the last log. The final log will always be restored with recovery if you want your database to be operational at that time.

Restore a Database and Logs with TSQL

You can perform all necessary restore operations with TSQL code as well if you prefer. You will need to execute a separate RESTORE statement for each backup that you want to restore. The basic syntax of the database restore is as follows, along with some of the most common options:

```
RESTORE DATABASE { database_name | @database_name_var }
  [ FROM <backup_device> [ ,...n ] ]
```

```
[ WITH
{
 [ RECOVERY | NORECOVERY | STANDBY =
 {standby_file_name | @standby_file_name_var }
 ]
| , <general_WITH_options> [ ,...n ]
]
[;]


--Restore Operation Options
 MOVE 'logical_file_name_in_backup'
  TO 'operating_system_file_name'
   [ ,...n ]
 | REPLACE
 | RESTART
 | RESTRICTED_USER

--Backup Set Options
 | FILE = { backup_set_file_number | @backup_set_file_number
}

--Error Management Options
 | { CHECKSUM | NO_CHECKSUM }
 | { STOP_ON_ERROR | CONTINUE_AFTER_ERROR }

<replication_WITH_option>::=
 | KEEP_REPLICATION
```

Notice the backup set options in the code. You will see an option in the form of FILE = backup_set_file_number. This option allows you to specify a specific backup in a media set based on its position number. For example, look at Figure 10.17. You will notice a Position column in the backup list. The number in this column represents that backup's position on the media. You need this information to ensure that you are restoring the correct backup from the media if there are multiple backups stored on the same media. You can also get this information using TSQL by using this code for each media file:

```
RESTORE Headeronly
FROM DISK='D:\DataBackups\Pubs_Full.bak'
GO
```

Data Administration

To illustrate, the following code will restore the pubs database with these options:

- The location of the backup media is d:\DataBackups\pubs_full. bak.

- The full database backup is the first backup in this file.

- This restore will overwrite the existing pubs database on this server.

- This restore will allow additional backups to be restored, so the database will be inaccessible until the process is complete.

```
USE master;
GO

RESTORE DATABASE pubs
FROM DISK = 'D:\DataBackups\Pubs_Full.bak'
WITH FILE = 1,
 REPLACE,
 NORECOVERY;
GO
```

Since the restore was executed with NORECOVERY, you are free to add additional backups as needed. If you were to look at the Object Explorer in the SSMS now, the pubs database would show in a restoring state. You may need to refresh the Database node to see this.

Now you can add the last differential backup. This is at position 3 on the backup file that you just took, since we can ignore the first differential backup. We still need to store in a NORECOVERY mode because we will add log backups after this, so we would use this code:

```
USE master;
GO

RESTORE DATABASE pubs
FROM DISK = 'D:\DataBackups\Pubs_Full.bak'
WITH FILE = 3,
 NORECOVERY;
GO
```

Notice that there is no need to use the REPLACE option because we are restoring a differential backup instead of a full backup. Also, you will see that there is no special indicator that this is a differential backup. The essential syntax looks the same as a full database backup. You are now ready to apply transaction log backups. The syntax is similar; you simply use RESTORE LOG instead of RESTORE DATABASE. The following code shows how to restore the first log file taken after this differential:

```
USE master;
GO

RESTORE LOG pubs
FROM DISK = 'D:\DataBackups\Pubs_Log.bak'
WITH FILE = 5,
  NORECOVERY;
GO
```

Finally, we can restore the final log. We will restore this log with RECOVERY to make the database accessible to users. In a real recovery scenario, this will usually be the orphaned log:

```
USE master;
GO

RESTORE LOG pubs
FROM DISK = 'D:\DataBackups\Pubs_Log.bak'
WITH FILE = 6,
  RECOVERY;
GO
```

Your database should now be fully restored and online for users.

Use Point-in-Time Recovery

Normally you will restore a transaction log to the latest possible point in time, capturing the log in its entirely. There may be some cases, however, when you want to halt the recovery at a certain point in time. For example, if someone inadvertently dropped a production table from the database, you may need to restore from a backup to recover the table. There are a couple of problems with this, however:

- If you capture the orphaned log and restore the entire log, you will simply repeat the drop operation and will gain nothing.

- If you do not restore the final log, you will lose any transactions that may have occurred between the last log backup and the point of the desired recovery.

Data Administration

PART III

The solution is to recover to a specific point in time. You can do this either with the SSMS or with TSQL code. In this case, assume that the inadvertent drop happened on April 12 at 3:11 p.m. You might choose to recover everything before that by using a load stop point of 3:09 p.m. This is a very simple operation in the SSMS, as illustrated in Figure 10.18.

Figure 10.18: Restoring to a point in time

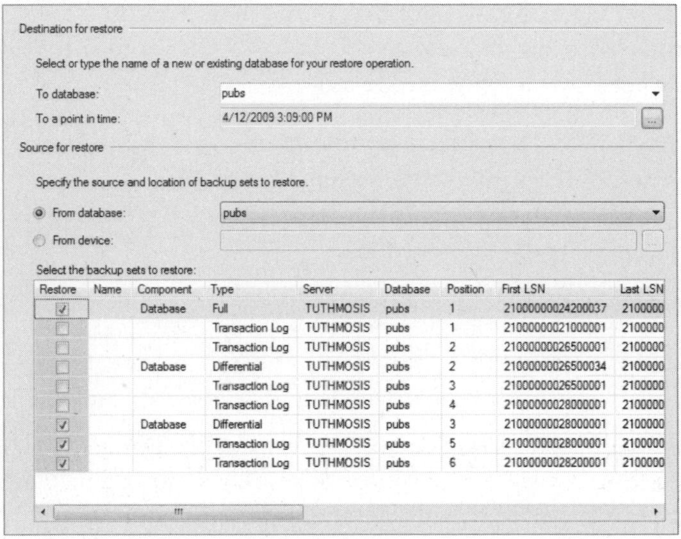

You will notice in this dialog that we have replaced the option for a point in time to stop at exactly 3:09 p.m. If you restore this last log with recovery, the server will roll back any uncompleted transactions at this point in time and make the database operational. There will be some data loss, but hopefully it will be minimized.

To perform the same action using TSQL code, you would perform all restores as before except for the log that contains the stopping point. The restore for that final log would look like this instead:

```
USE master;
GO

RESTORE LOG pubs
FROM DISK = 'D:\DataBackups\Pubs_Log.bak'
```

```
WITH FILE = 6,
 RECOVERY,
 STOPAT = 'Apr 12, 2009 3:09 PM';
GO
```

Another option that is only available in TSQL code is to restore to a transaction mark. For example, suppose you wanted to execute a statement and test the results but there is a possibility that you may need to recover to the point before the statement. You can mark the transaction that contains the statement in the log so that you can recover to that mark if needed. The code to mark the log looks like this:

```
BEGIN TRANSACTION MarkedTran
 WITH MARK 'Dangerous';
GO

-- Execute potentially recoverable code

COMMIT TRANSACTION MarkedTran;
GO
```

In this example, you have a transaction log mark called Dangerous that you can use for recovery. If you choose to recover up to and including the marked transaction, you could use this code:

```
USE master;
GO

RESTORE LOG pubs
FROM DISK = 'D:\DataBackups\Pubs_Log.bak'
WITH FILE = 6,
 RECOVERY,
 STOPATMARK = 'Dangerous';
GO
```

As an alternative, if you choose to recover to the mark but exclude the actual marked transaction, you can use this code:

```
USE master;
GO
```

Data Administration

PART III

```
RESTORE LOG pubs
FROM DISK = 'D:\DataBackups\Pubs_Log.bak'
WITH FILE = 6,
 RECOVERY,
 STOPBEFOREMARK = 'Dangerous';
GO
```

Another option is that if you happen to know the log sequence number (LSN) of the transaction in question, you can substitute the LSN for a named mark. That way, you can use this approach even if you did not make a mark in the log prior to the need for recovery.

PART IV

Performance and Advanced Features

Performance and
Advanced Features

PART IV

11

Monitoring and Tuning SQL Server

IN THIS CHAPTER, YOU WILL LEARN TO DO THE FOLLOWING:

Performance and Advanced Features

PART IV

I n this chapter we discuss monitoring and tuning for performance in server instances and databases. We use monitoring and tuning with SQL Server 2008 to see how an instance or a particular database is performing. Efficient and effective monitoring involves taking readings at various points in time throughout the day, including times of peak usage and times of low usage. Microsoft SQL Server, the Microsoft Server, and Windows operating systems work together to give us utilities that allow us to view the current condition of the database and to track performance as those conditions change. By monitoring SQL Server, you can determine whether or not you can improve performance, evaluate user activity, troubleshoot problems, and debug applications that may cause issues in your database operation.

Monitoring is very important in a SQL database environment because SQL Server provides a dynamic environment in which everything can change constantly. The way users connect to the database, resources are used by various components, and I/O functions can all change and vary as applications being used access the database resources. Monitoring is crucial and will allow you to decide if any changes are necessary in your Microsoft SQL Server 2008 environment.

You must have an organized methodology and follow several steps in order to effectively monitor and reveal any changes that may be required in your environment:

1. Determine your monitoring goals.

2. Select tools that you will use to monitor.

3. Identify the components to monitor.

4. Select the values or metrics for those components.

5. Perform the actual monitoring.

6. Analyze the data.

7. Improve your instance.

Monitor SQL Server

The very first step is always to establish the reason you are monitoring SQL Server. What are you trying to discover about your environment, or are you simply trying to establish a baseline for performance? Are

you attempting to address a specific problem that has occurred, or
are you trying to test the server under different loads? Perhaps you
need to discover if a particular maintenance schedule or backup plan is
effective in achieving the purpose for which it was created? You may be
making decisions concerning scaling up hardware or deciding to scale
out your environment. All of these are legitimate reasons to initiate a
monitoring program. Monitoring should always be performed before
any action is taken.

In the following sections, we will delve into the tools that can be used
for monitoring SQL Server.

Using the SQL Profiler

The SQL Profiler tracks engine process events, such as the start of a
batch for a transaction, enabling you to monitor the server and database activities. You can capture SQL Profiler data to a SQL Server
table or a file for later analysis. This allows you to replay the events
captured on the SQL server step-by-step so that you can see exactly
what happened. There are many ways to start SQL Profiler. First,
on the Start menu, point to All Programs ➤ Microsoft SQL Server
2008 Performance Tools ➤ SQL Server Profiler. You can also start
SQL Profiler in Management Studio by choosing the tools menu from
the menu bar and clicking the Profiler. To start the profiler from the
query editor on the menu bar, click New Query ➤ Trace Query in
SQL Server Profiler. Finally, a SQL Profiler can be started from within
the Activity Monitor by right-clicking a process and choosing Trace
Process in SQL Server Profiler. Running the SQL Profiler requires the
same user permissions as the Transact SQL stored procedures that are
used to create traces. Users must also be granted the ALTER TRACE
permissions to run the Profiler.

SQL Profiler can be used to create templates that define event
classes and data columns included in the trace. Once you decide
which template you wish to use, you can create one to run a trace
that records data for each selected event. You can use a template on
many traces even though the template itself is not executed. Within
SQL Server Profiler are several predefined templates. SQL Server
Profiler automatically defines the standard template as the default and
applies it to any new trace. However, there are some other predefined
templates that can also be used, as seen in Table 11.1.

Performance and
Advanced Features

PART IV

Table 11.1: SQL Profiler Predefined Templates

Template	Captures
Standard	Logins, logouts, completed batches, and connection information
TSQL	Transact SQL statements and time issued
TSQL_Grouped	Transact SQL statements and time issued, grouped by client/user
TSQL_Locks	Statements issued and exceptional lock events
TSQL_Replay	Information about SQL statements required for trace
TSQL_SP	Currently running stored procedures
TSQL_Duration	Client-submitted statements
Tuning	Stored procedures, batch execution, can create assessable output for Database Engine Tuning Advisor

In addition to traces from predefined templates, you can also create traces from blank templates, containing no event classes by default. Take the following steps to create a trace:

1. Start SQL Profiler and select New Trace from the toolbar or choose File ➢ New Trace.

2. Select the database to trace in the connection dialog.

3. Provide the trace name in the Trace Properties dialog (as seen in Figure 11.1). In this example, we are using Test_Trace_1. These are read-only values.

4. Select the template from the Use the Template drop-down menu.

5. Either choose the Save to File option and select a "Save As" name, or choose the Save to Table option and select the instance, database, and table to save to.

6. Select the time and day to stop the trace.

The Events Selection tab of the Trace Properties dialog, seen in Figure 11.2, allows you to select events and columns you wish to trace. To see a complete list, click the Show All Events check box and the Show All Columns check box. Events you can trace are grouped by type. If the Show All Events check box is selected, all groups that are available within SQL Profiler will be shown. If the Show All Columns check box is selected, each area in which events can occur will be displayed.

When a group is selected in this dialog, a label below the selection will be populated with information concerning the selected group. If you roll the mouse cursor over a column heading, the label below the group title will be populated with information concerning the event class. Once all required values have been selected, click the Run button to begin the trace.

Figure 11.1: The Trace Properties dialog

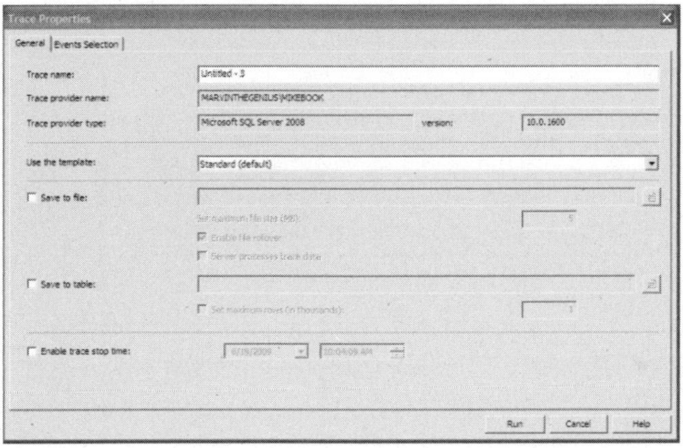

Figure 11.2: The Events Selection tab in the Trace Properties dialog

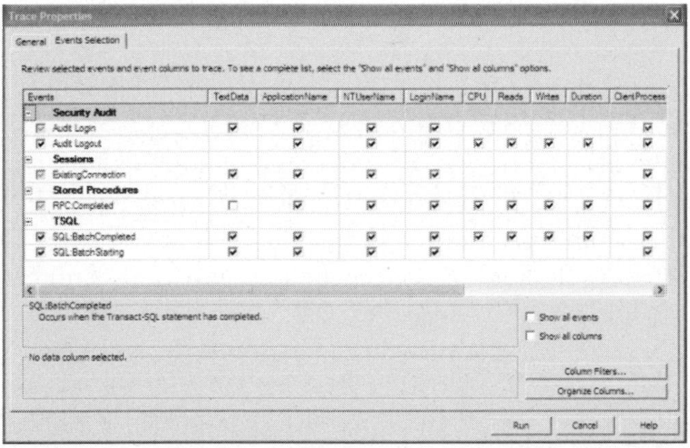

When a trace starts, the data is immediately captured. Traces can also be started by using a stored procedure. While a trace is running, you may only change its name property. You can pause a trace to prevent data from

being captured until the trace is restarted. Restarting the trace allows the operation and data collection to resume. No data collected by the trace will be lost by pausing the trace in its operation. While a trace is paused, you can change the name, events, columns, and filters. However, you cannot change the destination of the data the trace is collecting. A trace may also be stopped. When a trace is stopped, no data will be captured and the trace cannot be restarted without losing the data that has been collected so far. To restart a trace after it has been paused or stopped, simply choose File ➢ Run Trace in SQL Profiler. Figure 11.3 shows a trace in progress.

Figure 11.3: Trace in progress

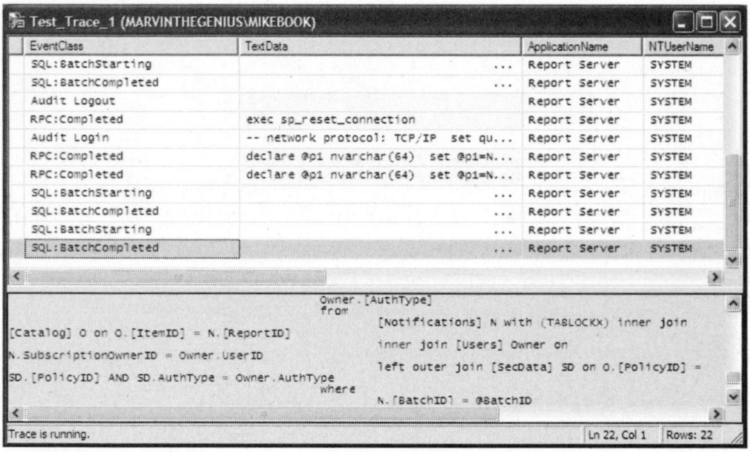

To view a trace in SQL Profiler after it has run, choose File ➢ Open ➢ Trace File. In the Open File dialog, click the trace that you want Profiler to open. If you have saved more trace results to a table than show on the File menu, point to Open ➢ Trace Table. You will then be prompted to connect to the server instance that holds your table. In the source table dialog box, select the database that contains the saved trace table from the list and click OK.

After opening the trace file or table, you can examine the collected data. Expand the node of the desired event class for more information on the specific object's events. You can search through the list of events or use the Find command on the Edit menu of SQL Profiler to speed up your search. Note the values in the Client Process ID and Start Time columns of events you trace—these can assist you in grouping events for analysis.

When you select a particular event in SQL Profiler, the details of the event populate the lower pane, as seen in Figure 11.4. This can be extremely useful in your analysis of events affecting your data environment.

Figure 11.4: Event data from a trace

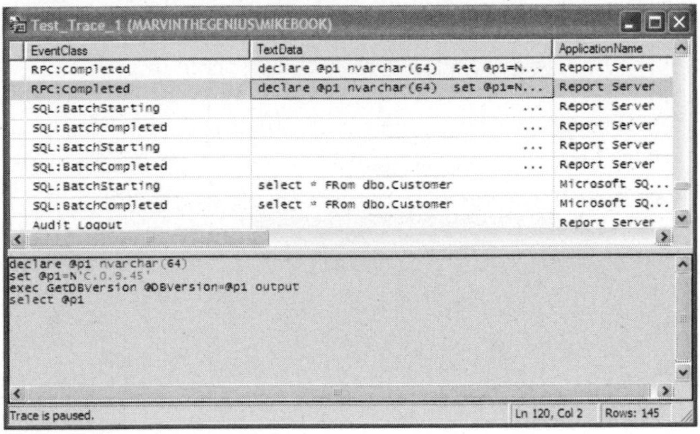

Using System Monitor

System Monitor is a tool primarily designed to track resource usage such as page requests and other predefined objects. It is built into the operating system and can monitor machines locally or remotely on instances of SQL Server with Windows NT 4.0 or later. The big difference between SQL Profiler and System Monitor is that SQL Profiler monitors the Database Engine events, whereas System Monitor tracks resource usage associated with server processes. To start System Monitor in any Windows XP environment, choose Start ➤ Run, type **perfmon** in the Run dialog box (System Monitor is sometimes referred to as Performance Monitor or perfmon), then click OK. System Monitor can also be started by choosing Control Panel ➤ Performance and Maintenance ➤ Administrative Tools. Then click or double-click the Performance icon to bring up System Monitor.

To start System Monitor in a Vista environment, choose the Start Globe button ➤ type **perfmon/res** in the Search dialog box (System Monitor is sometimes referred to as Vista Resource Monitor in Vista), then click OK. System Monitor can also be started by choosing Control Panel ➤

Performance and Advanced Features

PART IV

Administrative Tools ≻ Reliability and Performance Monitoring ≻ Start **perfmon** from the Monitor Menu. You will then see the screen represented in Figure 11.5.

Figure 11.5: Initial Performance Monitor Screen

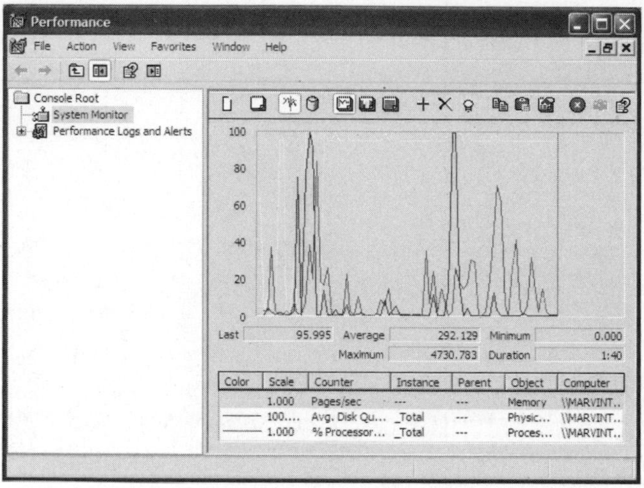

System Monitor works on system *counters* and *logs*. A counter is a type of listener dedicated to a specific object that exists in the server environment. A log is a record of values gathered by the counters selected. Counters are grouped according to the area they monitor. SQL Server counters are listed in Table 11.2.

Table 11.2: SQL Server Counters

Performance Object	Description
SQLServer: Access Methods	Searches through and measures allocation of SQL Server database objects (for example, the number of index searches or number of pages that are allocated to indexes and data).
SQLServer: Backup Device	Provides information about backup devices used by backup and restore operations, such as the throughput of the backup device.

Table 11.2: SQL Server Counters *(continued)*

Performance Object	Description
SQLServer: Buffer Manager	Provides information about the memory buffers used by SQL Server, such as free memory and buffer cache hit ratio.
SQLServer: Buffer Partition	Provides information about how frequently SQL Server requests and accesses free pages.
SQLServer: CLR	Provides information about the common language runtime (CLR).
SQLServer: Cursor Manager by Type	Provides information about cursors.
SQLServer: Cursor Manager Total	Provides information about cursors.
SQLServer: Database Mirroring	Provides information about database mirroring.
SQLServer: Databases	Provides information about a SQL Server database, such as the amount of free log space available or the number of active transactions in the database. There can be multiple instances of this object.
SQL Server: Deprecated Features	Counts the number of times that deprecated features are used.
SQLServer: Exec Statistics	Provides information about execution statistics.
SQLServer: General Statistics	Provides information about general serverwide activity, such as the number of users who are connected to an instance of SQL Server.
SQLServer: Latches	Provides information about the latches on internal resources, such as database pages, that are used by SQL Server.
SQLServer: Locks	Provides information about the individual lock requests made by SQL Server, such as lock time-outs and deadlocks. There can be multiple instances of this object.
SQLServer: Memory Manager	Provides information about SQL Server memory usage, such as the total number of lock structures currently allocated.

Performance and
Advanced Features

PART IV

Table 11.2: SQL Server Counters *(continued)*

Performance Object	Description
SQLServer: Plan Cache	Provides information about the SQL Server cache used to store objects such as stored procedures, triggers, and query plans.
SQLServer: Resource Pool Stats	Provides information about Resource Governor resource pool statistics.
SQLServer:SQL Errors	Provides information about SQL Server errors.
SQLServer: SQL Statistics	Provides information about aspects of Transact SQL queries, such as the number of batches of Transact SQL statements received by SQL Server.
SQLServer: Transactions	Provides information about the active transactions in SQL Server, such as the overall number of transactions and the number of snapshot transactions.
SQLServer: User Settable	Performs custom monitoring. Each counter can be a custom stored procedure or any Transact SQL statement that returns a value to be monitored.
SQLServer: Wait Statistics	Provides information about waits.
SQLServer: Workload Group Stats	Provides information about Resource Governor workload group statistics.

Table 11.3 lists the performance objects provided for Service Broker, which allows you to both send and receive asynchronous messages by using extensions in TSQL.

Table 11.3: Performance Objects for Service Broker

Performance Object	Description
SQLServer: Broker Activation	Provides information about Service Broker–activated tasks.
SQLServer: Broker Statistics	Provides general Service Broker information.
SQLServer: Broker Transport	Provides information on Service Broker networking.

Table 11.4 lists the performance objects provided for SQL Server Agent, the tool that allows for automation of tasks in a SQL environment.

Table 11.4: Performance Objects for SQL Server Agent

Performance Object	Description
SQLAgent: Alerts	Provides information about SQL Server Agent alerts.
SQLAgent: Jobs	Provides information about SQL Server Agent jobs.
SQLAgent: JobSteps	Provides information about SQL Server Agent job steps.
SQLAgent: Statistics	Provides general information about SQL Server Agent.

The following list gives the performance objects provided for SQL Server replication:

- SQLServer: Replication Agents
- SQLServer: Replication Snapshot
- SQLServer: Replication Logreader
- SQLServer: Replication Dist.
- SQLServer: Replication Merge

To add a counter to System Monitor, right-click in the counter area below the graph and choose a counter. To create an entire new set of counters and have them saved as a log, expand Performance Logs and Alerts, right-click Trace Log, and choose New. If you wish to set up a new counter log, right-click on Counter Logs and choose New. (The difference between a trace log and a counter log is that a trace log gathers data continuously until it's stopped, whereas a counter log is a set that can sample data at preset intervals.) When you right-click either option, you will be prompted immediately to name the log you have chosen. The counter log and the trace log each has its own set of dialogs.

The dialog for creating a new trace log is shown in Figure 11.6. The General tab includes a button called Provider Status. With this button, you can check on various data providers that you may be using. Checking the Show Only Enabled Providers check box will narrow down the list and provide a status of the providers. The General tab also provides the option of selecting Events Logged by System Provider or Nonsystem Providers. If you select Events Logged by System Provider, events tied to providers that the server has enabled by default will be traced. Choosing Nonsystem Providers will enable the Add button and allow you to select from a list of providers you wish to trace.

Figure 11.6: Creation of new trace log

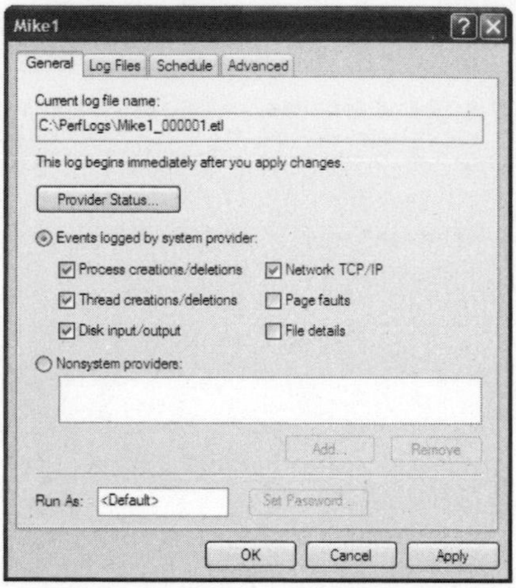

Figure 11.7 shows the Log Files tab. On this tab you can choose whether you wish to make your log file sequential or circular, how you want the files named, and whether or not logs should be overwritten. You can also add a comment to a log file. These choices are self-explanatory except perhaps whether logs are sequential or circular. A circular log will, when the maximum size is reached, overwrite itself to continue to record data. A sequential log will, when maximum size is reached, close down, and a new file will open to continue recording the trace.

Figure 11.7: Log Files tab

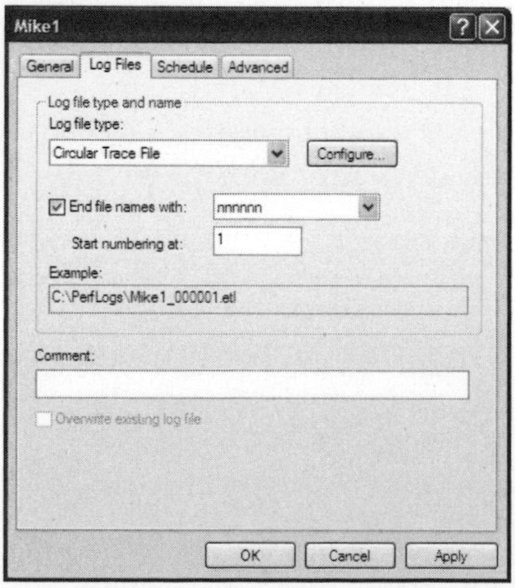

The Schedule tab allows you to set the time that you want the trace to run as well as stop. You can choose to continually start a new log if you have selected to stop the log after a specified time unit, as shown in Figure 11.8. There is no option to set up an interval schedule. If you wish to be able to schedule data collection at various intervals using your choice of counters, you should be using the counter log. This tab also gives you the option to run a command or script when a log file closes.

Figure 11.8: Schedule tab

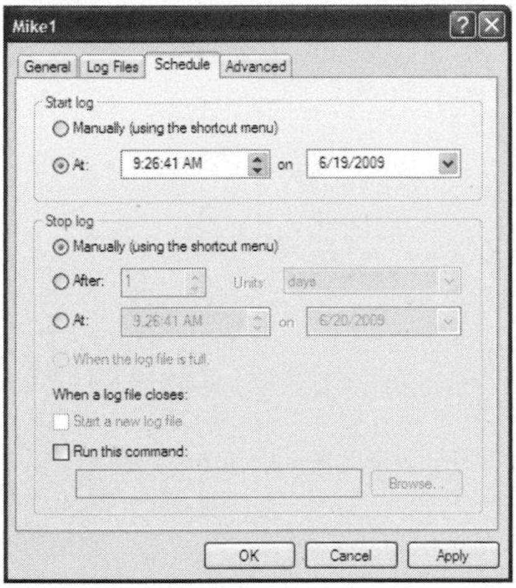

The final tab of the Create Trace dialog is the Advanced tab. On this tab you set up the buffers that are used for logging. This helps control your memory usage, but you must remember that by default, data will be dumped to the log file if the buffers are full. The log service will also override the settings on this tab if they do not meet tracing requirements. The default buffer size is set to 5KB, and the number of buffers is set to a minimum of 3 and a maximum of 25. You may also select the interval of transferring the data from the buffers to the log file. These settings should be changed only when it is required by your environment.

The dialog for creating a counter log has three tabs: the General tab, the Log Files tab, and the Schedule tab, as shown in Figure 11.9. The figure also shows the Add Objects dialog, which will pop up when you click the Add Objects button on the General tab. The two radio buttons at the top of the Add Objects dialog give you the option of choosing which machine you wish to run your counter log on. If you select the top radio button, Use Local Computer Counter Objects, then all of the objects you select will be on the machine you are currently using. Selecting the second radio button will allow you to select objects from other computers and SQL instances that you have permission to access. Remember, running a trace on a local machine can cause some "noise" in some counters. Below the drop-down that lists available machines is the Performance Objects list box. In this box you can select performance objects that you wish to add to your counter log. You can also highlight an object and click the Explain button to see more information about it.

Figure 11.9: Creating a counter log

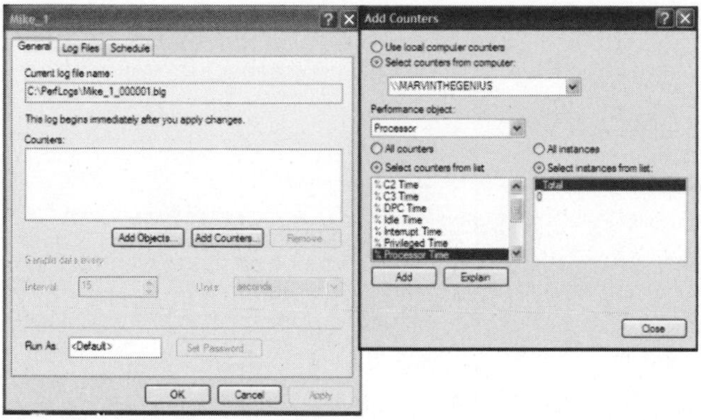

A selection dialog will appear when you click the Add Counters button (Figure 11.10). Here you have some of the same selections that you had in the Add Objects dialog. Below the selection drop-down box is a Performance Object drop-down box from which you can select a group of counters related to a single object. After you have selected the performance object, you either choose to add all counters you are interested in for that object or choose specific counters from the list. Below the list of counters are the familiar Add and Explain buttons. On the right side of the form you have the option to choose whether you wish your counters to monitor all instances or select specific instances from a list. For example, if you had more than one processor, you may wish to select which processor you want to watch.

> **NOTE** Remember that if you do not have an object installed, it will not appear in the list. For example, if you do not have SQL Server installed, you will not see any of the counters relating to the SQL Server object.

Figure 11.10: Add Counters dialog

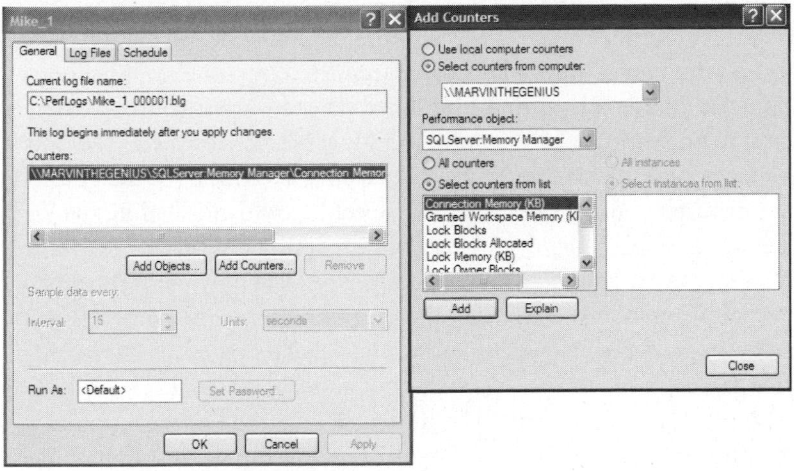

After you have made your selections, you are ready to decide the interval at which you want your data sample to be collected. Choices include seconds, minutes, hours, and days. Below the interval scheduling options, you have the option to run a counter log with user credentials of your choosing.

Now let's examine the Log Files tab (Figure 11.11). On this tab is the Log File Type drop-down menu; the options are Binary File, Circular Binary File, Text File (comma delimited), Text File (tab delimited), and SQL Database.

Figure 11.11: Log File Type menu drop-down menu on the Log Files tab

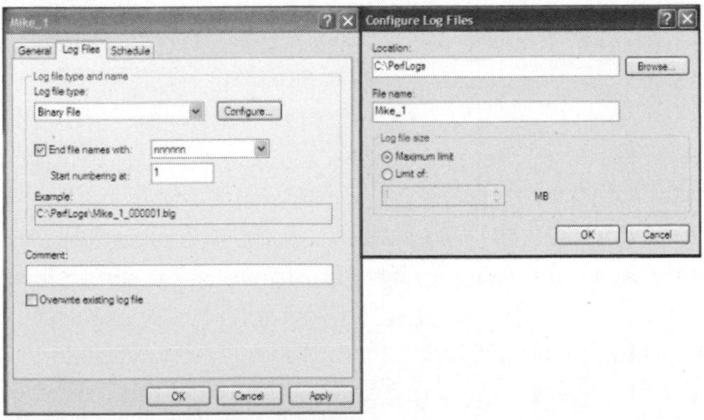

The binary file and circular binary file both consist of binary output, but the circular binary file will overwrite itself when its maximum size is reached. A text file, whether it is comma delimited or tab delimited, generates text output that can easily be imported into other applications. The SQL Database option gives you the ability to output your log to a SQL database destination. When the End File Names With check box is enabled, the filenames will end with the proper extension for the selected format. Figure 11.11 shows the default selection, which is ending the log filename with six digits and starting the numbering at one. The Example text box shows the results of your selections. At the bottom of the tab, you can add comments to your log files, and finally, as the name suggests, you can use the Overwrite Existing Log File check box to overwrite the existing log.

In Figure 11.12, you see the familiar Schedule tab in which you can set the time and duration you wish your counter log to run. Remember that on the General tab you set intervals for the collection of data by the counters you chose.

Figure 11.12: Counter log Schedule tab

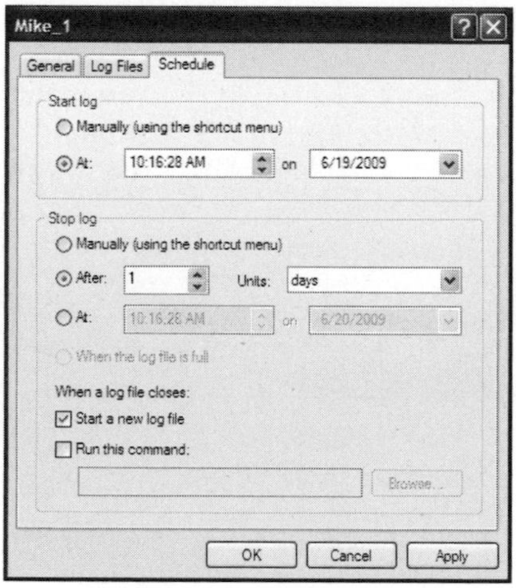

In most cases, SQL Server uses System Monitor to watch for server-level bottlenecks. This can be especially useful when you don't know exactly how a bottleneck is occurring on a system. How do you know whether to focus on fixing the first query, which requires a lot of CPU time, or the second query, which requires a lot of I/O time? Getting started with the System Monitor tool is a good way to begin breaking this down.

Ideally, you should use System Monitor to create a log of counters for a period of at least a day or more. You want to select a typical day with both busy and slow periods.

Following are some of the server counters that you would want to monitor:

- **Memory: pages/sec.** This should average around 20 or less. If you consistently have a higher value than that, you should increase the RAM on the server.

- **Memory: available bytes.** This should be greater than 5MB. SQL Server attempts to maintain 4 to 10MB of free physical memory. If it is consistently below 5MB, you can increase the RAM or lighten the load on the server.

- **Physical disk: % Disk Time.** This should run less than 55 percent. If this counter is higher than that for 10 minutes or more in a 24-hour period on more than one occasion, the server is likely experiencing an I/O bottleneck.

- **Physical disk: average disk queue length.** This should be below two per physical disk.

- **SQLServer: General Statistics.** This shows how many connections are using a particular server instance.

- **SQLServer: Access Methods – Page Splits/sec.** This indicates how effective your fill factor and pad index settings are in your database.

- **SQLServer: Buffer Manager: Buffer Cache Hit Ratio.** This monitors memory dedicated to SQL Server cache. Keep in mind that this value is based on the average buffers cache ratio since SQL Server service was last restarted.

It is also a good idea while we are discussing SQL Server memory manager counters to keep an eye on the Target Server Memory and Total Server Memory. Target Server Memory will tell you how much memory the SQL Server instance wants while Total Server Memory will tell you what is actually being used.

It should be mentioned here with System Monitor that a great deal of pertinent information can be gained by monitoring the Windows application event log. It provides an overall picture of events occurring on the server. This information is generally not available anywhere else, and you can use it to troubleshoot SQL Server–related problems.

Performance and
Advanced Features

PART IV

Using Activity Monitor

Another tool available to you in SQL Server Management Studio is Activity Monitor. This tool contains several sections to access various important SQL Server information areas. It's a great tool for getting a slightly more in-depth view of what's going on with your SQL Server instance. It is more detailed than Task Manager and Windows Resource Manager; however, there are many tools that when properly used will return a greater depth of detail. Activity Monitor is handy for getting a quick overview of where a problem might lie. This monitor returns data on the current state of your server instance.

To access Activity Monitor in SQL Server Management Studio, click Activity Monitor on the standard toolbar. To have Activity Monitor open automatically when Management Studio opens, choose Tools ➤ Options ➤ Environments ➤ General. In the At Startup box, select Open Object Explorer and Activity Monitor, as shown in Figure 11.13. To activate the selected change, close and reopen SQL Server Management Studio.

Figure 11.13: The Options dialog

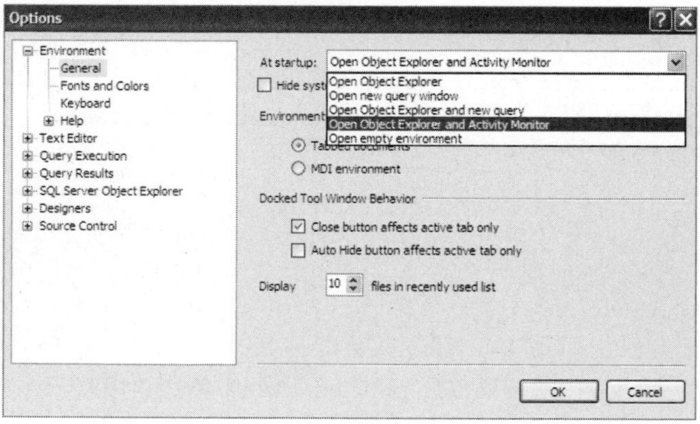

After it opens, the Activity Monitor can be observed and analyzed. The four graphs on the top of Activity Monitor in the Overview pane provide an active current readout of the server activity. Expanding each of the bands below grants you access to more detailed information. The Overview pane shows % processor time, waiting tasks, database I/O, and batch requests/sec. The section below the Overview pane can be opened up to view details about processes, resource waits, data file I/O, and recent expensive queries.

Processes detailed under the Processes band are separated by the ID of the session and include important details, as seen in Figure 11.14. Right-clicking, as seen in the figure, on a currently running process will give you the option of killing the process, tracing the process, or viewing the process details.

Figure 11.14: Viewing processes details

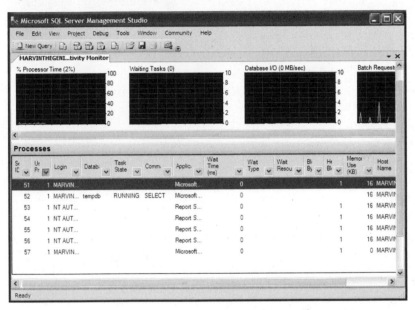

The Resource Waits band shows the waits separated by category. As seen in the Figure 11.15, it contains wait time in milliseconds, recent wait time, average waiter count, and cumulative weight time in seconds.

Figure 11.16 shows the Data File I/O where statistics and locations concerning your data files for each instance database are displayed. The table displays the database, then the filename and location, megabytes per second read, megabytes per second written, and response time.

The next band in Activity Monitor is Recent Expensive Queries, as seen in Figure 11.17, and it provides details concerning queries that are currently being run. Right-clicking on a query that is being executed will give you the choice of editing the text or showing the execution plan. Hovering the cursor over a query will display the SQL text of the query in question.

Performance and
Advanced Features

PART IV

Figure 11.15: Resource Waits band in Activity Monitor

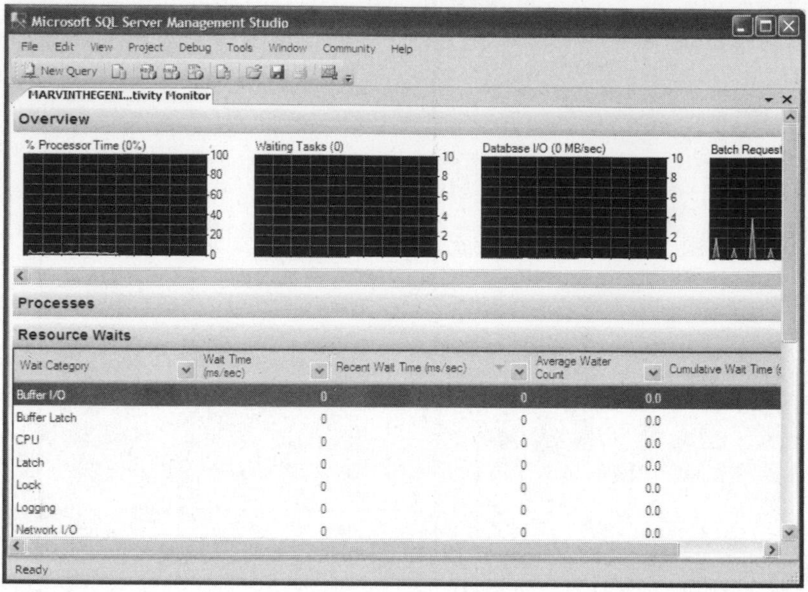

Figure 11.16: Data File I/O band in Activity Monitor

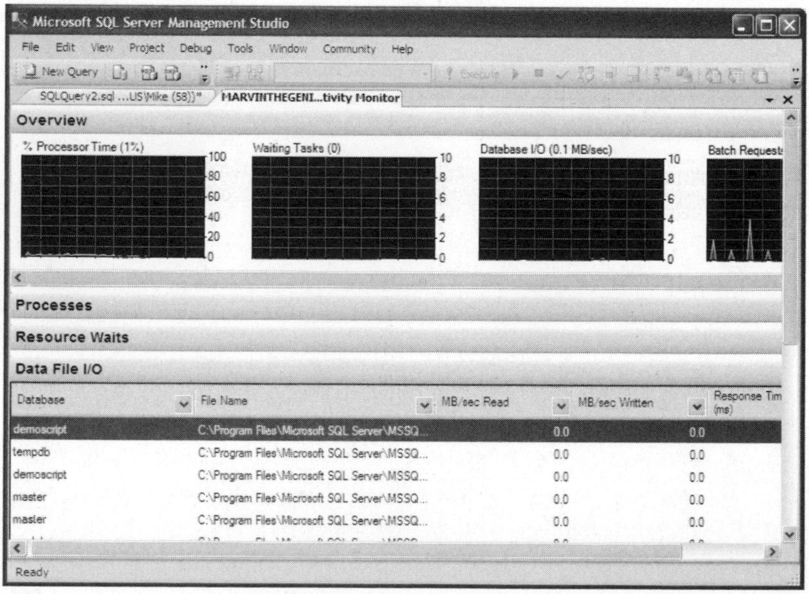

Figure 11.17: Recent Expensive Queries band in Activity Monitor

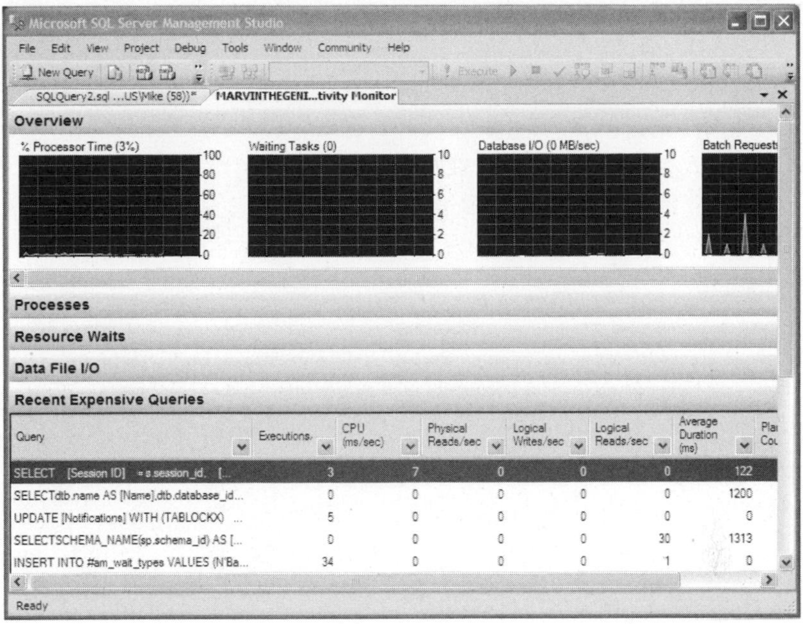

The Activity Monitor provides a graphic tool that allows you to interact with processes and important key points of your SQL 2008 environment. It is a quick view of database efficiency leading you to further detailed analysis and corrections.

Implementing DDL Triggers

Data Definition Language (DDL) triggers are designed to be invoked at the creation and drop statements of the database management objects. Unlike other triggers, which are created on tables, DDL triggers are created on individual databases or all databases in an instance. These triggers can be very useful in lobbying administrative events that occur within the instance. They are predominantly concerned with objects in a single database, such as tables, indexes, users, views, and so on. The area in which the trigger fires in response to an event is referred to as the DDL trigger scope. The possible scopes for a trigger are ON DATABASE and ON ALL SERVER. DDL triggers can be used to send messages upon the completion of a particular type of statement so that activity of that nature can be logged. To use DDL triggers in an auditing strategy, you

Performance and
Advanced Features

PART IV

must first make a table to record the actions fired from within a database. The following code will create just such a table:

```
USE demoscript;
GO
CREATE TABLE DDL_Audit
(ID          INT PRIMARY KEY IDENTITY(1,1),
Cmd      NVARCHAR(1000),
PTime    NVARCHAR(24),
HName    NVARCHAR(100),
LoginName   NVARCHAR(100)
);
GO
```

After making the table, it's time to create the trigger that will be specific to the demo script database in one file or on all DDL database level events.

```
CREATE TRIGGER DDLAudit ON DATABASE
FOR DDL_DATABASE_LEVEL_EVENTS
AS
DECLARE @data XML
DECLARE @cmd NVARCHAR(1500)
DECLARE @ptime NVARCHAR(24)
DECLARE @spid NVARCHAR(6)
DECLARE @loginname NVARCHAR(100)
DECLARE @hname NVARCHAR(100)
SET @data = EVENTDATA()
SET @cmd = @data.value('(/EVENT_INSTANCE/TSQLCommand/
CommandText)[1]'
, 'NVARCHAR(1000)')
SET @ptime = @data.value('(/EVENT_INSTANCE/PTime)[1]',
 'NVARCHAR(24)')
SET @spid = @data.value('(/EVENT_INSTANCE/SPID)[1]',
 'nvarchar(6)')
SET @loginname = @data.value('(/EVENT_INSTANCE/LoginName)
[1]',
    'NVARCHAR(100)')
SET @hname = HOST_NAME()
INSERT INTO dbo.DDL_Audit(Command, PTime,HName,LoginName)
 VALUES(@cmd, @ptime, @hname, @loginname)
GO
```

The purpose of this trigger is to capture the event data that is created once the trigger fires and parse out the data from the XML variable by inserting it into the appropriate columns of the DDL_Audit table. Once the trigger has been created, you can test to see if it is working:

```
UPDATE STATISTICS Production.Product
GO
CREATE TABLE dbo.Test(col INT)
GO
DROP TABLE dbo.Test
GO
-- View log table
SELECT *
FROM dbo.DDL_Audit
GO
```

Figure 11.18 shows the output when you choose to view the log table. The details displayed can assist you in analyzing which users are attempting to alter the database management objects within the scope of DDL trigger.

Figure 11.18: DDL_Audit table

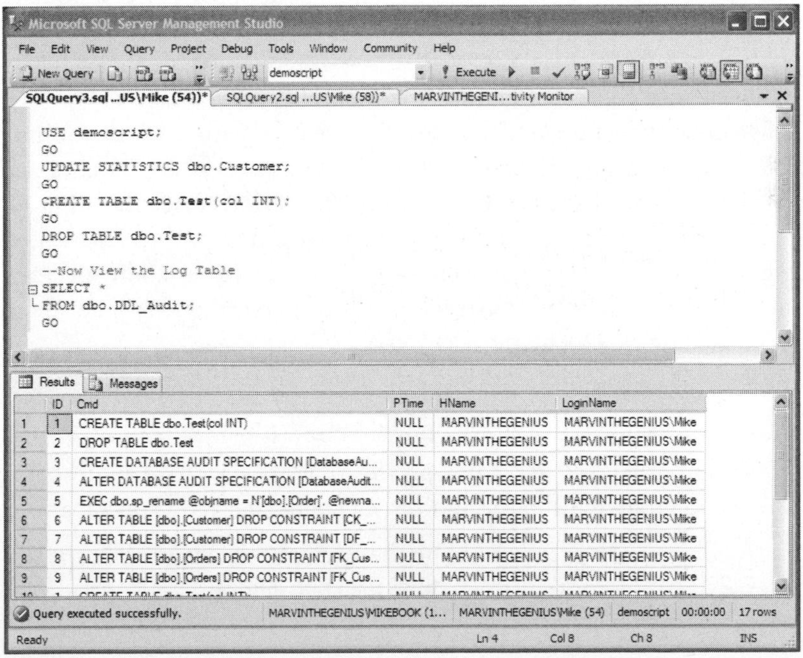

To view a list of all triggers that are available in the database, you can query the sys.triggers catalog view. The following code will enable you to do this:

```
SELECT name
FROM sys.triggers
```

Using SQL Server Audit

Auditing an instance of SQL Server or a SQL database involves tracking and logging events occurring in those systems. You can use several methods of monitoring SQL Server; however, in SQL Server 2008 Enterprise, you can also set up automatic auditing by using SQL Server Audit. There are several levels of auditing for SQL Server, depending on your standards and installation requirements. SQL Server Audit provides the tools and processes required to enable, store, and view various audits on various server and database objects. You can record server audit action groups per instance and either database audit action groups or database audit actions per database every time the auditable action is encountered.

An audit, by definition, is several elements combined in one package or a specific group of server actions or database actions. The components of an audit combine to produce an output that is referred to as an audit just as report definition is combined with graphics and data to produce a report.

When you define an audit, you must specify a location for the output, which is known as an audit destination. When the audit is created, it is disabled and does not automatically audit any action. Once the audit is enabled, the destination will begin to receive data from it. When you decide to create audits, you may choose to create a server audit specification, which will collect many server-level action groups, or a database audit specification, which you select.

The general process for creating and using an audit is as follows:

1. Create an audit, define the logging target, and enable the audit.

2. Create either a server audit specification or a database audit specification that maps to the audit; then enable the audit specification.

3. Read the audit events by using the Windows Event Viewer, the log file or viewer, or the fn_get_audit_file function.

If the database you wish to audit is using mirroring, the following settings must also be configured:

- The mirror server must have an audit with the same GUID to enable the database audit specification to write audit records. This can be configured by using the command CREATE AUDIT WITH GUID= <GUID from source Server Audit>.

- For binary file targets, the mirror server service account must have appropriate permissions to the location where the audit trail is being written.

- For Windows event log targets, the security policy on the computer where the mirror server is located must allow for service account access to the security or application event log.

To create and define an audit in Object Explorer, expand the security node, right-click Audits, and choose Create Audit. Figure 11.19 shows the Create Audit dialog. By default, the audit name is filled in with a date and a number generated by SQL Server. In the figure, we have left the default name, but you can change it as you wish. The Queue Delay setting is set in milliseconds and represents how long you are willing to wait if an event cannot be written to the chosen location. The check box below it is simply for shutting the server down should auditing fail. The next drop-down box is to select the location where you wish the log to be written. In this example, we have simply selected C:\Perflogs. If security log or application log is selected, you will not have the option of selecting a file location. If the Reserve Disk Space check box is selected, the space you are using is held for log usage and is unavailable if you allow unlimited file size. Once you have made your choices, click OK to create the audit. As you can see in Figure 11.19, the audit is primarily about where you want the output and the name of the log.

After the audit is created, you must enable it for it to be usable. This is a simple matter of right-clicking on the audit you wish to use and choosing Enable Audit. Once the audit is enabled, you will see a dialog stating the success of your action. Now you are ready to choose the scope to which you will apply the audit. You will start with Create Server Audit Specification, which will apply the audit to the entire SQL instance. Under the Security node in Object Explorer, just below the Audits node, is the Server Audit Specifications node. Right-clicking on this node and selecting New Server Audit Specification will bring up the Server Audit Specification Properties dialog shown in Figure 11.20.

Figure 11.19: Create Audit dialog

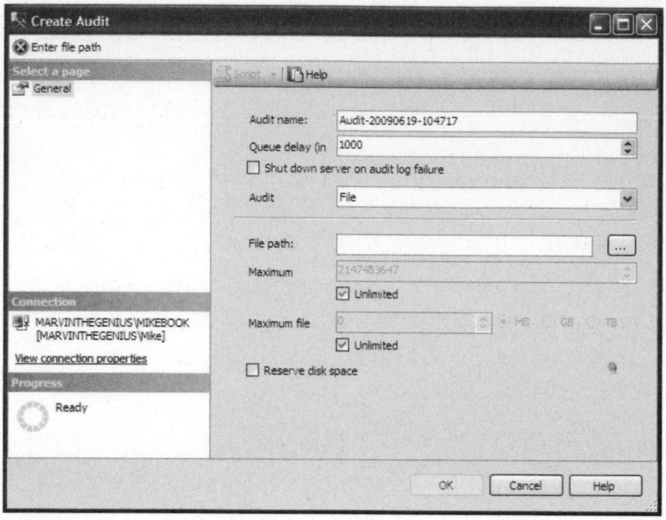

Figure 11.20: Server Audit Specification Properties dialog

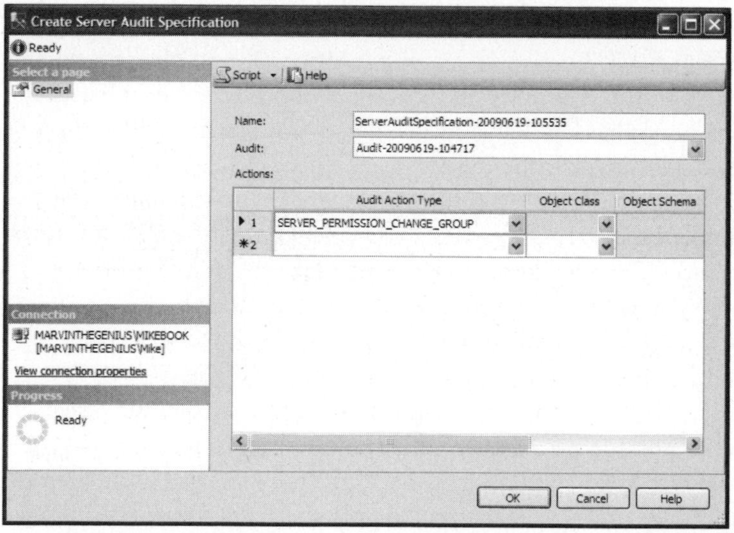

The first text box in the dialog allows you to establish the name. The Audit drop-down will show the audits that are available for you to use with the server specification. In the Actions area, the Audit

Action Type drop-down provides a list of server events that you can audit. The Object Class drop-down and the Object Schema, Object Name, and Principal Name fields are disabled and primarily used in a database audit specification. Once you've made your choices, click OK to create the specification. The specification must be enabled just as the audit was in order to be usable.

The other type of audit specification you can create is on the database. To create this type, you expand the Databases node, expand the database for which you wish to create the specification, expand the Security node, and at the bottom of the list, right-click Database Audit Specifications and select New Database Audit Specification. Figure 11.21 shows the dialog required to create the database audit specification.

Figure 11.21: Create Database Audit Specification dialog

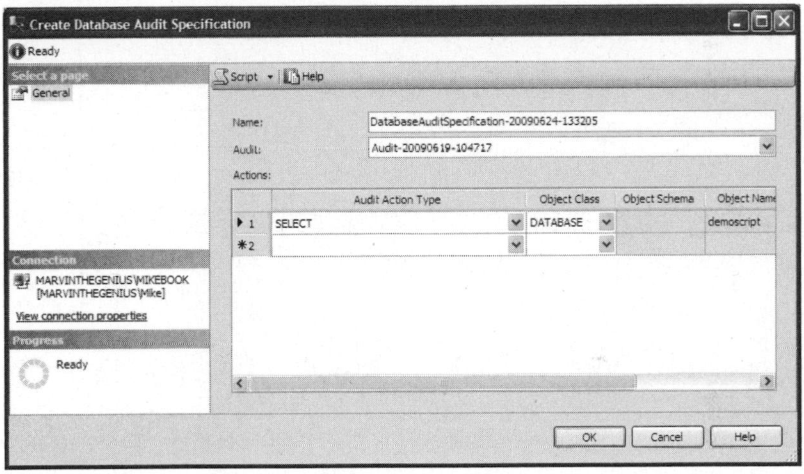

At first you have the opportunity to provide a name for the new specification. A drop-down will once again show the audits that you have created for use. The difference in this dialog as opposed to the server specification dialog occurs in the Object Class Schema Name and Principal Name areas. The Audit Action Type drop-down has actions associated with a particular database in which you are creating the specification. In this example, an action has been chosen. The Object Class drop-down provides the values of Database, Schema, and Object. The Object Class helps you refine the scope of what you plan to audit. If you select Schema, then the Object Schema field will be populated with the value, and then you can click the ellipsis next to the Object Name field and select a specific object from your Object Class drop-down. Finally, from the Principal Name drop-down, you can select which group you wish to audit. In our example, we are auditing the SELECT clause. If we wanted to audit everyone who ran a SELECT in our database, we would select the public role for our principal.

To see the audit logs, you just have to right-click on the audit itself, not the specification, and choose View Audit Logs. You will see an output similar to what we have in Figure 11.22. The audit session changes, and the select statements are shown clearly in the viewer.

Figure 11.22: Audit log output

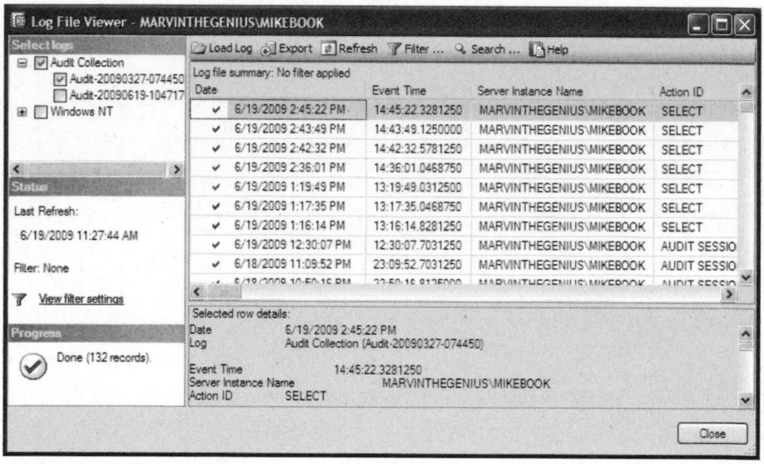

Tune SQL Server

After you have gathered a good sample of monitoring information, it's time to put it into practice. Improving performance of a SQL Server instance is referred to as *tuning*.

Using Resource Governor

Resource Governor is new to SQL Server 2008 and enables you to manage SQL Server workload and resources by specifying limits on resource consumption by incoming requests. Resource Governor defines a workload as a set of similarly sized queries that can and should be treated as a single unit. Although uniformity of your resource usage pattern is not required, it will likely give you more benefit from Resource Governor. The limits that you create for Resource Governor can be reconfigured in real time with minimal impact on the workload that is running. In environments where multiple distinct workloads are present on the same server, Resource Governor enables you to differentiate between these workloads and allocate shared resources as they are required based on the limits that you specify. These resources are CPU time and memory allocation.

The following three concepts are fundamental to understanding and using Resource Governor:

- Resource pools
- Workload groups
- Classification

Resource Pools

Two resource pools (internal and default) are created when SQL Server 2008 is installed. Resource Governor also supports user-defined resource pools.

The pool represents physical resources of the server. You can think of the pool as a virtual SQL Server instance inside an actual SQL Server instance. The full listing part does not overlap with other pools, which enables minimum resource reservation. The other part is shared with other pools, which supports the maximum possible resource consumption. The Resource Governor pool resources are set by giving a value to one of the following for each resource:

- MIN/MAX for CPU
- MIN/MAX for memory

The sum of the MIN values that are set across all pools cannot exceed 100 percent of the available server resources, and the MAX value can be set in the range anywhere between the MIN and 100 percent inclusive. If the pool has a nonzero MIN defined, then the effective MAX value of the other pools is readjusted because the minimum of the configured MAX value will have some of the MIN values subtracted from 100 percent.

Performance and
Advanced Features

PART IV

The internal pool represents resources used by SQL Server itself. This tool always contains only internal groups and cannot be changed. Resources used by the internal pool are not restricted. Any workloads for the pool are considered critical for server function, and the Resource Governor always allows the internal pool to borrow from other pools, even if that means a violation of the limits set for the other pools.

The default pool is for the user. Before you configure the default pool, it contains only the default group. The default pool cannot be created or dropped but it can be changed. The default pool can contain user-defined groups in addition to the default group.

Workload Groups

Two workload groups (internal and default) are created and mapped to their corresponding resource pools when SQL Server 2008 is installed. Resource Governor also supports user-defined workload groups.

A workload group serves as a container or holder for session requests that are similar according to a set of criteria and is similarly applied to each individual request. A workload group allows aggregate monitoring of resource consumption and an ability to use a uniform policy for all the requests of the group.

Classification

The Resource Governor supports what we call classification of incoming sessions. A classification is based on a set of user criteria contained in a function. The results of the function logic enable the Resource Governor to classify sessions into existing workload groups. You can write a scalar function that will assign incoming sessions to workload groups. Before you can use this function, you must complete the following actions: First, create and register the function using the ALTER RESOURCE GOVERNOR statement. Second, you must update the Resource Governor configuration using the ALTER RESOURCE GOVERNOR statement with the RECONFIGURE parameter.

In the context of Resource Governor, the login process for a session consists of the following steps:

1. Login authentication
2. LOGON trigger execution
3. Classification

When classification starts, Resource Governor executes the classifier function and uses the value returned by the function to send requests to the appropriate workload group.

To enable and begin using Resource Governor, open Object Explorer and expand the Management node; then right-click Resource Governor and choose Properties. Figure 11.23 shows the dialog to prepare for Resource Governor usage. The first drop-down box, Classifier Function Name, will be disabled until the Enable Resource Governor check box is checked. Once it is selected, you may choose the function that you have defined for classification.

Figure 11.23: Resource Governor Properties dialog

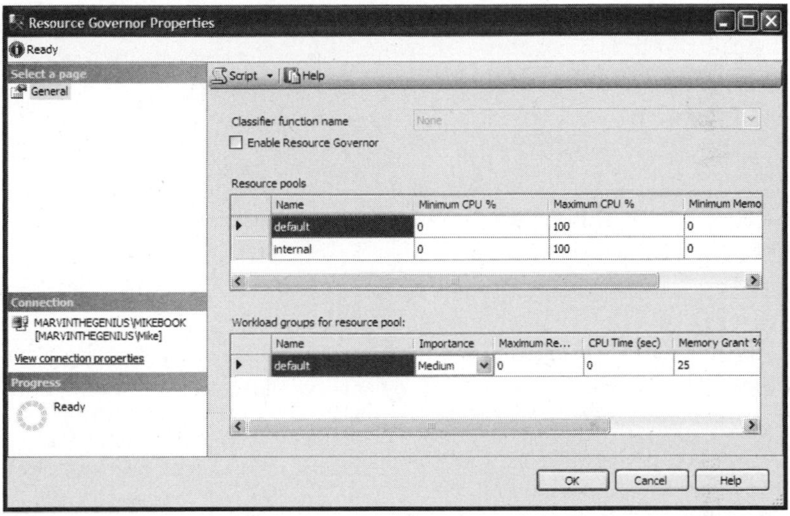

In the Resource Pools area, you can make both maximum and minimum settings for CPU and memory. These settings can be configured for both the default and internal resource pool within the limits that we discussed earlier. Below the Resource Pools area is the workload group for the resource pool default. Importance, Maximum Requests, CPU Time, Memory Grant, and Degree Parallelism all can be determined in this interface. Table 11.4 contains the definition of each of these settings. This table can also be found at http://msdn.microsoft.com/en-us/library/bb895389.aspx.

Performance and Advanced Features

PART IV

Table 11.4: Potential Workload Group Settings

Setting	Action	Description
Maximum memory	Increase or decrease	Increase. No effect on active queries, and these queries can obtain more memory if it is available. Decrease. Active requests are unaffected, but new requests will have less memory.
Maximum CPU time	Increase or decrease	Increase. No effect on active queries. Decrease. Causes an event to be fired for a query that is above the limit, but the query continues to run.
Resource time-out	Increase or decrease	Queries that are already waiting in the queue are not affected. New queries use the new setting.
Importance	Increase or decrease	Affects CPU distribution for Only queries in the workload group.
Maximum number of requests	Increase or decrease	Increase. No effect on existing queries. Decrease. Existing queries are unaffected, but new queries wait and may timeout.
Maximum degree of parallelism	Increase or decrease	Affects only the compile and execution of new queries.
Specified resource pool	Change	Active requests continue to use the existing resource pool and its settings. New requests use the new pool and its settings.

If you wish to create your own resource pool, right-click on Resource Governor under the Management node in Object Explorer and choose New Resource Pool. This will open the Resource Governor Properties page. In the Resource Pools grid, click the first column in the empty row that is labeled with an asterisk. This will be available only if you have checked the box to enable Resource Governor. Double-click the empty cell in the name column and type the name you want to use for the pool, and then click OK. Figure 11.24 shows a newly created application pool.

Figure 11.24: New application pool

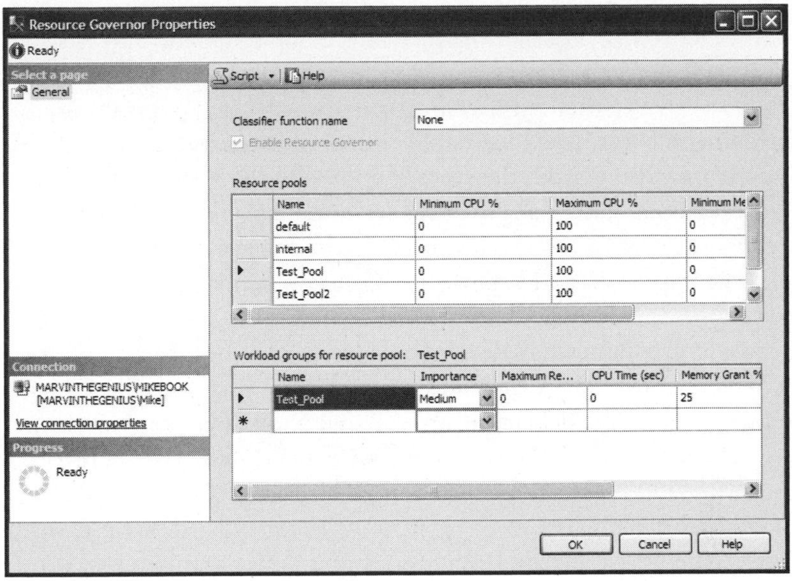

Managing Data Compression

SQL Server provides a feature that can assist you in maximizing database storage, called *data compression*. Data compression can be used on tables that have no indexes, tables with clustered and/or nonclustered indexes (including partitioned tables), nonclustered indexes, and indexed views.

You should use data compression because it will improve disk space utilization, reduce disk I/O for read and write operations, and make more room available in the buffer cache because the buffer cache will then contain compressed data. However, the disadvantage of using data compression is that there is a higher CPU load to be handled.

There are two modes of compression: at the row level and at the page level. When you enact compression, the database storage engine handles the algorithm, so there is no special code required in an application. After you enable compression in an object, anytime the data has to pass to and from the storage engine, it has to be compressed and uncompressed, respectively. Therefore, there is an extra CPU overhead involved, but the amount of disk I/O saved by compression makes up for the CPU costs.

Let's first look at an update statement with row-level compression enabled. Examining an update statement, a read is done before the write in order to identify that the record is being updated. This is so the relational engine will make a request to the storage engine, which will in turn retrieve that data record from the disk and put it into the buffer cache in compressed format. The record is uncompressed when the record transitions from the storage engine to the relational engine. The query, having gotten a row it wishes to update, now updates accordingly and passes the record back to the storage engine, where it is again compressed and kept in the buffer cache until the row is flushed to the disk in the compressed format.

In page-level compression, decompression does not occur until the page is nearly full because pages are allocated atomically, and partial compression of the page would yield no benefits. As with row-level compression, there will be increased CPU cost, but we have found significant improvements in large I/O bound workloads and getting data to and from the database more quickly.

To estimate the savings in storage space for tables and indexes, you can use either of two methods available to you. The first is sp_estimate_data_compression_savings, which is a built-in stored procedure. The following code shows how to use it:

```
USE AdventureWorks
GO
EXEC sp_estimate_data_compression_savings
    @schema_name = 'Production',
    @object_name = 'TransactionHistory',
    @index_id = NULL,
    @partition_number = NULL,
    @data_compression = 'ROW' ;
GO
```

The second method is to use the Data Compression Wizard, which will give you an estimate of space to be saved. To use the second method, expand the node for the database you wish to use, and then expand the tables list. Right-click the table and choose Storage Option ➢ Storage ➢ Manage Compression. This will begin the Data Compression Wizard. Once you click Next, you will see the dialog in Figure 11.25.

Figure 11.25: Data Compression Wizard

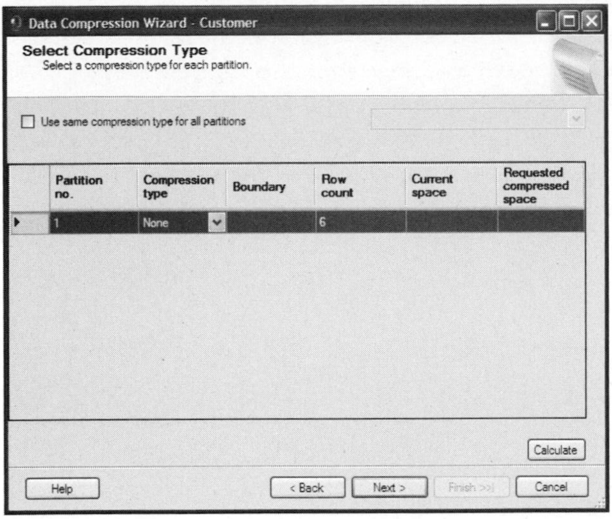

In this wizard, you can select the partition and compression type (Row, Page, or None). When you select the compression type and partition, click the Calculate button to see an estimate of your requested compressed space. The next page in the wizard allows you to choose your output for the compression script. You are also given the option of running the compression immediately or scheduling it for later. Clicking the Next button will give you a summary of the choices you have made in the wizard so far. Finally, click Finish to begin using your compression options.

Remember, do not make adjustments to an instance or database without first monitoring to figure out where the problems may lie. Taking the time to follow the procedures outlined at the beginning of this chapter will make your instance stable and more reliable.

12

Planning and Creating Indexes

Performance and Advanced Features

PART IV

The larger a database gets, the more difficult it is to efficiently extract information from the data store. Wading through every single data page in a data table requires extensive IO, and if you repeat this process again and again, you are wasting a lot of time and resources. It may even get to the point that your application is completely unusable for the end user because of the time that it takes to do even the simplest data operations.

The answer to the problem is to create an appropriate collection of indexes. Just as you can use an index in a book to locate specific information, so can a database index assist the query engine in locating specific information in the database. There are really two parts to this puzzle, however. First, you have to know which indexes to create. Second, you have to go through the mechanical process of creating the index.

It is not our intent in this chapter to provide a comprehensive overview of performance tuning. That is a subject best reserved for its own volume. We do, however, want to introduce you to basic index planning techniques, walk you through the mechanics of index creation, and then discuss some special cases regarding indexes that you might be able to use to improve overall database performance.

Understand Index Architecture

An important component of planning appropriate indexes is understanding the underlying storage architecture. Based on the way data is stored in SQL Server, some types of queries will lend themselves to certain index structures and, in some cases, perhaps no indexes at all. In the following sections, we will describe some of the index architectures you will see in SQL Server and how to use this knowledge of index architecture to plan your own index implementation.

Understand Index Storage

You may have heard it said that the natural state of the world is chaos. If that is true about the world in general, it must be doubly so for a database. Without any effort at maintaining structure and order, data engines tend to dump data into piles and expect you to sort through it later. This chaotic state of the database world is called a *heap*. You also have the option of creating a physical index on the data that clusters the data together based on a key. Heaps and clustered indexes are the two states in which a data page can exist.

Heaps

Think of a heap as an unordered collection of data pages. In its natural state with no indexes, every table is organized in a heap. When the table requires more data, it allocates another extent to the heap, adding to the number of pages in the pile. This is an efficient way to store data if you are concerned with the overhead of data storage. One data page is as good as any other, so the database can store the data wherever it finds room rather than having to store it in a particular place.

Tables that are organized in a heap have no specific sort or order for the data. To demonstrate, you will create a table with a heap by using a SQL query to copy data from one of the tables in the AdventureWorksDW2008 database to a new table using a SELECT INTO statement as follows:

```
USE AdventureWorksDW2008;

SELECT
  p.EnglishProductName,
  p.Size,
  p.Color,
  rs.OrderQuantity,
  rs.UnitPrice,
  rs.ExtendedAmount
INTO DemoSales
FROM FactResellerSales as rs
INNER JOIN DimProduct as p
  ON rs.ProductKey = p.ProductKey;
GO
```

The resulting DemoSales table is organized into a heap by default. To verify this, you can retrieve index information from the sys.indexes system view using the following statement:

```
USE AdventureWorksDW2008;

SELECT o.name, i.type_desc
FROM sys.indexes as i
INNER JOIN sys.objects as o
  ON i.object_id = o.object_id
WHERE i.type = 0;
GO
```

Performance and
Advanced Features

PART IV

In this query, an index type of 0 indicates that you are looking for only heaps. Every table that is currently organized as a heap will have an entry in the system catalog with an index type ID of 0, so you can always use this query to find out what heaps currently exist in your database.

When you query data from a table that is organized in a heap, the query engine does not have many choices as to how it will execute the query. With the data in no particular order, the data engine must examine every page in the heap to find the data to satisfy the query. This process of reading every page in the table is called a *table scan*. For most tables, resolving a query by using a table scan is very costly. The alternative is to use an index.

Index Structures

Indexes in SQL Server use a *balanced tree* structure, sometimes called a *B-tree* structure. Balanced tree indexes form a tree structure in which the data that you are indexing is on a group of pages called the leaf level. A narrowing structure builds on the leaf level until there is a single page called the *root*. The structure is called a "balanced" tree because every leaf page is exactly the same distance from the root as any other leaf page, creating a perfectly balanced structure. Figure 12.1 illustrates the general form of a balanced-tree architecture.

Figure 12.1: The B-tree index structure

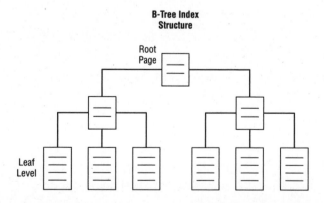

There are two basic kinds of relational indexes that use this balanced tree structure. The first is called the *clustered index*. This index represents the physical sort order of the data in the data table. There can only be one clustered index per data table. Second is the *nonclustered index*. This type of index builds a sorted key structure on top of the data page, so it does not directly impact the organization of the data page. Because of this, you can have multiple nonclustered indexes on a table.

In a balanced tree, the root page contains rows that store the first index value and a page pointer for each of the index pages in the level below the root. Each level will do likewise until you reach the leaf level, which might contain actual data or it might contain a key used to retrieve the actual data from a data page. This structure will work only if the leaf-level pages are arranged in a sorted order based on the index key.

To resolve a query with an index traversal, the query processor would begin at the root page and work its way down the levels, comparing the target value with the index keys in an attempt to narrow down the possible pages upon which the data could exist. The goal is to minimize I/O by eliminating pages from consideration without having to actually read them.

Get Index Information

Before you can effectively plan indexes, you must be able to retrieve information regarding index storage and allocation. There are a variety of techniques that you can use for this purpose. Particularly useful are IO statistics and showplan output.

Getting I/O Statistics

First, let's get a baseline. How many data pages are in the table that you are going to query. Assuming that you will query the DemoSales table, the following code will tell you how many data pages it is currently using:

```
USE AdventureWorksDW2008;
DBCC CHECKTABLE('DemoSales');
GO
```

Although your results will vary, you should get something like this:

```
DBCC results for 'DemoSales'.
There are 60855 rows in 788 pages for object "DemoSales".
```

Performance and Advanced Features

PART IV

Remember that each page read or written is considered one I/O. If we want to test our assumption, we can use the STATISTICS IO output to tell us exactly what our I/O was. To test this, use the following query:

```
USE AdventureWorksDW2008;
SET STATISTICS IO ON;
GO
SELECT COUNT(*) FROM DemoSales;
GO
SET STATISTICS IO OFF;
GO
```

This query will give you a message output that looks like the following snippet. Remember that if you are executing your results into a grid in the SQL Server Management Studio (SSMS), you will have to click on the Messages tab in the results pane to see this information. Note that we are presenting just the first part of the message here:

```
Table 'DemoSales'. Scan count 1, logical reads 788, physical
reads 0 …
```

- *Scan count* is the number of times the query processor had to scan the table, either as a full table scan or as an index traversal.

- *Logical reads* is the total number of data pages that the query processor had to read from memory to resolve the query.

- *Physical reads* is the number of pages that had to be read from disk into memory to make them available for the query processor. *Physical reads* of 0 in this case means that all of the required data pages were already in memory and there was no disk I/O necessary to resolve the query; in other words, there was a 100 percent cache hit for this query.

With this output, you can assume that the query was resolved by using a table scan. This is a good assumption for two reasons. First, the amount of logical I/O equals the number of pages in the table. Second, we have not created any indexes yet, so a table scan will generally be the best option; however, in some cases the query optimizer might instruct the query processor to create temporary indexes to make the query more efficient. If you suspect that the optimizer is choosing a table scan, you can verify this by using a showplan.

Using Showplans

Showplans come in many different forms. You can generate showplans graphically or you can generate them as text. You can generate the text-based showplan either as simple text or as XML. In SQL Server 2008, you can also view the estimated showplan (what the query optimizer thinks will happen) or the actual showplan (what actually happened).

You control the output of the text-based showplan through a connection SET statement. For example, to see the showplan for our previous query, you could use the following code. This output will be easier to read if you execute the query into text instead of into a grid:

```
USE AdventureWorksDW2008;
GO
SET SHOWPLAN_TEXT ON;
GO
SELECT COUNT(*) FROM DemoSales;
GO
SET SHOWPLAN_TEXT OFF;
GO
```

After displaying the code for which you are generating the showplan, the results will then give you output that looks something like the following. Again, your output may look a little different, but it will be similar:

```
|--Compute Scalar(DEFINE:
 ([Expr1004]=CONVERT_IMPLICIT(int,[Expr1005],0)))
 |--Stream Aggregate(DEFINE:([Expr1005]=Count(*)))
    |--Table Scan(OBJECT:
      ([AdventureWorksDW2008].[dbo].[DemoSales]))
```

The best way to read this output is from the bottom up. This output tells you that before doing any other processing, SQL Server had to do a table scan on the DemoSales table. In the context of that scan, SQL Server counted up the rows and then output the results. This output confirms that the processor did, in fact, execute the query using a table scan as we anticipated.

You can also get this information graphically. Sometimes a graph is easier to read than a text-based presentation. Either you can display the estimated execution plan without actually executing the query or you can include the actual execution plan with the query output. Figure 12.2 illustrates the process of displaying an estimated execution

Performance and
Advanced Features

PART IV

plan. Click the highlighted button to generate the plan. Notice that the tool tip on the button specifies an *estimated*, not an actual, execution. Clicking this button will not actually execute the query.

Figure 12.2: Generating the estimated execution plan

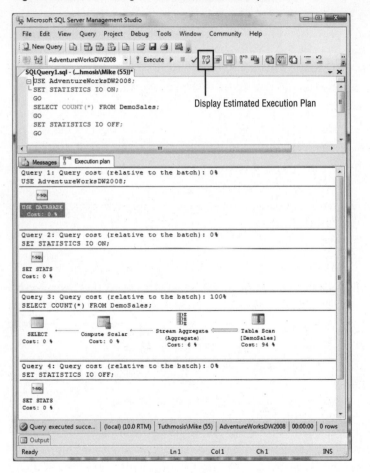

Because there are four queries in this batch, you see the execution plan for each query. Notice that the output provides a relative cost measure for each query in the batch. In this case, the cost of the USE statement is insignificant compared with the aggregate query. Each of the pictures in the output is a different operator in the query execution process. Each operator identifies the actual task that the query processor is executing. In this case, there are four operators:

Table Scan A Table Scan operator retrieves all rows from the table indicated in square brackets below the icon—in this case, DemoSales. If the query contains a WHERE clause, it will return only the rows that satisfy the clause.

Stream Aggregate The Stream Aggregate operator groups rows by one or more columns and then calculates one or more aggregate expressions returned by the query. Subsequent operators in the query can reference the output of this operator, or the results can be returned to the client.

Compute Scalar The Compute Scalar operator calculates the scalar aggregate of an expression—in this case, the results of the Stream Aggregate operator. Subsequent operators in the query can reference the output of this operator or the results can be returned to the client.

Select The Select operator returns the output of an expression to the client. In this case, the Select operator returns the results of the Compute Scalar operator. This is generally a terminal point in the query process.

After you have generated the estimated execution plan, you can hover your mouse over the icons to display more detailed costing information. For example, if you hover your mouse over the Table Scan shape in the results pane, you will get a pop-up window that looks like the one in Figure 12.3. This detail tells you what the query optimizer is assuming will happen when you execute this query.

Figure 12.3: Costing detail for the table scan

Table Scan	
Scan rows from a table.	
Physical Operation	Table Scan
Logical Operation	Table Scan
Estimated I/O Cost	0.586166
Estimated CPU Cost	0.067019
Estimated Number of Executions	1
Estimated Operator Cost	0.653185 (95%)
Estimated Subtree Cost	0.653185
Estimated Number of Rows	60855
Estimated Row Size	9 B
Ordered	False
Node ID	2
Object	
[AdventureWorksDW2008].[dbo].[DemoSales]	

Performance and
Advanced Features

PART IV

Look at the percentage associated with the operator cost. This is the percentage cost estimated to be attributed to this single operator in the set. You will also notice an estimated number of rows as well as a row size. The optimizer uses this information to determine what the I/O cost of the operator will be.

Plan Indexes

You have already seen how an index can provide much more efficient access to data than is possible with a heap. In most cases, you will want to have at least a clustered index on a table, if not multiple nonclustered indexes as well. The big questions then become how we should determine the best indexes to create, upon which field or fields we should create them, and how to effectively balance the costs and benefits of these indexes.

Evaluating Queries and Search Arguments

There are certain parts of a query that are going to provide the bulk of the information to the query optimizer. The WHERE clause and to a lesser degree the GROUP BY and ORDER BY clauses are particularly useful to the optimizer. The JOIN statements, specifically the correlated fields, are also useful. These parts of the query provide significant opportunity for the optimizer to reduce I/O by using an index and eliminating unnecessary page reads that might occur when performing a table scan.

The WHERE clause is where most of the data filtering takes place, and correctly structuring this clause is critical. This is where the optimizer will find the Search Arguments (SARGs), which are filter statements that you write in the very specific format of

```
Field <operator> expression
```

For example, assume that you wanted to filter an employee table based on a monthly salary greater than $1,000; however, the salary value stored in the employees table is expressed in annual terms. The following WHERE clause would be a valid SARG:

```
WHERE salary > 1000 * 12
```

Notice how the field is isolated on one side of the operator. If there is an index on the Salary field, SQL Server can evaluate that index as an option to improve the I/O score of the query. If you were to write the WHERE clause this way, it would be different:

```
WHERE salary/12 > 1000
```

In this case, the Salary field is not isolated. While there may be an index on salary, there is no index on salary/12, so SQL Server has no index that it can evaluate. If you take care to ensure that you write all filter criteria as SARGs, it will increase the probability that the optimizer will be able to use the indexes that you create on the filtered fields.

This applies to join operations as well. For example, suppose that in the Employee table you express all salaries in annual terms but in the Contractor table they are monthly values. You want to find the employees that you pay the same as the contractors in a matching list. If you write the JOIN clause like this, how will this affect the optimizer's options?

```
Employee as e INNER JOIN contractor as c
  ON e.salary = c.salary * 12
```

While this is a valid JOIN statement, the optimizer has no option to use any index on the Salary field of the Contractor table. It can still use an index on the Employee Salary field, however, because you have not manipulated this field in the JOIN clause.

Which Indexes Should You Create?

Which indexes should you create? That's simple: you should create the indexes that the query optimizer will actually use. You can usually determine this through trial and error, with a little bit of planning thrown in for good measure. To effectively plan your indexes, you must learn to look at your queries the way the optimizer will look at them. The optimizer is concerned with one thing only, resource consumption, primarily I/O.

To understand how the optimizer behaves, you have to know a few things about its design. When planning for index strategy, consider the following:

The optimizer favors throughput over response time.   There are two ways to think about performance. One way is response time: How long does it take for the query to return results to the user? The other is throughput: How do we push as much activity as possible through the server given a fixed amount of resources? The

Performance and Advanced Features

PART IV

answers to these two questions are often at odds with each other, but the optimizer will take an action that improves throughput before taking an action that improves response time.

The optimizer uses static statistics.   To make its I/O estimates, the optimizer uses distribution statistics. These statistics store information about the distribution of key values through the index and are critical to the accuracy of the optimizer. SQL Server stores these statistics, one per index, on pages that the optimizer consults when scoring an index. These pages are generally static. Although there are database options that you can enable to automatically update statistics during server idle time, you should get in the habit of regularly updating statistics yourself as a part of your regular maintenance process. Use the UPDATE STATISTICS statement to refresh the needed statistics pages.

The optimizer depends on a well-organized query.   Don't forget to review your queries to ensure that there are valid SARGs where needed. Also provide as much information as possible with regard to possible join relationships because they can give the optimizer more options for join orders. Because the optimizer can't optimize SARGs based on user-defined functions, be careful when using user-defined functions in joins or as SARGs. Be careful with the use of temp tables and table variables because queries against them are often not able to be optimized due to late binding. This is where the trial-and-error concept comes in really handy.

SQL Server uses one index per table.   In most situations, SQL Server will use only one index per table to resolve the query. Although there are a few exceptions to this rule, such as the optimizer's strategy for resolving OR operators, if you plan on one index per table, it will help you design the best indexes to meet the best aggregation of application needs. Try to get the most benefit from the fewest number of indexes.

To determine if the query optimizer is actually using an index for a query, consult the showplan output. Remember that if there is an index in the execution plan, you will see an icon in the plan that mentions the index. You may want to experiment with multiple index combinations to try to find the best aggregate collection of indexes. Remember that sometimes a *composite index*, one with more than one column in the key, can provide benefits for multiple queries. Although there are no hard and fast rules, here are some considerations for the best index selections. Start here and work your way out:

- Total I/O should never be more than a table scan. If using an index results in more I/O than a table scan, there is a problem.

- Clustered indexes generally work best for queries that select data based on range-based or nonunique searches.

- The maintenance cost of clustered indexes is very high. You should select nonvolatile columns for these indexes.

- Nonclustered indexes are generally best for very selective queries where you select a very small percentage of the data.

- Composite (multicolumn) indexes can often provide benefits for a broader range of queries, but they have a higher maintenance and storage cost.

- Consider indexes for fields frequently used in SARGs.

- Consider indexes for foreign key fields in join operations.

This is definitely just a starting point. Every database is different and will require different indexing tactics. We cannot underestimate the importance of experimenting with the showplan and I/O metrics to determine the best possible indexing strategies.

Create and Manage Indexes

Like most operations in SQL Server, you can create indexes in two ways. You can use either the SQL Server Management Studio (SSMS) visual interface or Transact SQL (TSQL) code. In the following sections, we will walk you through both approaches for creating both clustered and nonclustered indexes as well as special variations on these indexes.

Create and Manage Clustered Indexes

Remember that a clustered index represents the physical sort order for the data in the table. When you create a clustered index on a table, SQL Server reorganizes the heap into an ordered index leaf level. This can be time consuming, so be cautious about scheduling index creation processes. Creating indexes is generally a simple process. We will begin by illustrating this process with SSMS.

Creating a Clustered Index with SSMS

To begin, you must connect the Object Explorer in SSMS to the server you want to target. In this example, assume that you want to create an index on the DemoSales table in the AdventureWorksDW2008 database. Follow these steps:

1. Locate the appropriate table in the Tables folder of the AdventureWorksDW2008 database.

2. Expand the folder. You should see another folder inside labeled Indexes.

3. Right-click the Indexes folder and select New Index from the menu. This presents a New Index dialog like the one pictured in Figure 12.4. This is the General page of the dialog.

Figure 12.4: Creating a clustered index

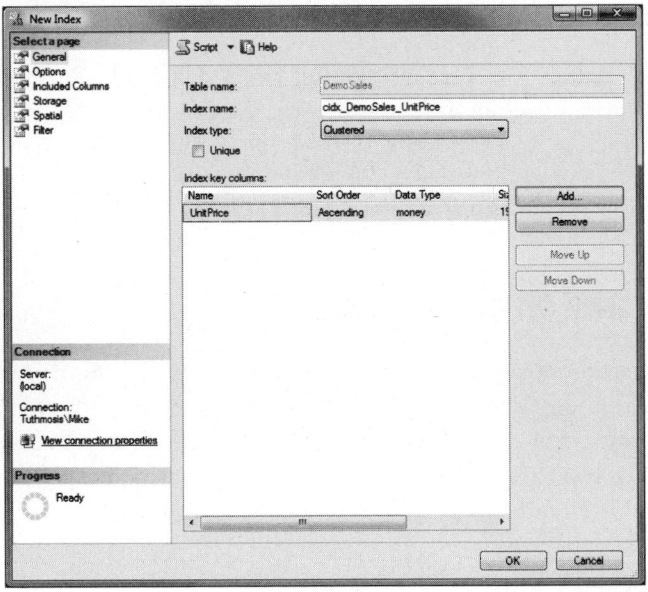

4. Name your index. Although there are no index-naming rules other than the standard SQL Server naming requirements, you should use something that is indicative of the type of index key structure. Here, the name cidx_DemoSales_UnitPrice indicates that this is a clustered index on the DemoSales table using the UnitPrice field as a key.

5. As you look over the dialog, you will also see the check box that allows you to mark the index as unique. This will prevent the index from accepting duplicate values for the key field(s).

6. To add a field to the index, click the Add button and select the field(s) from the pop-up window that appears. Selecting more than one field will make this a composite index. You will select only the UnitPrice field in this example.

7. Click on the Options page to display the dialog pictured in Figure 14.5. This page shows standard options such as locking, statistics recomputation, and fill factors. Many of these options, such as fill factors, can be modified after you build the index.

Figure 12.5: Index options

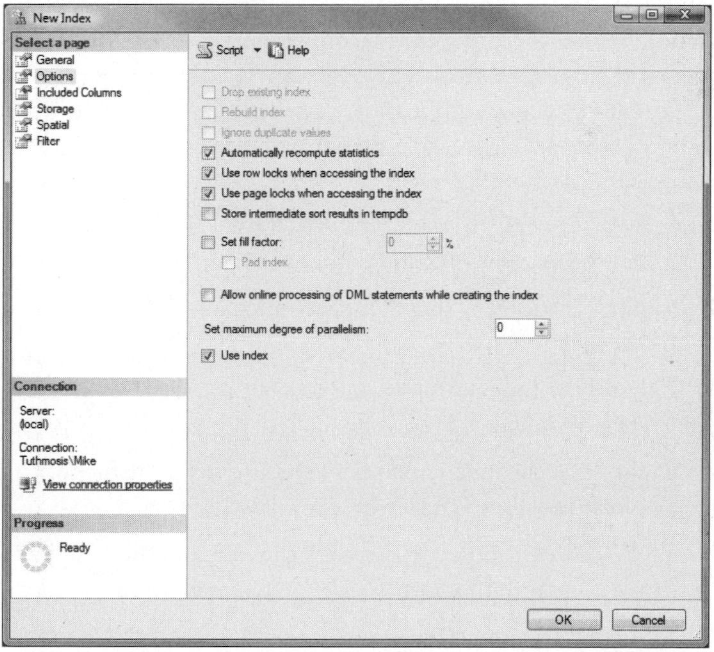

8. Look at the Storage page, which provides an interface where you can configure the physical filegroup or partition storage for the index.

> **NOTE** The Included Columns and Filter pages are relevant only for nonclustered indexes, which we will cover later in this chapter. The Spatial page is valid only with spatial indexes that support the geometry and geography data types new to SQL Server 2008. Those types are not covered in this book.

9. To create the index, click the OK button on the dialog. The new index will appear in the Indexes folder of the Object Explorer.

10. Note that you can alter the index at any time by navigating back to this dialog and changing the index options.

Disabling an Index with SSMS

Sometimes you may not want an index that you created to be accessible. This might be for performance reasons or perhaps you are trying to perform diagnostic or performance-tuning operations and need to exclude an index temporarily. Disabling an index will prevent the noise that the index may create when you're performing these activities. Follow these steps to disable an index:

1. Locate the appropriate table in the Tables folder of the AdventureWorksDW2008 database.

2. Expand the folder. You should see another folder inside labeled Indexes.

3. Expand the Indexes folder and locate the cidx_DemoSales_UnitPrice index.

4. Right-click the index and select Disable from the menu. Click the OK button on the Disable Indexes dialog.

5. To reenable the index, right-click the index in the folder and select Properties from the menu.

6. Select the Options page in the dialog. Locate the Use Index check box at the bottom of the page and select it.

7. Click OK to commit the action.

> **NOTE** Disabling a clustered index will prevent all access to the underlying table or view upon which the index is built. For this reason, disabling indexes is usually more useful on nonclustered indexes.

Dropping a Clustered Index with SSMS

Dropping a clustered index reverts the data storage to a heap, meaning that any inserts or updates are not required to be placed in index order. Also, SQL Server will delete the B-tree structure, so there will no longer be a mechanism for index traversal. Dropping an index is a simple process. To drop the index that you just created, follow these steps:

1. Locate the appropriate table in the Tables folder of the AdventureWorksDW2008 database.

2. Expand the folder. You should see another folder inside labeled Indexes.

3. Expand the Indexes folder and locate the cidx_DemoSales_ UnitPrice index.

4. Right-click the index in the list and select Delete.

5. Click OK to commit the action.

Creating a Clustered Index with TSQL

To create a clustered index, you will use the CREATE INDEX statement. The essential syntax of this statement is as follows:

```
CREATE [ UNIQUE ] [ CLUSTERED | NONCLUSTERED ] INDEX index_
name
  ON <object> ( column [ ASC | DESC ] [ ,...n ] )
  [ INCLUDE ( column_name [ ,...n ] ) ]
  [ WITH ( <relational_index_option> [ ,...n ] ) ]
  [ ON { partition_scheme_name ( column_name )
    | filegroup_name
    | default
    }
  ]
```

In this syntax, your relation index options (the section after the WITH clause) are as follows:

```
 PAD_INDEX = { ON | OFF }
 | FILLFACTOR = fillfactor
 | SORT_IN_TEMPDB = { ON | OFF }
 | IGNORE_DUP_KEY = { ON | OFF }
 | STATISTICS_NORECOMPUTE = { ON | OFF }
```

```
| DROP_EXISTING = { ON | OFF }
| ONLINE = { ON | OFF }
| ALLOW_ROW_LOCKS = { ON | OFF }
| ALLOW_PAGE_LOCKS = { ON | OFF }
| MAXDOP = max_degree_of_parallelism
| DATA_COMPRESSION = { NONE | ROW | PAGE}
```

Most of these options should look familiar because they correspond directly to the options on the pages in the index dialog you saw in Figure 12.5. The Options page contains most of the relational index options in this syntax, and the General page defines most of the basic settings, such as the index name and column list. The ON clause, which allows you to specify a filegroup or partition as the target of the index, is addressed in the Storage page of the dialog. The INCLUDE clause and the WHERE clause, which are valid for nonclustered indexes only, can be graphically configured in the Included columns and Filter pages, respectively.

This is very simple and precise syntax, and it allows you to create exactly the index you want and need. For example, to create a clustered index on UnitPrice in the DemoSales table, you would use this statement:

```
USE AdventureWorksDW2008;

CREATE CLUSTERED INDEX cidx_DemoSales_UnitPrice
ON dbo.DemoSales(UnitPrice);
GO
```

If the index already existed on the table and you wanted to drop it in order to re-create it, you could use the following statement. Note that you accomplish the same thing here with a rebuild, which is addressed in the ALTER INDEX syntax. The usual logic behind a DROP_EXISTING option is to change the column list or locations that cannot be addressed with a rebuild. Here is the statement:

```
USE AdventureWorksDW2008;

CREATE CLUSTERED INDEX CL_DemoSales_UnitPrice
ON dbo.DemoSales(UnitPrice)
WITH DROP_EXISTING;
GO
```

Altering a Clustered Index with TSQL

The ALTER INDEX syntax is a bit more involved because there are many options that you can modify when altering an index. The basic syntax of this statement is as follows:

```
ALTER INDEX { index_name | ALL }
ON <object> {
REBUILD | DISABLE | REORGANIZE
| SET ( <set_index_option> [ ,...n ] )
    }
```

The main body of this syntax allows you to do three things. You can rebuild the index, reorganize the index, or disable the index. You will address any other index options though the SET clause. These options are the same as those in the CREATE INDEX statement, so you can control things such as fill factors, statistics recomputation, and all the other options that you can control when creating an index.

Disabling a Clustered Index with TSQL

You can also disable an index with TSQL, although this is a one-way operation. You cannot reenable an index through TSQL. You must either use the technique mentioned previously using the SSMS or do an index rebuild in the TSQL by either executing a CREATE INDEX statement with a DROP_EXISTING option or using the ALTER INDEX with the REBUILD option. The basic syntax for disabling an index using the TSQL looks like the following example:

```
USE AdventureWorksDW2008;

ALTER INDEX cidx_DemoSales_UnitPrice
ON dbo.DemoSales
DISABLE;
GO
```

Dropping a Clustered Index with TSQL

This is very simple syntax, but remember that it has a significant impact on system structure. Just as with using SSMS, this one operation will remove the entire index infrastructure. Use the following code to drop the index:

```
USE AdventureWorksDW2008;


DROP INDEX DemoSales.cidx_DemoSales_UnitPrice;
GO
```

Create and Manage Nonclustered Indexes

Most of the mechanics of working with nonclustered indexes are identical to the corresponding operations with clustered indexes. The most substantial architectural difference between the two is that the nonclustered index does not impact the physical storage of the table. A nonclustered index can be created in two different operational scenarios:

Nonclustered index on a heap   If the data is organized in a heap, meaning that there is no clustered index, a nonclustered index leaf level contains a pointer to the heap for each index entry. After SQL Server uses the index to find the desired entry, it uses the pointer to access the underlying data from the heap.

Nonclustered index on a clustered index   If the data table contains a clustered index, the nonclustered indexes will use a clustered index key to locate the data rather than maintaining a pointer to the actual data. This improves the performance of index maintenance by not requiring all nonclustered indexes to monitor the location of every data row. However, for efficiency, if you plan to rebuild all of your indexes, you should rebuild the clustered index first and then the nonclustered because the nonclustered indexes depend on the clustered key.

Creating a Nonclustered Index Using SSMS

Most of the process is exactly the same as the process for creating a clustered index. The primary difference is the availability of a few features that are not available with clustered indexes. The following steps illustrate the process:

1. Locate the appropriate table in the Tables folder of the AdventureWorksDW2008 database.

2. Expand the folder. You should see another folder inside labeled Indexes.

3. Right-click the Indexes folder and select New Index from the menu. This presents a New Index dialog like the one pictured in Figure 12.6. This is the General page of the dialog. Note that the index type is set as nonclustered.

Figure 12.6: Creating a nonclustered index

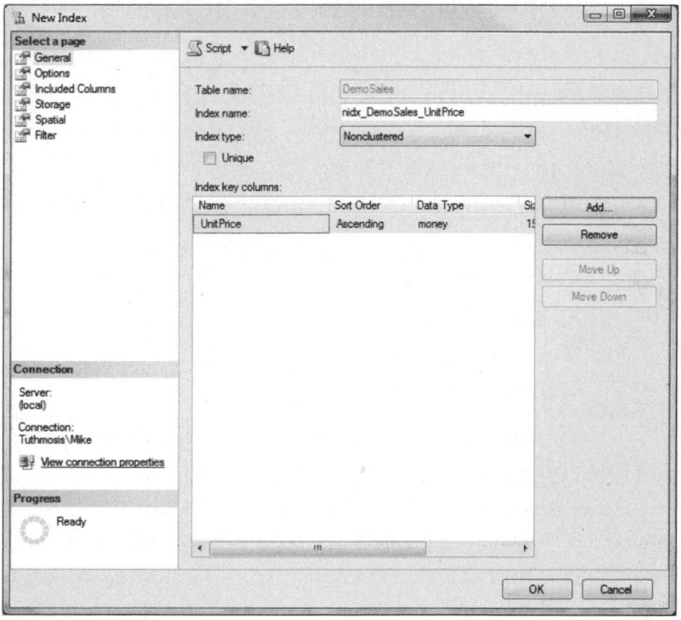

4. Click the Included Columns page. This page allows you to add columns to the index leaf level without actually making them part of the index key. This can be useful for creating *covering indexes*, which we will discuss later in this chapter in the section "Cover a Query."

5. Click the Filter page of the dialog. This page allows you to enter a filter expression to the index. For example, if you entered UnitPrice >= 10 as a filter expression, SQL Server would include only rows that meet the criteria in the index.

6. All of the other behaviors are the same as with clustered indexes. Click the OK button to commit the action.

All other actions, such as altering, disabling, or dropping nonclustered indexes, are essentially the same as the clustered indexes. Refer to the Create and Manage Clustered Index section on the clustered index operations for details.

Creating Nonclustered Indexes Using TSQL

The syntax for nonclustered indexes is, again, almost the same as clustered indexes, with the following exceptions:

- You do not have to include the word NONCLUSTERED in the CREATE INDEX statement. Nonclustered indexes are the default.

- You have the option of including nonindexed columns in the index leaf level.

- You have the option of applying an index filter if you do not want the index to include all of the rows in the table.

The following code illustrates the creation of a nonclustered index using TSQL code using these special features. This code creates a nonclustered index on the DemoSales table. The index key is UnitSales, but the leaf level of the index also includes the Size column. Only rows having a UnitSales value greater than or equal to 10 are indexed:

```
USE AdventureWorksDW2008;

CREATE INDEX nidx_DemoSales_UnitPrice
ON dbo.DemoSales(UnitPrice)
INCLUDE (Size)
WHERE UnitPrice >= 10;
```

Again, the other mechanics of nonclustered indexes are the same as their clustered counterparts. You can refer to the section "Create and Manage Clustered Indexes" for more details on those operations.

Use the Database Engine Tuning Advisor

Managing a complex portfolio of database indexes can be very challenging. The larger the database gets and the more interdependent the table structures become, the more challenging the process becomes. To assist you in this process, Microsoft includes a tool with SQL Server 2008 called the Database Engine Tuning Advisor. The purpose of this tool is to evaluate common workloads in conjunction with your database architecture to recommend an appropriate index portfolio.

The Advisor requires that you provide a workload that is representative of typical interactions with the database. You should create this workload before starting the wizard. The more complete this workload is, the better the analysis. This workload can be in the following formats:

- A trace file (.trc)

- A trace saved to a SQL Server table

- An XML workload file (.xml)

- A SQL script (.sql)

The following steps will guide you through the Advisor:

1. From the Windows Start menu, click Start ➤ All Programs ➤ SQL Server 2008 ➤ Performance Tools ➤ Database Engine Tuning Advisor.

2. In the Connect to Server dialog, connect to the server that hosts the target database.

3. Configure the Database Engine Tuning Advisor with the desired settings. Figure 12.7 provides an illustration for the following settings:

   A. The session name is set to Tuning Demo 1. Each session must have a unique name.

   B. The workload section points to a SQL script file.

   C. The workload executes in the AdventureWorksDW2008 database.

   D. Two tables in the AdventureWorksDW2008 are selected for analysis, DimEmployee and DimGeography. The Advisor will evaluate indexes for only these two tables.

4. Click the Tuning Options tab. This dialog, illustrated in Figure 12.8, provides the rules that the advisor will work with:

   a. A time limit setting. Some workflows may be large. This will limit analysis time.

   b. The next section allows you to decide which Physical Design Structures (PDS) the Advisor will consider for analysis.

   c. The third section provides options for evaluating partitioned indexes.

   d. The final section allows you to decide if you want to keep any of the existing PDS.

Figure 12.7: Configuring the Database Engine Tuning Advisor

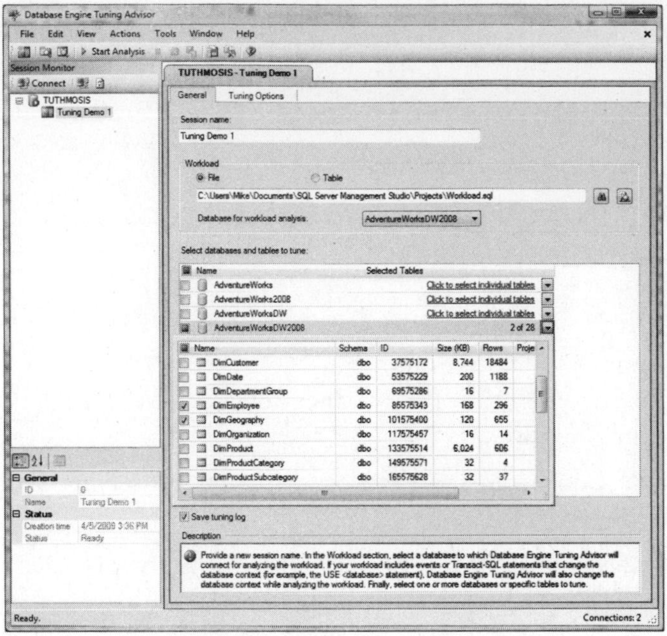

Figure 12.8: Setting tuning options

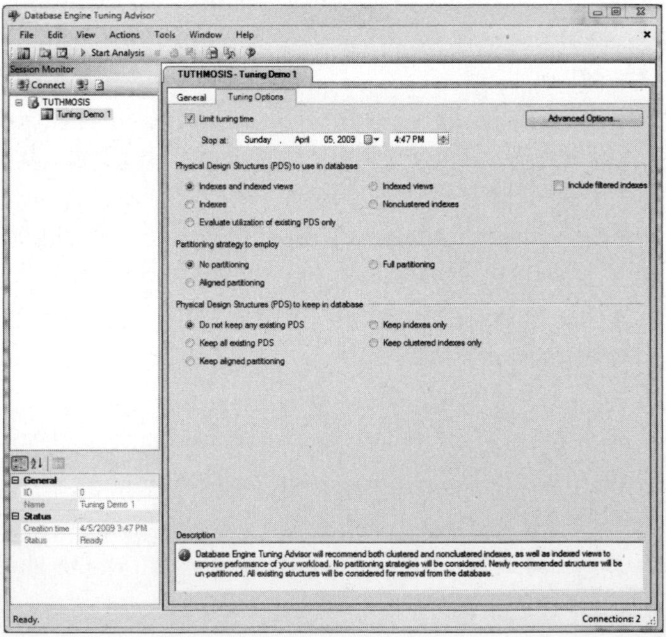

5. Click the Start Analysis button in the toolbar. This will add Progress, Recommendations, and Reports tabs to the dialog.

   a. The Progress tab displays the status of the analysis.

   b. The Recommendations tab, illustrated in Figure 12.9, provides a list of database objects and any tuning recommendations for those objects.

Figure 12.9: The Recommendations tab

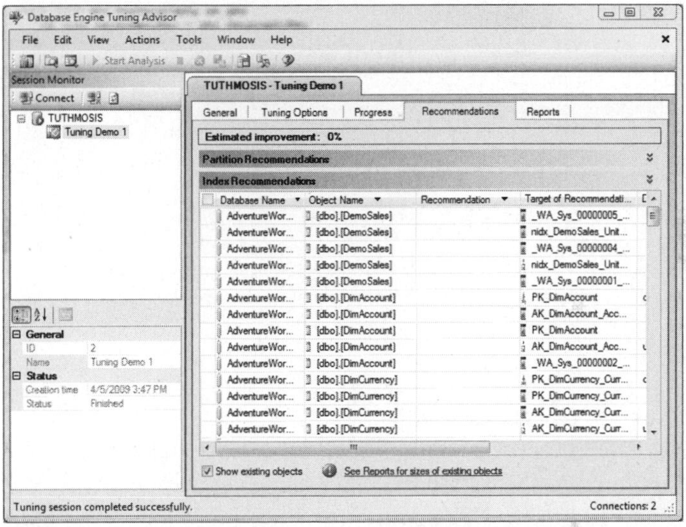

   c. The Reports tab, illustrated in Figure 12.10, allows you to select from a list of analysis reports to get more detailed information about the metrics behind the recommendations.

Manage Special Index Operations

As always, there are some exceptions to the rules. While most indexing strategies provide support for standard optimizer behavior, there are always special cases and they can have both positive and negative impacts on performance. Being aware of these special cases allows you to take advantage of performance opportunities and avoid potential pitfalls.

Figure 12.10: The Reports tab

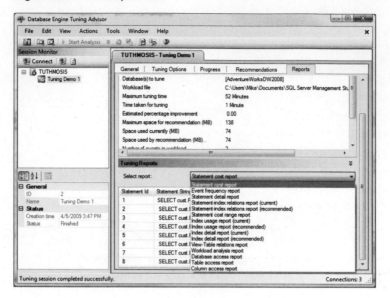

Cover a Query

Covering is the process of retrieving all necessary data from an index instead of going to the data page. This behavior is specifically related to nonclustered indexes. The concept is simple: Nonclustered index leaf pages contain more rows per page than the data page does. Because your performance objective is to reduce page I/O, reading pages with more rows means that overall you will read fewer pages. Therefore, if all the data you need is on the index page, why read the data page at all?

Assume for a moment that you have an employee table with an average row size of 100 bytes. This means that you can store about 80 rows on a data page. If you have 100,000 rows in the table, you need about 1,250 pages to store the data with no fill factor. If you ever do a table or clustered index scan on the table, you would execute 1,250 pages of I/O.

Now assume that you have a query that selects the first name and last name for each employee. If there is no WHERE clause in the query, this would require a data page scan. But what if you created an index on the firstname and lastname columns in the table? You might initially assume that because the query had no SARGs, the index would not be useful because it would provide no ability to filter the data. However, it might actually be of value to you.

Remember that all indexes at the leaf level will store the entire index key. If you create an index on the firstname and lastname columns, this entire key will exist in the nonclustered index leaf level for every row. Because the query only requires the firstname and the lastname data, why read the table when the query can get what it needs from the index? In this case, the index is said to "cover" the query and is called a *covering index* This situation is automatically detected and scored by the query optimizer as an option for query execution.

The I/O that you save may be significant. Assume that each index key uses 40 bytes of space for the index key and any other row overhead. This is a 60 percent savings on a per-row basis. Do the math and you will find that using the index would reduce the overall I/O to 500 pages.

If you create indexes with covering in mind, you could significantly reduce I/O by adding a few well-placed columns here and there in your indexes to ensure that you will get the benefit of covering. In the early days of SQL Server, you had to create composite indexes to get this advantage, meaning that all of the index fields had to be sorted and maintained when values changed. Now, however, you have the option of including nonindexed values in a nonclustered index by using the INCLUDE clause. They basically get to tag along for free, included with the index key but requiring no additional sort overhead.

To accomplish this, you can use the Included Columns page in the Index Properties dialog, or you can use the INCLUDE clause in the CREATE INDEX statement. Be careful not to include too many columns. There comes a point where too many columns create an index leaf level that is so large you lose the advantage of covering. When strategically placed, however, a covering index can be an incredible advantage over standard data page scanning.

Optimize Logical Operations

Logical operators such as AND, OR, and NOT pose particular challenges to the query optimizer. Remember that generally SQL Server can use only one index per table when resolving a query. Logical operators can either provide more information to the optimizer or doom you to a leaf level scan if the operator precludes the use of any specific index. These logical operators include the following:

NOT   The NOT operator usually has catastrophic effects on query optimization because it provides no argument containment. Unless there is another SARG that the optimizer can use to provide effective filtering, you will end up with a scan of some kind. Although this operator is sometimes a requirement, you should attempt to recode the query to avoid it whenever possible.

AND   The AND operator is the optimizer's best friend. This operator provides a collection of conditions that must all be true. If each of the conditions is a valid SARG, the optimizer suddenly has a choice of which index to use and will likely choose the index that provides the most selective filtering, thereby eliminating more I/O.

For example, if a query has two SARGs related with an AND operator, the optimizer will score each one. If the first SARG selects a fewer number of rows than the second and scores with less I/O, it will use that index to resolve the query and then apply the other condition to results of the index-based extraction.

OR   The OR operator can be problematic. If the filter criteria are not based on the same column, this operator provides no guarantee that a single index could access all qualifying data. For example, consider the following WHERE clause:

```
WHERE salary > 50000 OR department = 'Engineering'
```

Both of these criteria are valid SARGs, but using an index on one to filter the data would preclude some of the values that the other might need to capture.

Special *OR* Processing Strategy

Since OR operations are very common and can cause numerous performance problems in a query, SQL Server has a special way of handling optimization of OR operations. While generally a query can use only one index per table, one of the notable exceptions to this rule is the OR operator optimization. Consider the following query:

```
USE AdventureWorksDW2008;

SELECT EnglishProductName, UnitPrice, OrderQuantity
FROM dbo.DemoSales
WHERE UnitPrice >= 2000
OR OrderQuantity >= 20;
GO
```

This query could cause a real problem for the optimizer. Assuming that the DemoSales table had an index on both the UnitPrice and OrderQuantity columns, which one should it choose? Either way, both criteria could not be addressed by the same index, and this query would result in a table scan if SQL Server could use only one index.

The reality, however, is that you could easily rewrite this query as two separate queries with a union, as with the following code:

```
USE AdventureWorksDW2008;


SELECT EnglishProductName, UnitPrice, OrderQuantity
FROM dbo.DemoSales
WHERE UnitPrice >= 2000
UNION ALL
SELECT EnglishProductName, UnitPrice, OrderQuantity
FROM dbo.DemoSales
WHERE OrderQuantity >= 20;
GO
```

Now that SQL Server has two queries, it selects one index per table per query and unifies the results. In the old days, it was common practice to write all OR statements this way to promote better optimization. Now, however, SQL Server's query optimizer is smart enough to refactor this query for you. If you use OR statements in your query, SQL Server scores each section separately. If it can find a valid index for each section, it attempts to execute the query as a UNION. Of course, if even one section of the query would require a table scan, SQL Server will abandon this process and simply execute a table scan because a table scan is always the baseline I/O metric.

Optimize Join Operations

Join operations are a necessary evil in relational database architecture. While breaking data into multiple tables has positive impacts on data storage and maintenance, it can also cause performance bottlenecks. The correlation of tables together through common fields requires optimization that is conceptually similar to multiple dependent SELECT statements. While SQL Server has many different mechanisms that it can use to optimize joins, the general rule of thumb is to make sure you have adequate indexes.

Performance and
Advanced Features

PART IV

Choosing fields to index   JOIN statements correlate data through common fields. In most cases you use primary key/foreign key relationships to define the join columns. While creating a primary key automatically generates an index, the same is not true for foreign key constraints. Because the foreign key fields are frequently used in join operations, you should evaluate these fields for indexes. Omitting an index on the foreign field in a join will require SQL Server to find an alternate mechanism for optimizing the join. Most of the time, this will be less efficient than creating an index.

Choosing an index type   As you know, clustered indexes usually provide better raw performance than nonclustered indexes, but since you have only one clustered index per table, you should select it wisely. Sometimes a foreign key field is a good selection for this clustered index. Here are some factors that you should consider:

Join density   The general rule of thumb is that the more selective a query is, the more likely a nonclustered index will provide adequate performance. This is also true for joins. We measure this with a metric called *join density*. This is a measure of how many rows will be matched in a child table for each parent row.

For example, a one-to-one relationship would have a very low join density. One parent row always matches one and only one child row. The lower the join density, the less advantageous it is to use a clustered index on the related column. Using a nonclustered index will result in a small amount of extra I/O over a clustered index, but the difference is insignificant. The higher the join density, the more likely you will want to choose a clustered index.

Volatility   If the child column in the join is highly volatile, you might want to refrain from using a clustered index. SQL Server requires much more overhead to maintain a clustered index than it does a nonclustered index.

Comparative advantage   You must always remember that indexes do not exist in a vacuum. Indexes are part of a portfolio, and you must evaluate them that way. Every index has maintenance costs and can possibly impact the performance of other operations. You may want to use the Database Engine Tuning Advisor to assist you in managing the entire portfolio of indexes.

13

Policy-Based Management

Performance and
Advanced Features

PART IV

A new feature of SQL Server 2008 is Policy-Based Management. This feature allows administrators to set and enforce rules and conditions for SQL Server 2008 instances throughout the enterprise. Simply put, it allows for nearly any setting in an instance to be initially defined and then applied to almost any activity or setting in that same instance. These policies allow the DBA to specify rules for which objects and their properties are created or modified.

Understand Policy-Based Management

Policy-Based Management involves some new terms that should be defined before continuing:

target—SQL Server Management Objects (SMO) that are managed by Policy-Based Management. A target could be, for example, an index, a database, or a table.

facet—A set of properties for certain types of targets that can be managed by the established policy.

condition—A property expression that evaluates to True or False. These are mainly used to control properties of the facet in question.

policy—A Policy-Based Management condition and the expected behavior. A policy can contain only one condition and may be scheduled or on demand. Policies can be enabled or disabled. They can also be evaluated by a process we will discuss in the section "Evaluate a Policy."

NOTE   Here is a short overview of the operation of Policy-Based Management: You choose a target, open the facet of the target, define a condition, create a policy to implement the testing of the condition, and then set the particulars of the policy enforcement. Automated policies that are created in an instance will only allow, either by the use of graphical user tools or scripting, the creation or modifications that are in keeping with the policy condition. Any attempt to violate these polices will fail or be logged according to the appropriate evaluation models. This chapter covers many details of the new features of actual implementation.

To create or implement a policy, you must be a member of the PolicyAdministratorRole role in the msdb database. The actual interface of Policy-Based Management is accessed from the Object Explorer in the SQL Server Management Studio (SSMS). Open Object Explorer, expand the Server node of the instance you wish to manage, choose the Management folder, and then the Policy Management node. This will give you a view of the Policies, Conditions, and Facets nodes, as seen in Figure 13.1.

Figure 13.1: The Policy Management node

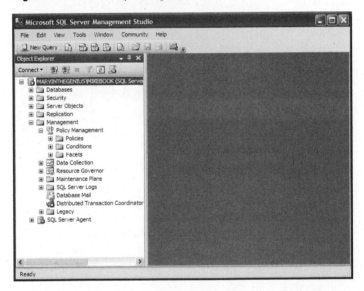

The nodes under Policy Management provide a view of the targets available to this instance of SQL Server 2008. As you can see in Figure 13.2, each of the targets represents a group of settings, or a facet, that you can direct or control with policies.

Right-clicking on a particular target and choosing Properties, in this case the Database target, provides a listing of those settings, as seen in Figure 13.3. These groups of settings are referred to as facets and contain properties that are used to specify a condition that will be checked by a policy. This is not the location where these settings will be changed. This is just a place to view them.

Performance and
Advanced Features

PART IV

Figure 13.2: Facets

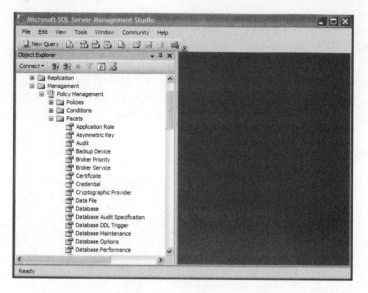

Figure 13.3: View Settings

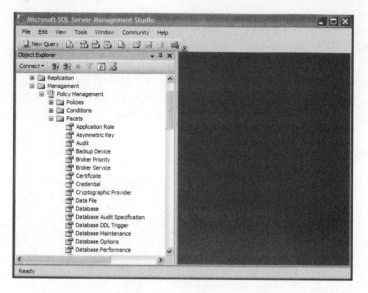

An example of a facet would be the AutoClose property. When AutoClose is set to ON, the database is shut down cleanly and its resources are freed after the last user exits. The database automatically reopens when a user tries to use it again. When AutoClose is set to OFF, the database remains open after the last user exits. In Policy-Based Management the value True would represent ON and False would represent OFF. A condition can consist of more than one value. If this is the case, they are typically joined by a logical AND or a logical OR.

Create a Condition

To begin using Policy-Based Management, you should first create a condition. This is done by right-clicking on the target for which you wish to create a condition and selecting New Condition. In this example, we have selected the Database target. The Create New Condition dialog box appears (Figure 13.4).

Figure 13.4: Create New Condition dialog

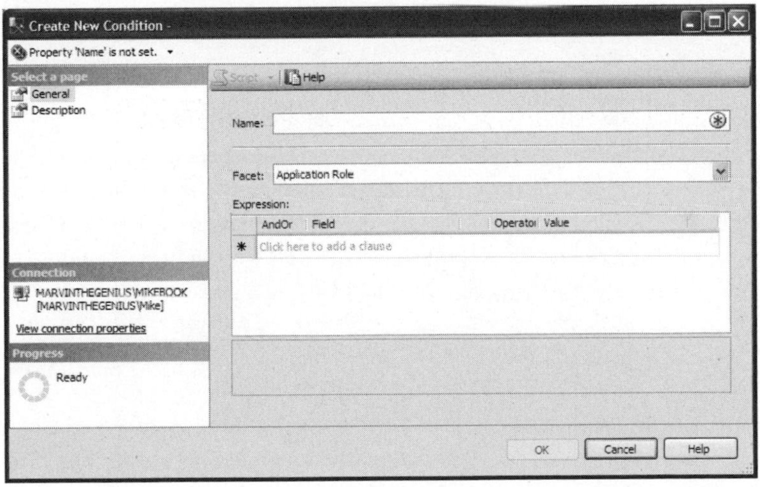

To create a condition, follow these steps:

1. Set the name property. In this example we've named the condition Auto Close Condition ON, as seen in Figure 13.5.

2. Ensure that the correct facet is selected. The value in the Facet drop-down list will already be populated. The Facet value is

Performance and
Advanced Features

PART IV

populated based on the target that was selected, which in this case was Database. You can change the facet, or group of settings for which you wish to create a condition, in this drop-down by selecting a different target, but for now we will stay with Database.

Figure 13.5: Create New Condition dialog with values

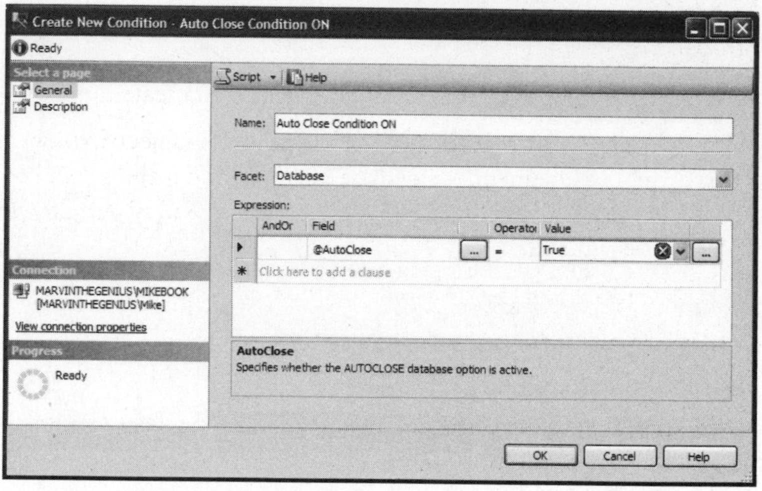

3. Select the clauses for your expression in the Expression area. The actual checking that the condition will perform will be established in this area. The first white cell in the center gray area states "Click here to add a clause." Click in that area and four cells and two buttons with ellipses appear:

   a. First is the AndOr cell, used to create a logical join between clauses.

   b. The next cell in the drop-down list is the Field heading. Here the list provides possible properties from the facet that apply to the target shown in the Facet drop-down list. In this example, the AutoClose property is selected. (Note the @ in front of each of the possible selections. This is typically used in SQL notation as a parameter designation.) The choice that is made in the Value cell will then be populated in the declared parameter.

   c. When you click the ellipsis button next to the Field column, a code editor window appears where you can write custom code for the condition.

    d. The next column is Operator and it's used to assign the value of the property that has been selected. The last cell is again an ellipsis that will open the custom code editor.

4. When you are finished, click the OK button to create the condition.

Create a Policy

The next step in Policy-Based management is to create a policy:

1. Right-click the Policies node in the SSMS Object Explorer (under the Management/Policy Management node) and select New Policy. Figure 13.6 shows the dialog that will be used to create the new policy.

2. At the top of the form, enter the name of the policy in the Name text box.

3. Click the Enabled check box to enable the policy.

4. Set the check condition. Any condition you have previously defined will be on this list, including the condition that was created earlier.

Figure 13.6: Create New Policy dialog

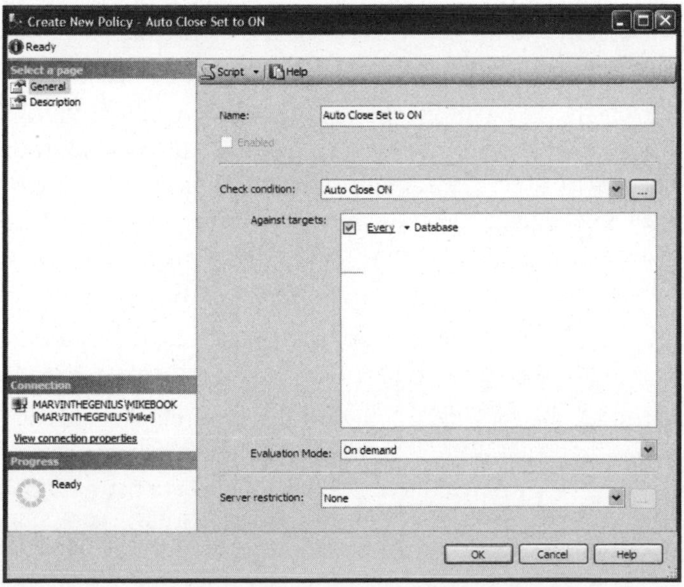

> **NOTE**   You can see that in Figure 13.6 the Enabled check box
> isn't selected. It will not be enabled unless the policy evaluation
> mode is an automated mode. This means that the evaluation mode
> could be On Schedule, On Change: Prevent, or On Change: Log
> Only. If the Policy Evaluation Mode property is set to On Demand,
> you won't be able to select the Enabled check box. The policy *will*
> be usable but will not be evaluated automatically.

5. Choose to check every database in the Against Targets list, or you
   can click the down arrow (between *Every* and *Database*) and define
   a condition. If you choose to define a condition at this point, it will
   automatically populate to the policy Against Targets list.

6. In the Evaluation Mode drop-down list, there are four possible
   choices, two of which are On Demand and On Schedule. These
   are available to nearly every condition, facet, and policy. They are
   the options that apply to the policy in the example. The other two
   modes are On Change: Prevent and On Change: Log Only.

   The On Change: Prevent mode uses Data Definition Language
   (DDL) triggers to prevent any object creation that would violate
   the evaluated policy. If the Nested Trigger server option is turned
   off in the database settings, this mode will not work. This mode is
   an automated mode that can be enforced automatically whenever
   an attempt at violation occurs. This is a great policy to define if
   the manipulation of objects by users is a problem in your data
   environment.

   On Change: Log Only is much like the On Change: Prevent
   mode; it will create an event log record of any attempt to violate
   the policy rather than simply preventing the action from occurring. On Change: Log Only and On Change: Prevent will only
   work if there is an existing aspect of SQL Server to enforce them.
   In other words, to use a DDL trigger, a DDL trigger must exist.

How can you find out which facets can be automatically enforced and
which can't? Use of the dynamic management view syspolicy_management_
facets gives you this information. By reading the following query, you see
that this view is available from the msdb database:

```
SELECT facet.name as 'Name of Facet',
OnDemand = CASE facet.execution_mode & 4 ;
              WHEN 4 THEN 'On Demand; On Schedule' ;
```

```
                        END,
    OnChangeLogOnly = CASE facet.execution_mode & 2   ;
                        WHEN 2 THEN 'On Change, Log Only' ;
                        END,
    OnChangePrevent = CASE facet.execution_mode &;
                        WHEN 1 THEN 'On Change, Prevent' ;
                        END
    FROM msdb.dbo.syspolicy_management_facets facet;
```

The query provides a table to show the facets that may use any of the automatic evaluation options. Opposite of the automatic evaluation option is the On Demand option, which requires manual involvement; it will evaluate the policy only when a user right-clicks on the policy in the SSMS Object Explorer and selects Evaluate from the menu.

The On Schedule option takes advantage of SQL Agent to execute a job on a particular schedule to check the policy. After selecting On Schedule from the Execution Mode drop-down list, you can click either the Pick or New button, as shown in Figure 13.7. This mode is an automated mode that can be enforced automatically.

Figure 13.7: On Schedule selection

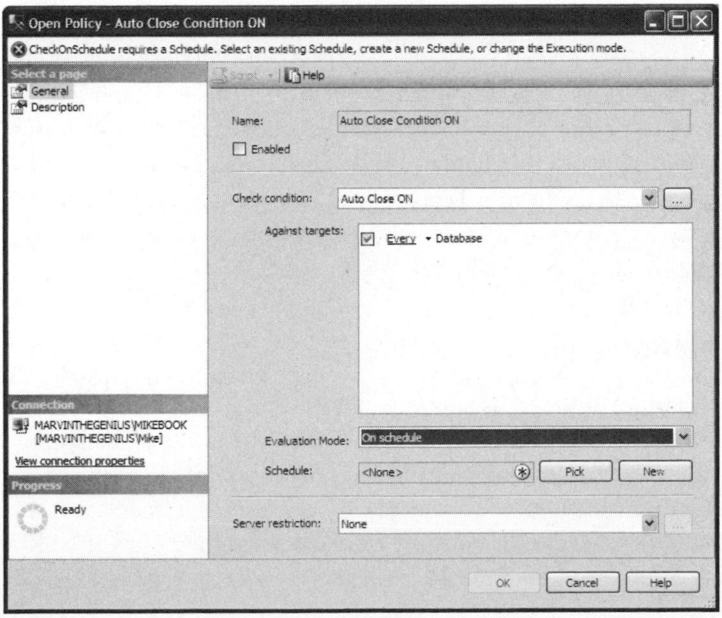

Performance and
Advanced Features

If you click the Pick button, you will see a dialog like the one shown in Figure 13.8. This dialog shows existing SQL Server Agent jobs that are scheduled and that you can add into the policy's evaluation. To pick an existing schedule, make a selection from the available options in this screen. SQL Server Agent will be further discussed in Chapter 14 "Automating with the SQL Server Agent Service."

Figure 13.8: Schedule picker

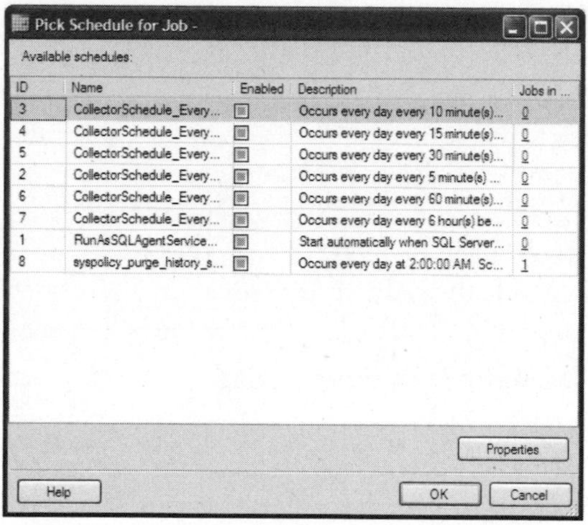

Alternatively, if you click the New button, you will see a dialog like the one shown in Figure 13.9. This scheduling interface is very intuitive and is discussed in depth in Chapter 14. Be sure to notice the Enabled check box next to the Schedule Type drop-down menu. If this is not selected, the schedule will not run. The Description box at the bottom of the dialog will sum up the choices you have made.

Evaluate a Policy

Evaluating a policy means applying the conditions that are defined in the policy to the instance of the database in question. In the case of an automatic evaluation, the conditions are applied upon any activity that would engage their testing.

You evaluate a policy on demand by right-clicking the policy in SSMS and selecting Evaluate. This generates a report as seen in Figure 13.10. The green check mark icon signifies that the policy evaluated to True for the databases shown.

Figure 13.9: New Job Schedule dialog

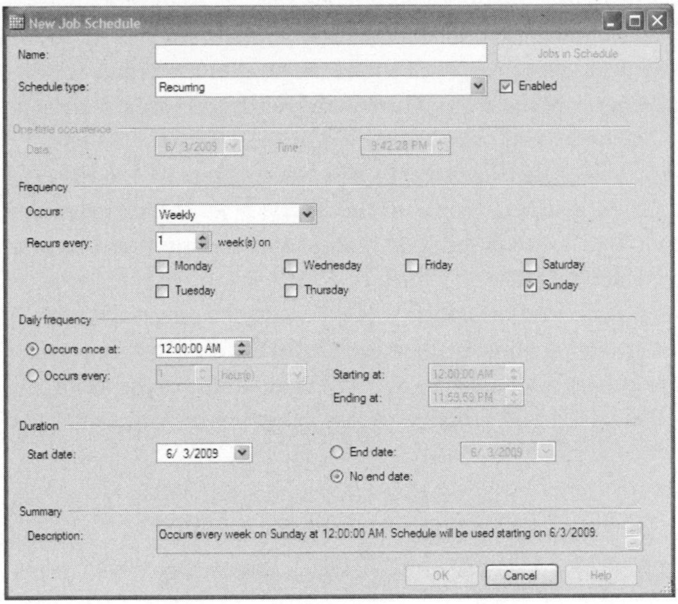

Figure 13.10: Evaluation results

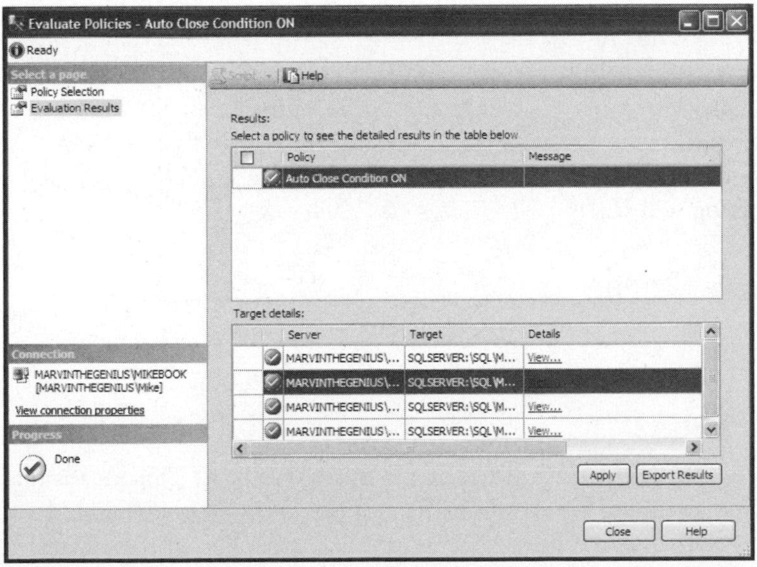

Right-click on the demoscript database in the SSMS Object Explorer and select Properties. Click the Options tab and change the AutoClose property to False. Evaluate the policy again and you will see the output shown in Figure 13.11. The circle with the X shows that the policy is not applied for the demoscript database. Shown above the icon area is a check box that allows the user to automatically fix a target where the policy evaluates to False. Checking this box will cascade check marks to the policy and also to the Target Details area of the dialog box. You can also use the Target Details area to select individual databases to which you want to apply the policy. Clicking the Apply button, which will be enabled when the check boxes are checked, will apply the policy to the selected targets. At any point in this dialog you can click the Export Results button, which will allow you to choose a location to save the evaluation results as an XML formatted file. It can be valuable to save a history of your evaluation results for a particular policy for later policy analysis.

Figure 13.11: Evaluation Results with failure

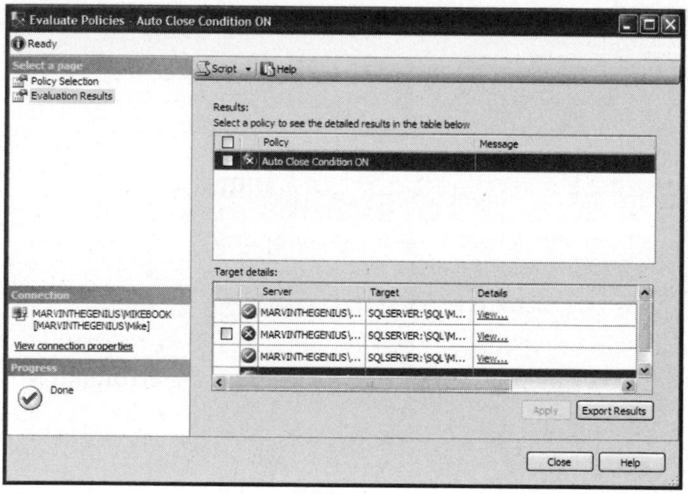

Policy Storage

When created, policies are stored in the msdb database. This means that if you change or add a policy, a backup of the msdb database should be performed, and as a good general practice, a backup of the master database should be performed as well. Backup policies, procedures, and techniques are discussed in Chapter 10, "Managing Data Recovery."

SQL Server 2008 includes policies that can be used to monitor an instance of SQL Server. By default, these policies are not installed in the Database Engine; however, they can be imported from the default installation location of `C:\Program Files\Microsoft SQL Server\100\Tools\Policies\DatabaseEngine\1033`. The files provide the policies available in an XML format. To import a policy from the afore-mentioned location, do the following:

1. Expand the Management node in Object Explorer.

2. Open the Policy Management node.

3. Right-click on Policies.

4. Choose the Import option.

You can also directly create policies by using the File ➢ New menu option in SQL Server Management Studio, and then saving them to a file. This enables you to create policies when you are not connected to an instance of the Database Engine.

Policy history for previously evaluated policies in the current instance of the Database Engine is maintained in msdb system tables. Policy history for policies previously applied to other instances of the Database Engine, Reporting Services, or Analysis Services is not retained.

Troubleshooting Policy-Based Management

Policy-Based Management, as with so many configuration-based protocols, can fail. Policy-Based Management will record errors to both the Windows event log and, for scheduled policies, the SQL Server Agent log. This logging will occur only if the policies are enabled or affect the expected target. If they fail to do so, it is not considered an error and is not logged.

Some of the errors that occur may be due to things as simple as the policy failing to be enabled. Other causes for the failure of an automated policy include a filter that excludes it, a target that does not subscribe to the policy group that includes the policy, and for the On Change: Prevent evaluation mode, the server broker eventing mechanism not monitoring the correct events.

To fix these issues, start checking whether or not the policy was actually executed. This can be done by checking the policy execution history in the `msdb.dbo.syspolicy_policy_execution_history` view. The output of this view is shown in Figure 13.12.

Performance and
Advanced Features

PART IV

Figure 13.12: The `policy_execution_history` output view

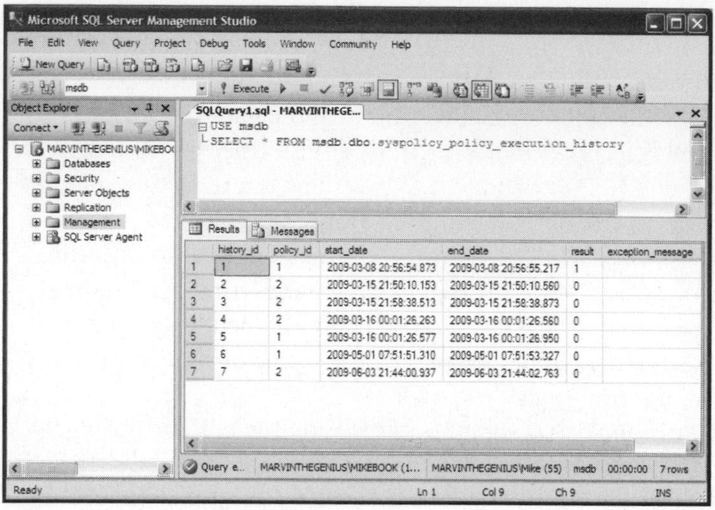

You can also view this information from within the SQL Server Management Studio by right-clicking on the Policies node under the Management heading and selecting View History. If you would like to test a particular policy, information can be found in the `msdb.dbo .syspolicy_policy_execution_history_details` view. These are management views that function in the same manner that meshing management views from SQL 2005 operate. But of course these views specifically relate to Policy-Based Management for SQL Server 2008.

If the policy uses the On Log: Prevent mode of evaluation, service broker will check whether the eventing mechanism is monitoring for the correct events. To troubleshoot this situation, follow these steps:

1. Verify that the transaction has committed and generated an event supported by the asset of the condition that the policy is defined on.

2. Then verify that the Service Broker queue is monitoring for the correct events by using the following query:

```
SELECT * FROM sys.server_event_notifications
WHERE name = N'syspolicy_event_notification' ;
GO
```

3. Check the evaluation engine by checking the Windows event log for Policy-Based Management errors to cover general evaluation information.

Manage Policies in the Enterprise

Using Enterprise Policy Management (EPM) Framework allows the DBA to extend the policy-based management that exists in SQL Server 2008 to control the application, evaluation, and creation of policies throughout the enterprise, including those from earlier versions of SQL product such as SQL 2000 and SQL 2005. EPM is a reporting solution that keeps track of the state in the enterprise against defined policies. The EPM framework will also allow a centralized means of collecting and evaluating policy information. With EPM reporting and administration across the multiple instances and environments, you will see management simplified in many ways by the virtue of the centralized reporting that the framework provides.

When EPM is implemented, it uses PowerShell to collect the policy evaluation information throughout the SQL Server enterprise environment. Implementing EPM requires at least one instance of SQL Server 2008. The PowerShell script will run from this instance through a SQL Server Agent job or manually through the PowerShell interface. The PowerShell script will capture policies evaluation output and insert the output into a SQL Server table. SQL Server 2008 Reporting Services will then deliver the information from a centralized table.

An EPM solution must have certain components configured in the environment and are executed from, as well as managed in, an instance of SQL Server 2008. The components that must be configured to use EPM are as follows:

- SQL Server 2008 instance to store policies

- SQL Server 2008 instance to act as the Central Management Server (CMS)

- SQL Server 2008 instance to execute the PowerShell script

- SQL Server management database and policy history table to archive policy evaluation results

- SQL Server 2008 Reporting Services to render and deliver policy history reports

Benefits of the EPM Framework

The EPM Framework can not only automate policy evaluation across an enterprise and centralize the collection of policy data, it can also provide reports to give a graphical representation of how departmental

Performance and
Advanced Features

PART IV

or organizational goals in the IT area are being met. Reports that are generated provide a drill-down capability that will give details of any problem area, such as these:

- Have backups been completed?
- Are we in compliance with security mandates?
- Are we in compliance with best practices?
- Are database management objects meeting schema and database generation requirements?

EPM compliance metrics are flexible enough to provide tracking of these questions as well as many industry standards. When properly implemented, these goals and metrics could be defined at many levels, rolling up to the overall key performance indicators (KPIs).

Figure 13.13 shows a sample report from the EPM framework titled "SQL Server Compliance Report." A SQL Server compliance report contains four areas of policy evaluation, including instance compliance, failed policy count by policy category, failed policy percentage by month, and last execution status. This sample report can be downloaded from http://www.codeplex.com/EPMFramework.

Figure 13.13: EPM SQL Server Compliance dashboard

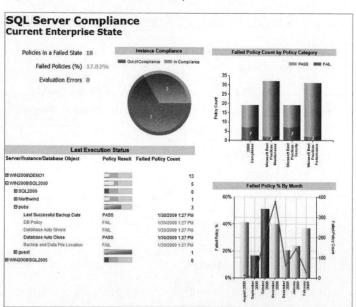

The HR in the upper left shows policy compliance overall by instance. In this report, policy checks were performed on three instances overall. Two instances failed policy checks and one instance passed. The last execution status report in the lower-left area provides drill-down details. Of the 18 failed policies, 13 were for the WIN2008\DEMO1 instance while 5 failures were reported for the WIN2008\SQL2000 instance.

We failed policy accounts in the upper-right breakdown of evaluation by policy category. The 18 failed policies are further broken down into policy categories such as 2008 compliance, Microsoft best practices: maintenance, Microsoft best practices: security, and Microsoft best practices: performance. Failed policy by month in the lower right shows compliance measured over time. Policy checking is shown in the blue bar graph. The blue line shows failed policy checks. The trend shows that over time, more policies are being checked with fewer failures.

The SQL Server compliance report can be used effectively and proactively to focus managing efforts to drive costs lower, limit exposure, and improve productivity. Moreover, productivity goals can be set in terms of compliance. Let's assume that we have an IT policy compliance target of 80 percent. Trending over time clearly shows an improvement in compliance. The last execution status showed a compliance rate exceeding the target at 82 percent. Next year's compliance target would be set higher, perhaps at 92 percent.

Table 13.1 shows various compliance areas that can be reflected in the current report. This chart is available from MSDN at `http://msdn.microsoft.com/en-us/library/dd542632.aspx`.

Table 13.1: EPM Report Compliance Areas

Policy area	Scenario	Comments	User-defined?	Version
Business	Backups complete	Have all my backups been completed?	N	All
Management	CLR	CLR enabled / disabled?	N	2005; 2008
Management	Naming convention	Naming convention compliance (for example, table names begin with tbl%)	N	All
Performance Best Practices	Data/log placement	Data and log on separate drives?	N	All

Performance and
Advanced Features

Table 13.1: EPM Report Compliance Areas *(continued)*

Policy area	Scenario	Comments	User-defined?	Version
Performance Best Practices	MAXDOP (Max Degree Of Parallelism)	For OLTP applications, set MAXDOP=1 For data warehouse and reporting workloads, set MAXDOP to half the number of CPUs	N	All
Performance Best Practices	64-bit memory workload	Applications with large queries (for example, data warehouse or reporting applications fit 64-bit profile	N	All
Security Best Practices	Passwords	Password complexity and expiration?	N	2008
Security Best Practices	SQL Mail	SQL Mail disabled?	N	All
Security Best Practices	Security model	Integrated security enabled?	N	All
Security Best Practices	xp_cmdshell	xp_cmdshell is a security exposure – is it disabled?	N	All
Regulatory – User-defined	PCI	Credit card security compliance	Y	All

Each policy area represented in the table can provide data to a central enterprise policy management report. Keep in mind that EPM primarily is a reporting service, designed to provide information about various policies and their implementations.

14

Automating with the SQL Server Agent Service

IN THIS CHAPTER, YOU WILL LEARN TO DO THE FOLLOWING:

Performance and Advanced Features

PART IV

T he job of the database administrator (DBA) is definitely challenging, and historically it has been a reactive one. You spend your life reacting to problems when they occur. In the past you may also have spent a great deal of time performing routine administrative tasks such as backup and restore operations and monitoring for imbalances in your server environment.

We well know that if any job can benefit from some simple automation, it is the database administrator's job. The ability to schedule repetitive maintenance tasks is advantageous, but a DBA that is more proactive, watching for problems and preempting them, will ultimately be rewarded with a superior infrastructure. The key to implementing automation in SQL Server is the SQL Server Agent service.

The SQL Server Agent is a multi-faceted tool that integrates tightly with SQL Server. It can handle numerous tasks, from issuing administrative alerts to taking preemptive actions, but ultimately the SQL Server Agent is all about automation. The more the service can handle, the less you have to handle.

Configure the SQL Server Agent Service

The SQL Server 2008 product consists of multiple Windows services. The most prominent is the SQL Server Service (MSSQLServer), which is essentially the Data Engine. The SQL Server Service provides all interaction with data and query processing. There are other services included with SQL Server 2008, however.

Another important service is the SQL Server Agent. This is the automation service. The role of the SQL Server Agent is to handle scheduling of activities and communicate information about those activities to relevant parties. To understand the SQL Server Agent, you first must understand the various artifacts that the agent controls. Then you can begin the process of configuring the service and creating the artifacts.

Understand Automation Artifacts

The functionality of the SQL Server Agent service revolves around some simple artifacts. If you can get a feel for the interplay between the various artifacts, you will be able to combine then into automation and communications models that will meet your administrative needs. As you look at these artifacts, remember that the ultimate goal of the SQL Server Agent is to facilitate proactive administration.

Jobs A job is a series of steps or actions that the SQL Server Agent service can execute. Each job consists of individual steps, and these steps can vary in terms of the technique they employ:

ActiveX script Using a scripting language such as VBScript or JScript (Microsoft's version of JavaScript), you can automate certain operations in SQL Server by using the SQL Server object models.

CmdExec A command executable, or CmdExec, task allows the SQL Server Agent to execute shell commands from within the SQL Server environment. This is a very useful technique when you need to communicate with the operating system environment as part of an administrative activity.

PowerShell PowerShell integration is in SQL Server 2008. PowerShell is an alternative to both ActiveX scripting and CmdExec coding in that it is a unified shell scripting tool that allows both operating system and application resources to be automated within a single scripting environment. The popularity of PowerShell scripting will certainly increase as its features gain broader acceptance.

Transact SQL (TSQL) The primary data manipulation tool in SQL Server is Transact SQL. TSQL is often the backbone of most jobs. Any time you need simple data interactions, the TSQL steps are the most efficient way to handle them.

SQL Server Integration Services (SSIS) package As we noted in Chapter 9, "Extracting, Transforming, and Loading Data," the SSIS is Microsoft's premier Extracting/Transforming/ Loading (ETL) service. Since these SSIS packages are likely to represent recurring administrative operations, the entire package can be organized as a single step in a job.

Schedules Schedules allow the SQL Server Agent to execute jobs at defined intervals. This allows automation of routine administrative tasks as well as recurring execution of other common data tasks, such as ETL operations. Schedules use one of the following structures:

- One time: Executes only once at a defined time
- Recurring: Executes repeatedly based on time and interval

- Autostart: Executes when SQL Server Agent service starts
- Idle: Executes when the CPU is idle; you can define the parameters of idle time

Operators   Operators are targets of communication. You can communicate with operators in three ways:

- Email: Through the Database Mail interface supported by SQL Server, you can send email messages to operators.

- Net send: Allows SQL Server Agent to send a pop-up message to a network workstation.

- Pager: Provided that an email/pager bridge system is installed and configured, you can specify a separate email address to be directed to a pager.

You can configure a single named operator with multiple configurations. For example, as a database administrator, you can configure SQL Agent Service so that you receive messages both by email and net send.

Alerts   An alert is a configured response to an event or condition. Alerts come in three varieties:

- SQL Server event: Alert based on a SQL Server error number or severity. You can filter out errors based on text in the error message.

- Performance monitor: Alert based on the value of a performance monitor counter. You can filter out by object, counter, and instance.

- Windows Management Instrumentation (WMI) event: A Query using WMI Query Language (WQL) to monitor system information through a WMI provider

You can configure alerts to respond in two different ways. First, you can configure a job to execute in response to an alert. Second, you can notify an operator in response to an alert. You also have the option of configuring both responses simultaneously.

Proxies   The SQL Server Agent service provides a new feature in version 2008 that allows for very tight security control over the execution of job steps: using artifacts called proxies. Each proxy defines a very specific set of permissions by impersonating an account through a credential. You can define as many proxies as needed. Each proxy is restricted to be available only to the SQL Agent step types that you specify. This allows you to ensure that each step executes with only the minimal permissions needed to perform the work.

Perform Basic Service Configuration

The SQL Server installer will include the SQL Server Agent service by default. During the installation of SQL Server, you had the option to select a Windows login account for the SQL Server Agent service (see Figure 1.8 in Chapter 1). You should evaluate the default configuration of the SQL Server Agent, however, before you assume that the service is ready to handle your production scenarios. To access the SQL Server Agent configuration options, execute the following steps:

1. Open the SQL Server Management Studio (SSMS) and connect to the Database Engine instance that hosts the agent you want to configure.

2. Expand the service instance node and locate the SQL Server Agent, as pictured in Figure 14.1.

Figure 14.1: Locating the SQL Server Agent node

3. Right-click the SQL Server Agent node and select Properties from the menu. This will open the SQL Server Agent Properties dialog that you will use to configure the service.

Performance and
Advanced Features

PART IV

The General Page

The first page of the Properties dialog defines the general runtime and logging behaviors of the agent. This dialog is pictured in Figure 14.2 for your reference.

Figure 14.2: The General page

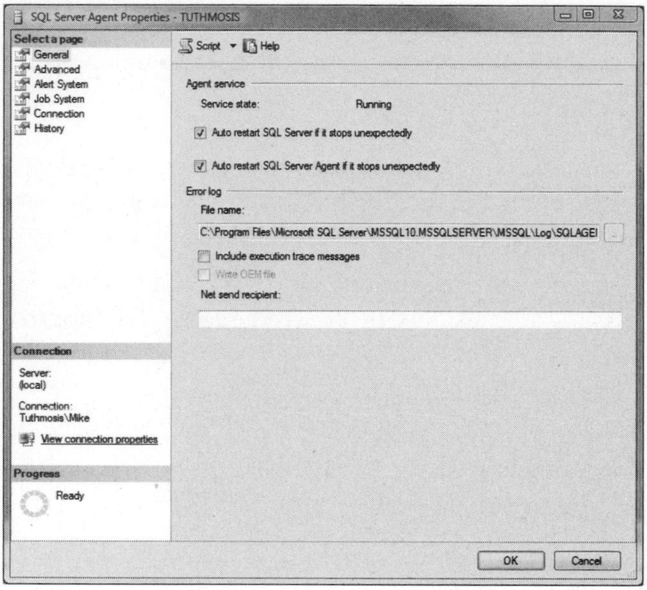

> **Agent Service** This section determines the runtime behavior of the service. In addition to an informational message telling you the current state of the service, you have options to configure restart behavior if the SQL Agent service or the entire SQL Server instance stops unexpectedly. Generally it is a good idea to leave these options enabled so that you do not have to enable them manually after a service comes back online.
>
> **Error Log** SQL Server Agent errors are logged at the location of your choice. Click the build button (with the ellipsis) next to the File Name box to browse to the error log location if you wish to select a location other than the default.

You can also choose to include the more verbose trace messages in the log. The trade-off is that while you get more information, it takes more disk space. If configured, this can also write an OEM version of the file that provides specific error information for OEM troubleshooting, but is usually not human readable.

Finally, you can configure a net send alert to inform an administrative workstation that SQL Server wrote an event to the log.

The Advanced Page

The Advanced page deals with the topics of event forwarding and CPU idle definition. Figure 14.3 illustrates this dialog.

Figure 14.3: The Advanced page

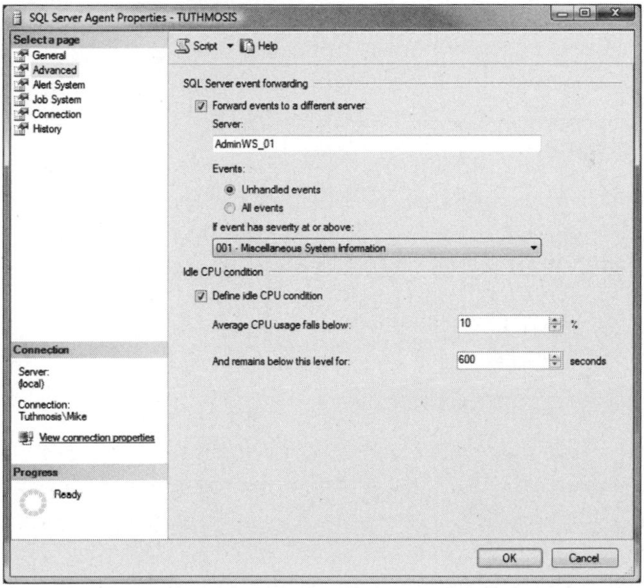

SQL Server Event Forwarding   It is possible to forward SQL Server events from one server to another. This promotes centralized handling of alerts. To enable this feature, select the check box labeled Forward Events to a Different Server, as shown in Figure 14.3. You will need to provide the name of the server to which the SQL Agent will forward the events. You can also choose to forward all events or simply unhandled events. Additionally, you can filter so that only

SQL Server events that exceed a configured severity level will be forwarded.

Idle CPU Condition If you configure a schedule to execute only during CPU idle time, you may want to be able to define exactly what that means. To override the default handling of CPU idle, click the check box to define the idle condition as shown. The configuration is based on two conditions:

- The percent of CPU usage

- The duration that the CPU usage stays below the percentage level

In this example, the average CPU usage has to fall under the 10% mark and stay there for 600 seconds (10 minutes) before the Agent will consider the CPU to be idle. If you have multiple CPUs or cores, this represents aggregate utilization.

The Alert System Page

Use the Alert System page to configure the behavior of SQL Server Agent alerts. The purpose of this page is primarily to handle alert delivery configuration. This page is illustrated in Figure 14.4 for your reference.

Figure 14.4: The Alert System page

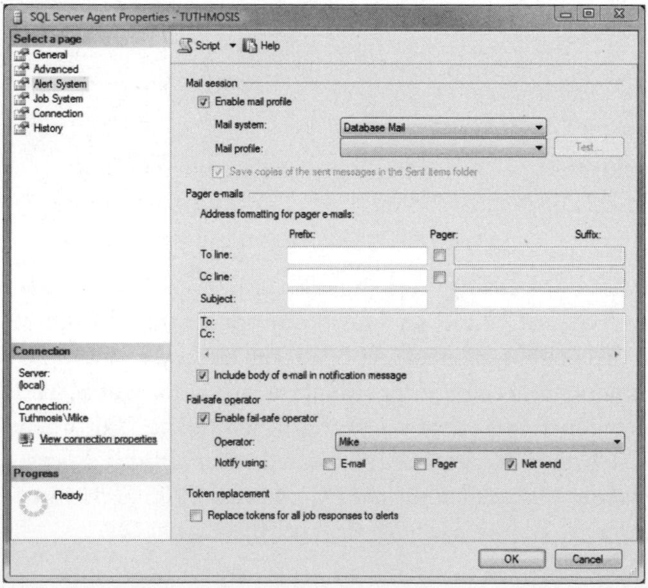

Mail Session This section allows you to specify which mail profile the SQL Agent will use. There are two configuration options. For legacy applications, you can configure a Microsoft Exchange–based profile. This is called SQL Mail. The preferred option is to use a Simple Mail Transport Protocol (SMTP) configuration, which is called Database Mail. We will show you how to configure the actual profiles later in this chapter in the section "Configure Database Mail."

Pager E-Mails Since every pager system is different, this section provides you with the ability to configure email formatting to work specifically with your pager system. If you are not using a pager system, you can ignore this section.

Fail-Safe Operator Since you can disable operators and also have the ability to define when pager operators will be on duty, it can be a good thing to define a fail-safe operator. If an alert is fired and the current configuration does not define an operator to receive it, the system will send it to the fail-safe operator. This ensures delivery of all messages to at least the fail-safe operator.

Token Replacement There is an advanced configuration that allows you to define tokens on job scripts using console output. This option allows you to capture that output in the text of the alerts. It is most useful when it is very important that the alert contains contextual information that is not available directly from the event.

The Job System Page

The Job System page provides some specialized configuration of the job system. This page is shown in Figure 14.5.

Shutdown Time-Out Interval If a job does not complete in a timely fashion, this option, expressed in seconds, will determine how long SQL Server Agent will wait before forcing the job to terminate.

Job Step Proxy Account SQL Server 2008 supports the concept of multiple proxy accounts so that when a job step executes, it can do so with a variety of preset security configurations. Older versions of SQL Server did not support this feature and could use only one defined proxy. This option provides backward compatibility for this behavior and is allowed only when the SQL Server 2008 SSMS is used to manage SQL Server Agent 2005 or earlier instances.

Performance and
Advanced Features

PART IV

Figure 14.5: The Job System page

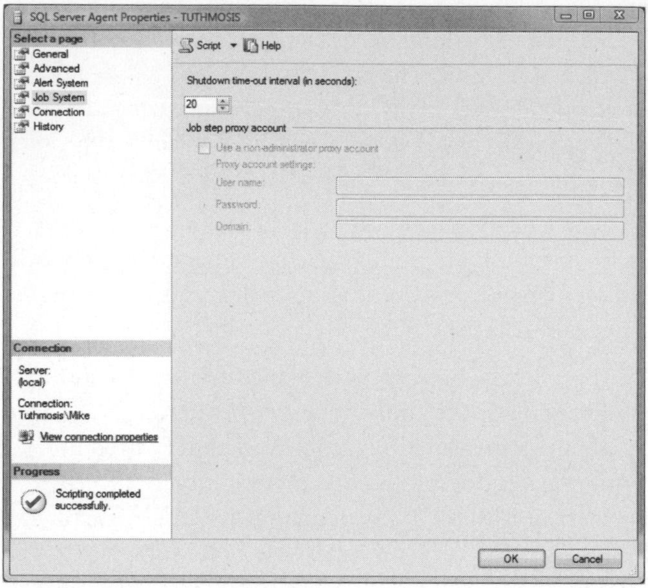

The Connection Page

The SQL Server Agent will need to connect to the SQL Server Data Engine regularly to execute database operations. The Connection page allows you to configure how the SQL Server Agent will make that connection. This page, illustrated in Figure 14.6, provides for two options.

Alias Local Host Server   If your local server configurations prohibit you from connecting to the local instance—for example, you have disabled the Browser service—you can define an alias for the server in the service configurations. You can then specify that alias here so that the SQL Server Agent can make the necessary connections.

SQL Server Connection   This setting will determine how the SQL Server agent will connect to the local data service instance. This option is dimmed out if the service is not configured to support non-Windows connections. Using Windows-based authentication is more secure and preferred. In that case, the SQL Server Agent service connects to the Data Engine using its own Windows account identity.

Figure 14.6: The Connection page

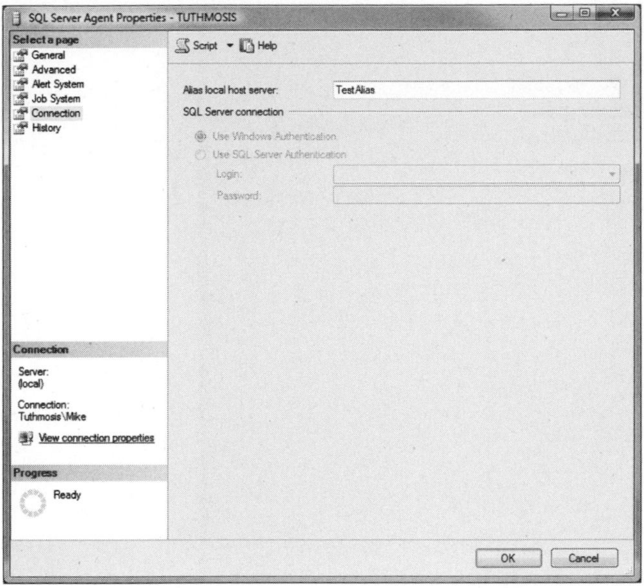

The History Page

The SQL Agent service maintains an historical log of jobs that it executes. This page, pictured in Figure 14.7, allows you to configure the behavior of that log.

You can limit the size of the history by removing events based on both log size and time. The first option restricts the size of the log based on total log rows as well as rows per job. The second option provides a setting to remove items from the log after a specifically configured amount of time.

Configure Database Mail

Allowing the SQL Agent service to send email to an operator is an important tool in database administration. Although we do everything we can to prevent problems from occurring, we need to be informed when problems occur or when certain events take place. In the past, SQL Server used a Microsoft Exchange–based email interface called SQL Mail. It was very proprietary and difficult to manage for someone that did not have Exchange experience. This option, although still supported, will be removed from subsequent releases of SQL Server.

Performance and Advanced Features

PART IV

Figure 14.7: The History page

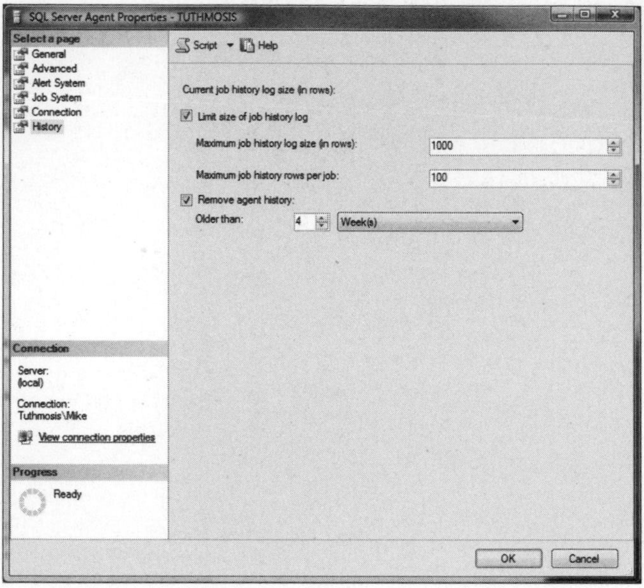

Instead, the preferred option now in SQL Server is to use an SMTP-based interface called Database Mail. This interface is easier to manage and allows for the SQL Server to use any nonproprietary SMTP-based email service. You can configure Database Mail by using a wizard. Follow these steps to start the wizard and configure the mail:

1. In the SSMS, locate and expand the Management node.

2. Inside the Management node, locate the Database Mail node. Right-click this node and select Configure Database Mail from the menu. This opens the introductory page of the wizard. Click the Next button to move to the next page.

3. The Select Configuration Task page, illustrated in Figure 14.8, allows you to specify the action you are taking with Database Mail. With this wizard, you can do the following:

   • Set up a new Database Mail configuration

   • Manage an existing configuration or account

   • Manage system security and configurations

4. Select the first option, Set Up Database Mail..., and click Next. If you get a message asking you if you want to enable the Database Mail feature, select Yes.

Figure 14.8: Selecting a configuration task

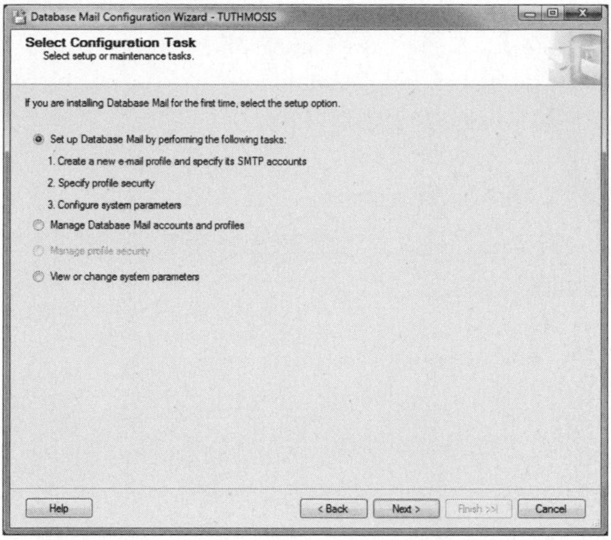

5. The New Profile dialog appears. Begin by clicking the Add button on the right side of the dialog to add a new SMTP account to this profile. If you do not have any existing accounts configured, this will open the New Database Mail Account dialog, pictured in Figure 14.9.

Figure 14.9: Creating a Database Mail Account

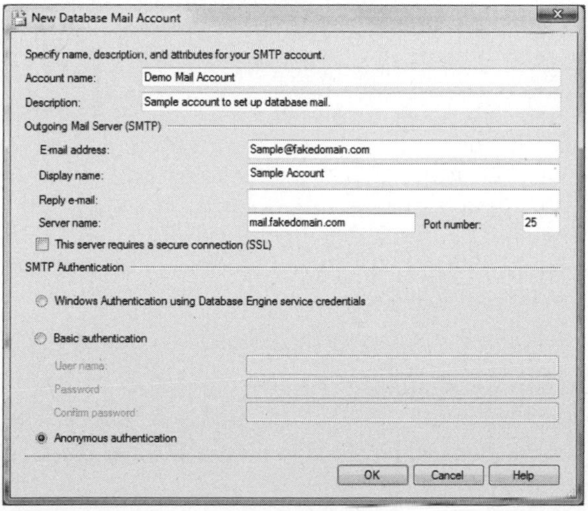

6. Enter the required information for the SMTP account that you wish to use. Click OK to accept the settings.

7. This will take you back to the New Profile dialog. Enter a profile name. The completed dialog should look like the one pictured in Figure 14.10. Click Next to continue.

Figure 14.10: Creating a new profile

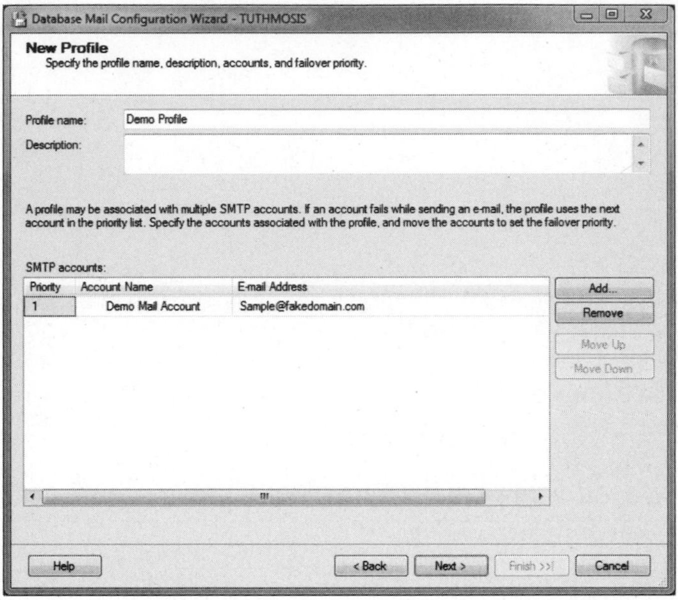

8. The next page of the dialog allows you to mark the profile as public for all users of the host or private to specific accounts. In our example, we will mark this as a public profile so that the dialog looks like the one pictured in Figure 14.11. Click Next to continue.

9. If you wish to change any of the other properties of the profile, this next dialog, pictured in Figure 14.12, will give you the opportunity. Click Next to continue.

10. On the final page of the wizard, click Finish to complete the process. Then click Close after the success report. To enable the profile for Database Mail, go back to the Advanced page of the SQL Server Agent properties, pictured in Figure 14.3, and select the Database Mail profile that you just created.

Figure 14.11: Managing Profile Security

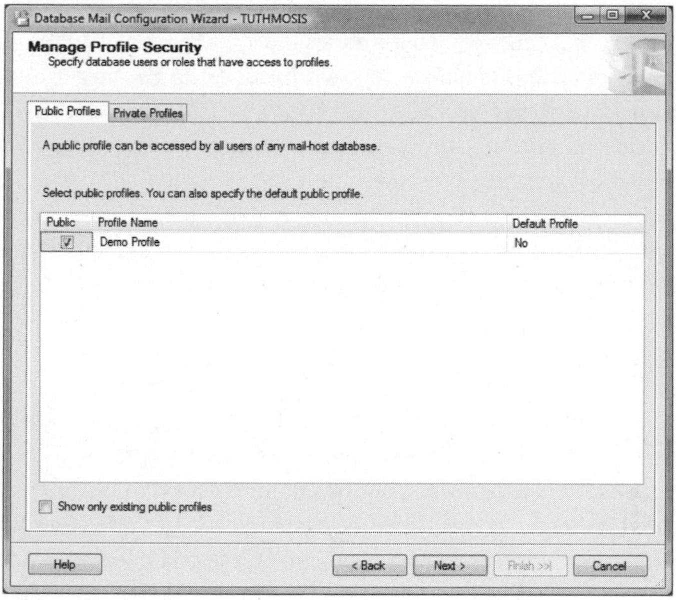

Figure 14.12: Configuring the profile

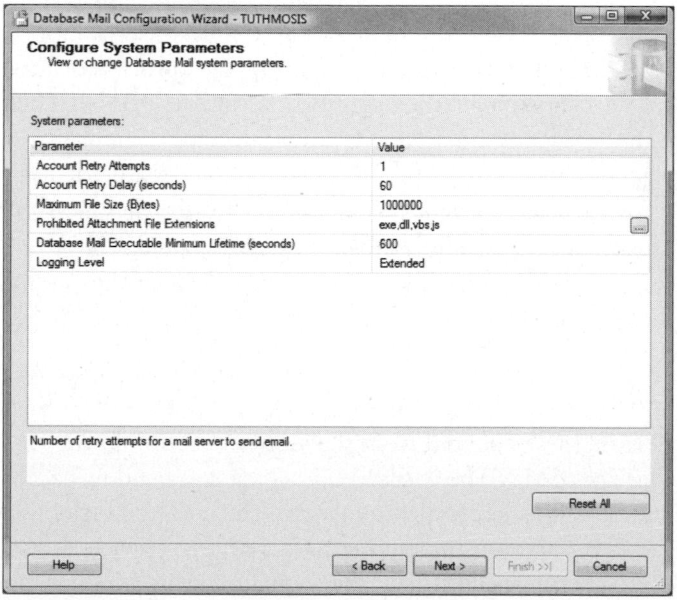

Create and Configure Automation Objects

The SQL Server Agent service manages many different objects on the server, each one responsible for its own function in the larger automation infrastructure. Mastering these objects is critical to effectively implementing an automation plan. In the following sections, we will look at the most important of these objects, specifically proxies, schedules, operators, alerts, and jobs. Finally, we will look at how you can simplify the process of creating a basic maintenance automation implementation by using the SQL Server Maintenance Plan Wizard.

Create and Configure Proxies

Although most of the processing that a SQL Server Agent automation structure will perform will be directed to SQL Server objects, there are often situations in which needed actions require access to resources that are outside of SQL Server at the operating system level. In these cases, authentication and permissions can be a problem. While you need to ensure that the SQL Server Agent can perform all of the necessary tasks, you must also restrict permissions to the minimum necessary to perform the actions. This is for security purposes. The SQL Server Agent offers this functionality through a proxy. Not all SQL Server Agent jobs require a proxy.

A proxy is really just the mapping of a SQL Server credential to a specific type of SQL Server Agent operation. This process occurs in two steps. You must first create the credential at the server level. Then you can map that credential to a proxy, which specifies the contexts and operation types with which you are allowed to use the credential. This will provide a trusted authentication identity for the tasks within SQL Server as well as a Windows identity for tasks outside SQL Server.

Create a Credential

A credential is a named reference to a Windows identity that you can use in SQL Server for authentication. Since this is a security object, you will create the credential from the security section in the Object Explorer of the SSMS. The first step is to create a Windows account with the permissions necessary to perform the required tasks, such as accessing a file system or interacting with a system service. Since this is a Windows version–specific task, the steps to do this will vary and we will not detail that process here. This is a task that will most likely be completed by a Windows system administrator.

To create the credential, follow these steps:

1. Locate the Security node in the Object Explorer. Expand the node and locate the Credentials node inside.

2. Right-click the Credentials node and select New Credential from the menu. Provide a name for your credential in the Credential Name text box.

3. Enter the name of the Windows account that you wish to map in the Identity text box. If you prefer to browse and select the Windows account, click the build button (the one with the ellipsis) next to the Identity text box.

4. Enter and confirm the password of the Windows account. The system will use this password when attempting to authenticate under this identity. The completed dialog looks like the one pictured in Figure 14.13.

Figure 14.13: Creating a credential

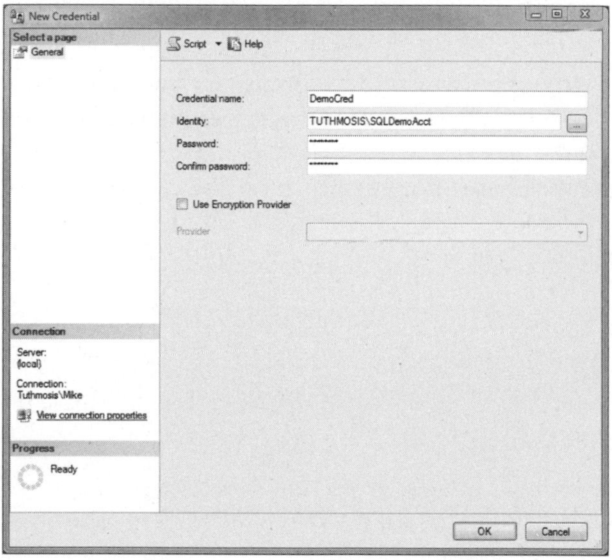

5. Click OK to accept the settings. You should now see the new credential in the list in the Object Explorer.

Now that you have created a credential, you can create the proxy. SQL Server 2008 supports the concept of multiple proxies, so you can have many different proxies, each of which represents a different authentication and set of permissions. When you create the proxy, you will specify the SQL Server Agent task types for which the proxy can authenticate. When you create SQL Server Agent jobs that require credentials, you will be able to use the proxy only with the configured task types.

To create a proxy, follow these steps:

1. Locate the SQL Server Agent node in the Object Explorer. Expand the node and locate the Proxies node.

2. If you expand the Proxies node, you will see a list of SQL Server Agent task types. Any proxy that you have configured for a specific task type will appear in the node list associated with that task. If you have associated a proxy with multiple tasks, it appears in multiple task nodes.

3. Right-click the Proxies node and select New Proxy from the menu to open the New Proxy Account dialog.

4. Enter a name for the proxy in the Proxy Name text box.

5. Enter the name of the previously created credential in the Credential Name text box and provide a description if desired.

6. Select the tasks for which you want this proxy to authenticate. If you click the Subsystem check box, all tasks will select. Figure 14.14 illustrates a completed version of this dialog. You will notice that we have selected only three task types in this example.

Figure 14.14: Creating a proxy

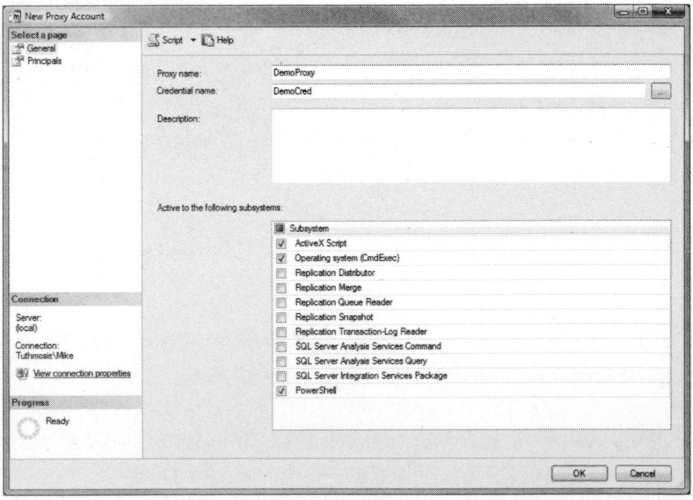

7. Click the OK button to accept the settings. You should now see the proxy nested in the appropriate nodes, as illustrated in Figure 14.15. Note that if you do not associate a proxy with any tasks, it appears in the Unassigned Proxies list.

Figure 14.15: Viewing assigned proxies

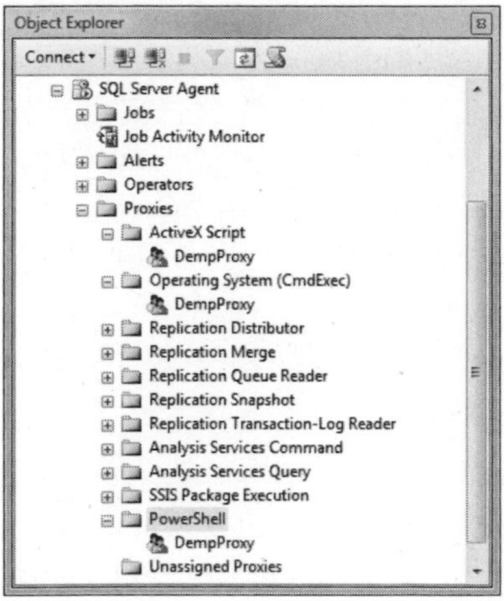

Create and Configure Schedules

One of the more important aspects of creating an automation infrastructure is determining the schedules for the planned processes. Although you can create these schedules "on the fly" as you create the automation jobs, taking a little more care to plan your schedules to maximize your resources is a very good idea. Try to determine when you have excess resource capacity and plan your processes around those times. If you create your schedules in advance, you will already have the timing infrastructure in place and be ready to go when you start to create the jobs.

To create a new schedule, follow these steps:

1. Locate the SQL Server Agent node in the Object Explorer. Expand the node and locate the Jobs node.

2. Right-click the Jobs node and select Manage Schedules from the menu to open the Manage Schedules dialog, pictured in Figure 14.16. This dialog lists all of the available schedules, allows you to enable or disable each schedule, and indicates the number of jobs currently assigned to each schedule.

Figure 14.16: The Manage Schedules dialog

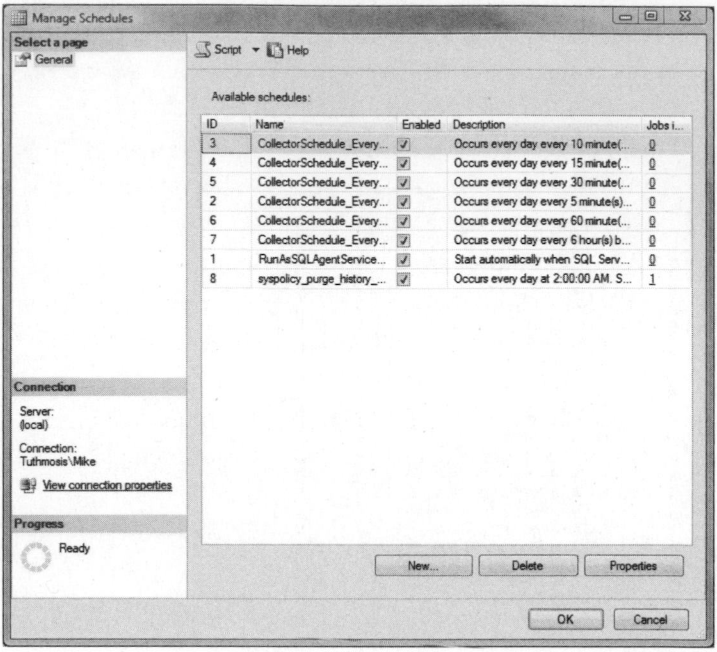

3. To create a new schedule, click the New button at the bottom of the dialog. This will open the New Job Schedule dialog. It looks different depending on the settings that you choose.

4. Click the Schedule Type list box to specify the type of schedule that you want. You will have four options:

Start Automatically When SQL Server Agent Starts Jobs assigned to this schedule will execute whenever the SQL Server Agent service starts. If the Agent service is set to autostart when the SQL Server Service starts, then these jobs will run accordingly. This schedule is useful for any jobs that you use to "initialize" the server environment.

Start Whenever the CPUs Become Idle Earlier in this chapter we showed you how to define the idle state for the CPUs. Jobs assigned to this schedule will execute whenever this condition exists. This schedule is useful for executing maintenance jobs that you want to execute during times of lower resource utilization.

One Time   Jobs assigned to this schedule will execute only once at the date and time specified in the dialog. Note that when you create this schedule, the configured execution date and time must be later than the current date and time.

Recurring   This is the most common schedule type. Jobs assigned to this type of schedule will execute on a recurring basis—daily, weekly, or monthly. The specific configuration of this schedule will depend on the interval that you choose.

5. If you select any schedule type other than recurring, there is very little additional configuration; however, the configuration for a recurring schedule type differs depending on the interval that you select:

    Daily   Figure 14.17 illustrates the dialog for a daily recurring configuration. Note that you can configure the daily reoccurrence as well as the frequency of occurrence within each day. You can set this frequency by hours, minutes, or seconds. Therefore, using this configuration, you can set schedules that vary significantly, such as, for example, once every 15 days or once every 15 seconds.

Figure 14.17: Configuring a daily schedule

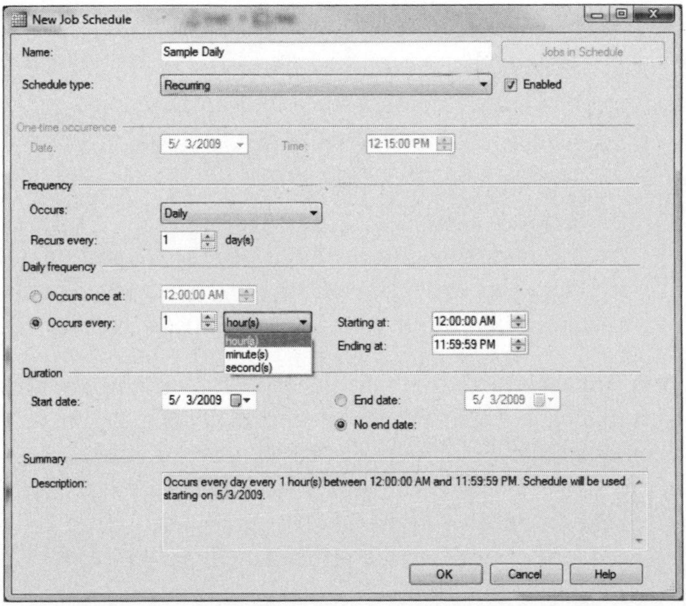

Weekly   Figure 14.18 illustrates the dialog for a weekly recurring configuration. You can select the day of the week that you wish to execute the job as well as the frequency in hours, minutes, and seconds.

Figure 14.18: Configuring a weekly schedule

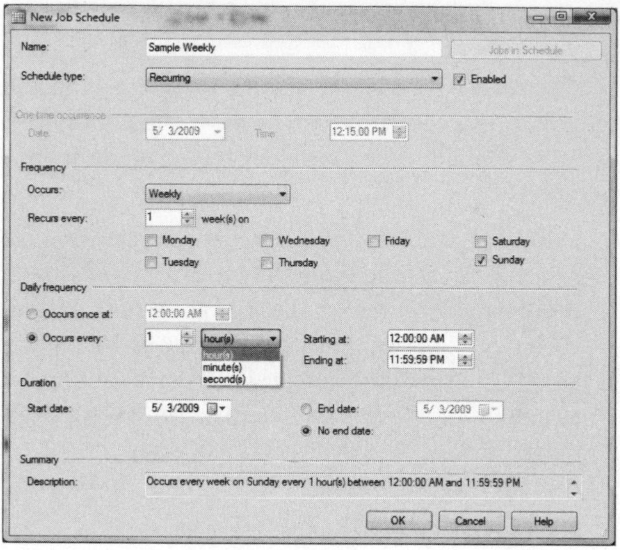

Monthly   Figure 14.19 illustrates the dialog for a monthly recurring configuration. You can select days of the month by date, as in the first day of every month, or by day, as in the first Monday of every month. On the selected day, you can again configure frequency by hours, minutes, or seconds.

6. After configuring the schedule, click the OK button to accept the settings. This will take you back to the Manage Schedules dialog and you will now see your new schedule in the list.

You can always edit the schedule later by selecting the schedule in the list and clicking the Properties button. This will take you back to the configuration dialog where you can make any changes required. You can also delete a schedule by selecting the schedule in the list and clicking the Delete button. Be careful about deleting a schedule that has referenced jobs. Removing the schedule will have the effect of canceling the scheduling of the jobs.

Figure 14.19: Configuring a monthly schedule

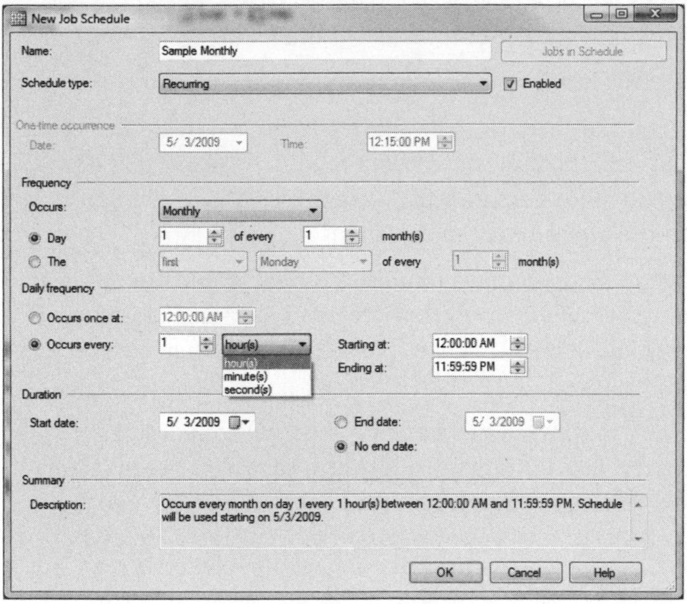

Create and Configure Operators

An operator is a person or device that SQL Server will inform when certain events happen in the SQL Agent service. These events can be an alert that there is a problem or simply a notification that a job has successfully completed. Operators can be configured to receive notifications via the following methods:

- Email
- Net send
- Pager (via pager email address)

You can configure operators to receive notifications as part of the job or alert configuration, and you can also create the operator as part of the job or alert configuration. To create a new operator, follow these steps:

1. Locate the SQL Server Agent node in the Object Explorer. Expand the node and locate the Operators node.

Performance and Advanced Features

2. Right-click the Operators node and select New Operator from the menu. This will open the New Operator dialog. By default you will be looking at the General page of the dialog.

3. Enter a name for the operator in the Name text box.

4. If you want the operator to be able to receive email alerts, enter the email address of the operator in the Email Name text box. This option requires that the SQL Agent service be configured for email as described earlier in this chapter.

5. If you want the operator to be able to receive notifications via net send messages, enter an appropriate machine name or address in the Net Send Address text box. Net send must be enabled on your network.

6. If you want the operator to be able to receive notifications via pager, enter the pager's email address in the Pager E-Mail name text box. SQL Agent Service must be configured for email and the appropriate email/pager software must be installed and configured.

7. If you configure a pager, you can set the pager hours in the lower portion of the dialog. The completed General page of the dialog should look like Figure 14.20. Note that this example configures only a net send notification.

8. Click the OK button to create the operator.

Figure 14.20: Creating an operator

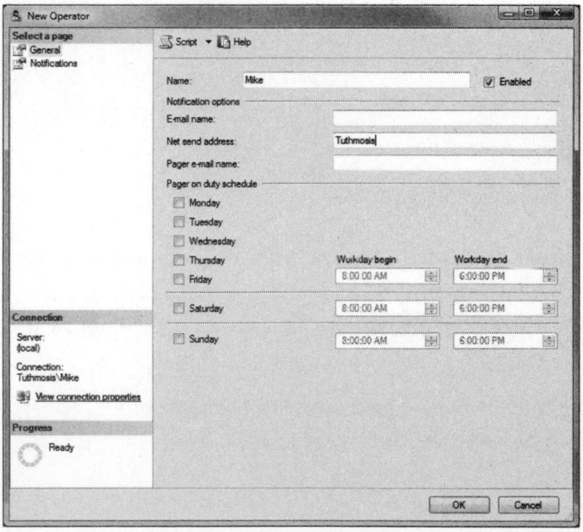

You can modify an operator at any time by opening the Operators node, right-clicking the operator, and selecting Properties from the menu. This will return you to the New Operator dialog. You can now view the existing notifications for the operator by selecting the Notifications tab and the notification history by selecting the History tab. Note that the History tab will only be visible when viewing an existing operator, and not when creating a new one.

Create and Configure Alerts

An alert is an event that indicates that some system activity has occurred or a system threshold has been reached. Typically, you will use alerts to trigger a notification to an operator or to start a job. This way you can inform an administrator of the potential problematic situation as well as start a series of tasks that can automatically remedy the problem. To create an alert, follow these steps:

1. Locate the SQL Server Agent node in the Object Explorer. Expand the node and locate the Alerts node.

2. Right-click the Alerts node and select New Alert from the menu. This will open the New Alert dialog.

3. Name the alert by entering a value in the Name text box.

4. Select the type of alert that you want to create. You have three options:

    SQL Server Event Alert This alert type allows you to respond to a SQL Server error. For example, error number 1205 is a deadlock error. If you wanted to raise an alert indicating that a deadlock took place in the AdventureWorks2008 database, you would configure the alert as illustrated in Figure 14.21. You could also raise an alert if any error occurs at a specified severity level.

    SQL Server Performance Condition Alert This alert type integrates with the performance monitor, allowing the system to trigger alerts when certain performance thresholds are reached. The object/counter/instance specifications are exactly the same as those that you use when you configure the performance monitor for system monitoring purposes.

Performance and Advanced Features

PART IV

Figure 14.21: Configuring a SQL Server event alert

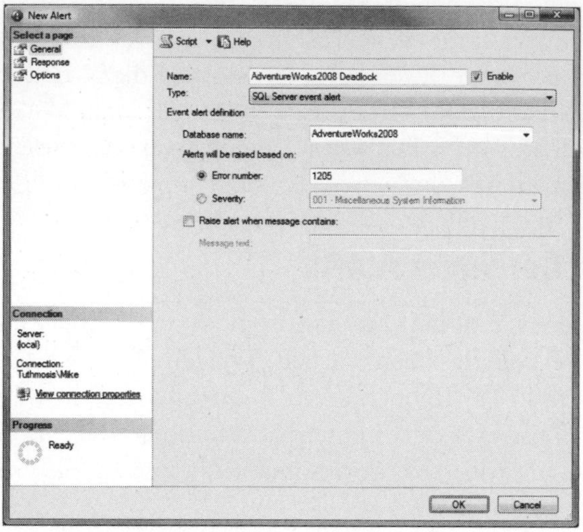

In the example illustrated in Figure 14.22, the alert fires when the percentage used on the transaction log for the AdventureWorks2008 database rises above 90%. In this example, you might consider creating a job that will back up the transaction log to prevent the log from expanding or triggering an error.

Figure 14.22: Configuring a SL Server performance condition alert

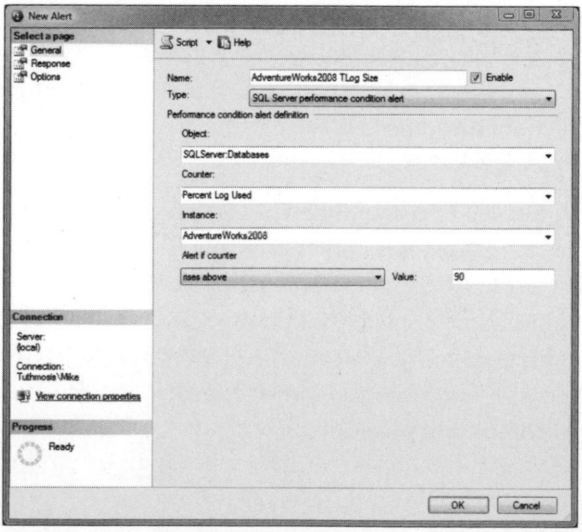

WMI Event Alert   The Windows Management
Instrumentation (WMI) interface uses Service Broker to fire
event notifications that can be trapped by the SQL Server
Agent service. To use this option, you must activate Service
Broker in all databases that will participate in the event processing. The specifics of WMI implementation are beyond the
scope of this book; however, there is significant documentation
on WMI available in the SQL Server Books Online.

5. Click on the Response page of the dialog to configure a notification or job response to the event, as illustrated in Figure 14.23. For
   example, if you wanted to notify the operator Mike whenever the
   transaction log expands beyond 90% used, you would configure
   the event as illustrated.

Figure 14.23: Configuring event notifications

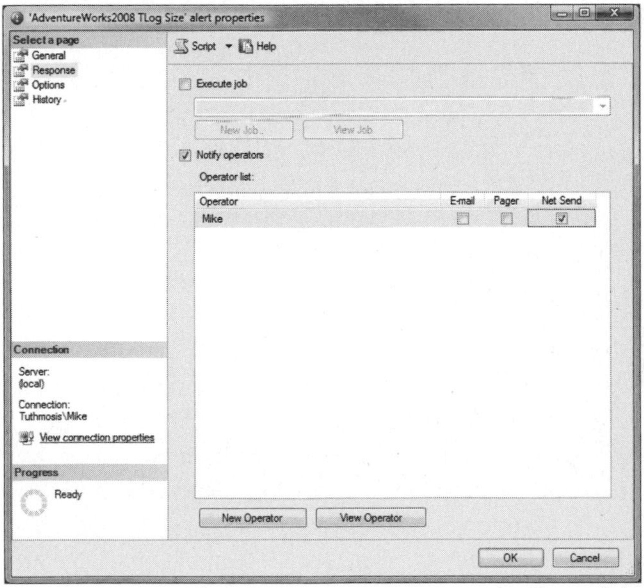

6. Click on the Options page to see the options illustrated in
   Figure 14.24. You can decide if you want to send the alert text to
   different notification targets as well as sending additional information about the event. You can also delay between response notifications to prevent the SQL Agent from spamming the operator.

Figure 14.24: Configuring event options

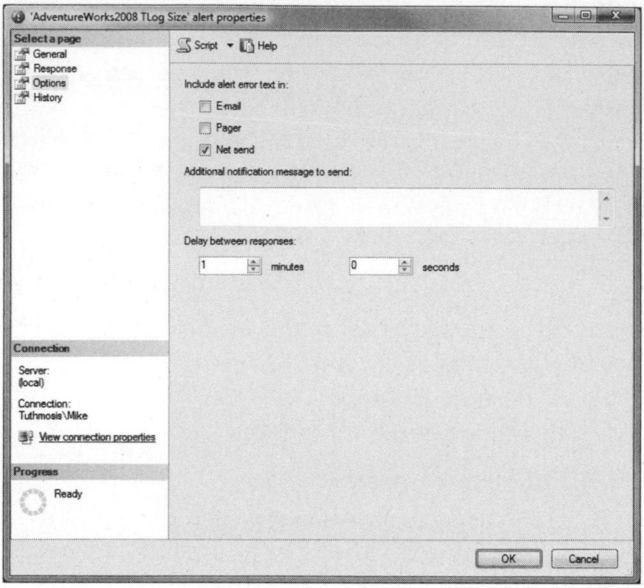

7. Click the OK button to create the alert. You should now see the new alert in the list under the Alerts node in the Object Explorer.

Create and Configure Jobs

Jobs are at the heart of the SQL Server Agent's automation infrastructure. The whole purpose of this environment is to automate routine tasks and to configure maintenance responses to system events. These actions require jobs. A job is a sequence of individual tasks that SQL Server will perform when the job is triggered. Since you have already created all of the other objects, such as operators, schedules and alerts, you should be able to assemble them into a complete package at this step, creating the job.

Creating the Job

To create a job, follow these steps:

1. Locate the SQL Server Agent node in the Object Explorer. Expand the node and locate the Jobs node.

2. Right-click the Jobs node and select New Job from the menu. This opens the New Job dialog. By default you will be viewing the General page.

3. Provide a name for the job by entering a name in the Name text box.

4. Specify a job owner. This is either a SQL Server or mapped Windows login account. You should select a non-user-specific account so that you do not have to transfer job ownership if the user login ever has to be deactivated.

5. You can specify a category and description of the job if desired. This is optional. The completed General page for this example is illustrated in Figure 14.25.

Figure 14.25: Setting general job properties

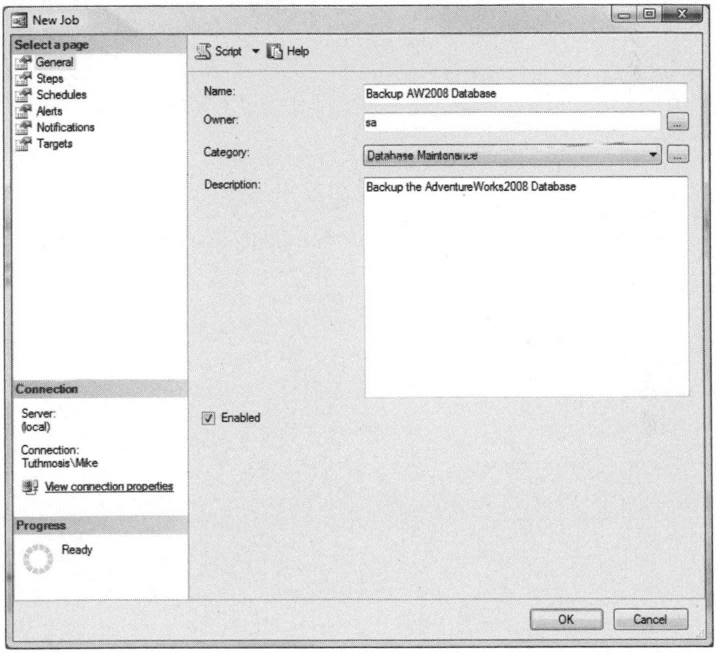

6. Click the Steps page to define the task steps in the job. At the bottom of this page, click the New button to create a new step. This opens the New Job Step dialog. Our example job will have two steps.

7. The first step will delete a file, if it exists, from the file system using a CmdExec. Specify a step name and CmdExec as the step type. If you configured the proxy as in the previous example, you should have two options in the Run As drop-down: SLQ Agent Service Account and DemoProxy. Configure the general page of this dialog as shown in Figure 14.26.

Figure 14.26: Setting general step properties

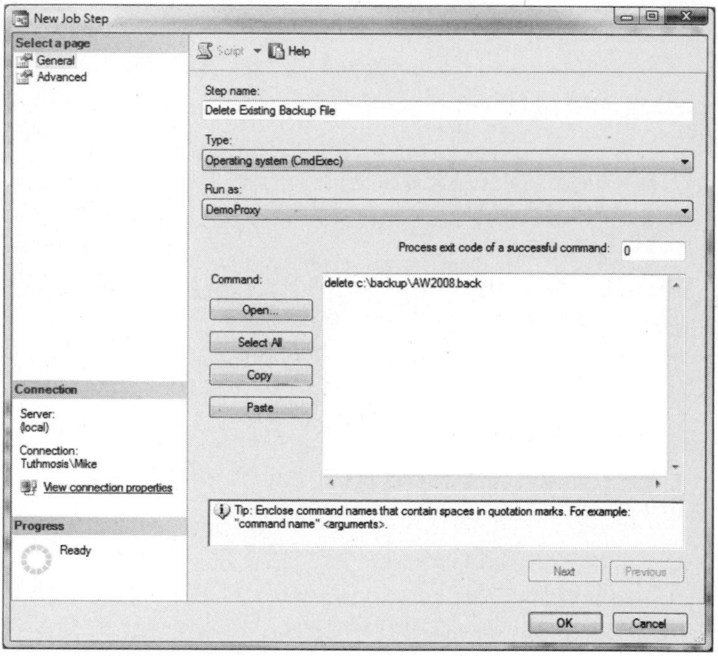

8. Click the Advanced page of the New Job Step dialog to configure job options. Configure the dialog as illustrated in Figure 14.27 so that if the step fails, the job will continue to the next step. Also click the check box at the bottom to include the step output in the history. Do not include any retries. Click OK to create the step.

9. You should now see your job step in the list in the New Job dialog. Click New to create the second job step. Configure the General page as pictured in Figure 14.28. Do not make any changes on the Advanced page. Click OK to create the step.

Figure 14.27: Setting advanced step properties

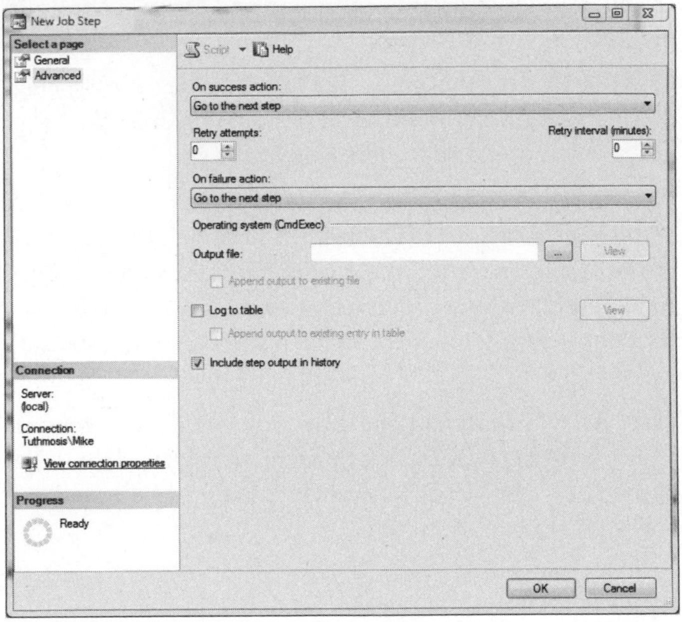

Figure 14.28: Creating the second step

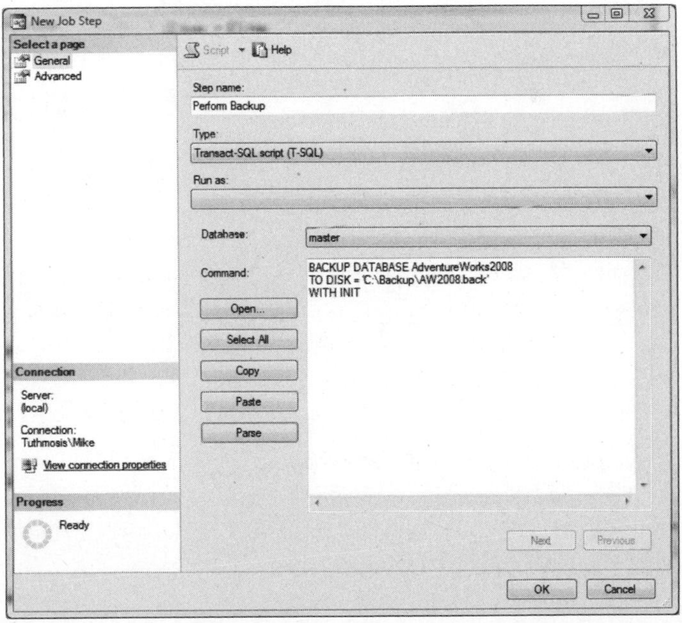

10. Note that on the Steps page of the New Job dialog, you can change the order of the steps; move them up and down by selecting a step and clicking the Move step arrows at the bottom of the dialog.

11. Click the Schedules page. At the bottom of the dialog, click the Pick button to view and select a desired schedule. You can also create a new schedule from here if you wish.

12. Click the Alerts page. Click the Add button to add a new alert. If you want to associate an existing alert with this job, complete the job and then return to the list in the Alerts node of the Object Explorer. Open the properties for the target alert and go to the Responses page. From here you can specify a job to execute if the alert fires.

13. Click the Notifications page. Select the notification formats that you want to use by selecting the appropriate check box. You can also write to the Windows event log. Figure 14.29 illustrates an operator configuration.

Figure 14.29: Setting notifications

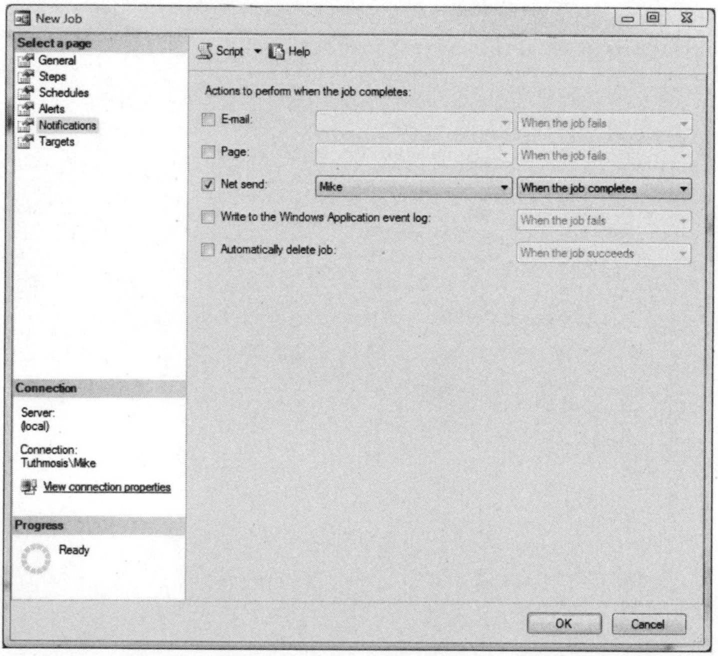

14. The final page, called Targets, is used when configuring a master events server infrastructure. This is an advanced configuration that we will not address in this book. For more information, locate the topic "Creating a Multiserver Environment" in the SQL Server Books Online.

15. Click OK to create the job. You should now see the new job in the list under the Jobs node in the Object Explorer.

Executing the Job

Because there is a schedule associated with the job, it will fire automatically as scheduled. Additionally, you can execute the job on demand by following these steps:

1. Locate the job in the list under the Jobs node of the Object Explorer.

2. Right-click the job and select Start Job at Step from the menu. This opens the Start Job dialog.

3. Make sure step number 1 is selected (or any other step if you wish to start in the middle of the job) and click the Start button. This will start the job.

4. A successful job execution will result in a dialog like the one in Figure 14.30. Click the Close button to close the dialog after viewing the results.

Figure 14.30: Reporting a successful job execution

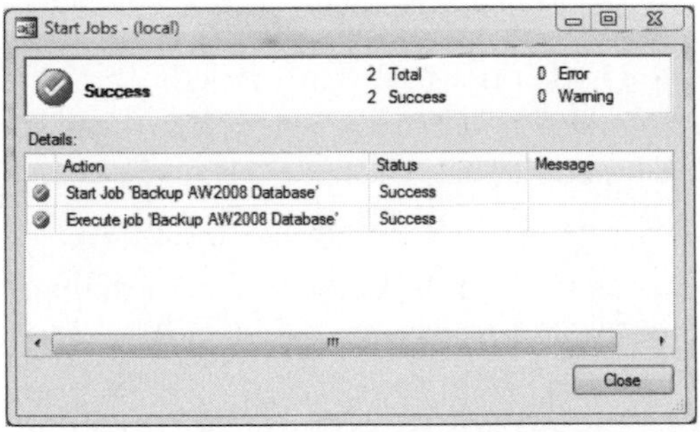

Viewing Job History

You can also view an execution history of any job. This is very convenient when troubleshooting jobs because error information contained in the history can provide the keys to repairing a job. To view the history, use these steps.

1. Locate the job in the list under the Jobs node in the Object Explorer.

2. Right-click the job name and select View History from the menu. This opens the Log File Viewer dialog for the job, shown in Figure 14.31.

Figure 14.31: Viewing job history

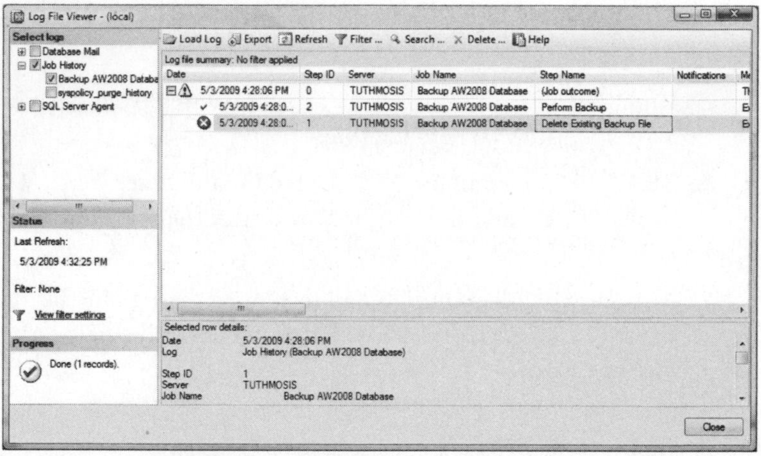

3. In this example, you will notice that step 1 failed. This is because the file that we attempted to delete did not exist at the time. However, because we configured the job to go to the next step on failure, the backup still executed and the job completed.

4. Click the Close button to close the Log File Viewer dialog.

Use the SQL Server Maintenance Plan Wizard

If your infrastructure is like most, the majority of the database automation requirements will be related to database maintenance. Simple tasks such as integrity checks, index rebuilds, and database backups are critical to any production system, but fortunately, they are also very simple to automate.

To make this process easier for the administrator, Microsoft provides a tool called the SQL Server Maintenance Plan Wizard. This wizard will create a maintenance automation package implemented through SQL Server Integration Services (SSIS) and scheduled by the SQL Server Agent service. While you can also create the maintenance plan manually, using the wizard provides a good starting point. You can then refine the process from there by working with the individual components of the plan. SSIS is described in more detail in Chapter 9, "Extracting, Transforming, and Loading Data."

Creating the Plan

To create a database maintenance plan, follow these steps:

1. Locate the Management node in the Object Explorer. Expand the node and locate the Maintenance Plans node.

2. Right-click the Maintenance Plans node. Notice that you have the option to create the plan manually or use the wizard. Select Maintenance Plan Wizard from the menu to begin.

3. Advance past the first informational page by clicking the Next button. The first step of the wizard is the Select Plan Properties page. Here you will set a name for the plan.

4. You can also decide how you want to handle the schedule. You have three options:

   - Separate schedules for each task
   - Single schedule for the entire plan
   - No schedule—manual execution only

   In this example, select the option for "Single schedule for the entire plan or no schedule" and click the Change button to set the schedule. This opens the Job Schedule Properties dialog, which looks like the dialog that we used earlier when creating a schedule.

5. Click Cancel on the Job Schedule Properties dialog and leave the execution at On Demand. The completed Select Plan Properties page will look like the dialog in Figure 14.32. Click Next to advance.

Figure 14.32: Select plan properties

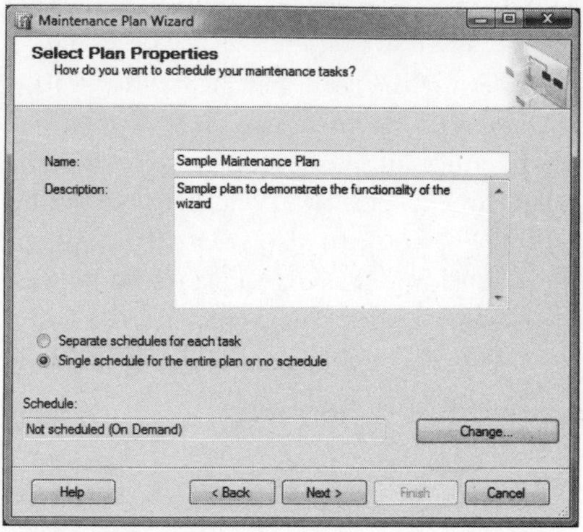

6. The next page allows you to select the tasks that you wish to execute in the plan. This example will perform a basic maintenance, as shown in Figure 14.33. As you can see, this approach allows you to create a plan as simple or as complex as needed. Click Next to advance.

Figure 14.33: Select plan tasks

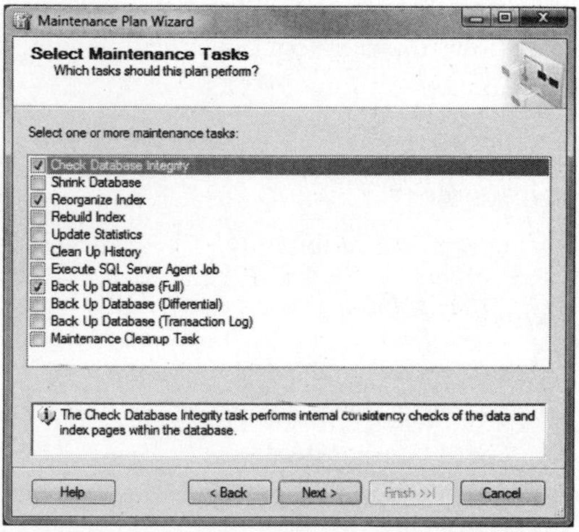

7. The next page allows you to change the execution order of the tasks. Note that if you selected the option to provide a separate schedule for each task, the buttons to move the tasks will be dimmed out. Figure 14.34 illustrates this page of the wizard. Click Next to continue.

Figure 14.34: Setting task order

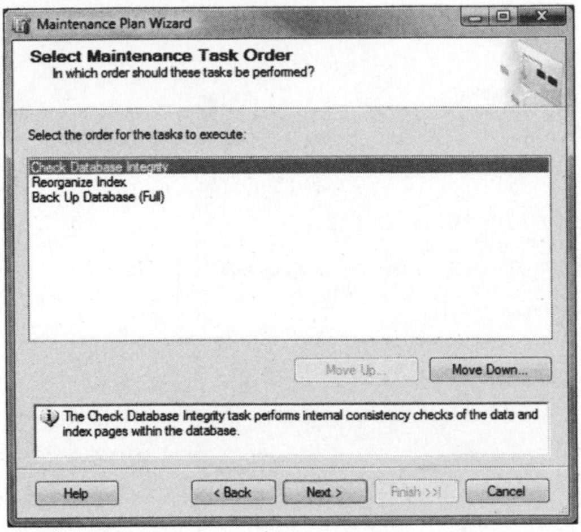

From this point on, the wizard pages will vary depending on the tasks selected. This example will include only the wizard pages for the tasks selected, but if you are familiar with the underlying tasks, the configuration pages should be easy to follow.

8. To define the context for database integrity checks, select the target databases by opening the drop-down list. This will open a dialog that looks like the one in Figure 14.35. In this example, we selected only the AdventureWorks2008 database. Click OK to close the pop-up window.

9. Back on the wizard page, you can also choose to include the indexes in the integrity checks. Figure 14.36 illustrates the completed page of the wizard. Click Next to continue.

Figure 14.35: Selecting target databases

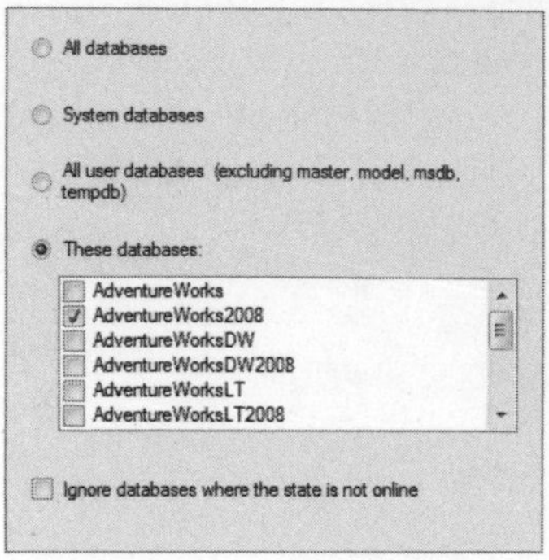

Figure 14.36: Defining integrity checks

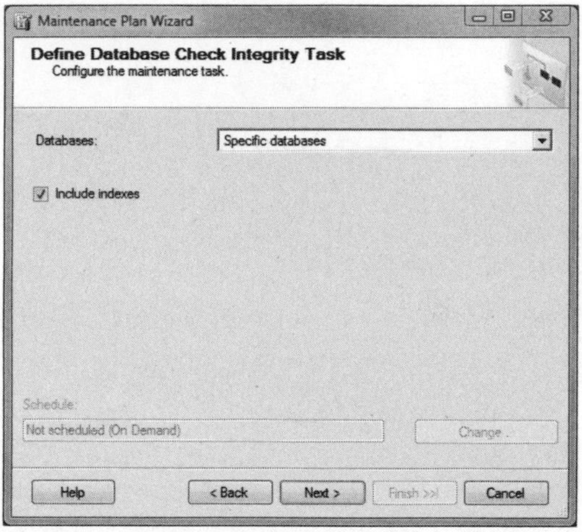

10. The next page provides details for the index reorganization task. Clicking the Databases drop-down list opens the same database selection dialog that we saw in Figure 14.35. Once again, select the AdventureWorks2008 database.

11. On the Object drop-down list, you can select Tables or Views to enable the Selection drop-down list, which allows you to select specific tables and views. If you choose the option Tables and Views, the wizard will reorganize all objects of each type. Figure 14.37 illustrates the completed page. Click Next to continue.

Figure 14.37: Select reorganization targets

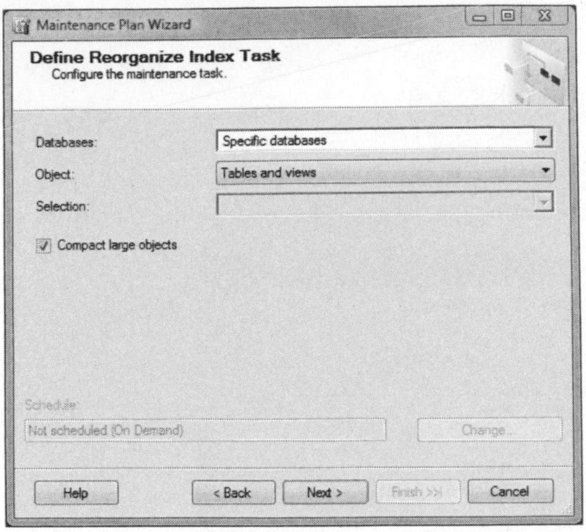

12. The next page in our example configures a full database backup task. (For details on the database backup options, consult Chapter 10, "Managing Data Recovery.") Our example is configured to back up a specific database (in this case, the AdventureWorks2008 database), as illustrated in Figure 14.38. Note that the target files for the backup will be auto-named by the maintenance plan. Click Next to continue.

13. To get a report of the plan execution, you can either specify a target location for the report or, if you have SQL Server configured for mail service, have the report emailed to you. Figure 14.39 shows the page configured to save the text file to a desired target location. Click Next to continue.

14. To complete the wizard, click the Finish button on the final page. Upon successful completion of the wizard, you will get a success report. Click the Close button to end the wizard.

Executing and Modifying the Plan

The plan will execute automatically based on the schedule if you set one. You can also execute the plan on demand by following these steps:

1. Locate the Maintenance Plans node and expand it. If the plan is not listed under the node, right-click the node and select Refresh, then expand the node.

Performance and Advanced Features

PART IV

2. Right-click the plan that you wish to execute and select Execute from the menu.

3. Upon completion of the plan, you will see a success report. Close the dialog to end the execution.

Figure 14.38: Configuring the database backup

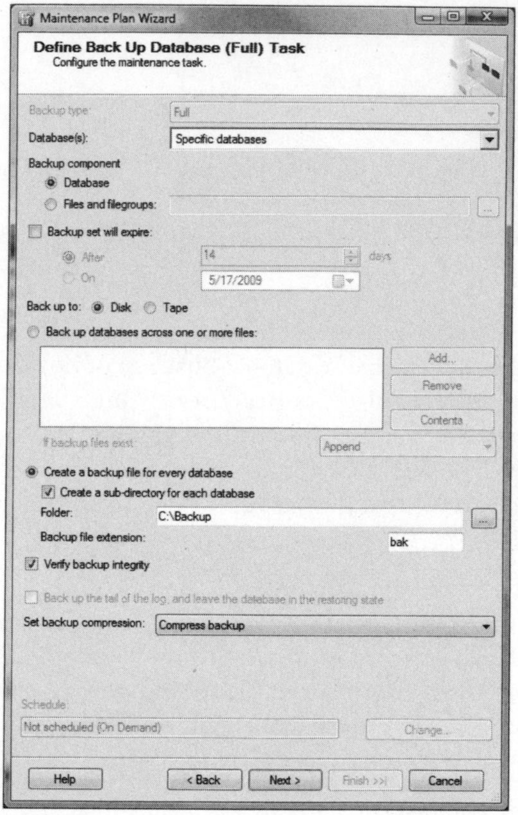

You can also modify the plan, but this will require some familiarity with the database maintenance tasks in SSIS. If you right-click the plan name in the list and select Modify from the menu, a maintenance plan design window opens. From here, you can modify schedules, add tasks, and change the properties of existing tasks.

Figure 14.39: Setting report options

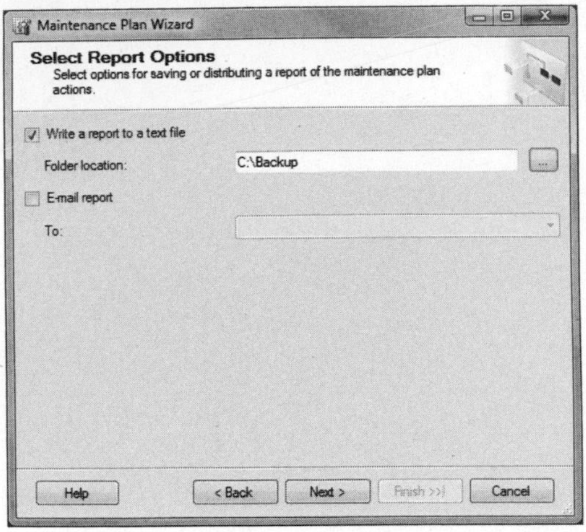

Index

Note to the reader: Throughout this index **boldfaced** page numbers indicate primary discussions of a topic. *Italicized* page numbers indicate illustrations.

C

L

M